The New Testament

Bart D. Ehrman, Ph.D.

THE
GREAT
COURSES

PUBLISHED BY:

THE GREAT COURSES
Corporate Headquarters
4840 Westfields Boulevard, Suite 500
Chantilly, Virginia 20151-2299
Phone: 1-800-832-2412
Fax: 703-378-3819
www.thegreatcourses.com

Bart D. Ehrman, Ph.D.

Professor, Department of Religious Studies
The University of North Carolina
at Chapel Hill

Professor Bart Ehrman is the Bowman and Gordon Gray Professor of Religious Studies at The University of North Carolina at Chapel Hill. With degrees from Wheaton College (B.A.) and Princeton Theological Seminary (M.Div. and Ph.D., magna cum laude), he taught at Rutgers for four years before moving to UNC in 1988. During his tenure at UNC, he has garnered numerous awards and prizes, including the Students' Undergraduate Teaching Award (1993), the Ruth and Philip Hettleman Prize for Artistic and Scholarly Achievement (1994), and now the Bowman and Gordon Gray Award for excellence in teaching (1998).

With a focus on early Christianity in its Greco-Roman environment and a special expertise in the textual criticism of the New Testament, Professor Ehrman has published dozens of book reviews and over 20 scholarly articles for academic journals. He has also authored or edited eight books, including *Jesus: Apocalyptic Prophet of the New Millennium* (Oxford University Press, 1999); *The New Testament: A Historical Introduction to the Early Christian Writings* (Oxford, 1997; 2nd ed. 1999); *After the New Testament: A Reader in Early Christianity* (Oxford, 1999); *The New Testament and Other Early Christian Writings: A Reader* (Oxford, 1998); *The Orthodox Corruption of Scripture* (Oxford, 1993); and (as co-editor) *The Text of the New Testament in Contemporary Research* (Eerdmans, 1996). He is currently at work on a new Greek-English edition of the Apostolic Fathers for the Loeb Classical Library (Harvard University Press).

Professor Ehrman is a popular lecturer, giving numerous talks each year for such groups as the Carolina Speakers Bureau, the UNC Program for the Humanities, the Biblical Archaeology Society, various civic groups, and universities across the nation. He has served as the President of the Society of Biblical Literature, SE Region; book review editor of the *Journal of Biblical Literature*; editor of the Scholar's Press Monograph Series *The New Testament in the Greek Fathers*; and co-editor of the E.J. Brill series *New Testament Tools and Studies*. Among his administrative responsibilities, he has served on the executive committee of the Southeast Council for the Study of Religion and has chaired the New Testament textual criticism section of the Society of Biblical Religion, as well as serving as Director of Graduate Studies at the Department of Religious Studies at UNC. ∎

Table of Contents

Table of Contents

Table of Contents

The New Testament

Scope:

The New Testament is undoubtedly the single most important book in the history of Western civilization, whether seen as a religious book of faith or as a cultural artifact. It is probably also the most widely disputed and misunderstood. The 24 lectures of this course will approach the New Testament from a historical perspective, bracketing questions of belief and theological truth to acquire a historically rich grounding for our understanding of these foundational documents.

The course will begin with four lectures on the historical context in which the New Testament was written, considering both the world of Greco-Roman pagan cults and the world of early Judaism—examining, that is, the beliefs, sacred spaces, liturgical practices, and distinguishing features of the religions surrounding the birth of Christianity.

In the second four lectures of Part I, we will examine the New Testament Gospels of Matthew, Mark, Luke, and John. These are our principal sources for knowing about the life and teachings of Jesus; they are also major literary works in their own right, each with its own perspective on who Jesus was and why his life and death matter. A major methodological concern will be to allow each of these books to speak for itself, rather than assume they all portray Jesus in the same way. Individual lectures will be devoted to establishing the distinctive portrayals of Jesus in each of the Gospels. An additional lecture will look at how Jesus is portrayed in two Gospels that did not make it into the New Testament, the Gospels of Peter and Thomas.

Part I concludes with four lectures that will take the results of our discussions and, in a sense, move behind them to see what we can learn about the historical Jesus himself and what he actually said and did. After considering what noncanonical sources (e.g., Roman and Jewish authors) say about Jesus, we will discuss the kinds of criteria historians have devised for using the Gospels not as literary texts but as historical sources for Jesus' life. We will then apply these criteria to reconstruct his actual words and deeds. We will see that the earliest records of Jesus are probably right in portraying him as a kind of apocalyptic prophet who anticipated that God would soon intervene in the course of history to overthrow the forces of evil and establish his good kingdom on earth and that people needed to repent in preparation for it. We will also consider the circumstances that led to his death at the hands of the Roman governor of Judea, Pontius Pilate.

In Part II of the course, we will move to consider the Book of Acts—the earliest surviving history of the early Christian movement—then the 21 epistles of the New Testament. Because 13 of these epistles claim to be written by the apostle Paul, we will spend some time trying to understand his life and theology. Paul was a Jew who converted to faith in Jesus after being a persecutor of the church. His letters are addressed to churches that he had founded, principally among Gentiles. In them, he spells out his convictions that a person can be made right with God only through the death and resurrection of Jesus (not, for example, through the Jewish Law) and draws numerous ethical and theological implications. Following our discussion of Paul's own letters, we will devote a lecture to considering the

relationship of Paul and Jesus, to see whether, as some people have claimed, Paul transformed the religion *of* Jesus into a religion *about* Jesus.

We will then consider other New Testament books that claim Paul as their author that modern scholars have concluded are, in fact, pseudonymous. Finally, we will move into a discussion of the remaining writings of the New Testament, including the books of 1 Peter and Hebrews and ending with a discussion of the book of Revelation, a book that continues to fascinate and intrigue modern readers. We will see that it, like all the other books of the New Testament, is best understood when situated in its own historical context—rather than taken out of context.

In short, this will be a historical introduction to the 27 books of the New Testament. The course will try to address such significant questions as who wrote these books, under what circumstances, and for what audience; we will consider what the books of the New Testament say, what they mean, and how historically accurate they are. Our ultimate goal is to come to a fuller appreciation and understanding of these books that have made such an enormous impact on the history of Western civilization and that continue to play such an important role for people today. ■

The Early Christians and Their Literature
Lecture 1

There can be no question that the Christian church since the 4th century has been the most significant social, economic, political, and cultural force in Western civilization. And the foundation of the church was and is the New Testament.

The New Testament continues to be a field of ongoing fascination, not just for Christian theologians, pastors, and believers, but also for professional historians and lay people interested in classics, history, and literature. Virtually all modern historians would agree that the New Testament has been the most significant book, or group of books, in the history of Western civilization. It continues to be an object of reverence and inspiration for millions of Christians today, a book that governs peoples' personal lives, shapes their religious views, and gives them a sense of hope. The New Testament also plays an enormous role in our political and social lives. The meaning of the book is not self-evident. The differenced interpretation are not just related to geography, culture, and history—they are also related to different understandings of the New Testament.

There are a number of ways we could approach the New Testament in this course. We could approach it from the perspective of the faithful believer. This is how most people who read the New Testament approach the subject. There are other equally valid ways of approaching the New Testament that do not require either that we all should agree about religion or even that we should agree to believe or disbelieve in the New Testament itself. It is possible to study the book from this cultural perspective of one interested in the development of Western civilization. There can be little question that this book stands at the foundation of Western civilization as we know it. Whatever you happen to think about the New Testament, there can be no question that the Christian church has, since the 4th century, been the most significant social, economic, political, and cultural force in Western civilization. And the foundation of the Church was and is the New Testament. We could study how it has played such a huge role in Western art or English literature.

Another way to approach this study is one that is directly concerned with understanding the New Testament in its own historical context. This is the perspective we will take in this course. To approach the New Testament from this historical perspective means suspending our own belief or disbelief in its teachings. We will work to understand how the 27 books that make up the New Testament came into being, to see who wrote them and why, and to determine what they might have meant to their original readers.

We need to consider several important pieces of background information on the New Testament in this first lecture, before plunging into our study. The New Testament comprises 27 books written by Christians of the 1st century, many of whom were said to be apostles of Jesus. The first to be written were produced about 20 years after Jesus' death; the latest, probably 70 years after. All of these books were originally written in Greek (not Hebrew or Aramaic, as many people think).

The 27 books of the New Testament are organized into four major groups. First are the four Gospels of Matthew, Mark, Luke, and John. These are the books that describe the birth, life, activities, teaching, death, and resurrection of Jesus. Virtually all of the stories that you've ever heard about Jesus come from these books. These books, then, narrate the *beginnings* of Christianity.

The second division of the New Testament consists of only one book, the Book of Acts (or the Acts of the Apostles). This is a historical account of the activities of Jesus' apostles and missionaries after his death. It is concerned, then, with the *spread* of Christianity.

The third part of the New Testament contains 21 epistles, 13 of which are ascribed to the apostle Paul, the others to others of the apostles. These are actual letters written by Christian authors to other Christian individuals or communities, instructing them in what to believe and how to act. These focus, then, on the *beliefs and ethics* of Christianity.

The final part of the New Testament consists of a single book, the apocalyptic Book of Revelation. This is a description of the end times, when God brings all his promises to fulfillment by destroying this world and bringing in a utopian kingdom. In contrast to the other portions of the New Testament, then, this book deals with the *culmination* of Christianity.

The 27 books of the New Testament were not the only ones written by the early Christians, but they were the ones that Christians of later times opted to include in their sacred canon. The decisions about which books to include did not come right away; throughout the 2nd and 3rd centuries, Christian leaders debated which books were to be accepted as canonical. There were other gospels, acts, epistles, and so on recording Jesus' words and deeds that are not in the canon. For example, the Gospel of Thomas seems to be in the Gnostic tradition. The Gospel of Peter contains an account of the Resurrection. It was not until the end

> **The 27 books of the New Testament were not the only ones written by the early Christians.**

of the 4th century A.D. that anyone came up with a list of New Testament books that corresponds exactly with our list of 27. This was in a letter written by Athanasius, an influential and powerful bishop of Alexandria, Egypt. The letter was meant to set the date of Easter that year (A.D. 367) and contained other pieces of pastoral advice, including which books should be included in the Scriptures.

The debates over which books to include involved a number of criteria. A book had to have been written by one of Jesus' apostles or a close companion of an apostle. In other words, it had to be very ancient, close to the time of Jesus. A book must have been widely read among the Christian churches throughout the world. Its teachings must coincide with those of the church at large; i.e., they had to be orthodox.

The question about whether the Christians who formulated the canon were right about their decisions is a historical one, not a theological one. Historians can appeal to evidence that we now have to decide such matters. For now, though, I want to stress that we will address this and all the other questions raised in this course strictly from a historical point of view, not a religious one. I will not try to promote belief or disbelief in these books. Instead, I will discuss what these books say, what their perspectives are, who wrote them, in what circumstances, to what audience, and for what reasons. These are historical questions. They may have implications for religious belief, but we will try to deal with them by looking at historical evidence. That will be the goal of the course: a historical introduction to the New Testament, a work of major religious, cultural, and historical significance that deserves our careful attention. ∎

Essential Reading

Brown, *The New Testament*, chap. 1.

Ehrman, *The New Testament: A Historical Introduction*, chap. 1.

Supplemental Reading

Gamble, *The New Testament Canon*.

Questions to Consider

1. Most people think of the New Testament as a religious book, the Christian sacred Scriptures. What reasons might people have for studying the New Testament if they are not religiously committed to it? How would a historical approach to the New Testament differ from a religious or theological approach?

2. What were the grounds adduced for including some books but not others in the New Testament? How, in your opinion, would modern-day understanding of the Bible be affected if some of these decisions were now called into question?

The Early Christians and Their Literature
Lecture 1—Transcript

I would like to welcome you to this course on the New Testament. I'm Bart Ehrman, Professor of Religious Studies at the University of North Carolina-Chapel Hill, where I have been teaching courses on the New Testament and early Christianity for the past 11 years. I have been engaged in the academic study of the New Testament for 25 years, and I must say that even though my views of the New Testament have changed rather drastically since I was a student in college, my fascination for this book has never waned.

The New Testament is probably the most revered and the most unknown book in our culture. This course of lectures is designed for people who want to learn something about it. Both people who don't know a lot about the New Testament but think that it is time that they did, and people who have studied the New Testament, who want to see what an academic approach to the New Testament might look like.

In this opening lecture I would like to explain why a study of this kind is worth our while and also explain how we will approach the New Testament, indicate what our objectives will be, and provide a few of the major points of background that are necessary to the beginning phases of our study. So, why is it important to engage in this kind of study? Virtually all modern historians would agree that the New Testament has been the most significant book in the history of Western civilization. It lies at the root of our form of culture, and it continues to be an object of reverence and inspiration for millions of Christians today. A book that governs people's personal lives—that shapes their religious views, that provides them with the sense of hope.

If you want to understand our culture, you have to know something about the New Testament. This is true for what we might call "high" culture, as well as "low." You simply can't read English literature from old English classics like "Beowulf" and "The Dream of the Rood" up through the 20th century without understanding the imagery drawn from the New Testament. The same can be said, of course, about Western visual art. In addition, the New Testament plays an enormous role in our political and social lives. Whether we like it or not, it's appealed to by the White House and by the U.S. Senate when trying to debate issues of foreign and domestic policy. It is used on both sides by people advocating their views on nuclear disarmament and abortion. And it has been invoked to support causes over the years that most people today would consider to be highly dubious morally: slavery in the South, military intervention abroad, the oppression of women everywhere. Obviously, despite its importance, the New Testament is a book whose meaning is not self-evident. This is perhaps most obviously seen simply on the denominational level. The difference between Greek Orthodox Priests, Appalachian snake handlers, mainline Presbyterians, and serious Pentecostals are not related just to geography, culture, and history; they are also related to different understandings of the New Testament. In some, the New Testament has brought a world of good into our civilization through its teachings of love and its promises of hope. And it has been used to promote evil in a wide range of hideous guises.

For all these reasons this book is worth our serious and sustained attention, whether we happen to believe in it or not. How, though, should we go about studying it? There are, in fact, several ways that we could approach the study of the New Testament in this course. We could, in theory, approach it from the perspective of the faithful believer wanting to learn what it says in order to know ourselves and what we should believe and how we should act. This kind of approach would probably be appropriate if we were in a church or a Sunday school. And it would probably be appropriate if we were in a private Christian college. Where I teach, though, at a state university, this is not really an appropriate approach, since I am not allowed constitutionally— at least as I understand the Constitution—to embrace a particular religious point of view when teaching my students about religion. Also, for this kind of course that we are doing here, the intention is to introduce the New Testament for all people—not simply for people who happen to be believers. Moreover I think that there are other equally valid ways of approaching the New Testament that don't require us to either agree about religion among ourselves or even to agree to believe or disbelieve in the New Testament. It is possible, in fact, to study the book not from the religious perspective of those that believe, but from a cultural perspective of one who is interested in the developing of Western civilization, and so this would be a second way to approach the study of the New Testament culturally.

There can be little question that this book stands for the foundation of civilization as we know it. Whatever you happen to think about Christianity yourself—whether you are ardent Roman Catholic, a strong evangelical, a mainline Methodist, a hard-core atheist, or an absolute pagan—there can be no question that the Christian church since the 4th century has been the most significant social, economic, political, and cultural force in Western civilization. And the foundation of the church was and is the New Testament. So we could see how the New Testament has been used through the ages—for example, through the Crusades or the Inquisition or the Protestant Reformation; or we could study how it has played such a huge role in Western Art or in English literature. As interesting as this kind of study may be, it also will not be the approach that will be taken during this course; for there is yet another way to approach the New Testament—one that will, as a side benefit, elucidate both the modern debates over the meaning of this book and the nature of its historical impact on Western civilization. This other way of approaching it has its more direct concern with understanding the New Testament in its own historical context. This approach involves studying the New Testament, then, from the perspective not of the believer, not of the cultural historian, but of the ancient historian. This is the approach that will be taken in this class. To approach the New Testament from the historical perspective means suspending our own belief or disbelief in its teaching and working to understand how the 27 books that now make up the New Testament came into being—to see who wrote them and why, to determine what they might have meant to their original readers. These are the sorts of questions that will absorb us in our subsequent lectures.

There are several pieces of important background information on the New Testament that we need to consider here in this first lecture before plunging into our study. One of the things that I am surprised continually is how little people know about the New Testament just in terms of its basic facts. This realization comes to me every year when I teach my large undergraduate course at Chapel Hill. This is a class with about 350 students in it, and every year I begin by giving a pop quiz in which I ask students some basic information about the New Testament. Questions like, "How many books are in the New Testament?" "What language were these books written in?" "When were these books written?" I also throw in some curve balls, and I ask them who wrote the Book of 1 Peter, who wrote the Book of 1 Timothy, and who wrote the Book of 1 Andrew—that's a curve ball because, of course, there is no 1 Andrew in the New Testament, but most of my students don't realize this. There are 11 questions on this pop quiz that I give to my students, and I tell them that if anybody gets 9 out of the 11 right, I will buy them a Mexican dinner at a local Tex-Mex restaurant. In my 11 years of teaching—I have classes every year of 350 students—in my 11 years of teaching, I've had only one student who has gotten 9 of 11 answers right of these very basic questions and background. And I am afraid that even though they are just 19- and 20-year olds, I'm afraid that their lack of knowledge, in fact, is typical, rather than atypical, of the population at large—and so I think I should here give some basic background information so that we are all on the same page about what the New Testament is all about in terms of basic information about it.

As I have already indicated, there are 27 books in the New Testament. All of these books were originally written in Greek. There are some scholars that think that some of these books may have been originally been written in Aramaic, but that is by far a minority opinion. These books, in the judgment of almost everybody who worked on them, were originally written in Greek. That is one of the interesting things about my students: Every time I ask them this question, only half of my students think that the New Testament was written in Hebrew, which has always struck me as odd. I have never quite understood it, but I suppose it is because they have seen enough TV shows on the Bible where they flash up screens of Hebrew text that they associate Hebrew with the Bible for some reason. The New Testament books were written in Greek, even though the books of the Old Testament, the non-Christian Testament, the Jewish Scriptures, were written in Hebrew. The books of the New Testament were all written during the 1st century A.D. or shortly thereafter. Most scholars would date the books of the New Testament from between the year 50 of the Common Era, or 50 A.D., up to about 120 A.D. To put that into perspective, virtually everybody thinks Jesus was born sometime around 4 B.C. and was probably executed sometime around the year 30 A.D., and so the books of the New Testament began to be written about 20 or 25 years after that and then continued to be written until about the year 120 A.D.

These are the earliest surviving books that we have from the Christians. There were other books written by Christians at the same time that have no longer survived, and there are some books written by Christians that were written near the end of the writing of the New Testament—books that still do survive but that did not make it into the New Testament.

Later on in this lecture, I will say a few words about how Christians had decided about which books to put into the New Testament and which ones not to put in. I should say again by way of background that Jesus himself did not write any of the books of the New Testament and, so far as we know, did not write anything. We don't know whether Jesus himself was able to write or not, but it is pretty clear that he didn't produce anything that has survived. Instead, the books of the New Testament are written by followers of Jesus. Some of the books are attributed to Jesus' own disciples.

The word "disciple" comes from a word which means follower. The disciples were earthly followers of Jesus, and sometimes the word "disciple" is used in a technical sense to refer to one of Jesus' Twelve—one of the 12 men whom Jesus picked in order to be his disciples on Earth. Some of the books of the New Testament are attributed to some of the disciples. For example, among our Gospels, we have Matthew, Mark, Luke, and John. Matthew and John are allegedly disciples of Jesus. Matthew was a tax collector who is referred to as one of Jesus' disciples. John is thought to be a person known as "The Beloved Disciple" in the Gospel of John.

I should say at this point, as I will point out in greater detail later in a later lecture, that these books themselves don't actually claim to be written by Matthew and John. In your English bibles today you will see a title "The Gospel According to Matthew," but that is not the original title to this book. The author himself didn't say, "This is the Gospel according to Matthew." Of course, if he were writing the book, he wouldn't say this is Matthew's gospel; he would simply say, "This is the Gospel," or he would say, "This is the Gospel of Jesus," or something. He wouldn't say, "This is the Gospel of Matthew." This is an attribution of the book to Matthew by somebody living later. In fact, this attribution first came about in the 2nd century. So that two of the books, two of the Gospels, are attributed to Matthew and John even though they don't claim themselves to be written by Matthew and John; these are two of the disciples.

Other books of the New Testament explicatively do claim to be written by people who were apostles. Now the word "disciple" means a follower of Jesus. The word "apostle" comes from the Greek word which means one who was sent. An apostle is somebody who understands him or herself to have been sent on a mission, and so there could have been—and there were—early Christians who understood themselves to have been sent by Jesus on a mission to spread his good news throughout the world. This would have included, for example, the Apostle Paul. Paul was not one of the original followers of Jesus. He was not a disciple, but he did understand himself to have been an apostle. And we will study Paul at some length in this course because 13 of our 27 books actually claim to be written by Paul. And so Paul, of course, is a very significant figure for the history of Christianity—but also especially for our understanding of the New Testament itself. We will also see that scholars have come to dispute whether Paul actually did write these books that are attributed to him. Thirteen books claim to be written by him, but scholars have reason for doubting whether all 13 actually were written by Paul or not. We will see this later in the course.

And so in the New Testament we have 27 books written in Greek from the 1st century—the books attributed to disciples or claiming to be written by apostles. These 27 books of the New Testament can be organized into four major groupings. The first major group would be the Four Gospels: Matthew, Mark, Luke, and John. The Four Gospels are the only books that we have in the New Testament that actually describe the life, activities, teaching, death, and resurrection of Jesus. Any stories that you have heard about Jesus that sound at all plausible historically, come from these four books. Probably every story you have ever heard and any teaching of Jesus that is found in the New Testament any activity of Jesus, any of his miracles—they are found in these four books: Matthew, Mark, Luke, and John. It's surprising, as we will see later in this course, that the other books of the New Testament say virtually nothing about Jesus' life itself. The stories of his life are found in these four books. Since they narrate Jesus' life from his birth to his death, these four gospels can be seen as narrating the beginnings of Christianity—and so, appropriately, they occur at the beginning of the New Testament.

The second division of the New Testament consists of only one book: the Book of Acts, or sometimes called the Acts of the Apostles. This is a historical account of the activities of Jesus' apostles and his missionaries after Jesus himself had died. It's concerned, then, with how these followers of Jesus propagated the faith as Christianity spread throughout the Roman Empire. The book begins after Jesus' death and resurrection. It narrates his ascension into heaven, and then it shows how the apostles were empowered to spread his gospel throughout the world. And so it is not about Jesus so much as it is about his apostles, and it is called the Book of Acts. Rather then dealing with the beginnings of Christianity as the Gospels, then, the second category book deals with the spread of Christianity.

The third group of books in the New Testament are the 21 Epistles or letters. These 21 Epistles or letters are actual pieces of correspondence sent by early Christian leaders to other individuals or other communities. Of these 21 Epistles, 13 (as I have indicated) are attributed to the apostle Paul. The others are attributed to others of the apostles, including James and Peter and John. These letters are written to address problems that had emerged in various Christian communities—problems having to do with what Christians ought to believe, how Christians ought to behave. Rather than dealing with the beginnings of Christianity and the life of Jesus or the spread of Christianity through the acts of the apostles, these 21 books are more simply focused on the beliefs and ethics of Christianity and are regularly turned to by Christians who want to know what ancient Christian beliefs were—doctrine and ethics.

The fourth part of the New Testament again consists of a single book, the book that probably is the source of most fascination by Christians still today: the Book of Revelation. The Book of Revelation is an apocalypse—in other words, it is a book which narrates events that are going to transpire at the end of time when God brings all of his promises to fulfillment by destroying this world and bringing in a utopian kingdom. It's an amazing book, the Book of Revelation. It is quite unlike anything that most of us ever read. Probably the closest thing to it that we read would be science fiction novels because it deals with sort of a supermundane reality, which can explain the reality here on Earth in which the Prophet actually ascends to another world and has encounters with supernatural beings and learns about the fate of Earth. This Book of Revelation then, rather than dealing the beginnings of the Christianity or the spread of Christianity or the ethics and beliefs of Christianity, deals with the culmination of Christianity at the end of the age when God intervenes on behalf of his people.

These, then, are the four major categories of the books within the New Testament. I've already indicated that these 27 books found in the New Testament were not the only books written by the early Christians. They were simply the books that later Christians decided to include in their sacred canon of scripture. The word "canon" comes from a Greek term which literally refers to a straight edge or a measuring rod. It came to be used to refer to a collection of books that would provide a kind of...would show the measure of a corpus of literature, the extent of a given body of authoritative texts. And so you can have a canon of any of kind of literature. A canon of Shakespeare, for example, or a canon of the Hebrew Bible.

The canon of the New Testament is the 27 books that Christians at later times decided were sacred books. One of the hardest things for my students at the undergraduate level to understand and to conceptualize is the fact that the 27 books of the New Testament were not always considered to be books of scripture. Even though today you can go to any bookstore and buy a New Testament and you will get the same 27 books in the same sequence, it wasn't always that way. In fact, there were long and hard debates about which books should be included within the canon of scripture. Throughout the 2nd and 3rd and even 4th centuries, Christians debated about the status— the canonical status—of books that had been written in the 1st century. And as I have indicated, we have some of these other books that now survive— books that make for very interesting reading.

For example, we have other gospels that are not found in the New Testament that also record Jesus' words and deeds. Probably the most significant archaeological discovery of the 20th century for the New Testament was the discovery of one of these other gospels that people commonly know about today. Thanks to this discovery, the Gospel called "The Gospel of Thomas" that some scholars have counted as the Fifth Gospel. The Gospel of Thomas is a very interesting book, and we will say some more about it later in the course. It is a book that consists of 114 sayings of Jesus, some of which sound like the sayings of Jesus in the New Testament Gospels, but other sayings that are, in fact, quite unlike the sayings of the New Testament. Some of these sayings sound like Gnostic teachings. Gnostic teaching, coming from the Greek word "gnosis." G-N-O-S-I-S. "Gnosis," which refers to knowledge. These teachings of Jesus seemed to presuppose a royal view that says that Jesus was a divine redeemer who came down from Heaven to reveal the truth that would set people free from the prison of this material world. Some of the sayings in this Gospel sound very strange to our ears today. One reason they sound so strange, though, is because we are not used to them because this Gospel didn't make it into the New Testament.

There are other Gospels that didn't make it into the New Testament that we have known about for a much longer time—for example, the Gospel of Peter. This is a book that actually claims to be written by Simon Peter, Jesus' own disciple. We didn't have access to this book until it was discovered at the end of the 19th century. One of the reasons it is so interesting is because in this Gospel, we have a narration of Jesus' resurrection itself. In the New Testament we have accounts of Jesus having been raised from the dead; we don't have any narration of him actually emerging from the tomb. The Gospel of Peter, though, does give a narration of this event. A fantastic account in which we are told that two angels came down from Heaven and entered into Jesus' tomb, and there emerged from the tomb three individuals. Two with their heads reaching up into heaven and one whose head reached up above the heavens. And behind the three, there emerges a cross from the tomb. A voice comes from heaven and says, "Have you preached to those who have fallen asleep?"—meaning those who have died. And the cross replies, "Yes." A terrifically interesting account that some Christians thought belonged in the New Testament, but eventually it was excluded.

We have a number of books—gospels, acts, epistles, apostleships which claim to be written to apostles and disciples—that did not get included. It was not until the 4th century A.D. that Christians came up with our list of 27 books. The first person to come up with the list that we have now was a bishop from the city of Alexandria, Egypt, a bishop whose name is Athanasius—a very powerful figure in early Christianity, who in the year 367 A.D. wrote a letter to his churches indicating, among other things, which books should be read as part of their worship services. He listed our 27 books. This is the first time that any Christian that we know of thought that these books and no others should be part of the Christian scriptures. Note the date: 367. This is 300 years after most of these books had been written. Three hundred years later, finally somebody decides these and only these should be among the books. And even then the issue wasn't decided because Christians continued to debate for decades which books should be included until finally everybody pretty much agreed on these 27 books.

The debates ranged over a number of issues. Christians by and large thought that books could be included in the list only if they were written by apostles or by companions of the apostles. Books could be included only, therefore, if they were very ancient—close to the time of Jesus. If a book had just been written recently, even if it was a very good book, it couldn't be included in the canon of scripture. Third, books had to be a book that was widely read throughout the Christendom; it couldn't just have appeal in just one locality. They needed to have widespread appeal to show that, in fact, there were books that were widely thought to have sacred authority. And fourth, most importantly, books that were to be included in the scriptures were books that had a correct teaching about doctrine. The teachings had to coincide with the teachings of the church at large. Probably the reason that books like the Gospel of Thomas and the Gospel of Peter were excluded was precisely because these books were not thought to be orthodox or correct in their teaching.

I want to stress that the question about whether these books were really written by apostles or really were ancient, those are historical questions, not theological questions. They have to be decided on the basis of historical evidence. That is the approach that we are going to be taking in this course, not asking whether theologically it makes sense. Yes, Matthew really wrote Matthew, or Paul really wrote the Book of Galatians. We are not going to be asking that question from a theological point of view, but from a historical point of view. I am not going to be trying to promote either belief of disbelief in these books. I will not be taking a religious point of view. I will be taking a historical point of view, discussing what these books say, what their prospective are, who wrote them, in what circumstances, for what circumstances, for what audiences, and for what reasons. This, then, will be a historical approach to the New Testament.

In conclusion, the books of the New Testament are major religious, cultural, historical artifacts, and they merit careful attention whether or not we happen to be Christian believers in these books. The 27 books of the New Testament are our earliest surviving documents that come from the early Christians, for the most part. These books—many of them which claim to be written by Jesus' own apostles—came to be regarded as sacred scripture by Christians. In this course we will be studying these books for what they can tell us about Jesus and his followers from the 1st century, and we'll be approaching them from a strictly historically prospective. We will begin our study then in the next lecture by considering the historical context within which these books were written. Because from a historical approach to the New Testament, the only way to understand them is to situate them within their own historical context.

The Greco-Roman Context
Lecture 2

Since context determines the meaning of all of our words and our actions, we need to ask what the context of a historical document was if we are going to understand it.

To begin our study of the New Testament, we must first place it in its own historical context. If we don't know the context of a work, we take it out of context. And if we take it out of context, we change its meaning. This is one of the reasons so many people have so many disputes about the meaning of the New Testament. I can show the importance of context for understanding using two illustrations. The context of a word or group of words is always crucial for interpretation. What would it mean, for example, if I said, "I love this course"? Well, it would depend on where I am, what I am doing, and what the word *course* means (course of a meal, golf course, college course) or how I inflect the word *love*. The same is true of everything in our existence, not just words, but also actions and even gestures. Because context determines the meaning of all our words and actions, we need to ask what the context was in which Jesus lived and the books of the New Testament were written.

Scholars usually refer to the religions of the New Testament world as Greco-Roman cults, commonly called *paganism*. I can begin our study by defining two key terms and providing some historical background. When scholars use the term *Greco-Roman world*, they are referring to the lands around the Mediterranean from roughly the time of Alexander the Great, c. 300 B.C., to the time of the Roman Emperor Constantine, c. A.D. 300. Alexander (356 B.C.–323 B.C.) was the great world military genius who conquered most of the Mediterranean, from his native land Macedonia to the Near East, including Egypt, Palestine, and Persia. As he conquered, he spread Greek religion and culture (learned from his tutor, Aristotle), so that by the time of the New Testament, nearly 300 years later, most of the highly educated elite throughout the Mediterranean spoke Greek, in addition to their native languages. The New Testament, as already pointed out, was originally written in Greek. The Greek word for Greece is *hellas*. The *Hellenistic* world is, therefore, the world that adopted Greek culture in the wake of Alexander's conquests.

The Romans eventually conquered most of these lands a couple of centuries after Alexander. Palestine (modern-day Israel) was under Roman control during the time of the New Testament. Jesus himself was born during the reign of the first Roman emperor, Caesar Augustus, himself a conqueror who brought peace to the Mediterranean area after years of social strife. Caesar Augustus, also known as Octavius, was a great general who overcame the internal divisions and social strife in Rome and had himself proclaimed its emperor. This began a long period characterized, for the most part, by internal peace and prosperity in the confines of the Roman world, which eventually stretched all the way from England to Syria and included North Africa and Egypt. The countries throughout the area were brought under Roman rule and forced to pay tribute to Rome in exchange for services rendered; Roman troops guarded the borders on the frontiers. Augustus thus inaugurated the *Pax Romana* (the "Roman Peace"), which was to last for about 200 years. The Roman world enjoyed a common language, coinage, and law and had a good road system and other benefits of civilization. These factors helped the spread of Christianity.

Corel Stock Photo Library.

Beginning with the rule of Caesar Augustus, Rome began a long period characterized by internal peace and prosperity.

The Empire did not convert to Christianity for several

centuries. The first Christian emperor was Constantine, who lived in the 4th century A.D. Before that time, virtually everyone—except for the Jews and the small group of Christians—adhered to local and state religions, or cults. These people—non-Jews and non-Christians—are often called *pagans* by modern scholars. Note that this term does not have derogatory connotations in this context. A *pagan* was simply someone who subscribed to any of the polytheistic religions found throughout the empire. These religions are called *cults* not because they were dangerous and marginalized; the word *cult* is simply an abbreviated form of the term *cultus deorum*, Latin for "care of the gods" (just as *agriculture* is "care of the fields"). These religions were concerned with caring for the gods so that the gods would, in exchange, care for the people.

For many people today, only one religion can be "true." Most ancient people didn't see it this way at all.

One way to understand the religious cults scattered throughout the Empire is to contrast them with what we think of as religion today. For most people today, it only makes sense that there is only one God. For most ancient people this didn't makes sense at all; in fact it was nonsense. People throughout antiquity were polytheists, believing in many gods. There were, of course, the "Great gods," known to us through ancient mythology—Greek gods, such as Zeus, Ares, and Aphrodite, or their Roman equivalents, Jupiter, Mars, and Venus. There were also numerous local gods who protected and cared for cities, towns, and villages; even less powerful gods who were localized in forests, rivers, and roads; family gods who cared for the home; gods who oversaw every human function and activity—the crops, the cupboard, the hearth, personal health, childbirth, and so on.

For many people today, only one religion can be "true." Most ancient people didn't see it this way at all. Because there were lots of gods, there was no reason to think that one was better for everyone than any other or that only one was to be worshipped and praised. They were all gods, so they all deserved to be worshipped. For this reason, the religions of the Greco-Roman world were far more tolerant of one another than most religions of our world today. Following one religion did not prevent you from following any other as well. You could worship as many gods as you chose. Everyone was expected to worship the state gods. These gods had made the Roman Empire great and, of course, they deserved to be worshipped. Not to do so was to oppose the state they had created, which was a political offense. These gods were often worshipped at major state festivals, which were eagerly awaited and enjoyed as vacations from work to be spent feasting and drinking with family and friends. The Christians, of course, refused to participate in these forms of pagan worship, which ultimately is why they came to be persecuted.

For most people today, religion is a matter of constant attention, thought, and devotion. It is a daily routine. For most ancient people, religion was a periodic matter. The gods did not demand constant devotion, just sacrifices at set times in the calendar and on other occasions as the need arose. There was no sense that one had to engage in daily devotion. In fact, for the most part, the gods were completely uninterested in how one lived one's daily life. Ancient people were concerned with ethical behavior, but the gods weren't. Ethics was, therefore, a matter of philosophy, not religion. Very few ethical activities were considered relevant to religion. Religion was almost exclusively a matter of ritual performances of sacrifice and prayer.

For most people today, it only makes sense that religion is a matter of proper belief. Oddly enough, most ancient people didn't see it that way. Odd as it might seem to us today, it didn't much matter to the ancients what you *believed* about the gods—only how you worshipped them through cultic acts. There weren't set doctrines to be believed, sacred books to study, or creeds to recite. As a result, there was no such thing as a heretic, or false believer, in these religions. You either practiced the religions or you didn't.

Religion is also a question of securing the afterlife for people today. Most ancient people, as it turns out, didn't believe in the afterlife. For them, religion was a question of securing the favor of the gods in the here and now. When life is lived close to the edge, and you can't really control major factors in your life—such as warfare, health, rain, and crops—then you need help from someone who *can* control them. The gods can and do. By worshipping the gods, you convince them to help you win your battles, secure the love of a particular woman, keep healthy, and grow your crops.

For many people today, God is far beyond humans in every way; most ancient people did not conceive of the divine realm as completely separated from the human by an unbridgeable chasm. There was a hierarchy among the gods themselves, a kind of divine pyramid, with the most powerful god at the top, the state gods below him, various local gods below them, family gods still further down, and so on. The more powerful gods were also more remote. Near the bottom of this divine pyramid were beings who were much more powerful than us, but much less powerful than the full gods. These were people that we might call divine men—humans who were born to the union of a god and a mortal—who were either more powerful than the rest of us, like Hercules, or more awe-inspiring, like the Emperor Augustus, or more wise, like the Greek philosopher Plato. There were stories, in fact, of divine men who were miraculously born, who could perform such divine miracles as healing the sick and raising the dead, who delivered divine teachings to their followers, and who at the end of their lives ascended to heaven to live among the gods forever (e.g., Apollonius of Tyana). This may sound familiar, because there are stories in the New Testament of Jesus doing all these things. For us today, these stories are completely unique, unlike anything else in our experience. For people in the Greco-Roman world, though, these stories would have made perfect sense. The existence of such divine men was widely recognized throughout their context. ∎

Essential Reading

Ehrman, *The New Testament: A Historical Introduction*, chap. 2.

Supplemental Reading

Lane Fox, *Pagans and Christians*.

Shelton, *As the Romans Did: A Source Book in Roman Social History*.

Turcan, *The Cults of the Roman Empire*.

1. Explain why "context" is so important for meaning. Think of some examples from your own experience in which a misunderstanding occurred because somebody took a word or action out of context.

2. Summarize the most important ways that religion in the Greco-Roman world was so different from what most people today think of as 'religion.' How can "common sense" in one context seem to be "non-sense" in another?

The Greco-Roman Context
Lecture 2—Transcript

In our last lecture, I showed that the New Testament consists of 27 books that were written by the earliest Christians. These books were later formed into a canon of scripture by the 4ᵗʰ century. Christians were thinking that these books consisted of sacred books that were inspired to provide information for Christians about what to believe and how to behave. I argued in that lecture that these books can be studied not only as religious books of faith, but also as historical documents. That'll be the approach we take in this course of lecture—trying to understand the New Testament from a historical point of view, suspending our own beliefs or unbelief about what it happens to say.

The place to begin the historical study of any document is to set it within its own historical context. If we don't know the context of the work, we will take it out of context; and if we take it out of context, we will change its meaning. This is one of the reasons why so many people have so many disputes about the meaning of the New Testament. As you can see at any time when you turn on your television to watch television evangelists or hear somebody on the radio, people from different perspectives have widely different views of the New Testament. It's not simply because of their own perspectives; it's also because most people don't try to understand what the New Testament might have originally meant within its own context. If you change the context of something, you change what it means. This is a point I try to teach my students, and I have to admit it is rather difficult to convince them, but I try to do so by showing several illustrations from their own lives of how things in different context mean different things.

This is true not only of words, but also of actions—and let me give you two illustrations to make my point before getting on to show what the historical context of the New Testament itself was. Take any group of words: words that would be commonly sensible within a particular context—where if you change the context, you change what they mean. Suppose you heard somebody say, "I love this course." Well, what is the context within which they are saying these words? If you hear somebody saying that while walking out of a classroom on the university campus—"I love this course"—well, it would make perfect sense what it means. It would mean that the person has a real affection for the professor or for the syllabus or they really like this course of study that they are engaged in. What if you hear the same words by somebody who's on the back nine of the local golf course, who is about to break par? "I love this course." Well, same words, but it means something quite different. What if you hear from a precocious young woman who is sitting at a posh restaurant in the middle of a five-course meal and she says, "I love this course?" Well, you might think, of course, that these things all mean basically the same thing—somebody loves something that they call a course. What if, though, you are in a boring classroom and you've got a professor who is droning on and on, and a student in the back row leans over to somebody else and says snidely, "I love this course," and snickers? Same words, but in fact it means just the opposite. It would mean in fact, "I hate this course." It depends on the context and how something is said. Words mean what they do depending on their context.

So, too, with gestures, actions, deeds—everything that we experience means something within its own context. What if you see somebody, standing upright with their arms raised up over their head and their index finger pointed up? What does it mean? Well, it depends. Is this a spectator at an air show? "Look what's happening!" Is it an athlete on a basketball court after they won the national championship? "We're Number One!" Is it a fervent Pentecostal at a revival meeting? "There's one way to Heaven." Or is it a desperate second grader on the back row who has had too much orange juice for breakfast and needs to do something about it quick? A gesture means what it does depending on its context; so, too, with everything in our experience.

Since context determines the meaning of all of our words and our actions, we need to ask what the context of a historical document was if we are going to understand it. And so for this class, what was the context within which Jesus himself lived and the books of the New Testament were written? I won't be able to say a lot about the context of the New Testament in this lecture—that would, in fact, require a course of 24 lectures of its own simply to begin to cover the waterfront—but I can at least say a few things in this lecture about the religious environment of the Greco-Roman world. In the next lecture, then, I will talk more specifically about Judaism, the religion that Jesus himself was born into and most of the New Testament authors originally adhered to. Scholars usually refer to the religions of the New Testament world as Greco-Roman cults—commonly called paganism.

I want to begin by defining three key terms. The term "Greco-Roman world," the term "paganism," and the term "cult." This first term will take a little bit of time to unpack. The Greco-Roman world. When scholars use the term "Greco-Roman world," they are referring to the land around the Mediterranean from roughly the time of Alexander the Great, who lived around 300 B.C., to the time of the Roman Emperor Constantine, who lived around A.D. 300. Alexander the Great: Alexander was born in the year 356 B.C., the son of Philip of Macedon, who was the ruler of Macedonia. Upon his father's execution, Alexander took over and engaged in a military campaign in which he conquered most of the Mediterranean area, from his native land, Macedonia, down into Greece and then further east, including Egypt, Palestine, and Persia. Alexander had, as a youth, studied under the Greek philosopher Aristotle. Under Aristotle, he had acquired an appreciation of Greek culture, Greek religion. As he conquered lands around the Mediterranean, Alexander promoted the adoption of Greek culture in these various lands. He built Greek cities—cities according to the Greek model—in which there were gymnasia and temples and various other Greek institutions. He urged the adoption of Greek language among the elite of these various cities. Generally he tried to propagate Greek culture so that he was not only conquering places, he was trying to subdue them culturally so as to unify the areas that he conquered under one common Greek culture. This is significant, of course, for the New Testament. As I have pointed out already, the New Testament itself was written in Greek. Well, why in Greek? Because Palestine and the lands around the Mediterranean where these various books were written were already under the influence of Alexander's Greek culture. The Greek word for Greece is "*hellas*." The Hellenistic world is, therefore, the world that had adopted Greek culture in the wake of Alexander's conquests.

The Romans eventually conquered most of these lands a couple of centuries after Alexander. Originally Rome had been a kingdom and started off as a small village that was eventually ruled by kings. By the time of the New Testament, it had been a republic for 500 years, meaning it had been ruled by a senate. And just before the New Testament period, it had become an empire ruled by an emperor, principally, rather than the senate. The 1st century B.C. had been a time of significant upheaval within the Roman world. Civil wars, including such things as the assassination of Julius Caesar, whose adopted son—his nephew, named Octavius—some years after Julius' assassination quelled the civil wars and, as a great general, brought peace and prosperity to the empire. He himself, in fact, was proclaimed then as the first emperor— Octavius, renamed Caesar Augustus. Under Caesar Augustus, there was a time of peace and prosperity within the confines of the Roman World. This was a world that eventually stretched all the way from England in the west to Syria in the east and stretched from North Africa in the south and Egypt on up into what would be today the central states of Western Europe. The countries throughout the area were brought under Roman rule and were forced to pay tribute to Rome in exchange for services rendered. Roman troops guarded the borders on the frontiers.

The Roman economy was agrarian. There wasn't much industry. The way people in Rome maintained their wealth and obtained their wealth was through owning land. The empire itself was supported by requiring tribute from its subject states—tribute usually in the form of crops and taxes that would then buy the various things that Rome wanted. Rome itself, of course, the City of Rome, was a magnificent place which had been funded by the provinces who were forced to pay tribute to them. It's a mistake to think that the Romans had their armies throughout the entire empire. They had their armies situated on the frontiers to guard against invasions from other places. This was a time, begun by Caesar Augustus, of peace within the empire. On the borders of the empire, of course, there continued to be wars. There is a significant war we are going to talk about later in this course within Palestine itself in which there is a Jewish uprising against the Romans that led to the destruction of the capital of Jerusalem and the burning of the temple in Jerusalem. But for most of the empire, for most of time, there was relative peace. Caesar Augustus inaugurated what people have since called the *Pax Romana*, the Roman peace, a 200-year period of peace and prosperity within the empire.

Pax Romana—I tell my students, by the way, that if you have a perfectly good English term for a concept, that you are much better off using the Latin to show that you have been through the university. So we don't call this the

Roman peace—we call it the *Pax Romana*. There are a number of benefits associated with the *Pax Romana*. Throughout the entire empire, people could speak the same language rather than promoting the adoption of Latin, which was Rome's own language. The Romans continued the use of Greek throughout the empire so that people could travel the entire expanse of the empire and make themselves understood by speaking Greek, much as today, people can speak English in large stretches in Europe. There was a common coinage throughout the empire so that one did not have to have a currency exchange whenever one crossed over a boundary. There were roads that the Romans built for their armies that made travel possible. There was relative safety through the empire—and peace. These were all benefits brought to that part of the world through the *Pax Romana*. They were benefits that helped—eventually helped—Christianity to spread throughout the empire because Christians could take advantage of the situation in order to propagate their faith.

If Christianity starts with Jesus and his apostles in the 1st century, it did not have a huge impact on the Roman World for several centuries, as we will see in the later lecture. The first emperor to convert to Christianity was the Emperor Constantine in the 4th century. Prior to that time, virtually everyone in the Roman World, except for the Jews and, of course, the small group of Christians, adhered to local and state religions or cults. These people, the non-Jews and the non-Christians, are often called "pagans" by modern scholars. I need to be clear on this context that the term "pagan," when used by historians, does not have derogatory connotations. It does not mean the same thing as I mean when I call my next-door neighbor a pagan. A pagan in this context was simple somebody who subscribed to any of the polytheistic religions found throughout the empire. These religions are often called cults, not because they were dangerous and marginalized; the word "cult" itself is short for the Latin term *cultus deorum*, Latin for "care of the gods." Just as in English we have the term "agriculture," which means "care of the fields," you can have *cultus deorum*, care of the Gods. These are cults, then, because they are concerned with caring for the needs of the gods. How is that done? Principally through sacrifices and prayers.

One way to understand the religious cults scattered throughout the Roman Empire is to contrast them with what we might think of as religion today. For most people today it only makes sense to say that there is one god. If there is any god, there is one god. For most ancient people, that common sense, in fact, was nonsense. Most ancient people couldn't understand at all the idea that there would be only God—most people throughout antiquity. The fact is virtually everybody throughout antiquity, except for the Jews and then the Christians, were polytheist, believing in many gods. There were, of course, the Great Gods, known to us today through ancient mythology, Greek Gods like Zeus and Aries and Aphrodite, or the Roman equivalents Jupiter and Mars and Venus. But there were lots of other gods: Gods that were local deities who protected and cared for cities or towns and villages; even less powerful gods who were in charge of smaller places—gods in charge of the forest or the river or of a road; families had their own gods—gods who oversaw every human function and activity, the crops, the cover, the harvest, the personal health of a family member, childbirth; gods in charge of virtually every function. These ancient religions, then, first of all differ from ours in that they subscribe to polytheistic views.

Second of all, most people today think that only one religion can possibly be true; if one religion is true, than others have to be false. Ancient people simply didn't see it that way. Since there were lots of gods, there was no reason to think that one god was any better than any other god, or that only one god was to be worshiped and praised. They were all gods, and so they all deserved to be worshiped. For this reason, the religions of the Greco-Roman world were far more tolerant of one another than most religions are in our world today. We might think of Roman religion as being intolerant because of what we know happened to Christians who were persecuted by Romans. I will say some things about that in a later lecture. By and large, a more striking feature of Roman religion was that it was highly tolerant precisely because it was so widely polytheistic. You can worship any gods you wanted to, in any way you wanted to, and nobody else really much cared. Everyone was, of course, expected to worship the state gods. These were the gods that had made the Roman Empire great, and so, of course, they deserved to be worshiped; and if you refused to worship them, then you must have some ulterior motive for refusing. In other words, it was seen to be a political offense not to worship the state gods. These gods were often worshiped at major state festivals, which were looked forward to and enjoyed as a time of vacation from work and a time with family and friends, a time to feast and to drink. Christians, of course, refused to participate in these state cults because they thought that to worship these other gods was to compromise one's commitment to the true God. Most other people—in fact, virtually everybody else—though, didn't see a problem with worshiping the state gods along with the local gods and along with their family gods.

So, first point, ancient religions were polytheistic. Second point, they tended not to look upon one religion as true and others as false. Third point, for most people today, religion is a matter of constant devotion to God. For ancient people, on the other hand, religion was a periodic matter—not a matter of continual devotion, but a matter of periodic attention to the gods. These gods didn't demand constant devotion. They simply demanded sacrifices at set times in the calendar and as the occasion arose. Most gods, in fact, in the ancient world, were completely uninterested in how people lived their daily lives. They were uninterested in how people lived their daily lives. This is not to say that ancient people were unconcerned with matters of ethics. Ancient people were concerned about ethics as much as we are today. But in this ancient world, ethics were a matter of philosophy, not a matter of religion. There were very few ethical activities that were considered to be relevant to religion. Religion, then, was almost exclusively a matter of ritual performances of sacrifice and prayer, not of daily devotion.

Fourth, for most people today, it only makes sense to say that religion is a matter of proper belief. What you believe is what matters about religion. Oddly enough, for most ancient people, this wasn't the case at all. Far less important than what you believed about the gods was that you performed the proper cultic acts in their honor. Sacrifices of animals and foodstuffs and prayers performed at home, occasionally at the local temple, and on big occasions, at civic festivals. Odd as it might seem to us today, in the ancient world it didn't much matter what you believed about the gods, only how you worshiped them through cultic acts. And so there weren't set doctrines to be believed. There weren't sacred books to study. There weren't creeds to recite. As a result, there was no such thing in these religions as a heretic or a false believer. You either practiced them or you didn't.

Fifth, for many people today, the question of religion is a question of securing the afterlife. In other words, for many people, religion today is a matter of acquiring proper fire insurance. Most of my students think that if there's no afterlife, then there is no point of religions. If you are not going to go to Heaven if you are good, or go to Hell if you are bad, then why not party all the time? Ancient people, interestingly enough, didn't see it this way at all. As it turns out, most people in the ancient world didn't even believe in an afterlife. There is talk about afterlife in some literary text from the ancient world, but recent studies of inscriptions on tombstones and other material remains demonstrate pretty clearly that most people thought that when you died, that was the end of the story. Why, then, would you bother to be religious? For most ancient people, religion wasn't a matter of the afterlife, it was a matter of securing the favor the gods in the here and now. These were people who lived life close to the edge, for the most part. In a world where there are no modern methods of irrigation; when there are not massive possibilities of transportation of goods; when there isn't any advanced technology or sophisticated machinery; when there isn't modern medicine, things are very different. This is a world in which getting a tooth abscess will normally kill you. This is a world in which every adult woman of childbearing age has to bear an average of five children in order to keep the population constant. This is a different world from ours, in which life is lived on the edge. The worship of the gods is not meant to secure the afterlife; it is to secure the present life. By worshiping the gods, you can convince them to help you win your battles; secure the love of the woman next door; keep healthy; grow your crops. You can sustain life in their present.

Sixth, for many people today, God is far beyond us in every imaginable way. God is the creator above all who has an unbridgeable chasm between where he is and what he is and what we are. The ancients didn't quite see it that way. The ancients did, of course, think of the divine realm was something fantastically great, but there was not an unbridgeable chasm between the gods and humans. As I have already indicated, within the polytheistic system, there is a kind of a hierarchy of the gods. We might think of it as a kind of divine pyramid with the most powerful god or gods at the very top. Some ancient pagans did believe in one ultimate god who was over all. Under this great god there were the other gods—say, the gods of Mount Olympus that we know about from mythology. The state gods who are far beyond what we can imagine in terms of power and strength. Below these gods there are very local gods who aren't quite as powerful as the state god. Below them would be the family gods and various other smaller local gods. All of these gods of course are far beyond human capacity. But near the bottom of this divine pyramid, there is another kind of layer of divine beings that are a lot more like us—in fact, people who might be called divine men. Divine men—human beings who are borne to the union of a god and a mortal, who are more powerful than the rest of us—someone like Hercules or the Greek Heracles, or someone who is completely awe-inspiring like the Roman emperor, or someone who is supernaturally wise like Plato. Ancient people believed that there were, in fact, divine humans.

I sometimes begin my classes on New Testament at Chapel Hill by talking about an individual we know about from about 2,000 years ago, who was a remarkable person. Even before he was born, his mother had a visitor from Heaven telling her that her son wasn't going to be normal human being, he was going to be the son of God. His birth was attended by supernatural signs. As a child, he showed himself to be quite a prodigy, impressing the religious leader of his own day. As an adult, he left home and engaged in an itinerant preaching ministry in which he went from village to town trying to convince people that they could give up on the material things of this world and simply be concerned about the spiritual things of life. He acquired a number of followers who became convinced that he wasn't a mortal—that he was divine. And he did miracles to help them believe what they believed about him. He was able to heal the sick and cast out demons and raise the dead. At the end of his life, his enemies decided to bring him up on charges before the Roman authorities before whom he appeared. But even after he left this world, his followers continued to believe in him. Some claim that they saw him alive after he had ascended to Heaven—that he appeared to them to convince them that there is a life after this death. Some of them later even wrote books about him, but I doubt if any of you have read the books.

In fact, as with my students in Chapel Hill, you probably don't know who I have been talking about. I've been referring to Apollonius of Tyana, a pagan philosopher, a worshiper of the Greek gods. Apollonius of Tyana lived at about the same time as Jesus—the 1st century of the Common Era. His followers believed that he was the son of God. They knew about Jesus. They thought that Jesus was a magician and that he practiced magic and that he was a hoax. Well, the followers of Jesus thought this about Apollonius of Tyana.

We have stories like those of Apollonius and like those of Jesus of people who are born supernaturally, who could do miracles, deliver supernatural teachings, who then ascended into Heaven. Why? Because these people thought there wasn't an unbridgeable chasm between the gods and humans, that, in fact, that were some commerce between the divine realm and human realm. These stories about divine men like Apollonius of Tyana and others may sound unusual to us. We know only stories about Jesus that sound like this, but in the ancient world there were lots of people who had stories told about them of this sort. People in the ancient world would make perfect sense about the stories of Jesus because in fact they knew of other divine men who were widely recognized as having commerce with the divine realm.

And so let me just wrap this up. In this lecture we have seen the importance of establishing the historical context for Jesus and his followers, including those among his followers who eventually wrote the books of the New Testament. It is important to understand the emergence of the Christian religion within this context of other religions of the Greco-Roman World—religions that were thoroughly polytheistic and, by and large, that were widely tolerant of one another. These other religions focused on cultic acts of sacrifice in the temples to the gods and on prayers rather than on doctrines. They were religions that focused on the activities of the gods in the present, in the here and now, rather than in the afterlife. And they thought that there were divine humans who were manifest among us. Far and away, though, the most important religion for understanding the context of Jesus and early Christianity is Judaism, a religion that stood apart from the pagan religions of its environment. In the next lecture, we will explore some of the important features of this ancient Jewish religion.

Ancient Judaism
Lecture 3

The first distinctive aspect of Judaism was they were monotheists. Second of all, Jews believed that this one God, the creator of all, had made a covenant with his people.

In the last lecture, we saw that we must place the New Testament in its own historical context to understand it. Ancient Judaism is an important part of that context. Even though ancient Judaism is sometimes portrayed, even by scholars, as being completely unlike any other religion in its environment, a moment's thought shows that cannot have been the case. If it were completely different, no one could have recognized it as a religion. Imagine how you would describe an Austin-Healy Sprite to someone who had never seen one before or who didn't know what a sports car was—or even a car. In fact, Judaism had a number of points of contact, or broad points of similarity, with other religions of the Greco-Roman world. Like pagans, the Jews believed in a divine realm, inhabited by one supreme God but also by other divine beings of less power, beings such as angels, archangels, and demons. Like pagans, Jews had sacred places devoted to their worship of this god, where sacrifices could be made and prayers recited. Like pagans, Jews saw worship as principally involving cultic acts—animal sacrifices and prayers in accordance with ancient tradition—meant to propitiate God and demonstrate devotion. Like pagans, most Jews were more concerned with life in the present than in life after death. God was the God of this world, and he was concerned about how his people lived in it.

At the same time, there were significant differences between Jews and everyone else in the Greco-Roman world. To understand Judaism more fully, we should talk about these areas of distinctiveness. Possibly the most distinctive feature of ancient Judaism, in contrast to the various forms of paganism, is that it was monotheistic. Some pagans, as we've seen, thought there was one God who was above all others, but Jews took this even further. There was only one true God who was to be worshipped and served; this was the God who had created the universe. He was more powerful than all the other gods which were widely thought to exist, even among Jews.

He was not the god of a particular locality, even though originally he may have started out as the local deity of the land of Judah. He was so holy, so distinct from everything else, that not even his name could be pronounced.

Jews, therefore, spelled his name in a way that could not be pronounced (the *tetragrammaton*; i.e., the "four letters" that were God's personal name). He was the only one that was to be worshipped.

Jews believed that this one God had made a covenant—a treaty or a pact—with the ancestors of the Jewish people. He had agreed to protect and honor them, so long as they agreed to worship him and

Early Judaism was not a monolith, any more than today's Christianity is a monolith. In fact, there were many kinds of Jews in the 1st century who believed different things and practiced their religion differently.

behave as he instructed them. This covenant was first made with the father of the Jews, Abraham. It was confirmed under Moses, the great Savior of Israel. After Moses led the Exodus out of Egypt, God gave him his Law on Mount Sinai. The Law of Moses, in other words, represented the obligation of the Jews to God, governed by the covenant.

This Law came to be embedded in writings, particularly the first five books of the Hebrew Bible, also known as the Torah. These books (Genesis, Exodus, Leviticus, Numbers, Deuteronomy,) as a group are sometimes also known as the Pentateuch, a word that means "the five scrolls." In the modern world, Christians have sometimes misunderstood the importance of the Law in Judaism. It was never meant to be an undoable list of dos and don'ts that Jews had to keep (even though they were unable to) in order to have salvation. Instead, the Law was seen as the greatest gift God had ever given to humans—his own direction on how to worship him and live together. Following the Law was the greatest joy, because doing so meant yielding oneself to the all-powerful and loving God who ruled the universe and called his people out of slavery. Following the Law was a *requirement* for salvation, not a *response* to salvation. Included in the Law, of course, were the Ten Commandments, and laws that were designed to make Jews distinct from other peoples. For example, Jews were to circumcise their baby boys; they were not to work on the Sabbath, the seventh day of the week; and they were to observe kosher food laws, not eating, for example, pork or shrimp.

One other distinctive feature of ancient Judaism involved its places of worship, especially the Temple in Jerusalem. This was the one and only Temple, a glorious place in the days of Jesus. It was large enough to encompass 25 football fields and it was expensive: Parts of it were overlaid with gold. It was the only place in Judaism where animal sacrifices could be offered to God. Because animal sacrifices were so much a part of the religion, the Temple was a central place for all Jewish worship. It was located in Jerusalem, the capital of Judea. Jews would flock from all over the world to worship at the Temple.

Most Jews in the 1st century, though, did not live anywhere near Jerusalem but had scattered throughout the Mediterranean at different periods of foreign conquest. Because the Temple was so remote for most Jews, the

In 1947, a library of religious scrolls for an Essene community were discovered in the Qumran Caves.

practice of having local places of worship, called *synagogues* (from the Greek term meaning "gathering together"), had developed by the time of the New Testament.

Early Judaism was not a monolith, any more than today's Christianity is a monolith. In fact, there were many kinds of Jews in the 1st century who believed different things and practiced their religion differently. One way to illustrate the variety of early Judaism is to talk about four of the major groups that we know about from the time of Jesus. These were the Pharaisees, Sadducees, Essenes, and the Fourth Philosophy. Not every Jew belonged to one of these groups. These aren't like Christian denominations (almost all Christians belong on one level to one or another) but like local civic organizations (the Elks, the Chambers of Commerce, the Rotary clubs; some people belong to them but most don't). They are useful to examine, though, because they reveal some aspects of early Jewish diversity.

The best known group was the Pharisees, who contrary to modern misperception, were not professional hypocrites. They were a committed group of Jews who believed in following God's law, as revealed in the Torah, absolutely as far as possible, and who devised certain "oral" laws (as opposed to the written—and sometimes ambiguous—Law of Moses) to help them do so. These oral laws and debates about them eventually came to be written down by later rabbis, or Jewish teachers, about 200 years after Jesus, in the book called the *Mishnah*, the heart of the very large collection of Jewish lore and learning called the Talmud. In short, in their religious outlook, the Pharisees stressed the Law.

The Pharisees were sometimes opposed by the Sadducees, who did not subscribe to the oral Law. We are not well informed about the Sadducees, because none of them left us any writings. It appears, though, that the Sadducees were made up of the upper-class aristocracy of the Jews. Many of them were priests in the Jewish temple and served as the liaison with the ruling power, the Romans. In their religious outlook, the Sadducees stressed the Temple and the need to perform the sacrifices to God as prescribed in the Law.

The Essenes were a group of highly religious Jews who believed that the rest of the people of Israel had fallen away from God and had, therefore, become impure. Essenes worked to preserve their own purity, apart from the impurity of those around them. Occasionally, they founded their own monastic communities where they could live together and worship God. One such community was at a place called Qumran, where the Dead Sea Scrolls, a library of an Essene community, were discovered in 1947. In their religious outlook, the Essenes stressed the need to maintain their own purity in view of the fact that the world as we know it was soon going to come to a crashing halt, when God intervened in history and overthrew the forces of evil (which included most of the other Jews).

Another group of Jews is sometimes called, simply, the Fourth Philosophy. This group comprises a number of groups of Jews who believed that God had given them the land of Israel and that it should be taken back by force from those who currently ruled it.

One kind of ancient Jewish perspective has proved particularly important for understanding the historical Jesus and the New Testament: Jewish apocalypticism. We know about this particular world view from a number of sources, including the biblical book of Daniel; some non-biblical Jewish books from the time; including the book of 1 Enoch; and the Dead Sea Scrolls. This was a widespread form of Jewish belief, held to, for example, by various thinkers among the Pharisees and the Essenes. The major tenets of this form of Judaism were as follows: (1) Apocalypticists held to a dualistic view of the world. There are two fundamental forces of reality, the forces of good and evil. History itself was seen dualistically. We are now living in the evil age, but there is a good age that is yet to come. (2) Apocalypticists were pessimists, to the extent that they thought life in this world could not be improved by human effort. The forces of evil were in control and were going to make life worse and worse. (3) But there was a day of reckoning coming, in which God would judge this world and overthrow the forces of evil. (4) This coming judgment of God was imminent. In the words of one prominent Jewish apocalypticist: "Truly I tell you, some of you standing here will not taste death until they see that the Kingdom of God has come in power." These are the words of Jesus, one of the best known Jewish apocalypticists from the ancient world. ∎

Essential Reading

Cohen, *From the Maccabbees to the Mishnah.*

Ehrman, *The New Testament: A Historical Introduction*, chap. 2.

Supplemental Reading

Sanders, *Judaism: Practice and Belief.*

Sandmel, *Judaism and Christian Beginnings.*

Questions to Consider

1. In what ways was ancient Judaism like and unlike Christianity as practiced in the modern world?

2. Summarize the major tenets of Jewish apocalypticism. Are there any major religious groups in the modern world that seem to embrace a similar point of view?

Ancient Judaism
Lecture 3—Transcript

In the last lecture, we saw that in order to understand the New Testament, we need to place it within its own historical context; and so we considered the pagan religions of Greco-Roman World, and we saw how they differed from modern religion in their emphasis on polytheism, their stress on diversity, tolerance, cultic acts, and life in the present. We now can move to the religion of particular importance for the understanding of Jesus and the New Testament— the religion of ancient Judaism.

Even though Judaism is often portrayed, even by modern scholars, as being completely unlike any other religion in its ancient environment, a moment's thought shows that this could not have been the case. If Judaism were completely unlike every other religion, it wouldn't have been recognized as a religion at all. We can only recognize something in relationship to other things that are within our own experience.

Let me illustrate this point. Sometimes, in order impress my students, I tell them that when I was in college I drove an Austin- Healey Sprite. Unfortunately this doesn't impress anyone because my students don't know what an Austin-Healey Sprite was, and so I have to explain to them; but I explain it in terms that they can understand. So sometimes I will tell them Austin-Healey Sprite was kind of like an MG; in fact, it was the same car as the MG Midget. Well, what if they don't know what an MG Midget was? Then I would say an MG Midget was like a Mazda Miata. Now most of my students know what a Mazda Miata is, but if they don't, I have to explain. Mazda Miata is a sports car. Well, what if they don't know what a sports car is? A sports car is a small car, a two-seater that usually sits low to the ground and is considered sporty. Well, what if they don't know what a car is? Well, they do—but what if they didn't? Well, a car is like a horseless carriage. What if they don't know what horses are, or carriages are? The way you explain something is by explaining in terms that somebody already understands. Imagine how you yourself might try to explain what an aardvark is to somebody, or what a kumquat is. You have to explain things in terms that people already understand because the only way we understand anything is in its relationships to other things that are like it.

Judaism was like other religions of the ancient world in many respects. To be sure, it was also different, but it had some similarities. Like pagans, ancient Jews believed in a divine realm that was inhabited by one supreme god, but they also believed that there were other divine beings of lesser powers—beings like angels and archangels and demons, seraphim, and cherubim. In other words, they also had a divine realm that could be structured as a kind of pyramid with, of course, the one true God at the top.

These Jews had sacred places there especially devoted to their worship of this god, where sacrifices could be made and prayers could be recited. Like pagans, Jews saw worship as principally involving cultic acts—animal sacrifices, and prayers in accordance with their ancient tradition. Sacrifices and prayers that were meant to perpetuate God and demonstrate their devotion to him. Like pagans, most Jews were far more concerned with life in the present rather than life after death. God was the god of this world, and he was particularly concerned about how people lived within it. And so there are a number of very basic similarities between Jews and pagans in the ancient world.

At the same time, there were significant differences between Jews and everyone else, and so to understand Judaism more fully, we should talk about areas of distinctiveness—areas of Judaism that made it unlike other ancient religions, realizing, of course, at the same time, that there was a good deal of diversity among all the pagans and also within Judaism. And so what are the distinctive features of Judaism?

First, possibly the most distinctive feature of ancient Judaism in opposition to various forms of paganism is that Judaism was monotheistic. Some pagans, as we have seen, thought that there was one god who was above all others, but Jews took this even further; there was only one God who's to be worshiped and served. This was the God that had created the universe. This God was more powerful than all the other gods. Most Jews, at a very early period, did believe that there were other gods. Evidence for this is found in the Bible itself—in the Hebrew Bible, the Ten Commandments. The first of the Ten Commandments says, "You shall have no other gods before me," which presupposes that the other gods existed, they simply weren't to be worshiped as the head of the gods of Israel. At an earlier time, most Jews did believe that there were other gods, but that only one God was to be worshiped. By the time of the 1st century, the time of the New Testament, though, many Jews had come to believe that there was really only one ultimate God. This God was not the god of a particular locality as many pagan deities were. Originally, the Jewish God may have been a local deity, namely the deity of the land of Judah. The name "Jew," by the way, comes from the fact that, originally, Jews came from Judah. Eventually, when Jews were dispersed outside of their homeland, Judah, they continued to worship the god of Judah, and so were known by other people as Jews—people who worshiped the god of Judah. This god, by the 1st century, was not about to be a local god, but a universal God who had created the world. This God was far beyond anything people can think or imagine. He was so holy, so distinct from everything else that not even his name could be pronounced. Jews, therefore, spelled God's name in a way that couldn't be pronounced. This is the famous tetragrammaton—the four letters which consist of God's name. The four letters which represented God's personal name that was never to be pronounced, this one God who was so holy and so far removed from us, who had created the world was the only one to be worshiped.

And so the first distinctive aspect of Judaism was they were monotheists. Second of all, Jews believed that this one God, the creator of all, had made a covenant with his people. The term "covenant" means a treaty or a pact. Jews believed that God had made a covenant, a treaty or pact, with the ancestors of the Jewish people. He had agreed to protect and honor them, so long as they agreed to worship him and behave in the ways that he instructed them. This covenant, as recorded in the Hebrew Bible, was made with the Father of the Jews, Abraham. It was confirmed, though, under Moses, the great savior of Israel, whom God had raised up to deliver his people out of their slavery in Egypt. After Moses led the exodus out of Egypt, God gave him his Law on Mount Sinai. This was the Law that was to direct the worship and communal life of God's people—Israel. And in fact, this Law comprises the third major distinctive aspect of Judaism: the Law of Moses represented the covenantal obligation of the Jews to God. This Law came to be embedded in writings, particularly the first five books of the Hebrew Bible, which are sometimes simply called the Torah. The word *Torah* is a Hebrew word, which means literally guidance or direction; or, somewhat more woodenly, it means law. And so the Torah is often used simply as the designation of the Law of Moses, the Torah. The word is sometimes also used to refer to the first five books of the Hebrew Bible in which this law can be found: Genesis, Exodus, Leviticus, Numbers, and Deuteronomy. These five books as a group, sometimes called the Law. Sometimes they're known under their Greek name, *Pentateuch*. "*Pentateuch*"—Greek for the five scrolls."

I want to take a brief excursion to explain that many Christians in the modern world haven't understood the importance of the Law within Judaism. Many Christians have been raised to think that the Law was some kind of undoable list of "Dos and "Don'ts", which had to be followed in order to obtain salvation, but since it was undoable, couldn't be followed for salvation; so the Jews were stuck with a law they couldn't keep, which therefore ended up leading them into damnation. In fact, Jews never saw the Law as an undoable list of "Dos and Don'ts." Instead, the Law was seen by most Jews as the greatest gift God had ever given to humans. This was God's direction on how to worship him and on how Jews could live together in their communities. Jews saw the Law as the greatest joy because following the Law meant yielding oneself to the all-powerful and loving God who ruled the universe and had called his people out of their slavery. Following the Law was not a requirement for salvation for ancient Jews; following the Law was a response to the salvation that God had already given his people.

Included in the Law, of course, were not just the Ten Commandments, but also laws that were designed to make the Jews distinct from other people. Jews, for example, were to circumcise their baby boys. They were not to work one day out of seven, on the Sabbath. They were to observe special food laws—keeping kosher—not eating, for example, pork or shrimp. These were laws that were designed to keep Jews distinct from other peoples.

And so distinctive aspects of Judaism: monotheism, the covenant, the Law. Fourth, have distinctive places of worship; especially, Jews in the 1st century worshiped in the temple in Jerusalem. Pagan religions had temples where sacrifices were performed and prayers could be said to the gods. Jews, unlike other people, had only one temple where sacrifices could be performed. It was a temple that was located in accordance with the Law itself—the Torah itself—in the city of Jerusalem. This was a fabulously large and glorious place in the days of Jesus. It was large. If you have visited the temple's remains in Jerusalem today, you will know how large it was. The wall surrounding the temple encompasses an area that was large enough to place 25 American football fields in. These were big walls, 10 stories high. The inner parts of the temple were magnificently done in the days of Jesus. Parts of it were overlaid with gold. It was an extremely expensive and glorious sight that Jews would come from all over the world to visit and to worship in. This was the only place in Judaism where animal sacrifices could be offered to God. Moreover, since animal sacrifices were so much a part of the religion (according to the Law, people were to sacrifice animals), the temple, then, was the central place for all Jewish worship. As I've indicated, it was located in the capital city of Judea, Jerusalem. Jews would come to Jerusalem to worship in the temple from all over the world, especially during annual festivals like the Passover feast, which commemorates the exodus of the people of Israel from Egypt under Moses.

Most Jews in the 1st century, of course, didn't live anywhere near Jerusalem, but they had scattered throughout the Mediterranean at different periods of foreign conquest. Since the temple was so remote for most Jews, since most Jews could never go there, if they could go, maybe they could go once during their lifetime.

Since it was so remote for most Jews, they developed, by the time of the New Testament, a practice of having local places of worships called synagogues. The word "synagogue" is a Greek term again, which simply means "a gathering together." A synagogue was a place where Jews could gather together for prayer and the study of the Torah. A synagogue at this time could be formed wherever there was a quorum of ten adult men. There were no sacrifices performed in a synagogue. Instead, the synagogue was a place of prayer and the reading and interpretation of Torah undertaken on the Jewish day of rest, the Sabbath. And so the fourth distinctive characteristics of Jews—their distinctive places of worship.

To this point I've described some of the basic features of Judaism, both how it is similar to and different from pagan religions of the ancient world. Many people make the mistake of thinking that Judaism in this ancient world was some kind of monolith, that there was one thing called Judaism. In fact, Judaism in the 1st century was no more monolithic than modern Christianity is today. People are more widely aware in our context of the diversity of modern Christianity. There are similarities between Greek Orthodox priests and Appalachian snake handlers, but, in fact, there are a lot of differences, too, that are often more striking. Ancient Judaism, in many ways, was even more diverse than modern Christianity. I won't be able to explain all the diversity of early Judaism now. I do want to illustrate it, though, by talking about some of the major aspects of Judaism that we know about that represent its diversity.

One way to illustrate its diversity is to talk about the four major groups that we know about from the time of Jesus. I should emphasize that it's not the case that every Jew belonged to one of these four groups. There were Jews that believed all sorts of strange things that don't sound much like what we think of as Judaism, that didn't belong to these four groups. These four groups all agreed on the basic tenets of Judaism that I have laid out, but there were striking differences among them. The four groups that I will be talking about are the Pharisees, the Sadducees, the Essenes, and what's called the Fourth Philosophy.

The best-known group were the Pharisees. The word "Pharisee" probably comes from an ancient Persian word which means separated ones. This group was called Pharisees because they were separated off from other people because of their eminent holiness. Pharisees have been widely misunderstood, again, in modern Christian circles. Many people associate the term Pharisee with hypocrite. In fact, in some modern dictionaries, one of the tertiary definitions of Pharisee is hypocrite, which is an interesting designation when you think about it. It would be comparable to having a dictionary in 2,000 years defining Episcopalians as drunkards or Baptists as adulterers. Of course, there are probably drunkards among Episcopalians and adulterers among Baptists, but defining them in those terms is a little bit odd. Same thing with Pharisees. Pharisees were not professional hypocrites, or as I tell my students, they didn't have to take a "Hippocritic" oath to be a Pharisee. The Pharisees were, in fact, a highly committed group of Jews who believed in following the Torah, God's law, absolutely as far as possible. They believed that the Law had been given by God to direct the people of Israel. Therefore, this Law had to be followed. It is a blueprint, in a sense, for how people ought to live their lives.

The problem with the Law of Moses for many Jews in the 1st century was that this law was not explicit in how it ought to be followed and, in many places, is completely ambiguous. For example, the Law says that a person is to honor the Sabbath day and keep it holy. Well, what does that mean and how does one do it? Most Jews thought that this meant you shouldn't work on the Sabbath. Fine, but what does it mean to work? Well, if you are a farmer, probably working would involve harvesting your crops; well, you shouldn't harvest crops on the Sabbath, then. What if you aren't really harvesting your crops, but you just want something to eat and you go into your field and pick some grain to eat it? Is that work or not? Well, some people would consider that to be comparable to harvesting and some wouldn't. Well, the decision has to be made if you are to keep the Sabbath day holy or allowed to go into your field on the Sabbath and eat grain. Some people said, "Yes;" some people said, "No." What if you go through the field on the Sabbath, and you don't actually eat the grain, but you walk through and you knock some of the grain off—is that permitted? Well, on one hand that's kind of like harvesting because you are taking the grain from the stalk; but on the other hand it's obviously not work. So is it permitted or not? A decision has to be made. The Pharisees were concerned to make the right decisions, and so they developed a set of laws that are sometimes called the Oral Laws that would help them interpret the written Law of Moses. These Oral Laws, and the debates about these laws, were eventually written down nearly 200 years after Jesus in a book that is now called the "Mishna," which is the heart of the large collection of Jewish lore and learning called the "Talmud." Pharisees were behind the collection of these Oral Laws that were intended to help Jews follow the written Law of Moses. Nothing necessarily hypocritical about this particular activity, they simply wanted to do what God had told them to. In short, in their religious outlook, Pharisees stressed the Law.

The Pharisees were sometimes opposed by the second group, known as the Sadducees, who did not subscribe to the Oral Law. We are not well-informed about the Sadducees because none of them left us any writings. It does appear though that Sadducees were made up of the upper-class aristocracy of the Jews. Many of them appear to have been priests in the Jewish temple, and since they compromised the aristocracy, many of them served as a kind of liaison with the ruling power—the Romans. In their religious outlook, since the Sadducees were connected with the temple, Sadducees had appeared to have stressed temple sacrifice and the need to perform sacrifices as God had prescribed within the law. So you have Pharisees stressing the Oral Laws, and Sadducees who don't accept the Pharisees' Oral Laws but, instead, stress sacrifice in the temple.

A third group is called the Essenes. Ironically, the Essenes are the one group of the four that are not mentioned in the New Testament, but that are the group that we are best informed about because of recent archaeological discoveries. The Essenes were a group of highly religious Jews who believed that the rest of the people of Israel had fallen away from God and become impure. Essenes worked to preserve their own purity apart from the impurity of those around them. Occasionally, they founded their own monastic communities where they could live together and worship God. Their stress is on ritual purity in the face of impurity around them. One such monastic community that the Essenes founded was located in a place called Qumran, where the Dead Sea Scrolls were discovered in 1947. The Dead Sea Scrolls were a library of an Essene community located to the northwest of the Dead Sea. This library has been significant for a number of reasons. For one thing, it included some very ancient texts of the Hebrew bible. In fact, the texts of the Hebrew Bible, the manuscripts of the Hebrew Bible found in the Dead Sea Scrolls, are a thousand years earlier than other surviving manuscripts that we have for the Hebrew Bible; so they are extremely important to reconstruct what the original Hebrew Bible might have said. Even more importantly for our context, the Dead Sea Scrolls contain documents produced for and by this Essene community itself, so that by reading these documents, we can discover what rules this community followed in its communal life together. The books also contain hymnals—books of songs—commentaries on scripture, and interesting prophetic descriptions of future events. In their religious outlook, the Essenes stressed the need to maintain their own purity in view of the fact that the world as we know it—well, at least as they knew it—was soon going to come to a crashing halt. They believed that God was going to intervene in history, overthrow the forces of evil—including the forces that had inspired many Jews, the Jewish leaders, especially their enemies, the Sadducees.

The fourth group of Jews is sometimes simply called the Fourth Philosophy. This Fourth Philosophy comprised of a number of groups of Jews who believed that God had given them the land of Israel, who also believed that since a foreign power dominated the land, that God had given them the authorization and the power to overthrow the domineering force. In other words, the Fourth Philosophy proposed to engage in violent resistance to foreign powers dominating the land. Eventually, the Fourth Philosophy had its way; in the year 66 A.D., just a generation after Jesus' death, there was a revolt against the Romans that broke out, leading to a three-and-a-half year war that ended in the destruction of Jerusalem and the burning of the temple. The religious outlook of the Fourth Philosophy then centered on the Jewish homeland as given to the Jewish people, that should not be ruled by any foreign power.

To this point, I've talked about some of the major aspects of Judaism and some of the diversity. I want to end this lecture by talking about one particular kind of Jewish perspective that has proven particularly important for understanding the historical Jesus and the New Testament. This is a perspective that modern scholars have called "ancient Jewish apocalypticism." We know about Jewish apocalypticism from a number of ancient sources, including some books of the Hebrew Bible, like the Book of Daniel, and some non-biblical books including those of the Dead Sea Scrolls. This appears to have been a widespread form of belief among many ancient Jews. Held by some Pharisees, maybe a lot of Pharisees; held by Essenes and by others.

The major tenets of this form of Judaism are as follows. First, apocalypticists held to a dualistic view of the world. They believed that there were two fundamental components of reality—the forces of good and the forces of evil—and everything and everybody aligns themselves with one or the other of these forces. Moreover, history itself was seen dualistically. We are now living in an evil age, ruled by the forces of evil, including the Devil and demons and sin and disease and death. These are all powers opposed to us that are ruling this world. But there is an age that is coming that will be good, an age in which God will overthrow the forces of evil and establish his good kingdom here on Earth. And so the first point, apocalypticists were dualists, believing in cosmic forces of good and evil, and in two ages, this evil age and the age to come.

Apocalypticists were pessimists. They didn't believe that there was much possibility of improving life in this world through human efforts. The forces of evil were in control of this age and they were going to make life worse and worse.

But, third, God was going to vindicate his name at the end of this age. There is a day of judgment coming in which God would judge this world and overthrow the forces of evil. All people would be judged; not just those that are alive, but also those who have died. People shouldn't think that they can side with the forces of evil and prosper, rise to the top of the heap and then die and get away with it. God isn't going to allow anybody to side with evil and get away with it. At the end of this age, there would be a resurrection of the dead, when God would force all people to face judgment, either for reward or punishment. He would then bring in his good kingdom. When would this happen?

Fourth point, this coming judgment of God was imminent; it would happen very soon. In fact, it was right around the corner. In the words of one famous Jewish apocalypticist of the 1st century, "Truly I tell you, some of you standing here will not taste death before they see that the kingdom of God has come into power." These, in fact, are the words of Jesus, one of the best-known Jewish apocalypticists from the 1st century. "Truly I tell you," says Jesus, "this generation will not pass away before all these things take place." Apocalypticism is going to be a very important aspect of Judaism for us to consider in the context of the New Testament.

Quickly, in conclusion, if we are to understand Jesus and the New Testament, we have to situate it within its own historical context of the 1st century Judaism. Jews were like pagans in many respects, but they were also distinct, especially in the emphasis on monotheism—the one God, the law that he gave, the covenant that he gave. In addition, they had distinctive places of worship. We have seen the diversity of the Judaism in the four major parties, the Pharisees, Sadducees, Essenes, and Fourth Philosophy. But especially we have seen one of the distinctive emphases of Judaism, that of Jewish apocalypticism, a view that dominated the teaching not only of the Dead Sea Scrolls and other works of the time, but, as we will see, the teachings of Jesus and his followers.

The Earliest Traditions About Jesus
Lecture 4

Are [the Gospels] historically accurate biographies of Jesus written by people who saw him do the things that he did, or are they filled with legends and myths? Are they well-intentioned fictions created by his well-intentioned followers? Are they fact, fiction, or a combination of both?

To this point in the course, we've examined the background of Jesus and the New Testament, focusing on the religions of the Greco-Roman world and, in particular, early Judaism. With this lecture, we'll move on to the New Testament itself, beginning with the first four books of the New Testament, the Gospels of Matthew, Mark, Luke, and John. Before plunging into these texts, though, we should make some initial inquiries into what kind of books these are. Are they historically accurate biographies of Jesus written by people who saw him do the things he did? Are they filled with legends and myths? Are they well-intentioned fictions created by his well-intentioned followers? Are they fact, fiction, or a combination of both?

One way to begin is by discussing some significant historical data—the dates of the Gospels in relationship to the events that they narrate. Virtually everyone agrees that Jesus died sometime around the year 30 A.D. Moreover, for a variety of reasons that we don't need to go into here, almost all scholars of every persuasion agree on the approximate dates of the Gospels. Mark was probably the first to be written, c. 65–70 A.D.; Matthew and Luke were probably next, c. 80–85 A.D.; and John was probably last, c. 90–95 A.D. What scholars don't always agree on is the significance of these dates. For our purposes here, I want us to consider the time gap between the death of Jesus and the first accounts of his life. The gap is 35 to 65 years, which is significant for understanding the character of these earliest accounts. This would be akin to writing the first accounts of the presidency of Lyndon B. Johnson at the turn of the 21st century—with no written sources from the time.

It is important to understand what was happening during all those years. For the New Testament, the most important events during those years involved the spread of the Christian church. Christianity started, immediately after Jesus' death, with a handful of his followers, perhaps only 20 or so. Within 40 or 50 years, however, this tiny band of disciples had multiplied themselves many times over and spread the new religion based on Jesus in major urban areas throughout the Mediterranean. In this age before the possibilities and problems created by mass media, Christians necessarily propagated the religion by word of mouth. Obviously, the stories about Jesus changed, given the fact that they were being told in different languages in different places. As we will see, there is historical evidence that the stories did change in many ways.

There are some standard objections to the idea that the stories about Jesus changed as they circulated by word of mouth throughout the empire. Many people—perhaps somewhat unreflectively—assume that the stories couldn't have been changed in such a relatively short time, especially when eyewitnesses were around to verify the accounts. But stories *can* change overnight (as anyone who has ever been in the news can readily attest), and eyewitnesses often disagree among themselves about crucial points concerning an event (cf., testimony in a court case). Finally, almost no one who was telling these stories could have checked with eyewitnesses, even if had they wanted to, in this world before e-mail, the Internet, the telephone, the telegraph, or even the Pony Express.

The most common objection is that people living in oral cultures had better memories than most of us and could be counted on to tell stories exactly as they heard them, time after time, without changing them in the least. Unfortunately for this view, anthropological studies of the past 20 years have shown convincingly that this isn't the case at all. In fact, the concern for verbal accuracy that is behind this theory is a concern found exclusively in written cultures where accounts can be checked to see if they are consistent. In oral cultures, the natural assumption is that stories *are* to be changed, depending on the audience and the situation.

In fact, as scholars have long known, the question about authorship of the Gospels is not that simple. All four books were written anonymously. They were not ascribed to Matthew, Mark, Luke, and John until some time in the 2nd century A.D., decades after they were written. There are good reasons for doubting that these traditional ascriptions are accurate. Even though Jesus and his own disciples spoke Aramaic, these books are written in Greek. Jesus' own disciples, at least according to the New Testament accounts, were mostly lower-class, uneducated peasants (according to Acts 4:13, both Peter and John were known to be illiterate); the Gospel writers were highly educated and literate. All of the books are written in the third person, making no direct references to the authors' own involvement with Jesus. The books were later ascribed to apostles by Christians interested in securing their authority as Scripture. But these traditional ascriptions are late and questionable.

Who, then, were the authors? We can't really say, except that they were relatively highly educated and literate Greek-speaking Christians who lived several decades after Jesus. The authors had heard numerous reports about Jesus' life that were passed down year after year among his followers and wrote some of these reports down. If this is so, then it seems likely that the Gospel accounts themselves preserve traditions that have been changed over time. Is there any evidence for this view or is it pure conjecture?

Although it is undoubtedly true that the Gospels of the New Testament contain stories about Jesus that are historically accurate, other stories appear to have been modified by Christians in the process of retelling.

The evidence for this view is preserved in the Gospels themselves. Sometimes the Gospels tell the same story, so we can compare the stories to see if they are consistent. If not, then obviously someone has changed the story. This can be illustrated with just a single extended example, which involves a very simple question: When did Jesus die? Each of the Gospels, of course, narrates the events surrounding Jesus' death, and two of them, our earliest Gospel, Mark, and our latest, John, provide a precise dating of the event. All four Gospels indicate that Jesus died during the Feast of the Passover, the annual festival celebrated in Jerusalem to commemorate the events of the

Exodus. The festival had as its background the stories of God's deliverance of his people Israel from their slavery in Egypt through Moses, as recorded in the book of Exodus in the Hebrew Bible. In the 1st century, Jews would come from all over the world to Jerusalem for this feast and would purchase a lamb to be eaten at the celebratory meal. The lambs were sacrificed in the Temple on the afternoon before the Passover meal was eaten. That day was called the "Day of Preparation for the Passover." The lambs were taken home to be prepared for the meal, which was then eaten after it got dark—that is, on the day of Passover itself. It's important to recall that in Jewish reckoning, a new day begins, not at midnight, as for us, but whenever it gets dark. (That's why the Jewish Sabbath begins, even today, on Friday evening at dark and continues through Saturday, until it gets dark again.)

In the earliest account of Jesus' last days, found in Mark, the sequence of events is clearly laid out. The day before his arrest, Jesus' disciples ask him where they are to prepare the Passover meal (Mark 14:12). He gives them their instructions. That night they have the meal, during which Jesus instills the symbolic foods with new significance. ("This is my body," he says over the bread, and "This is the cup of the new covenant in my blood," he says over the cup.) Afterward, Jesus goes out to pray, is betrayed by Judas Iscariot, is handed over to the Jewish authorities for trial, and spends the night in jail. The next morning—i.e., the morning of Passover, the day after the lambs were slain—he appears before the Roman governor, Pontius Pilate, who finds him guilty of criminal charges and orders him executed. Jesus is immediately taken off and crucified at 9:00 a.m.

Our last Gospel of the New Testament, John, has a sequence of events that is in many ways similar but contains some striking differences. Here, too, Jesus has a last meal with his disciples, but there's no word of it being a Passover meal. The disciples, in this Gospel, never ask where they are to prepare Passover, and Jesus does not speak about the symbolic foods in a new way. Again, after supper, he goes out to pray, is betrayed by Judas, is arrested, and spends the night in jail. The next day he appears before Pilate and is ordered to be executed. We're told exactly when this happened in John 19:14: "And this was on the Day of Preparation for the Passover, at 12:00 noon." But how could it be the Day of Preparation for the Passover? According to Mark, Jesus lived through that day, had the Passover meal with his disciples that night, and was put on the cross the next morning, on the day of Passover itself. In John's Gospel, though, Jesus was executed before the Passover meal even began.

How does one reconcile this discrepancy? It probably cannot be reconciled literally. It is worth noting that the Gospel of John, which has Jesus die on the afternoon of the day before the Passover (the Day of Preparation), precisely when the lambs were being slaughtered, is the only Gospel of the New Testament that explicitly identifies Jesus himself as "the Lamb of God that takes away the sins of the world" (John 1:29, 36). Is it possible that John has changed historical data to make a theological point, that he's changed the day and hour of Jesus' death precisely to show that Jesus really was the Lamb, who was slain on the same day and at the same hour (and at the hands of the same people—the chief priests!) as the Passover lamb?

These kinds of changes in the accounts of Jesus' life appear throughout the pages of the New Testament Gospels. Changes can be seen, for example, in the accounts of Jesus' birth in Matthew and Luke. Both Gospels record incidents that later were combined into the well-known "Christmas" story. But the Gospels are at odds on a number of points: Did Joseph and Mary originally live in Bethlehem, as in Matthew, or in Nazareth, as in Luke? Were they in Bethlehem just for a temporary visit or was that their home? Did they return to Nazareth a few weeks after Jesus was born or stay in Bethlehem for a long time, until the "wise men" appeared? Did they flee to Egypt or head back north to Nazareth?

In short, although it is undoubtedly true that the Gospels of the New Testament contain stories about Jesus that are historically accurate, other stories appear to have been modified by Christians in the process of retelling. Part of our task, later in this course, will be to decide which accounts can be accepted as historically accurate and which ones cannot. For the time being, we will bracket the question of their historical accuracy and examine each Gospel as a piece of literature—seeing what it has to say about Jesus and trying to understand how he is portrayed theologically by those who told the stories about him. ∎

Ehrman, *The New Testament: A Historical Introduction*, chap. 3.

1. Which arguments strike you as the strongest that early Christians modified their traditions about Jesus? What kind of counter-arguments might someone adduce?

2. Does it matter to you if the accounts of the New Testament are historically accurate? Why or why not?

3. If Christians modified the traditions about Jesus that have come down to us in the New Testament, how do you suppose we might get behind their modifications to see what Jesus really said and did?

Lecture 4: The Earliest Traditions About Jesus

The Earliest Traditions About Jesus
Lecture 4—Transcript

To this point in the course, we have examined the background of Jesus and the New Testament, focusing on the religions of the Greco-Roman World and, in particular, early Judaism. With this lecture we will begin to move on to the New Testament itself, beginning with the first four books of the New Testament—the Gospels of Matthew, Mark, Luke, and John. Before plunging into these texts, we should make some initial inquiries into what kind of books these are. Are they historically accurate biographies of Jesus written by people who saw him do the things that he did, or are they filled with legends and myths? Are they well-intentioned fictions created by his well-intentioned followers? Are they fact, fiction, or a combination of both?

One way to begin is by discussing some significant historical data—the dates of the Gospels in relationship to the events that they narrate. Virtually everyone agrees that Jesus died sometime around the year 30 A.D. Some people think that he might have died in the year 29, some 32, some 33, but pretty much everybody agrees it was some time around the year 30. The Gospels were written probably 35 to 65 years after Jesus' death. Scholars debate the dates of the Gospels, but most scholars are reasonably sure that Mark was the first to have been written, probably around the year 65 to 70 A.D. Matthew and Luke were probably next, written possibly in 80 or 85 A.D. The Gospel of John was probably the last Gospel to be written, sometime around 90 or 95 A.D. On these dates pretty much all scholars agree.

What scholars don't agree on is the significance of these dates. For our purposes here, I want to think about the time gap between the death of Jesus and the first accounts of his life. As I have pointed out, it is a time gap of between 35 and 65 years. This gap is significant for our understanding of the character of these, our earliest accounts. To put the time gap in modern terms, if the earliest Gospel about Jesus was written 35 years after his death, that would be comparable to having the first account of the presidency, the early years of the presidency, of Lyndon Johnson being written this year. Now you think, "Well that wouldn't be such a big time gap because I remember quite well Lyndon Johnson's presidency." But imagine somebody writing about the presidency of Lyndon Johnson with no earlier written sources, somebody today recording what Lyndon Johnson did 35 years ago. That is the shortest time gap between Jesus and the Gospel of Mark. What about the longest gap, between Jesus and the Gospel of John? Sixty-five years. That would be like somebody today writing for the first time an account of somebody who was, say, a preacher who was the height of his career during the Great Depression, for the first time. Thirty-five to 65 years separate the life of Jesus from the earliest accounts we have of him.

It seems to me that this time gap is significant, and I want to explain why. The explanation has to do with what was happening during all these years between the year 30 and the year 65 to 95. Of course there are a lot of things happening in the Roman Empire during those decades. For our purposes, the most important thing that was happening is that Christianity was spreading through the empire. According to our surviving sources, Christianity started immediately after Jesus' death with a handful of his followers. According to the Book of Acts, our earliest account, Jesus had 11 remaining followers among his disciples after his death (because Judas had killed himself) and a handful of women. So, say 20 followers. These followers were located in Jerusalem. They had been people who had accompanied Jesus on his ministry throughout his life. Between that point of time and the end of the 1st century, Christianity had spread to the major urban areas of the Mediterranean as Christians propagated their belief in Jesus as the Son of God who had died for the sins of the world. Within 40 or 50 years this tiny band of, say, 20—possibly a few more, possibly a few less—disciples had multiplied themselves many times over, having spread the new religion based on Jesus throughout the cities of the Mediterranean.

In this age before the possibilities and problems posed for us by mass media, Christians necessarily propagated their religion by word of mouth; that is, by telling stories about Jesus from one person to the next—stories about who Jesus was, what he thought, what he did, how he died. People were trying to convert others to Christianity, and the only way to do it effectively was to tell somebody the stories. We don't have evidence of people doing massive revivals or tent meetings. We don't have evidence of people having big campaign rallies in the coliseum trying to convert people to Christianity. It appears to have been a one-on-one sort of propagation of the faith. People then, are telling stories about Jesus in order to convert others; and then when people are converted, they form church communities, and stories continued to be told within the churches. This is happening not just in Jerusalem; it's happening throughout the cities and villages of Judea, up in Samaria, up in Asia Minor, over in Macedonia and Achaia (which is modern-day Greece), over in Italy, possibly in North Africa, certainly in Egypt. Throughout the Mediterranean, people are converting to Christianity and telling the stories about Jesus.

Who is telling the stories? That is a key question for our discussion of the Gospels, which are written 35 to 65 years after the death of Jesus. Given the fact that the stories are being told throughout this entire region, they are obviously being told in different languages in different areas. I think we are probably safe to say that the people who are telling the stories about Jesus, by and large, were not Jesus' own followers. They must have been people, by and large, who had been converted to believe in Jesus after the fact.

Let me illustrate how the process worked by simply coming up with a hypothetical example. Imagine for a second that you are a businessman who lives in the city of Ephesus in Asia Minor. Someone has come through town on business, or for some other business, and has met you and told you stories about the Son of God in Judea who did miracles and delivered great teachings but then was crucified by the Roman Governor of Judea. You hear more stories, and the more you hear, you decide that you are interested in believing in this person, and you convert yourself to becoming a Christian. You go home and tell your family some of the stories you have heard. Say your wife converts, or your husband. Your spouse goes next door, tells the neighbors some of the stories, they become convinced, they convert; one of the neighbors is this businessman who goes off to Smyrna and tells some of the stories there and people in Smyrna convert, and then they convert their family members. Those final family members, from whom did they hear the stories? Well, they heard it from the businessman who came to town. He came from Ephesus to Smyrna. Well, where did he hear the story? Well, he heard it from you, a spouse. Where did your spouse hear the story? Well, she heard it from you. Where did you hear the story? You heard it from somebody that came into Ephesus. Where did he hear the stories?

Well, you see as it goes on; as people propagate the faith, necessarily the people telling the stories are the people who had converted on the basis of the stories they heard. But these stories cannot have been told by the eyewitnesses themselves because the religion is propagating too quickly for it to be based simply on eyewitness testimony. Since it is increasing geometrically, the people telling the stories are people who were not there to see these things happen and didn't know anybody who had been there to see these things happen. I don't mean to say that Christianity immediately overtook the world and half of the empire converted within 40 or 50 years; it simply didn't happen that way. As we will see later in the course, the empire itself didn't convert until much, much later. But there were pockets of Christians who started emerging during these years in different locales throughout the Mediterranean.

Now, for what we want to talk about in this lecture, the key question is, what happened to the stories as they were being narrated by these people at this time, throughout the Mediterranean? My contention is that, in fact, the stories got changed as they were told time and time again. The stories about Jesus were modified as people recounted these stories year after year after year. Sometimes, of course, these changes of stories would have been purely accidental, just as every story gets changed when it is told by word of mouth from one person to another. Possibly you have had children who on a birthday played the game "Telephone." You have a group of kids who sit in a circle, and one child tells the next child a story, who tells it to the next child, who tells the next child; it goes around the circle, and by the time it comes back to the person who originally told the story, it's a different story. If it didn't work like that, it would be rather a silly birthday game to play. If you hear the same story you just told there wouldn't be much excitement in that. Stories get changed when they are told by word of mouth. Imagine playing the game Telephone, not in some living room on some summer day among people the same socioeconomic class, just 12 kids class sitting in your room. Suppose, in fact, the game Telephone is played for 50 years where people tell the stories one person to the next in different countries using different languages, where you have thousands of players; what happens to the stories? My assumption is that the stories get changed.

In addition, I would assume that sometimes people change the stories because they wanted to change the stories. After all, people are telling stories about Jesus in order to convert others to believe, and once they believe, they are trying to convince them of certain things to believe and certain ways to act. The stories are told in order to promote faith in Jesus and to promote the right kind of faith in Jesus. Is it possible that sometimes the stories were changed precisely in order to make Jesus look even better than he did before? Or to stress a particular theological point about Jesus' importance? As we are going to see in a moment, there is, in fact, historical evidence that stories were changed in these ways.

There are some standard objections to the idea that the stories about Jesus came to be changed as they circulated by word of mouth throughout the empire. Let me give you a couple of the standard objections. First, many people—somewhat unreflectively, I think—assume that stories couldn't have been changed in such a relatively short amount of time, especially when there were eyewitnesses around to verify the accounts. The logic of this is that if there were eyewitnesses someplace, then if stories were told, the eyewitnesses would have checked to make sure that the stories were kept in line with the way things really happened. I said I think this is a bit unreflective precisely because I don't think it takes very much time to change a story, and because the presence of eyewitnesses usually has nothing to do with the accuracy of an account. Stories can change overnight; anybody in the news knows this. I occasionally get in the news, in a newspaper article or on the radio or something, and inevitably what is reported is simply wrong. I have colleagues, in fact, who refuse to do any interviews with newspapers or on radio precisely because they can't expect to be quoted correctly, or some of their views would be misrepresented. It happens overnight, even today in the age of mass media. Moreover the presence of eyewitnesses simply cannot guarantee the accuracy of accounts, especially in a world before e-mail, the Internet, the telephone, or even the Pony Express. There is no way to make sure that the eyewitnesses are always around to guarantee the accuracy of reports.

The second objection that people commonly raise to the idea that stories of Jesus got changed is that in ancient society, which were oral cultures, people had better memories than those of us do today, who are based in written cultures. People living in oral cultures, according to this theory, had an ability to tell stories accurately time after time. They were trained to do this, they had better memories, and therefore when people told stories they automatically did so with accuracy. Unfortunately for this view, anthropological studies done in the past 20 years have shown convincingly that this is not the case at all. That, in fact, the very concern for verbal accuracy that lies behind this theory is a concern that's found exclusively in written cultures. The logic is that only in written cultures can one check to determine the accuracy of something that's said. Since you can check in written cultures, there arises a sense that things ought to be accurate. But in oral societies, as it turns out, there is no natural assumption that stories should remain unchanged. These anthropological studies have shown convincingly that, in fact, in oral cultures, the assumption is that stories should be changed depending on the audience to which a story is told. And so stories appear to have been changed as they were told word-of-mouth from one person to another in this kind of oral culture. But why would the fact that stories got changed over time normally have any effect on the Gospels? After all, the Gospels were not written by hypothetical businessmen living in Ephesus, but by the disciples of Jesus and their close followers—that is, by eyewitnesses and those who knew eyewitnesses—were they not? In fact, as scholars have long known, the question of the authorship of the Gospels is not that simple.

All four of our Gospels in the New Testament, Matthew, Mark, Luke, and John, were written anonymously. As I indicated in the last lecture, these books later came to be ascribed to people named Matthew, Mark, Luke, and John. In other words, to two of Jesus' disciples, Matthew, the tax collector, and John, the beloved disciple, and to two friends of the apostles, Mark, who was thought to be secretary for the apostle Peter, and Luke, who was thought to be a traveling companion of the apostle Paul. Later they were attributed to two disciples, Philip and John who had died earlier. These ascriptions, though, are not original to the Gospels themselves, and they did not occur until the 2nd century—a hundred years after the Gospels themselves were written. In fact, none of the gospel writers identifies himself by name, and these ascriptions and their assumptions are based in some ways on Jesus and His followers originally spoke Aramaic, a language that is closely related to Hebrew, the Gospels we now have painted ... these were written in Greek, not the language of Jesus' own followers themselves—Jesus' own disciples, at least according to the New Testament ...

accounts, were, by and large, lower-class uneducated peasants. According to the Book of Acts Chapter 4, both Peter and John, two of Jesus' principal disciples, were known to be illiterate—the literal meaning of the word used in Acts 4:13. Peter and John were illiterate. The Gospel writers, on the other hand, are highly educated and literate. In addition, all of these Gospels are written in the third person. Never in these books does an author say, "then Jesus and I went up to Jerusalem," and then we did this, that, or the other thing." The stories are never described in the first person, always the third person. These books, then, do not appear to have been written by Jesus's own disciples. They were later ascribed or assigned to later Christians, Christians who were interested in securing their authority as canonical scripture. These and their ascriptions, though, are late and questionable.

Who, then, were the authors of these books? Well, the most I really say in that we can say is that these books were written by relatively highly educated and literate Greek-speaking Christians living several decades after Jesus, who had heard numerous reports about his life as these reports had been passed down for forty years among his followers. They then wrote some of the stories that circulated in this way, and it is by these highly-educated Christians preserve them that had been carried over time. I have absolutely any evidence of all I have to base it on, but I am just telling you there are who have no interesting ideas no them have been. But there is evidence that the Gospels somehow might have been changed over time, we are going to see. I am not sure that here critically reading professionally, but then I'm going to try to read them and tell you that historians can with mostly available to scholars. I am going to characterize by looking at historical facts about life. They have not that I want to look at nonhistorical relevant issues like a relatively certain history, what can I say in that might suggest how and when it was done.

[...] and then there are those talking going into this issue and it is based in these [...] that Christian documents also contain that which seem to be questionable, but trying to make a big point. But in history studies, sometimes [...] and as an investigating a certain issue, they may be highly significant that when someone has an issue about the case with a very [...] of serious issues of being able to the best study of the historical [...] they are able to the way in ancient situation can [...] history books in the context

Historians are like that. They have to look for little things, fingerprints, strands of hair, in order to explain something big that has happened. And so this might seem like a little issue, but it has big implications.

When did Jesus die? Well, each of the Gospels, of course, narrates the event. Two of them, our earliest Gospel, Mark, and our latest Gospel, John, provided a precise dating for it. All four Gospels indicate that Jesus died sometime during the feast of the Passover, the annual festival that was celebrated in Jerusalem by Jews to commemorate the events of the exodus from Egypt. The festival had as its background the stories of God's deliverance of his people from Egypt—from their slavery in Egypt—under Moses, as recorded in the Hebrew Bible in the Book of Exodus. In the 1st century, Jews would come from all over the world to celebrate this feast. When they came to Jerusalem, they would purchase a lamb that would be eaten at the celebration in the evening. The lambs were sacrificed in the temple on the afternoon before the Passover was actually eaten. The day when the lambs were sacrificed is, therefore, called the Day of Preparation for the Passover. Now it is important for what I am going to say to recall that, in Jewish culture, recognizing a new day begins not at midnight as it does for us, but whenever it gets dark. That's why Jewish Sabbath begins, even now, on Friday evening at dark and then continues through Saturday, until it gets dark on Saturday. The lambs during the Passover feast, then, were sacrificed on the Day of Preparation for the Passover. They were taken home, they were cooked for the evening meal, and when it got dark then, it was the next day, and they would eat then, the Passover meal on the day of Passover.

Return now to the Gospel accounts. In the earliest account of Jesus' last days, the account found in Mark; the sequence of events leading up to Jesus' death are clearly laid out. The day before Jesus is arrested, Jesus' disciples asked him where he wants to prepare to eat the Passover meal. Mark Chapter 14, Verse 12: "Where would you have us prepare the Passover?" He gives them their instructions. That night—in other words, on the day of Passover—that night they have the meal in which Jesus takes the symbolic foods of the Passover feast and instills new significance in them. He takes the unleavened bread and says, "This is my body, which is given for you." He takes the cup of wine and says, "This cup is the new covenant in my blood." Afterwards, Jesus goes out to pray; he is betrayed by Judas Iscariot and handed over to the Jewish authorities for trial. He spends the night in jail. The next morning—that is, the morning after the Passover lambs have been eaten—Jesus appears before the Roman Governor, Pontius Pilate, who finds him guilty of criminal charges and orders him executed. Jesus is immediately taken off and crucified, and we are told when this was—9:00 in the morning, according to Mark Chapter 15, Verse 25. This is a very clear dating of when Jesus died.

Our last Gospel, the Gospel of John, also provides the precise dating for the events. The sequence of events in John is in many ways similar to that found in the Gospel of Mark, but there are striking differences as well. Here, too, in John, Jesus also has a last meal with his disciples, but there is no word of it being a Passover meal. The disciples in this Gospel never ask where they are to prepare the Passover, and Jesus doesn't speak about the symbolic foods, giving them new significance. After the supper in John, Jesus again goes out to pray, he is betrayed by Judas, he is arrested, he spends the night in jail. The next day he appears before Pontius Pilate and is ordered to be executed, and we are told precisely when it happened. John Chapter 19, Verse 14: "This was on the Day of Preparation for the Passover at 12:00 noon." The Day of preparation for the Passover? How could it be the Day of Preparation for the Passover? According to Mark's Gospel, Jesus lived through that day; he had the Passover meal with his disciples that night and was put on the cross the next morning on the day of Passover itself. In John's Gospel, though, Jesus was executed before the meal even began.

How does one reconcile this discrepancy? Well, it probably can't be reconciled literally, although people try all the time. It is worth noting, though, that the Gospel of John, which has Jesus die on the afternoon before the Passover, has him die precisely when the lambs of God were being slaughtered—the Passover lambs, being slaughtered in the temple. Moreover, this Gospel is the only Gospel that refers to Jesus himself as the Lamb of God who takes away the sins of the world. John Chapter 1, Verse 29, and again six verses later, John Chapter 1, Verse 36. In other words, in John's Gospel, Jesus is identified as the Lamb of God, and in John's Gospel, Jesus dies precisely on the day and at the time that the lambs were being killed in the temple. Is it possible that John has changed a historical datum in order to make a theological point? That he has changed the day and hour

not simply to recount events from Jesus' life, but also to explain to the readers who he was and why his death mattered.

Mark sets a tall order for himself at the very outset of his Gospel by his initial description of Jesus as "the Christ, the Son of God" (1:1). These designations may not seem surprising to us, because Christians today naturally think of Jesus as the "Christ." But for people in Mark's world, this description would have seemed rather shocking. The term *Christ* is Greek, and means literally "anointed." It is, in fact, the exact Greek equivalent of the Hebrew word *messiah*. It would have seemed shocking as a description of Jesus in particular, because everyone—Mark, his readers, and just about anyone who knew about Jesus—realized that Jesus had been crucified as a criminal. Jews who were expecting the messiah were expecting a figure of grandeur and power, perhaps a great military leader such as King David or a cosmic figure who would come from heaven in a mighty act of judgment against the forces of evil. As far as we know, there were no Jews before Christianity

who thought that the messiah would be a figure who suffered and died. Quite the contrary, the messiah was to overthrow his enemies to bring in God's kingdom. Mark's book is designed to show how Jesus could be the messiah despite the fact— or rather, even more shocking still, *because* of the fact—that Jesus was crucified. For Mark, Jesus was the messiah *because* he suffered and died.

Mark begins his narrative through a series of stories that are meant to demonstrate Jesus'

Doré Bible Illustrations, Courtesy of Dover Pictorial Archive Series.

Jesus preaching to the multitudes.

credentials as the uniquely authoritative Son of God. He is announced by a Jewish prophet, John the Baptist, as the fulfillment of the Jewish Scriptures (Mark 1:2–3). After he is baptized by John, he goes into the wilderness to do battle with the devil and the wild animals and returns unscathed. He immediately begins his public ministry by acting in ways that reveal his great power. You would think that with all these miracles, people would recognize Jesus for who he is.

But one of the major points of this Gospel—unlike some of the other Gospels—is that no one recognizes Jesus. Consider how people react to him in the first half of the Gospel: His family thinks that he's gone out of his mind (3:21). The people from his hometown can't understand what he's doing, because to them he's just the carpenter down the street (6:1–6). The leaders of his own people, the Jews, think that he's

> **Mark's Gospel was ... written by a Greek-speaking Christian who had inherited a number of traditions about Jesus. This author, though, did not simply repeat these traditions ... Mark's account is much richer and contains more nuance than that.**

possessed by the Devil (3:22). Most striking of all, his own disciples are explicitly said not to understand who he is (6:51–52; 8:21). Who, then, does know that Jesus is actually the Son of God in this Gospel? When you read the first half of the Gospel carefully, you may be surprised.

When Jesus is baptized, the voice comes from heaven saying, "you are my beloved son" (1:11). God knows who Jesus is and because the voice in this account comes to Jesus (and only to Jesus), it's clear that Jesus knows. When Jesus casts out demons, they declare him to be the Son of God (3:14). So they know. Obviously Mark knows, because he's writing these things, and presumably you know, because you're reading them. But no one else seems to know.

All that changes in the middle of the Gospel, in a sequence of stories that show that some people, at least the disciples, begin to get some kind of an inkling of Jesus' identity. At almost the midway point of the Gospel comes the most interesting miracle in the entire narrative, an account of a man who

Supplemental Reading

Hooker, *The Message of Mark*.

Kingsbury, *The Christology of Mark's Gospel*.

Questions to Consider

1. What do people today generally mean by the term *messiah* and how does this contrast with the meanings that were more common in ancient Judaism?

2. Why do you suppose Mark portrays the disciples of Jesus as so ignorant of who he really was?

Lecture 5: Mark—Jesus the Suffering Son of God

Mark—Jesus the Suffering Son of God
Lecture 5—Transcript

We have seen in our study of the Gospels to this point that these accounts represent not only genuine historical recollections of what Jesus said and did, but also stories that were modified. Sometimes modified significantly, sometimes slightly, as people told and retold the stories about Jesus. Since the Gospels have both kinds of tradition in them, both historically accurate accounts and accounts that have been changed, we have two fundamental tasks before us as we engage in our studies of these texts. First, we have the task of looking at each account as a piece of literature to see what its own take on Jesus was, what its own perspective on Jesus was. Secondly, we will have the task of getting behind the portrayal of Jesus in each of these accounts to see what Jesus himself was really like. I look at these as the literary and the historical tasks of the historian.

We will begin with the literary task, devoting a lecture to each of the four Gospels of the New Testament, and then a lecture to Gospels that didn't make it into the New Testament. After we have looked at each one individually for its literary portrayal of Jesus, then we will be able to move behind the accounts to reconstruct what Jesus himself actually said and did. To engage in the literary task of studying the Gospels, it will be important for us to consider the distinctive emphases of each account. There is not just one Gospel of the New Testament, but four. And as we will see, each of the four has something special to say about Jesus. Because these four differ—sometimes in slight ways, sometimes in major ways—it is important that we take them on their own terms. If we conflate the four into one Gospel, then we destroy the distinctive meaning of each one. This can be seen by any interpretation of the Gospels that takes two accounts that have discrepancy and mashes the two accounts together so that you then have one account. Sometimes people speak, for example, of the seven last words of the dying Jesus. These seven last words of the dying Jesus come from taking the four Gospel accounts, in which Jesus says things while being crucified in different Gospels, and putting them together so that Jesus says all seven things. The problem is that each of the Gospels records a specific idea about Jesus in the things that they have him say at the end, so that when you put all four of them together, the distinctiveness of each account is lost, as we will see in subsequent lectures. At this point I simply want to stress that we need to consider each of the Gospels on its own terms, without appealing to other Gospels to help us explain the Gospel that we are trying to study at any point.

We are going to begin our study with the first Gospel to be written, the Gospel of Mark. The Gospel of Mark is attributed in Christian tradition to a man named John Mark, the personal secretary of the Apostle Peter. As I indicated in the last lecture, we don't actually know who this author was. The attribution to Mark does not occur until 70 or 80 years after the book itself was actually written. All we know about this author is that he was a relatively highly educated Greek-speaking Christian who was writing some 35 to 40 years after the events that he narrates. Most scholars date this book to the year 65 or so, so possibly as late as 70, possibly a few years even earlier—say 55 to 60 years after Jesus' own death. This author appears to have based his book—that is, he had been in circulation for some time. He did not base his narrative on eyewitness accounts but simply as he heard them circulating his own community...

"Christ" is a Greek term which literally means anointed one. In fact, it is the exact Greek equivalent of the Hebrew word *moshiach*—messiah, so that the Greek Christ means the Hebrew Messiah. This is a designation or a title, not a name. I need to emphasize this with my students, my undergraduates, because they don't realize that Christ isn't a name. But I have to tell them with Jesus Christ, "Christ" is not his last name. It is not Jesus Christ born to Joseph and Mary Christ. It means Jesus the Messiah.

Why would this have been a surprising or problematic designation for Jesus? Well, precisely because of what people thought the Christ or the Messiah was to be. This would have been a shocking description of Jesus in the ancient world precisely because everyone—Mark, his readers, and everyone who wasn't his reader—knew that Jesus had been crucified as a criminal. The Jews were not expecting a crucified criminal as the Messiah. Quite the contrary. Those Jews who were expecting a messiah—and not every single Jew was, but many Jews possibly were—those Jews who were expecting a messiah were expecting a figure of grandeur and power, that is, a great military leader, someone like King David, or a cosmic judge who is coming to come from heaven in judgment against the Lord, and the future priest that are born in wisdom. Jews who expected a messiah possibly would have had a worldly figure who would rule the world, a stately and after being baptized goes off into the wilderness where he does battle with the devil and the wild animals, returning from the wilderness unscathed. He immediately begins his public ministry by acting in ways that reveal his great power.

The early accounts of Jesus here in Chapter 1 of Mark are meant precisely to show that he is a man who has God's authority behind him. The first thing that he does is he calls some disciples. He walks along the Sea of Galilee, and he sees there two brothers, Simon and Andrew, fishing. And he calls to them, saying, "Come follow me and I will make you fish for people," or traditionally, "I will make you fishers of men." Immediately, these men, who have never laid eyes on Jesus before, drop their nets and follow him. Right afterwards, Jesus sees two other brothers fishing, James and John, and again he calls to them, they leave behind their father Zebedee in the boat with the other workers, and they drop everything to follow Jesus. Jesus calls people, and they follow without asking questions. This is showing his authority. He not only is an authoritative leader, he is also an authoritative teacher. Jesus, we are told in the next two verses, teaches the crowds, and they are amazed because he teaches as one who has authority. His authority is not only over people that he leads, and over people that he teaches; Jesus has authority even over demons and illness. We are told in the next stories that Jesus casts out demons, evil spirits that inhabit bodies. Jesus has authority over them; he casts them out and people are amazed because of his authority. He then heals people who are sick, so much so that people come from all around; there is no room even before the door. He heals all those who are sick. These stories in Chapter 1 of Mark are designed to portray Jesus as the authoritative Son of God. His commands are heeded by all. He teaches with unparalleled authority. He has power even over the demons and over human illness.

You would think that with all of these miracles, people would recognize Jesus for who he is. One of the striking points of Mark's Gospel, which makes it stand in contrast with other Gospels is that, in fact, in this Gospel, virtually nobody recognizes Jesus, despite the miracles that he does. Consider, first, how people react to Jesus in this Gospel. Of course there are people who are being healed by him; they must know who Jesus is. People are seeing him do miracles; they must know who he is. What does Mark tell us about how people understand Jesus? Well, in fact, it's quite striking; virtually no one understands Jesus' identity, especially in the first half of this Gospel. Chapter 3, Verse 21, we are told that his family comes to seize him from the public eye because they think that he has gone out of his mind. His own family.

I should point out that in this Gospel there is no account of Jesus being born to a virgin in Bethlehem. This Gospel begins with Jesus being baptized by John the Baptist, so there is no account here of Mary knowing anything about Jesus before his birth. But you think, "Yes, but she did know about it because of Matthew and Luke." But remember, we have to read each Gospel on its own terms. Mark's Gospel is written to people who don't know Matthew and Luke. Matthew and Luke hadn't been written yet. If you are reading this Gospel and sticking to this text, in this book his family thinks that he is crazy. Not just his family; we are told in Chapter 6 that people from his hometown don't understand what he is doing, since to them, he is simply the carpenter down the street. He has been delivering these fantastic teachings, and people come and they are amazed. Who is this? This is the carpenter; how does he teach such great words? Even though he grew up with them, they don't understand who he is. Not just his family and his townsfolk, even the leaders of his own people don't understand who he is. Jesus casts out a demon and people are wondering, Could this man be the Messiah? The Jewish leaders, though, insist—Chapter 3, Verse 22—that the reason he is able to cast out demons is because he is empowered by the Prince of Demons, the devil. The Jewish leaders think that he is inspired by the devil. Most striking of all, Jesus' own disciples are explicitly said not to understand who he is in two accounts in this early part of the Gospel. The first half of the Gospel, we have accounts of the disciples who have witnessed what he has done, failed to understand who he is, and the narrator explicitly tells us that they don't understand.

One time he is on the boat and the storm has come up, and he says to his disciples to beware of the leaven of the scribes and the Pharisees. They think, "Ah, oh, this means that we should have brought some bread along because Jesus has been talking about leaven." And they feel, "We blew it this time. We didn't bring any bread on the boat, and he is upset with us." This is right after Jesus two times has multiplied loaves of bread for the multitudes, feeding 5,000 at one time and 4,000 another time with just a few loaves of bread. The narrative ends when the disciples think, "Oh, we should

... so far in the reading, by Jesus saying "Don't you yet understand ... about the bread? I can provide bread?" but they don't understand ...

A couple of chapters later in Chapter 8, we have another account of the disciples emphatically being said to not understand who Jesus is. Chapter 4, ... Jesus has just performed another miracle, and again the disciples ... telling a long speech ... is not ... about; and Jesus has to ask ... "Do you not yet understand?" ... reveals ... they don't understand ...

context, by the way, a passion prediction...passion in this context, as I tell my students, doesn't refer as to what happens in the dormitories on Friday night. Passion in this context comes from the Greek work *pasco*, which means to suffer. The passion of Jesus is the suffering of Jesus, is the narrative of his suffering and death. A passion prediction, then, is a prediction of this coming death. On three occasions, Jesus predicts his coming death—Mark Chapter 8, Verse 31; Chapter 9, Verse 31; and Chapter 10 Verses 33 and 34. What is striking is after each of these predictions, the disciples demonstrate their complete inability to understand what Jesus is saying. They spend their time talking about who among them is the greatest and who will be the most powerful in the coming kingdom after each prediction. They engage in this kind of dialogue. They don't realize that Jesus is not going to overthrow the Romans; he is going to be crushed by them, and following him means experiencing his fate.

Mark's Gospel has sometimes been called "a passion narrative with a long introduction." Fully 6 of the 16 chapters of this book deal with the final week of Jesus' life, leading up to his death. After 10 chapters of teaching the multitudes, healing the sick, casting out demons, and even raising the dead, Jesus goes to Jerusalem for the Passover. He spends, then, a week there preaching in the temple. He has a last meal with his disciples, after which he is betrayed by Judas, arrested by the authorities, denied by Peter, put on trial by the Jewish leaders, and then brought before the Roman governor Pilate, who condemns him to die on a cross. Then comes the climax of the narrative, the point of which everything else has been driving up to this stage: Jesus' death itself. Up to this point, no one seems to have recognized who Jesus is. And even those who, like the disciples, have some kind of partial understanding of Jesus have not fully realized that, even though he is the Messiah, he needs to suffer and die. At the end it seems that not even Jesus himself is so sure. Three times he prays that God will remove this fate from him, as if the Messiah could escape suffering. At the end, he is completely silent as if in shock. As he hangs on the cross, he has been silent through the entire proceeding, everybody has mocked him, and at the end, hanging on the cross, he cries out, "Eloi, Eloi, lama sabachthani"—"My God, my God, why have you forsaken me?" He then dies.

Even if Jesus has doubts at the end of this Gospel, though, the reader does not. Mark gives two clear indications in the very next two verses what this death was all about, Mark Chapter 15, Verses 38 and 39. The first thing that happens when Jesus dies, we are told that the curtain in the temple is torn in half. This was the curtain that separated the area of the temple called "the Holy of Holies" from everything else. The Holy of Holies was a room in the temple which was the most holiest of rooms because it was thought that there was where God's presence dwelt on Earth. No one could go into that room, except for once a year, the high priest would go into that room to perform a sacrifice for the people before God. Mark says that curtain is ripped in half, meaning that now God is no longer separated from his people because of Jesus' death. The death of Jesus brings salvation. This is a death that had to happen. Moreover, the second thing that happens is that somebody recognizes it. No one throughout this entire Gospel has realized that Jesus is the Messiah, the Son of God who has to suffer, until the end. Interestingly, it is not one of Jesus' family members or townsfolk, not one of the Jewish leaders, and not even one of his disciples. It is the pagan centurion who has just crucified him, who sees him die and then calls out, "Truly this man was the Son of God." Jesus is the Son of God in this Gospel not despite the fact he died, but because he died on the cross. His identity is then finally confirmed at the end of the story. Three days later, Jesus' women followers go to the tomb, and they find it empty. There is a man there who tells them that he has been raised from the dead. Interestingly, in keeping with the theme that Jesus was completely misunderstood all along, we are told that the women then flee the tomb and don't tell anyone about it because they were afraid.

The original version of the Gospel of Mark ended there with the women not telling anybody anything. At a later time, in the early Middle Ages, some Christian scribes who copied the Gospel of Mark added an ending to this account: twelve verses in which Jesus actual does appear to his disciples, convincing them that he is alive. Scholars, though, are convinced that this additional ending to Mark's Gospel was not original. The disciples never did understand, even though the reader does.

Let me sum up, in conclusion, the major points I have made about this Gospel. Mark was the first Gospel to be written, by a Greek-speaking Christian who had inherited a number of traditions about Jesus. This author

as one of his sources, one of the ways to study his Gospel is to see how it's different (this is termed "redaction criticism"). This Gospel has been traditionally ascribed to Matthew, the disciple of Jesus who was known to be a tax collector; we do not, however, know the author's actual identity. He does not appear to have been an eyewitness to Jesus' life, but rather a Greek-speaking Christian writing around 80–85 A.D., a half century or so after the events that he narrates.

Matthew's Gospel offers a distinctive portrayal of Jesus. On the one hand, as you might expect, Matthew has a similar view to Mark. Here, too, Jesus is the messiah, the Son of God, whose entire life looked forward to his death, which was necessary to bring salvation. But there are different emphases in places, as becomes apparent at the very outset of the Gospel. This Gospel is distinguished by its stress both on the Jewish-ness of Jesus and on his opposition to Judaism as he found it. This Gospel emphasizes, far more than Mark, that Jesus was the Jewish messiah, sent from the Jewish God, to the Jewish people, in fulfillment of the Jewish Scriptures. He gathered Jewish disciples and taught them that they had to follow the Jewish Law. At the same time, Jesus opposed the Jewish teachers of his day and condemned the way they practiced their religion. This combination of a strong affirmation of Judaism as it ought to be and a vitriolic condemnation of Judaism as it is actually practiced makes Matthew's portrayal of Judaism so distinctive.

Matthew's emphasis on Jesus' own Jewish-ness can be seen in passages found in Matthew that are not found in his earlier source, Mark. It is important to stress the methodological point. By adding stories to the account of Mark that he had in front of him, Matthew has altered somewhat the overarching perspective. Matthew begins his Gospel not with the baptism of Jesus, as in Mark, but with a genealogy that traces his line of descent. The very first verse intimates the stress of this Gospel: Jesus descends from Abraham, the father of the Jews, and David, the great King of the Jews, whose descendant, commonly called the Son of David, was to be the messiah. The genealogy itself establishes Jesus' credentials as standing in the messianic line and does so in a striking way. Matthew has organized "who begat whom" into three sets of 14 generations: 14 from the father of Israel, Abraham, to the King of Israel, David; 14 from the King of Israel to the destruction of Israel by the Babylonians; and 14 from the destruction of Israel to the messiah of Israel—

Jesus. This sounds almost too good to be true, as if divine providence has itself decided when the messiah must come and Jesus appears just at the right moment. The problem, though, is that to make the sequence of three sets of 14 work, Matthew has had to do some creative editing. A comparison with the Hebrew Bible shows that he has dropped some names out of the genealogy—e.g., in v. 8, Matthew says that Joram was the father of Uzziah, when in fact, he was his great-great-grandfather. Why would Matthew change the genealogy? Apparently, so he could show that Jesus appeared just at the right moment, when the messiah was supposed to appear. Whether Matthew's genealogy is historically correct is not really the point of his narrative. The genealogy is meant to say something about Jesus: Jesus really was the Jewish Messiah descended from the venerable Jewish line of King David.

Jesus' Jewish-ness continues to be at the forefront in the stories that come next, stories also not found in Mark, of Jesus' miraculous birth (see Matthew 1:18–23). Probably the most striking thing about these stories as found in Matthew, which are different from Luke's account, is that they mirror the accounts of the birth of Moses in the Hebrew Bible. A boy is born under a hostile regime (Egypt, Rome); the ruling power wants to destroy him (the Pharaoh, Herod); he is divinely protected; he sojourns in Egypt; he leaves Egypt; goes through the water (the Exodus of the Red Sea, the waters of baptism); and goes up onto a mountain (Mount Sinai, the Sermon on the Mount) to deliver God's law. It appears that Matthew wants to portray Jesus as a *new* Moses, a new savior of the people of Israel.

Some people have pointed out the striking fact that there are five major blocks of Jesus' teaching in Matthew, the first of which is the Sermon on the Mount in chapters 5–7. Most of this material is not found in Mark (it comes from Q). Why five blocks of teaching? Is it to form a parallel to the five books of Moses, the Pentateuch? Notice further, though, that all the events of the story (e.g., Jesus' conception by a virgin [Isaiah 7:14], his birth in Bethlehem, his flight to Egypt) are all explicitly said to fulfill Scripture. The emphasis is clear: Jesus is the Jewish messiah sent from the Jewish God in fulfillment of the Jewish Scripture.

This ... a prophet like Moses, will deliver his teaching to us ... This ... in the first major block of teaching. Here Jesus goes up on a ... and delivers his teaching (like Moses going up to Mount Sinai to receive ...

camels" (23:24). They are portrayed as godless and heartless, blind leaders who know the right thing to do but don't raise a finger to do it.

Because of this harsh opposition to the Jewish leaders, this Gospel is sometimes read as being anti-Jewish, but that may be taking the matter too far. The closest thing to any real opposition to Jews per se comes in Matthew's account of Jesus' trial before Pilate. In this account, Pilate declares Jesus innocent and washes his hands of his blood, while the Jewish crowds assume responsibility for Jesus' death, crying out "his blood be upon us and our children" (27:25). Even here, though, the real culprits are portrayed as the Jewish *leaders* who have stirred up the crowds.

In conclusion, these are the main points we've seen in our consideration of Matthew's distinctive portrayal of Jesus. As in Mark's Gospel, Jesus in Matthew is portrayed as the Son of God who must die for the sins of the world. But here the stress is much more on the Jewish aspects of who he was. For Matthew, Jesus was the Jewish messiah sent from the Jewish God to the Jewish people in fulfillment of the Jewish Law. Jesus—as messiah—gave the true interpretation of the Jewish Scriptures to his Jewish followers, who were then expected to fulfill the Jewish Law, even better than the scribes and Pharisees. ■

Essential Reading

The Gospel of Matthew.

Brown, *Introduction to the New Testament*, chap. 8.

Ehrman, *The New Testament: A Historical Introduction*, chap. 7.

Supplemental Reading

Brown, *Birth of the Messiah*.

Carter, *What Are They Saying About the Sermon on the Mount?*

Senior, *What Are They Saying About Matthew?*

1. Many people today consider Judaism and Christianity to be two completely distinct religions. How would Matthew react to this view?

2. If Matthew were so insistent that Christians needed to follow the Jewish Law, does that mean Christians today should refuse to work on the Sabbath (Saturday) and should keep kosher?

3. Matthew's thorough opposition to the Jewish establishment has been used over the centuries as justification for acts of anti-Semitism. In what sense should Matthew himself be held responsible for such acts of hatred? Is there some sense in which he himself should be seen as anti-Semitic (even though he does stress Jesus' own Jewish-ness)?

to change. So by looking at the changes, you can see what the author's vested interests were. That is the approach we will take in this lecture towards the Gospel of Matthew, trying to see how Matthew differs from Mark in order to see what Matthew's distinctive emphases were.

By way of background, let me remind you that this Gospel has been attributed traditionally to Matthew, the disciple of Jesus who was known to be a tax collector. We don't actually know what the author's identity was. He doesn't appear, though, to have been an eyewitness to Jesus' life. As I pointed out earlier, this book was written anonymously. There are no first-person narratives in this account, and if scholars are right to say that this author used Mark for many of his stories, it's hard to imagine that the author himself was an eyewitness, as if he had to rely on somebody else for recounting what Jesus had done when he had seen it himself. For these reasons, scholars are fairly unified in thinking whoever the author was, he was not one of the disciples. He appeared to have been a Greek-speaking Christian living around 80 or 85 A.D., about a half-century or so after the events that he narrates.

Matthew's Gospel provides a distinctive portrayal of Jesus. On the one hand, as you might expect, Matthew has a similar view to Mark. Here too as in Mark, Jesus is the Messiah—the Son of God—whose entire life looks forward to his death, which was necessary to bring about salvation. Matthew has many of the same stories and therefore much of the same theology as Mark. But there are different emphases in this Gospel as well, as it becomes apparent at the very outset. In brief, the distinctiveness of this Gospel has to do with its stress both on the Jewishness of Jesus and on his opposition to Judaism as he found it. This gospel emphasizes far more than Mark that Jesus was the Jewish Messiah sent from the Jewish God to the Jewish people in fulfillment of the Jewish Scriptures. He gathered Jewish disciples and taught them that they had to follow the Jewish Law. At the same time, Jesus opposed the Jewish teachers of his own day and condemned the way that they practiced their religion. It's this combination of a strong affirmation of Judaism as it ought to be, and a vitriolic condemnation of Judaism as it actually was practiced, that makes Matthew's portrayal of Jesus so distinctive.

Matthew's emphasis on Jesus' own Jewishness can be seen in passages that are found in Matthew that are not found in his earlier source, Mark. Let me stress again this methodological point; by adding stories to his source, Matthew has altered somewhat the overarching perspective. We saw that Mark began his Gospel with the baptism of Jesus by John. Matthew doesn't begin his Gospel that way; instead, Matthew begins his Gospel with a genealogy that traces the descent of Jesus. Now genealogies are not among the most favorite readings of most students of the Bible; "Who begat whom." I have to assure my own students, though, that the genealogy in Matthew, which is only 16 verses long, doesn't compare at all with some of the genealogies you get in the Hebrew Bible. First Chronicles, which begins with nine chapters of genealogy, is a lot more names. Here though, simply 16 verses that are well-chosen verses because the names in this genealogy are a key to Matthew's own emphasis, as it becomes clear at the very beginning. Matthew's gospel begins with a verse, "The book of the generation, or the genealogy of Jesus Christ, the son of David, the son of Abraham." He begins his gospel by stressing the intimate connection between Jesus and David and Abraham. David, of course, was the great king of the Jews who lived a thousand years before Jesus, the great king whose descendent was supposed to be another king, a ruler of the Jews, commonly known as the son of David, the Messiah. Abraham was the father of the Jews, from whom all Jews trace their lineage. In other words, this very first verse is stressing that Jesus is Jewish, descended from Abraham, and that he is the Messiah, descended from David.

The genealogy itself goes on, then, to establish Jesus' credentials as standing in the Messianic line of the Jews; and it does so in a striking way. The genealogy begins, "Abraham begot Isaac, Isaac begot Jacob, and Jacob begot Judah and his brothers," and then it goes on down to, "Jesse begot David the king. David the king begot Solomon of her that had been the wife of Uriah. Solomon begot Rehoboam," etc. And it goes on down to Jachonias who is begotten along with his brothers by Josiah at the time of the captivity to Babylon. After the captivity to Babylon, "Jachonias begat Salathiel. Salathiel begat Zorababel," etc. on down to "Matthan begat Jacob; and Jacob begot Joseph the husband of Mary, of whom was born Jesus who is called the Messiah." In other words, it is who begat whom from Abraham to David to the captivity in Babylon, down to Joseph who is married to the

These stories of Jesus' birth in Matthew, unlike in Luke, are interesting because they mirror the accounts of Moses. In Moses, too, a child is born under a hostile regime—Egypt, rather than Rome. In Moses' case, as well, the ruling power wants to destroy him. In Moses' case, too, he is divinely protected. He sojourns in Egypt. He leaves Egypt. He goes through the water; in Moses' case, of course, it's the water of the Red Sea during the Exodus. In Jesus' case, immediately after the stories of his birth, he is baptized. In other words, it skips all those years between his infancy and his adulthood. The next story, though, is he goes through the waters of baptism, and then he goes out into the wilderness to be tempted, just as Moses and the children of Israel, who go into the wilderness for 40 years, and Jesus' 40 days in the wilderness. And then Jesus comes from the wilderness and goes up onto the mountain to deliver his teachings, his new Law, just as Moses went up on Mount Sinai to deliver God's Law. My point is that Matthew has told the stories about Jesus' birth precisely in order to call to mind the birth of Moses.

Why the birth of Moses? Because for Matthew's Gospel, Jesus is a new Moses, a new savior of the people of Israel; not one who stands in contradiction to or in contention with Moses himself, but a new Moses who fulfills the Law of Moses and delivers its correct interpretation. Matthew doesn't understand the choice for people in his day to be between Moses and Jesus. Matthew, as we are going to see, is not propounding that followers of Jesus have to reject Judaism. On the contrary, followers of Jesus, according to Matthew, have to affirm Judaism; but it's Judaism as interpreted by Jesus. It's not a choice between Moses and Jesus; it's a choice between Moses without Jesus or Moses with Jesus. And, according to the Gospel of Matthew, it is only Moses with Jesus that is the proper interpretation of the Law of Moses itself.

Some people have pointed out the striking fact that in Matthew's Gospel, unlike Mark and unlike Luke, in Matthew's Gospel there are five major blocks of Jesus' teaching, the first of which is the Sermon on the Mount in Chapters 5 through 7. This material, much of it is not found in Mark; most of this material comes from "Q." But why are there five blocks of his teaching? Is it to form a parallel to the five books of Moses, the Pentateuch? It's a possibility.

It is important, further, to recognize that these stories of Jesus' birth in Matthew's Gospel are all explicitly set to fulfill the scripture. We are told by Matthew that Jesus was born of a virgin, and we are told why; because, according to Isaiah Chapter 7, Verse 14, "A virgin shall conceive and bear a child, and you shall call him Emmanuel." There is question of whether Isaiah itself was referring to the birth of a child through a virgin. When you read the text in Hebrew, in fact, it doesn't say, "A virgin will conceive and bear a child." The Hebrew says, "A young woman will conceive and bear a child," but the Christian quotation of it in Matthew indicates that she was to be a virgin. Jesus' birth fulfills scripture. He is born in Bethlehem. Why? Well, Matthew says, because it is according to the prophet Micah, who says that the savior will come from Bethlehem. He flees to Egypt. Why? Because, as I have indicated, scripture says. Josiah Chapter 11, Verse 1: "Out of Egypt have I called my son." At every point, the events in Jesus' birth are said to fulfill scripture. Why is this emphasis found in Matthew, and only in Matthew? Precisely because Matthew is trying to show that Jesus fulfills everything God predicted in the scriptures.

Jesus, in other words, is the Jewish fulfillment of Jewish Law, given by the Jewish God. He is the one who, like Moses, will deliver God's Law to his people. This emphasis on the Law that Jesus gives is particularly found in the first block of his teaching, the so-called "Sermon on the Mount." Jesus goes up on a mountain, much as Moses went up to Mount Sinai, and then delivers his teaching. He begins the Sermon on the Mount, not by espousing an entirely new teaching, but interpreting for his hearers the teachings of Moses in the so-called "antitheses," the antitheses of the Sermon on the Mount. The Sermon on the Mount is Chapters 5 through 7 of Matthew. The antitheses are part-way through, after he has given the Beatitudes, where he begins to interpret what Moses said and then gives his own reading of what Moses means. Jesus says, for example, "You have heard it said that you shall not murder and that whoever murders shall be liable to judgment. But I say to you that everyone who gets angry with his brother will be liable to judgment. You have heard it said that you should not commit adultery. I say to you that you should not even lust after a woman in your heart. You have heard it said, 'an eye for an eye and a tooth for a tooth.' I say to you, turn the other cheek." Jesus gives a Law of Moses and then gives his interpretation of the Law of Moses. These teachings are called antitheses because Jesus sets his own understanding of this teaching in opposition to other understandings of the teaching. It is not that Jesus is contradicting what Moses himself said; in other words, Jesus doesn't say, "Moses said you shall not murder, but I say you should." These antitheses, instead, are giving alternative interpretations of the law of Moses, which get beyond the literal level, down to the point of the spirit of the Law. "Moses said don't kill; I say don't even get angry. Moses said don't commit adultery; I say don't even lust." Jesus wants his followers to follow, not only the letter of the law, but its very spirit.

Some readers find the demand to be so strict that it can't really be serious. Jesus can't

Jewishness of Jesus himself is counterbalanced by Jesus' forceful opposition to the Jewish leaders, whom Jesus does not think follow the Law very well. In fact, Jesus portrays them as hypocrites who demand that people follow the law, but don't do so themselves. Particularly striking is Chapter 23. Chapter 23 of Matthew shows Matthew's vehement opposition to the scribes and Pharisees. Where Jesus calls his opponents, the Jewish leaders, "whitewashed sepulchres." They are cleaned on the outside but filled with rot and corruption inside. People there are hypocrites who teach one thing but do the opposite.

Luke—Jesus the Savior of the World
Lecture 7

Luke portrays Jesus as a Jewish prophet whose salvation goes to the whole world to bring salvation, not just to Jews, but also to Gentiles, in fulfillment of the plan of God.

L uke has a distinctive emphasis of his own. On the one hand, like Mark, Luke portrays Jesus as the Son of God whose death fulfilled the Scriptures. But he does not stress the failure of everyone to recognize Jesus—in fact, Jesus is worshipped even as an infant. Like Matthew, Luke maintains that Jesus is the messiah. But Luke does not stress that Jesus was the new Moses who demanded that his followers adhere to the Jewish Law. Instead, Luke stresses that Jesus' salvation comes not just to the Jews, but to all people. This is not to say that Jesus is not portrayed as Jewish here. Jesus is portrayed as a Jewish prophet (that is, one who knows God's will and has been called by God to proclaim it to his people) who has been rejected by the Jewish people. It is precisely because he is rejected by Jews that Jesus' message of salvation is taken to the non-Jewish people, that is, the Gentiles.

In exploring Luke's Gospel, we can begin by considering some background information. As with the other Gospels, this one is anonymous. Tradition has ascribed it to a Gentile physician named Luke, known to have been a traveling companion of the apostle Paul. Whether we can trust this 2nd-century tradition or not continues to be a matter of debate among scholars. This Gospel was written in Greek, apparently at about the time of Matthew (80–85 A.D.). There is little to suggest that Matthew and Luke knew each other's work, but they both appear to have had access to a copy of the Gospel of Mark and the lost source of Jesus' sayings called Q. One of the things that makes this Gospel distinct is the fact that its author wrote a second volume: the Book of Acts—our only surviving account of the history of earliest Christianity after the death of Jesus up through the ministry of the apostle Paul.

One way to approach Luke's account is by comparing it with the narratives we have already studied. Luke's preface is like prefaces found in the works of other ancient historians (1:1–14). He tells us his sources of information, which are written accounts and oral tradition. Luke does not think favorably of his predecessor Gospel writers. He dedicates this work to "Theophilus," perhaps a pagan Roman administrator of status or perhaps a fictional recipient whose name means "loved by God" or "lover of God." Even though Luke did not use Matthew as a source, a comparison of the two can reveal some of Luke's special emphases.

Like Matthew, but unlike Mark, Luke provides a genealogy of Jesus. This genealogy is strikingly different from the one found in Matthew. In fact, in places it is quite literally a different genealogy—all the way from Jesus' father's father back to King David. (The attempt to reconcile these differences by saying that Luke's genealogy gives the family tree of Mary rather than of Joseph overlooks the rather obvious fact that it claims to give the ancestors of Joseph.) More significantly, Luke does not stress Jesus' ties to David and Abraham. Instead, Luke's genealogy goes as far back as one can imagine: to the progenitor of the human race, Adam (3:23–38). Unlike in Matthew, then, the emphasis here is not that Jesus is closely connected to the Jewish people through the king of Israel all the way back to the father of the Jews. Luke emphasizes that Jesus is closely connected to the entire human race through the father of us all. For this author more than any other we've seen, Jesus' salvation comes to the entire world.

This stress can be found throughout Luke at critical junctures, as can be seen by comparing several episodes with those found in Mark. About halfway through Jesus' ministry in Mark, he goes to his hometown and preaches in the synagogue, only to be rejected by his own people, who can't understand how a simple carpenter can speak such words of wisdom (Mark 6:1–6). Luke has the account, but changes it significantly (Luke 4:16–30). The first thing to notice is that in Luke, this episode occurs as the very first event in Jesus' ministry. The story is used, in other words, to set the stage for all that is to come. Moreover, the account is much longer in Luke, who has Jesus read from the prophet Isaiah, then claim that these very predictions are fulfilled in him. Unlike in Mark, Jesus likens himself to two prominent prophets of the Hebrew Bible, Elijah and Elisha, who were sent (to the chagrin of their compatriots) to minister to both Jews and Gentiles. The people in the synagogue become outraged at Jesus' claims about himself and not only abuse him verbally, as in Mark, but also attempt to kill him (4:29–30). This foreshadows what is to come in the rest of Luke's narrative. As in Mark, Jesus does great miracles and delivers authoritative teachings, in preparation for his death in Jerusalem. Even more so in Luke, however, he is portrayed as a Jewish prophet who has been rejected—to the death—by the Jewish people so that his message can go beyond the bounds of Judaism to the Gentiles and the whole world.

Jesus, then, is principally portrayed by Luke as a rejected Jewish prophet. He is born like a prophet. Like Matthew, Luke has a birth narrative in which Jesus is born of a virgin, Mary, in Bethlehem. But here the emphasis is not on his fulfillment of Scripture (Luke never explicitly stresses Scripture), nor on his similarities to Moses (Luke lacks the stories of Herod's trying to kill the child, the flight to Egypt, and so on). Instead of reminding one of Moses, Luke's birth stories recall the birth of another famous Jewish prophet, Samuel, to the extent that Mary's song of thanksgiving to God mirrors the song sung by Samuel's mother, Hanna, in the Hebrew Bible (Luke 1:46–55; cf., 1 Sam 2:1–10).

Jesus is principally portrayed by Luke as a rejected Jewish prophet.

Jesus preaches like a prophet, as we have seen in the sermon in Nazareth. He claims that the prophecies have been fulfilled in him. He portrays himself as a prophet like Elijah and Elisha. Jesus also heals like a prophet. The story of his raising the dead son of a widow at Nain (found only in Luke 7:11–17) is remarkably similar to the story of the prophet Elijah's raising the dead son of a widow at Zarephath (1 Kings 17:7–24). The crowds acknowledge the significance of what Jesus has done on the occasion: "a great prophet has risen among us" (Luke 7:16).

And finally Jesus dies like a prophet. Jesus explicitly says (only in Luke) that he must go to Jerusalem to be killed because that's where the prophets die (Luke 13:33). Because he's a prophet who fully knows God's will, Jesus shows no real agony or indecision before his death in Luke. This can be seen by contrasting Luke's "Garden of Gethsemane" scene with the one found in Mark. In Luke, Jesus is calm and in control, even in the period of greatest temptation. Luke's portrayal of Jesus' death is completely different from the one in Mark. Rather than being silent and shocked, feeling forsaken of all, even God, in Luke Jesus dies in complete control of the situation, in full confidence of God, knowing what must happen and why. As a prophet, he knows what must happen. Most strikingly—and unlike Mark—Jesus speaks early, often, and confidently throughout his way to Calvary and during the crucifixion.

This emphasis on Jesus as a prophet—one who knows God's will and is sent to proclaim it—coincides with another emphasis in Luke, that everything that happens to Jesus and his followers happens according to God's plan. Luke frequently speaks of the "plan" or "will" of God. Nothing happens in this Gospel that hasn't been foreseen. In particular, in Luke's Gospel, unlike Mark's, there's no emphasis on the apocalyptic notion that the end of the world is imminent. This can be seen in the ways Luke modifies Jesus' words about the coming end (cf., Mark 9:1 and Luke 9:27 or Mark 14:62 and Luke 22:69). No longer is there a sense that the end will come while the disciples are still alive. For Luke, the Kingdom of God was already at hand in Jesus. For Luke, the end could not come immediately (as well he knew, by then, that it hadn't), because first the Gospel had to be taken into all the world to allow the Gentiles time to hear and repent. That is what Luke's second volume (Acts) is about—how God planned the salvation brought by Jesus to be taken throughout the world.

Because the world is to go on for a long time, it's not surprising that Luke has a stronger social agenda than the other Gospels. Jesus stresses the poor and needy in his teachings. (Compare, for example, the Beatitudes. In Matthew, it's "Blessed are the poor in spirit" and "Blessed are those who hunger and thirst for righteousness [Matthew 5:3–11]." In Luke, it's "Blessed are you poor" and "Blessed are you who hunger and thirst [Luke 6:20–26]." Also compare the Parable of the Good Samaritan.) Jesus emphasizes more the rights and needs of women (cf., Luke 10:38–42, a story found only in Luke, in which Martha is praised for not being concerned with her "womanly" duties but for learning from the teacher, presumably along with the other disciples.)

In conclusion, Luke is both like and unlike the two other Synoptic Gospels. Like both Mark and Matthew, Luke describes Jesus' public ministry as one filled with miraculous feats and marvelous teachings, and he, too, sees the importance of Jesus' death for God's plan of salvation. Rather than stressing Jesus as the misunderstood Son of God, as in Mark, or as the Jewish messiah who insists that his followers keep the Jewish Law, as in Matthew, Luke portrays Jesus as a Jewish prophet whose salvation goes out to the whole world, to bring salvation to both Jews and Gentiles, in fulfillment of the plan of God. ■

Essential Reading

The Gospel of Luke.

Brown, *Introduction to the New Testament,* chap. 9.

Ehrman, *The New Testament: A Historical Introduction*, chap. 8.

Supplemental Reading

Brown, *The Birth of the Messiah.*

Juel, *Luke–Acts: The Promise of History.*

Powell, *What Are They Saying About Luke?*

Questions to Consider

1. How might the fact that Luke produced a *two*-volume work affect the way we should interpret either volume? Should we, or can we, read one volume in light of the emphases of the other?

2. If Luke were writing principally to show that Jesus was the savior of the entire world, why would he emphasize so strongly that he was a *Jewish* prophet?

3. Do you see the three different accounts of Jesus that we have examined as complementary to one another or contradictory? Is it possible for them all to be historically accurate, if they tell the same stories but give different accounts? Do you see any explicit discrepancies?

Luke—Jesus the Savior of the World
Lecture 7—Transcript

To this point in the course, we have been looking at the Gospels of the New Testament as literary productions. We haven't yet begun to ask the question about what Jesus himself really said and did. Instead, we have been looking at the distinctive portrayals of Jesus in each one of the Gospels. We've seen that Mark portrays Jesus as the Son of God who, contrary to widely held expectations, must suffer for the sins of the world. Matthew agrees with this perspective, but adds a strong emphasis that Jesus was the Jewish Messiah, sent in fulfillment of the Jewish scriptures, a new Moses, who expected his followers to keep the Jewish Law.

We turn now to the third of the Synoptic Gospels, the Gospel of Luke, who, like Matthew and Mark, has a distinctive emphasis of his own. On the one hand, like Mark, Luke would portray Jesus as the Son of God whose death fulfilled the scriptures; but he does not stress the failure of everyone to recognize Jesus the way that Mark did. In fact, in Luke's Gospel, Jesus is worshiped already as an infant. Like Matthew, Luke will maintain that Jesus is the Messiah, but he does not stress that Jesus was the new Moses, who demanded that his followers adhere to the Jewish Law. Instead, Luke stresses that Jesus' salvation comes, not just to the Jews, but to all people. I don't mean to say that Jesus is not portrayed as Jewish in the Gospel of Luke, for, in fact, he is portrayed as a Jewish prophet. That is, as a man who knows God's will and has been called by God to proclaim this will to his people. Jesus, in this Gospel, is portrayed as a Jewish prophet sent to the Jewish people, who is rejected by them. Because he is rejected by the Jews, his message of salvation then can go to the non-Jews—that is, to the Gentiles. That is the overriding thesis of the Gospel of Luke.

I want to begin our consideration of this Gospel, again, by looking at some background information. As with the other Gospels we have considered, this one, too, is anonymous; the author didn't tell us his name. Traditionally, the Gospel has been ascribed to a man named Luke, who was a gentile physician who was a traveling companion of the Apostle Paul. This tradition goes back to the 2nd century. Whether or not we can trust the tradition is a matter of debate among competent scholars. Like the other Gospels, this one was written in Greek. Apparently it was written at about the same time as the Gospel of Matthew, possibly 80 or 85 A.D. There is little to suggest that Matthew and Luke knew each other's work, but they do both appear to have had access to the Gospel of Mark and to the lost sources of Jesus' sayings the scholars have called "Q".

One of the things that makes the Gospel of Luke distinct is the fact that this author wrote a second volume, the Book of Acts, that we will be considering later in the course. The Book of Acts, which is our only surviving account of the history of earliest Christianity after the death of the Jesus, up through the ministry of the Apostle Paul. In this later lecture, we will look at how this second volume, the Book of Acts, continues on many of the themes and emphases of this first volume, the Gospel of Luke. In this lecture, we will be focusing exclusively on the Gospel of Luke.

One way to approach Luke's account is by comparing it with the narratives that we have already considered, those of Matthew and Mark. I want to make this kind of comparison, not so that we can see how Luke should be interpreted in light of Matthew and Mark; in other words, I don't want to conflate the accounts together and pretend they are all saying the same thing. Quite the contrary, I want to look at the accounts in comparison with one another precisely to show how Luke is different from the other two, so that we can detect what his distinctive emphases are.

The first thing that strikes one in making a comparison between Luke and the other Gospels is that he begins in a completely different way from Matthew and Mark. Luke begins by giving a kind of preface, an overview of his account, a preface that is very much like prefaces that you find in other works of ancient historians. Luke begins by saying, "Whereas many have undertaken to produce a narrative of the matters that have been fulfilled among us just as they were handed on to us from the beginning by eyewitnesses and ministers of the word, it seemed good to me also, most excellent Theophilus, to produce an accurate account having followed all things carefully, so that you might know the certainty of the matters that had been fulfilled among us." Those are the first four verses of Luke's Gospel. It's a very interesting preface for several reasons. First, as I have pointed out, this preface is like prefaces found in other works of ancient historians, which might suggest that Luke was taking the historical nature of his narrative a little more seriously than other ancient Gospel writers that we have. He is trying to mimic the style of ancient historians. Second, he tells us what his sources of information were. This is a typical move among ancient historians. His narrative will be based on accounts that he has seen, written reports; people before him have undertaken to writing these accounts. He has seen these accounts. And secondly, ultimately, all of these accounts go back to eyewitness reports. In other words, Luke has before him written Gospels and oral traditions. Third, it is striking that Luke does not think favorably of his predecessors. He indicates that others have tried to write an account, but now he wants to write one that is accurate so that his recipient will know the certainty of what happened before. In other words, he is casting some slight aspersions, perhaps, on some of his predecessors, which is particularly interesting if, in fact, Mark was one of those predecessors, because that might suggest that Luke didn't think Mark had done an adequate job. Of course that is implied, as well, by the fact that he has changed Mark so significantly. If he liked Mark the way it was, he would have simply copied Mark and published it as is.

He dedicates this book to Theophilus. We don't know Theophilus was. It is typical for historians to dedicate their work to a patron, someone who provides financial support for the author. Theophilus may have been a patron of Luke. Some scholars have thought that Theophilus might have been some kind of Roman administrator that Luke is giving this book to. The reason for thinking that is because he calls Theophilus "most excellent Theophilus," and that term "most excellent" is used in the Book of Acts for Roman Administrators. So possibly this is a pagan Roman that Luke is writing for. While that is a possibility, and a number scholars think that this is what's going on here, it seems to other scholars somewhat unlikely that a book of this size is being handed over to some pagan Roman official, as if he would have time, or the desire, to read it. There is another explanation for what Theophilus is. The term "Theophilus," in fact, comes from two Greek words which mean beloved of God, or lover of God. It is possible that, in fact, Luke has devised a fictional recipient of this book, one who is loved of God. In other words, that he is writing for Christians in his own community, who are beloved of God, or who are lovers of God. That makes somewhat better sense, because most of these early Christian writings, in fact, probably all of these Gospels, were probably directed to the Christians who were reading them, rather than to outsiders, say, as missionary literature. And so it may be that Theophilus is simply a code name for the Christians who are receiving this book.

Once we get beyond the preface, we can see other differences between Luke and the other Gospels. First, let me point out a striking difference between the Gospel of Matthew. It's not that Luke used Matthew as a source, as I have indicated, but they do have some similarities, and so it is interesting to look at their differences. One of the striking differences between Luke and Matthew has to do with the genealogy that Matthew uses to begin his Gospel. Mark didn't have a genealogy. Matthew had one, and it turns out that Luke had one as well. But what is striking is that, in comparison with Matthew's, Luke's is a different genealogy of Jesus. The genealogy that Luke gives is found in Chapter 3. In Chapter 3 we are told that Jesus was supposedly the son of Joseph, who is the son of Eli, who is the son of Matthat, who is the son of Levi, etc., etc., and it keeps on going back. Matthew's genealogy, if you recall traced Jesus back to King David, and from King David back to Abraham, the father of the Jews. The stress in Matthew's genealogy was the Jesus is Jewish, descended from the father of the Jews and the great king of the Jews, that he was the Messiah from the Davidic line. Luke, interestingly, doesn't go back just to David and Abraham; it goes back all the way to Adam, as in Adam and Eve.

This is a terrific genealogy. I have an aunt who is a genealogist, who is quite proud of the fact that she has been able to trace my family origin back to the Mayflower. The Mayflower—that's nothing! This genealogy traces Jesus back to Adam—Adam and Eve. But why? If Matthew's genealogy was meant to show the Jewishness of Jesus, because he is related to David and Abraham, Luke's genealogy is designed to show Jesus' humanity. He is not the savior just of the Jews; he descends from the entire human race. He's the savior of the entire…of all humankind. That's Luke's emphasis that we see just in the genealogy. Let me say again that this genealogy is different from Matthew, not simply because it goes all the way back to Adam; if you read the beginning part of this genealogy, you realize that, in fact, it is a complete different genealogy. It traces Jesus' lineage through Joseph, as does Matthew. But Joseph, in this genealogy, has a different father, and a different grandfather, and a different great-grandfather. The names are different all the way from Joseph back to David. Some people have tried to reconcile this by saying that Matthew's genealogy is giving the genealogy of Joseph, and Luke's genealogy is giving the genealogy of Mary, which is a clever solution; that would explain why you would have the different names. Unfortunately for that thesis, when you read the text itself, it is quite clear that, in fact, Luke's genealogy is the genealogy of Joseph. Apparently, Matthew and Luke simply inherited their genealogies from different sources. The stress that Luke places in the genealogy on Jesus being the savior of the entire human race can be found throughout Luke's Gospel at a number of critical junctures. That can be seen, above all, by comparing several episodes of Luke with those that are found in Mark, which is one of his sources.

One of the most interesting stories to compare between Luke and Mark has to do with an event that takes place halfway through Mark's Gospel, in which Jesus goes to his hometown of Nazareth and preaches in the synagogue, only to be rejected by his townsfolk, who can't understand how a simple carpenter like Jesus can speak such words of wisdom. That's found in Mark Chapter 6, Verses 1 through 6. Luke also has this account, Luke Chapter 4, Verses 16 through 30, but he's changed it in significant ways. The first thing to notice is that in Luke's Gospel, this rejection of Jesus occurs as the very first thing that happens in Jesus' ministry. It doesn't happen halfway through the account; it is the first thing that happens. Why does Luke transpose the account to the very beginning? Because in Luke's Gospel, this is going to set the stage for everything else that is to come. Moreover, in Luke's account, the rejection of Jesus in Nazareth is much longer than in Mark. Luke lengthens the account by having Jesus read from the prophet Isaiah in the synagogue. Jesus goes to the synagogue, and he gets up to read the scriptures. The attendant hands him a scroll of Isaiah. Jesus reads the scroll, and it's a passage which says that "the spirit of the law is upon me because he had announced me to preach to the poor. He has sent me to proclaim forgiveness to the captives, sight to the blind," etc. And then Jesus sits down—this is found only in Luke, not in Mark—Jesus sits down and says—everybody is looking at him—and he says, "Truly I tell you today, this scripture has been fulfilled in your hearing." Jesus explicatively claims to fulfill the prophet Isaiah. He is the prophet that Isaiah has anticipated.

The people wonder what Jesus can possibly be talking about, and then Jesus goes on and likens himself to two prophets of the Hebrew bible, Elijah and Elisha, whose stories in the Hebrew Bible include accounts of them going out to help people who were non-Jews, even when Jews were suffering. There is a drought in the land, according to 1 Kings, and Elijah, rather than going to stay and to help out a Jewish family, goes to a pagan family, a widow in Zaraphat. Elijah is sent to heal a leper, not a Jewish leper. Jesus likens himself to Elijah and Elisha, and his audience knows full well what he is talking about. He is saying that he has come to minister, not to Jews, but to Gentiles. The reaction is immediate; they take him out of the synagogue, they take him up to a high hill, and they are going to try to cast him off, but Jesus then walks through their midst. It's an interesting account because it sets the stage for what's going to happen in Luke's Gospel and then the Book of Acts. Jesus comes to his people; he proclaims his message for salvation, that he is the one who fulfills the prophets. They reject him, and because they reject him, his message then goes to the Gentiles. Jesus, throughout this account, is portrayed as a rejected Jewish prophet.

There are several ways that Luke portrays Jesus as a prophet in narratives that are unique to Luke. First, Jesus is born like a prophet. Like Matthew, Luke has a birth narrative. We saw that Matthew's narrative emphasized that Jesus is like Moses, and it emphasized that Jesus fulfilled scripture. Luke also has an account of Jesus being born to a virgin, Mary, in Bethlehem. But here the emphasis is quite different. Here, what one sees when one reads the account is not that Jesus is fulfilling scripture in the sense that you have in Matthew. Instead, what you have a sense of is that Jesus is being born like prophets are born. Specifically, when Mary conceives Jesus, she breaks out into a song in which she praises God for bringing down the high and raising up those that are low. It's a song that sounds almost exactly like the song of Hannah in the Hebrew Bible (1 Samuel Chapter 2). Hannah, who gave birth to the first major Jewish prophet, Samuel. Mary's song, in other words, is to call to mind the song of Hannah. Why? Because Luke is trying to emphasize that Jesus is born like the prophets are born. He is not only born like a prophet, he preaches like a prophet, as we saw in the sermon that he gave in Nazareth. He claims that the prophecies have been fulfilled in him, and he likens himself to Elijah and Elisha, these two great prophets of the Hebrew Bible. All of these stories, let me emphasize, are unique to Luke; you don't find them in Matthew and in Mark. Third, Jesus heals like a prophet heals. There is a very interesting account in Luke Chapter 7, Verses 11 through 17, found only in Luke, of Jesus raising from the dead the dead son of a widow at a city called Nain. When you read the account, if you know the Hebrew Bible well enough, it sounds very similar to the account of Elijah raising the dead son of a widow in the city of Zarephath (1 Kings Chapter 17). In fact, the similarity of the miracle is not lost among the people who witness it in Luke's Gospel. Chapter 7, Verse 16: "the crowd acknowledged the significance of what Jesus has done on the occasion by saying, 'a great prophet has risen among us.'"

He is born like prophet, he preaches like a prophet, he heals like a prophet, and, perhaps most significantly, Jesus dies as a prophet in Luke's Gospel. Jesus explicitly says, only in Luke, that he must go to Jerusalem to be killed because that's where the prophets die (Luke Chapter 13, Verse 33). He's a prophet, so he must go to Jerusalem, because that's where prophets are killed.

Because Jesus has been portrayed as a prophet in his death, Luke modifies some of the traditions about the passion narrative itself, in some very interesting ways. Jesus knows what is going to happen to him in Luke's Gospel. Because he knows, it doesn't appear that Jesus is experiencing real agony in this Gospel the way he does in the others. This is one place, in particular, where it is important not to conflate the accounts and pretend that they are all saying the same thing. If you read Luke's account, just on its own terms, you don't have the sense of Jesus going through real agony up to his death. You can see this in two different narratives.

When Jesus goes out to pray prior to his arrest, in Mark's Gospel, Jesus goes to the garden of Gethsemane. He is extremely distraught; he tells his disciples that his soul is troubled unto death. He tells them to wait for him. He goes off. He falls on his face. He prays three times, "God, take away this cup from me." Luke has the same narrative; but Luke doesn't say that Jesus is distraught. Jesus, in this narrative, doesn't say to his disciples, "My soul is troubled unto death." He goes to pray, but he doesn't fall on his face; instead, he kneels down. Instead of praying three times, "God, take away this cup from me," he says "If it be your will, take this cup from me," and he prays it only once. There is not the same sense of agony here at all.

The idea of Jesus not being in real distress and agony going up to his death is seen even more clearly in the account of Jesus' own crucifixion in Luke's Gospel. Again, it is worthwhile comparing what Luke says with what his predecessor, Mark, had said. Remember Mark's account, Jesus appears before Pontus Pilate; he is accused of being the King of the Jews. He is basically silent through the entire proceeding; he only says two words in Mark's Gospel. Pilate says, "You are the King of the Jews," and Jesus says, "If you say so." He goes to his place of crucifixion, and he is silent the entire way in Mark's Gospel. He is nailed to the cross, in Mark's Gospel, is silent the whole time. People are passing by, people are mocking him, and he says nothing, even on the cross, until the very end. In Mark's Gospel, when everybody has betrayed him, denied him, mocked him, in Mark's Gospel, to the very end, he is hanging on the cross, and he cries out, "Eloi, Eloi, Lama Sabachthani"—My God, my God, why have you forsaken me?—and he dies. In Mark's Gospel, Jesus appears to be in doubt and wonders why God himself has forsaken him at the end. It's a stark contrast with Luke, if Luke has changed the story.

In Luke's Gospel, Jesus is not silent on his way to crucifixion. He is walking with the cross, and he sees some women weeping on the side of the road. And he turns to them, only in Luke's Gospel, and he says, "Weep not for me, but weep for yourselves and for your children for the fate that is to befall you." More concerned about these women than himself. In Luke's Gospel, while he is being nailed to the cross, he is not silent. Instead, he prays, "Father forgive them; they don't know what they are doing." While he is hanging on the cross in Luke's Gospel, he is not silent; he has an intelligent conversation with one of the other people being crucified with him. Now, in Mark's Gospel, both robbers mock Jesus. In Luke's Gospel, only one of them mocks him. The other one tells him to be quiet because Jesus hasn't done anything to deserve this. And then this robber turns to Jesus and says, "Lord, remember me when you come into your kingdom," and Jesus replies, "Truly, I tell you today, you will be with me in paradise." Most striking of all, at the end in Luke's Gospel, instead of crying out, "My God, my God, why have you forsaken me?" Jesus doesn't cry that out at all; instead, Jesus says, "Father, into your hand I commend my spirit," and he dies.

I mentioned in an earlier lecture the tendency of readers to assume that Jesus said all of these things on the cross. So you have the seven last words of the dying Jesus, where he says the words in Mark, and the words of Luke, and of Matthew, and of John; you brought them all together, and you have seven of the words. In fact, these are distinctive portrayals. Luke is not portraying Jesus the way that Mark is, as somebody who is in agony and uncertainty at the end. In Luke's Gospel, Jesus is going to his death knowing full well what's happening to him and why it is happening to him and what's going to happen to him; after it happens to him, he is going to wake up that day in paradise, and this robber is going to be with him. Jesus is a prophet who is fully certain about God's will for him and the future of the Earth. For that reason, Jesus doesn't go to his death in agony.

So Jesus is portrayed as prophet in Luke, one who is born as a prophet, one who preaches as a prophet, one who heals as a prophet, and one who dies as a prophet. This emphasis on Jesus as a prophet, one who knows full well what God's will is and who is sent to proclaim it, coincides with emphasis found throughout Luke's Gospel. In particular, it coincides with an emphasis, found distinctively in Luke, that everything is going according to God's plan. "The will of God," "the plan of God," are terms that one finds throughout Luke's Gospel. Moreover, interestingly, in this Gospel, there is no emphasis (the way there is in Mark) that the end of the world is supposed to happen right away. Mark's Gospel, on a couple of occasions that we will refer to later in the course, refers to the circumstance that the end is immediate. Jesus tells his disciples in Mark, "Some of you standing here won't taste death before you see that the kingdom of God has come in power."

The kingdom of God is going to come in power, and you are going to be alive to see it. Luke changes that verse to, "Some of you standing here won't taste death before you see the kingdom of God." Nothing about it coming in power. Luke does think that the disciples saw the kingdom of God because, according to Luke, Jesus' own ministry is the kingdom of God. Luke says, in Chapter 17, "The Kingdom of God is in your midst," or is among you. For Luke, there's not going to be an end of the age the way we think of; the

Kingdom has already arrived, in some sense. So, too, in the trial before the high priest in Mark's Gospel, Jesus says to the high priest, "You will see the Son of Man coming on the clouds of heaven." Luke has the same verse, but he changes it to, "From now on, the Son of Man will be seated at the right hand of power." It's not that the high priest is going to see the cosmic judge come from Heaven: it's that from now on, Jesus will be exalted.

Jesus, as a prophet in Luke, knows that the end isn't going to come right away. The reason it is not going to come right away is because God wanted to allow time for the message of Jesus to go out into the world, so that salvation can come to Gentiles, as well as to Jews. That's what the second volume, the Book of Acts, is going to be about, the salvation of God that goes to Gentiles. Well, it takes time for salvation to go throughout the world, and so, of course, in this Gospel, you can't expect the end to come right away. First there has to be time for the establishment of the church. Since Luke thinks there is going to be a long period of time before the coming of the end, Luke, more than the other Gospels, has a strong social agenda.

Unlike the other Gospels, Jesus stresses the importance of taking care of the needs of those who are poor and oppressed and outcast. You get some of this in the other Gospels, but in Luke, it's even much more strongly stated. Compare the Beatitudes in Matthew and in Luke. In Matthew, Jesus says, "Blessed are the poor in spirit." In Luke, he says, "Blessed are you who are poor," in other words, poverty itself is a problem. In Matthew, "Blessed are those who hunger and thirst for righteousness." In Luke, it's, "Blessed are you who hunger and thirst." In other words, in Luke's Gospel, rather than being concerned just about spiritual matters, Jesus is concerned about material matters as well, including the needs and rights of women. In Luke's Gospel, there is a higher emphasis on the need for Christian communities, the followers of Jesus, to take care of the needs of women, who were, of course, an oppressed group in ancient societies.

In conclusion, Luke is both like and unlike Matthew and Mark, the two other Synoptic Gospels. Like both of the others, Luke describes Jesus' public ministry as one that is filled with stupendous miraculous deeds and marvelous teachings. Here, too, we see the importance of Jesus' death for God's plan of salvation. But instead of stressing Jesus as the misunderstood son of God, as in Mark, or as the Jewish Messiah who insisted that his followers keep the Jewish law, as in Matthew, Luke portrays Jesus as a Jewish prophet whose salvation goes to the whole world to bring salvation, not just to Jews, but also to Gentiles, in fulfillment of the plan of God.

John—Jesus the Man from Heaven
Lecture 8

The Gospel of John, the fourth Gospel, [is] a book that is so different from the other three that, sometimes, it is known amongst scholars as a "maverick" Gospel.

To this point, we have considered the portrayals of Jesus in Matthew, Mark, and Luke, books called the Synoptic Gospels because they have so many traditions in common that they can be "seen together." Despite their numerous similarities, we have seen that they each have a distinctive emphasis in the portrayal of Jesus. Traditionally, the book has been ascribed to John, the son of Zebedee, one of Jesus' closest disciples. This ascription cannot be found until near the end of the 2nd century; the book is, in fact, anonymous. In the earlier sources, the disciple John is portrayed as a lower-class peasant from Galilee, who presumably spoke Aramaic, not the Greek in which the Gospel is written. Moreover, John is said in the New Testament itself to have been illiterate (Acts 4:13). It seems unlikely that he was directly responsible for writing this book, which appears to have been produced near the end of the 1st century (90–95 A.D.). As was the case with the other Gospels, we'll continue to call this one "John" in lieu of a better option.

In very rough outline, John is like the other Gospels. Here, too, is an account of Jesus' ministry of teaching and healing, leading up to his death and resurrection in Jerusalem. Moreover, John shares several stories with the other Gospels, especially in the Passion narrative.But the differences between John and the Synoptics are nonetheless striking. This can be seen just in terms of its contents. John lacks most of the stories that form the backbone of the Synoptic Gospel portrayals of Jesus. Among those notably absent from John are accounts of Jesus' birth, his baptism by John, his temptation in the wilderness, his proclamation of the coming Kingdom of God, his telling of parables, his casting out of demons, his transfiguration before some of his disciples, his institution of the Lord's Supper, his prayer in the Garden of Gethsemane, and his trial before the Jewish authorities. These stories form the heart and core of the Synoptic accounts of Jesus' life, but none of them is found in John.

On the other hand, John has numerous stories of his own, not found in the Synoptics. Some of Jesus' most startling deeds are found only here; for example, the turning of the water into wine (2:1–12) and the raising of Lazarus from the dead (11:1–44). Some of Jesus' most memorable teachings are also found only here; for example, his conversation with the Jewish rabbi, Nicodemus, in which Jesus says, "you must be born again" (3:3) and his famous "I am" sayings, in which he identifies himself as the only one who can bring salvation: "I am the light of the world," "I am the bread of life," "I am the resurrection and the life." Some of the differences between John and the Synoptics have been seen by readers over the years as actual discrepancies. We've seen one example already: John appears to have Jesus die on a different day and at a different time than the Synoptics (on the afternoon before the Passover meal was eaten in John; on the morning after in the Synoptics). Another example that is commonly cited involves Jesus' cleansing of the temple, which in John occurs not during the final week of Jesus' life as in the Synoptics, but at the very beginning of his ministry (2:13–22).

In some ways, even more revealing of the distinctiveness of this Gospel are the differences in emphases that it places on material shared with the other Gospels. In all four Gospels, for example, Jesus is portrayed as a miracle worker, but the reasons for his miracles are quite different in John than in the Synoptics. The Synoptics show Jesus doing miracles to help people in need; he explicitly refuses to do them to prove his own identity. For example, in Matthew, after Jesus has healed a blind man, some people believe that he must be the messiah. The Scribes and Pharisees approach him, asking him to do a "sign" to prove it to them. He refuses, saying, "no sign will be given to this evil and adulterous generation" (Matthew 12:39). A similar message is given in the Synoptic account of the Temptations in the wilderness. At one point, Jesus is tempted to jump from the Temple to be miraculously swept up by the angels before hitting the ground—evidently to prove to the Jewish worshippers gathered there that he is the one sent from God. Jesus spurns this desire as a Satanic temptation (Matthew 4:5–7).

In John, rather than spurning the temptation to produce a sign for his onlookers, Jesus does miracles precisely to prove his identity. In fact, in John, his stupendous deeds aren't called miracles but signs. At one point, Jesus says that his signs are designed to make people believe and that people won't be able to believe without the signs (4:54). The Gospel itself indicates that the signs of Jesus are written to make people believe (20:30–31). It is striking that neither Jesus' refusal to offer a sign nor the temptation narrative appears in John.

In the Synoptics, Jesus' miraculous deeds are done in response to a person's faith; in John, they are meant to generate that faith. In the Synoptics, Jesus refuses to do miracles to prove who he is; in John, he does them for just that reason. These differences can be seen in two separate accounts, one in Mark, one in John, of Jesus raising a person from the dead at the request of a family member: the raising of Jairus's daughter in Mark 5 and the raising of Lazarus in John 11. The stories are striking in their basic formal similarities. In both, a family member asks Jesus to come to help a sick person before it's too late, but he does not arrive in time and the person has died in the meantime. In both accounts, onlookers mock Jesus for thinking that he can now do something about the death, and he speaks of the person as "sleeping" (a Greek euphemism for having died). In both accounts, he goes to where the person is and commands him or her to arise; the person arises, and Jesus orders the onlookers to take care of his or her physical needs.

In view of the strong formal similarities of the stories, their differences cannot help but attract our notice. In Mark's account (Mark 5), Jesus goes as soon as he is summoned, privately entering the girl's room, taking only the parents and three of his disciples, and ordering the witnesses strictly not to tell anyone what they have seen. In John's account (John 11), Jesus intentionally does not go to Lazarus when he is ill, because, as he tells his disciples, he wanted Lazarus to die so that he could raise him from the dead as a public display of his power. He comes then to Lazarus's tomb with the crowds surrounding him and commands Lazarus to rise from the dead. To the amazement of the crowds, Lazarus comes forth. In one account, Jesus orders secrecy; in the other, he makes his miracle a public display of power. In one story, he refuses to do miracles to convince people of who he is; in the other, that's precisely what he does. It's no accident that Mark has the one story and John has the other. In the Synoptics, Jesus refuses to establish his credentials through his miraculous deeds; in John that is why he does them.

This difference corresponds to a second difference in emphasis. In both the Synoptics and John, Jesus engages in public teaching. But the content of his teaching is significantly different. In the Synoptics, Jesus teaches about the coming Kingdom of God through parables. This is portrayed as a future kingdom, in which God will provide fullness of life to all who repent in preparation for its coming. This teaching is predominantly done through parables, short, simple, and symbolic illustrations of spiritual truths. According to Mark 4, Jesus taught the crowds only through telling parables. Jesus never instructs his disciples on his own identity as one who is divine.

> **John's Gospel is quite unlike the others, both in its content and its emphases.**

In John, though, that's virtually *all* he talks about: who he is, whence he has come, how he relates to God the Father, and how he is the one sent from God to bring salvation to the world. Strikingly, Jesus never proclaims a future coming kingdom in John, a kingdom in which all the wrongs of this world will be made right. He never tells a parable in John. Jesus instead speaks about his own identity. He is the one from God, who is in fact equal with God, who can bring eternal life to those who believe in him. In the Synoptics, the focus of Jesus' teaching is God and the kingdom he is about to bring in the future; in John, the focus is on Jesus himself and the eternal life that he brings here and now.

These two differences in emphases are linked together in John's Gospel. Jesus teaches principally about himself and does miracles to provide the evidence. Jesus says that he is the "bread that brings life" and he feeds the multitudes to prove it (chap. 6). He says that he is the "light of the world" and he heals a blind man to prove it (chap. 9). He says that he is the "resurrection and the life" and he raises a man from the dead to prove it (chap. 11). Jesus here is much more than the man we find in the Synoptics. He is God come to earth to provide salvation to the world. This same sense is not found in the Synoptics. This emphasis, so unlike the Synoptics, is found in the beginning of the Gospel, in the "prologue," which indicates that Jesus is the Word of God who existed from the beginning of all things, through whom God created the universe, who has now become a human being (1:1–14). That's why, throughout the Gospel, anyone who sees Jesus is said to have seen the Father, whoever does what he commands does the will of the Father, whoever rejects him has rejected the Father (14:10–14; 3:18). No longer is Jesus simply God's misunderstood messiah or prophet; now he is, himself, fully divine. As he says here, "I and the Father are one" (10:10) and, as Thomas confesses, "My Lord and my God" (20:28).

In conclusion, I think it's safe to say that John's Gospel is quite unlike the others, both in its content and its emphases. John lacks a number of the accounts found in the Synoptics and contains numerous memorable stories preserved in his Gospel alone. Even more significantly, John provides a completely different portrayal of Jesus. No longer is he merely a compassionate miracle worker who responds to people's faith and proclaims the coming kingdom of God, a prophet rejected by his own people. He is not even the Jewish Messiah sent from the Jewish God in fulfillment of the Jewish Scriptures. Now Jesus himself is divine, who spends his entire public ministry teaching that he is the one sent from God for the salvation of the world and who does miracles to prove that what he says is true. ■

Essential Reading

The Gospel of John.

Brown, *Introduction to the New Testament,* chap. 11.

Ehrman, *The New Testament: A Historical Introduction*, chap. 10.

Supplemental Reading

Kysar, *John the Maverick Gospel.*

Sloyan, *What Are They Saying About John?*

Smith, *The Theology of John.*

1. How might the differences between John and the Synoptics affect the question of whether this book was actually written by Jesus' own disciple, John, the son of Zebedee?

2. In what ways do modern Christian understandings of Jesus as both God and man seem more closely tied to the portrayal of Jesus in John than in the Synoptics?

3. Discuss whether the more exalted view of Jesus found in the Gospel of John can be reconciled with the portrayals of Jesus found in the other Gospels. If Matthew, Mark, and Luke also thought of Jesus as divine, why was this not a major emphasis in their accounts? Or did they think so at all?

John—Jesus the Man from Heaven
Lecture 8—Transcript

To this point we have been considering the portrayals of Jesus in Matthew, Mark, and Luke, books called the Synoptic Gospels because they have so many traditions in common that they can laid side by side and be seen together—the literal meaning of the word "synoptic." Despite their numerous similarities to one another, we have seen that these three Gospels each has a distinctive emphasis in its portrayal of Jesus. This is even more true of the Gospel of John, the fourth Gospel, a book that is so different from the other three that, sometimes, it is known amongst scholars as a "maverick" Gospel. Traditionally, the Gospel has been ascribed to John, the son of Zebedee, one of Jesus' closest disciples. This ascription cannot be found until near the end of the 2nd century. As with the other Gospels, this book is anonymous; the author doesn't name himself. And, interestingly enough, the name John, son of Zebedee, doesn't occur in this Gospel at all, which people who thought that it was written by John have taken to be an act of modesty on the author's part; and people who thought that it wasn't written by John have taken it as an indication that, in fact, John wasn't very important to this author, which just shows that evidence can be read any way a person likes.

In any event, the ascription of John didn't occur till near the end of the 2nd century, and there are some reasons for thinking that John, the son of Zebedee, did not write the book. In our earlier sources where John is portrayed, John himself, as a lower-class peasant from Galilee, who, presumably, since he was a Jewish peasant from Galilee, spoke Aramaic. Since he was lower class, he probably wasn't well educated or literate, and so the idea that he composed an entire book in Greek seems somewhat unlikely, given his own circumstances. Moreover, we know from the New Testament itself that John was thought to have been illiterate. Acts Chapter 4, Verse 13, calls him that, and there is nothing to counter that evidence, at least in our earlier sources. For these reasons, it seems somewhat unlikely that John was directly responsible for writing this book, which appears to have been produced near the end of the 1st century, possibly around the year 90 or 95 of the common era A.D.—65 years or so after Jesus himself had died. As was the case with the other Gospels, I'll continue calling this one John in lieu of a better option.

In very rough outline, John is like the other Gospels. Here, too, is an account of Jesus' teaching and healing, leading up to his death and resurrection in Jerusalem. Moreover, John shares several stories with the other Gospels, especially in the passion narrative. In other words, in very broad terms, this is similar to the other Gospels. But the differences between John and the Synoptics are particularly striking. I want to spend most of this lecture talking about the differences between John and the Synoptics as a way of highlighting John's own distinctive emphasis about Jesus. First, I want to talk about the differences in contents between John and the Synoptics.

It is striking that John lacks most of the stories that form the backbone of the Synoptic portrayals of Jesus. When you think through a skeletal outline of what Jesus does in the Synoptic Gospels, you would have many of the following stories. In two of them, of course, Matthew and Luke, he is born of a virgin in Bethlehem. In all three of the Synoptic Gospels, he begins his public ministry by being baptized by John. He then is tempted by the devil in the wilderness. He comes out of the wilderness and proclaims the coming kingdom of God, principally, according to the Synoptics, by telling parables. He does many miracles, particularly casting out demons. Halfway through the Synoptic Gospels, he is transfigured before his disciples; he takes Peter, James, and John up onto a mountain, and he begins to radiate his glory before them. He is transfigured in their presence. At the end of his life, he institutes the Lord's Supper. He has a prayer in the garden of Gethsemane, praying to be removed, to have "this cup" removed from him. He appears, then, before Jewish authorities, who hand him over to Pontus Pilate at the trial before the Jews.

It is striking that these accounts that form the backbone of the Synoptic Gospels are absent from John. There is no account of his birth. There is no explicit detailed narrative of his baptism. He does not go into the wilderness to be tempted. He does not proclaim the coming kingdom of God. He never tells a parable. He never casts out a demon. He's not transfigured before his disciples. He doesn't institute the Lord's Supper. He doesn't pray to have his faith removed from him in the garden of Gethsemane. He doesn't have a trial before the Jewish authorities. These things are not found in John. Just in terms of what John lacks, then, this is a very different Gospel from the Synoptics.

What, then, does he have if he is lacking these basic stories? Well, John has numerous stories of his own, stories that aren't found in the other three. Some of Jesus' most startling deeds are found in John, and only in John, including the first miracle that he does, which is the most popular miracle on college campuses. Jesus is at a party; they have run out of wine, and Jesus turns the water into wine so that they can continue their celebration, John Chapter 2, found only in John. Or probably his most graphic miracle that you will see in all of the Jesus movies produced out of Hollywood, the raising of Lazarus from the dead, John Chapter 11, found only in John. Not only are many of his most startling deeds found only in John, so, too, are many of his most memorable sayings or teachings found only here. For example, in Chapter 3, Jesus has a conversation with a Jewish rabbi, Nicodemus, in which he says the famous line, "You must be born again," or sometimes translated, "You must be born from above." Jesus' famous "I am" sayings, found only in the Gospel of John, in which Jesus identifies himself as the only one who can bring salvation. Jesus says, "I am the light of the world." "I am the bread of life." "I am the resurrection and the life." Sometimes he simply says, "I am." "Before Abraham was, I am," possibly a reference to the passage in the Hebrew Bible where God identifies himself to Moses as, "I am." Moses says, "Who shall I tell the children of Israel have sent me?" and God says, "Tell them that I am have sent you." In John's Gospel, Jesus says, "Before Abraham was, I am," possibly claiming some kind of equality with the God of the Hebrew Bible.

Many of Jesus' remarkable teachings, then, as well as many of his deeds, remarkable deeds, are found only in John. These are differences in content between John and the Synoptics, and I should point out that people have long noticed some of these differences in content as being actual discrepancies between John and the other Gospels. We see one example already. In an earlier lecture, where I showed that, in John's Gospel, Jesus actually dies on a different day and at a different time of the day than in the Synoptics. In John's Gospel, Jesus dies on the afternoon before the Passover meal was eaten, in order to show, I think, that Jesus is executed when the lambs are being killed in the temple, because Jesus himself, for John, is the Passover Lamb. In the Synoptic Gospels, Jesus survives that day, has the meal that evening, and then is executed the following morning. Another example that is commonly cited involves Jesus' cleansing of the temple, which is the final event of his public ministry. A major event in the synoptic Gospels, Jesus cleanses the temple the last week of his life, and that is what leads to his arrest and trial. John also has a cleansing of the temple, but it happens at the very beginning of his ministry, John Chapter 2; it is not the last thing. In John's Gospel, the ministry actually lasts something like three years. We know that in John because John mentions three separate Passover feasts. The cleansing of the temple happens at the very beginning, before this entire ministry, as opposed to the Synoptics, where it happens at the end.

There are ways, by the way, to try and reconcile anything in the Bible that appears to be a discrepancy. One way to resolve this particular problem is people say, "Well, Jesus did it twice, at the beginning of his ministry and at the end of his ministry." That kind of explanation works in some circumstances. My favorite explanation for that kind of reconciliation of the discrepancies is that in one of the Gospels, Mark, Jesus tells Peter that "before the cock crows, you will deny me three times," and in another Gospel, Jesus says, "Before the cock crows twice, you will deny me three times." Well, how do you resolve this? Well, Peter denied Jesus six times— three times before the cock crowed and three times before it crowed twice. It works to reconcile the account, but it leads to difficulties of its own.

Back to John. In some ways, even more striking, in terms of the distinctiveness of this Gospel, then, the differences in contents involved the differences of emphases between John and the Synoptic Gospels. The differences in emphases are really quite striking and can alert us to some of the distinctive features of this portrayal of Jesus in the fourth Gospel. I want to talk about differences of emphases in two major areas; first, different understanding of Jesus' miracles, and second, different understanding of his teaching.

So, first the miracles. In all four Gospels, Jesus is portrayed as a miracle worker. But the reasons for his miracles are quite different between John and the Synoptics. The Synoptic Gospels portray Jesus as doing miracles in order to help people in need, but he explicitly refuses to do miracles in order to prove his own identity in Matthew, Mark, and Luke. For example, in Matthew's Gospel, after Jesus has healed a blind man, some people come to believe that he must be the Messiah. The scribes and Pharisees approach

Jesus asking him to do a sign to prove his identity to them. Jesus explicitly refuses, saying, "No sign will be given to this evil and adulterous generation" Matthew 12:39. Jesus refuses to do a miracle as a sign of who he is.

A similar message is given in the Synoptic account of the temptations in the wilderness. Jesus is tempted three times by the devil: first to turn the stones into bread; then to worship Satan so as to inherit the Earth; the third temptation, at least in the sequence in Luke's Gospel, is that Jesus is tempted to jump off of the temple. The devil takes him to the pinnacle of the Temple, the very top, and he tells him to jump. I am not quite clear what the temptation is here. One could see why it would be tempting to take stones and turn them into bread and eat them if you are hungry, and you can see the temptation of inheriting the Earth. But what's the temptation of jumping off of a high building? The key seems to be where this building is. It's the temple in Jerusalem, where, presumably, there are Jewish worshippers gathered down below. The devil tempts Jesus that if he jumps off the building, God will send the angels to swoop down and catch him before he hits the bottom. In other words, Jesus is being tempted to prove that he is somebody special before God by doing a miracle. Jesus spurns the desire to jump off the building as a satanic temptation.

In the Gospel of John, rather than spurning temptation to produce a sign for his onlookers, Jesus does miracles precisely in order to prove his identity. In other words, whereas in the Synoptics, Jesus won't do signs, that is what Jesus does in John. Interestingly, in John's Gospel, Jesus' great deeds are not called miracles the way they are in Matthew, Mark, and Luke. They are explicatively called "signs." Signs of what? Signs of who Jesus is. In John's Gospel, at one point, Jesus indicates that his signs are designed to make people believe, and that people won't be able to believe without the signs, John Chapter 4, Verse 54. The Gospel itself indicates that the signs of Jesus are written in order to make people believe, John Chapter 20, Verses 30 and 31. In John, Jesus does miracles as signs to get people to believe. It is striking that neither Jesus refusing to do a sign, found in Matthew, nor the temptation narrative, found in the Synoptics, can be found in John. So, whereas in the Synoptic Gospels, Jesus' miraculous deeds are done in response to a person's faith, in John they are meant to generate their faith. In the Synoptics, Jesus refuses to do miracles to prove who he is. In John, he does them for just that reason.

These differences highlighting the different understandings of the miracles in John and the Synoptics can be highlighted by looking at two separate accounts, one in Mark and one in John, of Jesus raising a person from the dead. The two accounts are the raising of Jairus' daughter in Mark Chapter 5 and the raising of Lazarus in John Chapter 11. What I want to do is, see, compare and contrast these two accounts because both of them involve the resurrection of a dead person; but they show the distinctive emphasis of the Synoptics on the one hand, and John on the other, precisely in their differences. There would be no point in comparing these two accounts if they weren't basically similar in a broad form of way, as, in fact, they are. Just to show you, formally, how similar they are, in both accounts, both the raising of Jairus' daughter in Mark 5 and the raising of Lazarus of John 11, in both accounts a family member requests Jesus to come to help a sick person before it's too late. But Jesus doesn't arrive in time, and the person has died in the meantime. In both accounts, onlookers mock Jesus for thinking that he can now do something about it, since the person has already died. But in both accounts, Jesus speaks with the person as "sleeping," which is a Greek euphemism for having died. In both accounts, Jesus goes to where the person is, and he commands them to rise. They do so. He then orders the onlookers to take care of their other physical needs.

In view of the strong formal similarities of the stories, their differences cannot help but attract our attention. The differences, in fact, are quite striking. In Mark's account, Mark Chapter 5, Jesus goes as soon as he is summoned to the daughter of Jairus. He privately enters the girl's room. He takes only the parents and three of his disciples with him, apart from the crowds, and he orders the witnesses strictly not to tell anyone what they have seen. Okay, that's Mark's account. In John's account, Jesus intentionally doesn't go to Lazarus when he is ill because, as he says to his disciples, he wants Lazarus to die. This is one of the most striking verses in the entire New Testament, one that often gets translated...the difficulty gets translated away. But it literally says in Chapter 11, Verse 5, "Jesus has just learned that his friend Lazarus is sick unto death," and the text says, "now Jesus' loved the..." now this is the sisters of Lazarus, "Jesus loved Martha and her sister and

Lazarus. So when he heard that he was sick, he remained where he was for two more days." In others words, Jesus wants to stay away, and he goes on to tell his disciples why he wants to stay away; because, he says, "This illness is not unto death; it is for the glory of God, so that the Son of God might be glorified by it." For Jesus to be glorified, Lazarus has to die. And so Jesus intentionally remains away. When he comes to the tomb of Lazarus, rather than doing a miracle in secret, in private, with just a few people present, as in Mark, Jesus puts on a large display. The crowds are surrounding him, he goes to the tomb and he commands, "Lazarus, come forth." Lazarus rises from the dead; to the amazement of the crowd, he emerges from the tomb.

So in one account Jesus orders secrecy, don't tell anyone, he does it in private. In the other, he makes his miracle a public display of power. In one he refuses to do miracles to convince people of who he is. In the other, that is precisely what he does. It's not an accident that Mark has one of the stories and John has the other. In the Synoptic Gospels, Jesus refuses to establish his credentials through his miraculous deeds. In John, that's why he does them.

This difference, this different understanding of Jesus' miracles, corresponds to a second difference in emphasis between John and the Synoptics. In both John and the Synoptics, of course, Jesus engages in public teaching. But the content of the teaching is strikingly different between John and the Synoptics. In the Synoptic Gospels, Jesus teaches about the coming kingdom of God by telling parables. This is portrayed as a future kingdom that is coming in which God will provide fullness of life to all who repent in preparation for its coming. This teaching of the coming kingdom of God in the Synoptic Gospels is taught predominantly through parables, that is, through short, simple, symbolic illustrations of spiritual truths. In fact, according to Mark Chapter 4, Jesus taught the crowds no other way than through telling parables. This is the only way he taught the crowds, according to the Gospel of Mark. It is particularly worth noting that in Matthew, Mark, and Luke, where Jesus teaches about the coming kingdom, Jesus never instructs his disciples on his own identity as one who is divine. You simply won't find any teaching of Jesus about who he is, as one who is divine, in Matthew, Mark and Luke. In John, on the other hand, that's virtually all that he talks about. Who he is, whence he has come, how he relates to God the father, how he's the one sent from God to bring salvation to the world, that's what

Jesus teaches in the Gospel of John. In John, Jesus never proclaims a future coming kingdom, a kingdom in which all the wrongs of this world will be made right. He never tells a parable in the Gospel of John. Instead, he speaks about his own identity; he is the one who has come from God; who is, in fact, equal with God; who can bring eternal life to those who believe in him. Thus, whereas in the Synoptic Gospels, the focus of Jesus' teaching is God and the kingdom that God is about to bring in the future, in the Gospel of John, the focus of the teaching is Jesus himself and the eternal life that he brings in the here and now.

These two differences and emphases are linked together in John's Gospel. In John's Gospel, Jesus teaches principally about himself, and he does miracles in order to provide the evidence, in contrast to the Synoptics, where Jesus doesn't teach about himself and refuses to prove who he is through miracles. In John, he teaches about himself, and the miracles are the proof. For example, in John Chapter 6, Jesus has a discourse in which he says, "I am the bread that brings life." In other words, he is the one that can bring sustenance to humans, which he is thinking of not simply in terms of keeping them alive in the here and now, but he is the one that can bring life giving bread; in other words, bread for eternal life. More strikingly in the same chapter, he does a miracle to prove that he is the bread of life because that's when he multiplies the loaves for the multitudes, so that the miracle is closely linked to his teaching about himself. The miracle proves that he is the bread of the life because he can multiply the loaves.

Similarly, in John Chapter 9, Jesus says, "I am the light of the world," meaning that he is the one that brings illumination, the illumination that brings eternal life. And then he proves that he is the light of the world by healing a blind man. A man is born blind, they bring him to Jesus, and he heals him to the astonishment of all those around. Afterwards, the scribes and the Pharisees are upset. They wonder how this could have possibly have happened. It turns out that this happened on the Sabbath day. They question the man, "Who has healed you?" He says, "Well, Jesus healed me." They said, "He couldn't have healed you because it's a Sabbath, and that would mean that he is a lawbreaker, and a lawbreaker obviously can't be empowered by God." And he replies, "Well, I don't know who you think he is, but he certainly healed me," and they have this little controversy. The point of the miracle, though, is that Jesus says that he is the one that can provide light, and then he proves it by giving this man his sight. So, too, in Chapter 11, Jesus says, "I am the resurrection and the life," meaning that by believing in him, a person will be raised for eternal life, and then he proves it by raising Lazarus from the dead. The miracles and the teachings of Jesus are brought together in the Gospel of John, so that what he says about himself is proved by his miraculous deeds.

Jesus, in both his teachings and his miracles, is much more, in John, than the man that we find in the Synoptics. In John's Gospel, Jesus is God come to Earth to provide salvation to the world. In the Synoptics, you don't have a sense of Jesus himself being divine; you do get that sense in the Gospel of John. Let me say that, in the Synoptics, of course, Jesus is portrayed as the Son of God, as the Messiah, as the son of David. These are not titles, though, that 1st century Jews would have thought that indicated that Jesus is divine. The fact that he is the Son of God doesn't make him divine; this is a reference to the Hebrew Bible where all sorts of people are called the Son of God. For example, Solomon, whom God says "will be my son; I will be his father" 2 Samuel Chapter 7, Verse 14. The Son of God is the king, but he's a mortal, he's a human. In the Synoptics, Jesus is a mortal, he is a human, even when he is born of a virgin in Matthew and Luke. The idea in Matthew and Luke is not that Jesus is born of a virgin because he pre-existed, was born of a virgin as a way of entering into the world. Read Matthew and Luke carefully; there is no sense that he pre-existed. The birth, the virgin birth, is how he came into being. Not so the Gospel of John, which doesn't have a virgin birth. In the Gospel of John, Jesus is, in fact, a pre-existing being who has become flesh.

This emphasis is found already at the beginning of John's Gospel in the prologue of John Chapter 1, Verses 1 through 14. This is a kind of a beginning of the Gospel, sort of preface or prologue of the Gospel, that sets the tone for what is going to happen subsequently throughout this book. A very famous beginning, in which the author alludes to the book of Genesis. The book of Genesis, of course, begins, "In the beginning, God created the heavens and the earth." The Gospel of John says, "In the beginning was the word. The word was with God and the word was God. This one was in the beginning with God. All things came into being through him and apart from him; nothing came into being which came into being. In him was life and his life was the light of humans. And the light shines in the darkness; and the darkness has not overcome it." Jesus is God's own word, God's manifestation of himself, his external being. We are told in Chapter 1, Verse 14, that this word of God, this manifestation of God, became flesh and dwelt among us. The pre-existent word of God becomes a human being, and, in fact, it's Jesus. That's why, in this Gospel, everyone who sees Jesus is said to have seen the Father John Chapter 14; whoever rejects Jesus has rejected the Father, John Chapter 3. No longer is Jesus, in this Gospel, simply God's misunderstood Messiah or prophet. Now he himself is fully divine. As he himself says in this book, "I and the Father are one" John Chapter 10. Or as Thomas, confessing at the end of the Gospel when he sees Jesus raised from the dead, Thomas says, "My Lord and my God" John Chapter 20. Jesus here is divine.

In conclusion, I think it is safe to say that John's Gospel is quite unlike the others, both in its content and its emphasis. John lacks a large number of the accounts found in the Synoptics and contains numerous memorable stories preserved in its text alone. But even more significantly, John provides a completely different portrayal of Jesus from the other Gospels. No longer is Jesus merely a compassionate miracle worker who responds to people's faith and proclaims the coming kingdom of God; a prophet rejected by his own people; or even the Jewish Messiah, sent from the Jewish God in fulfillment of the Jewish Scriptures. Now he himself is divine, the one sent from Heaven who spends his entire public ministry teaching that he is the one sent from God for the salvation of the world, and one who provides miracles in order to prove that what he says about himself is true.

Noncanonical Gospels
Lecture 9

While these other Gospels are, for the most part, much later in date and more legendary in character than the New Testament Gospels, they nonetheless are significant for scholars of the New Testament.

We have now completed our examination of the New Testament Gospels of Matthew, Mark, Luke, and John. It would be a mistake to think that these were the only accounts of Jesus' words and deeds produced by the early Christians. We have seen, for example, that two of the Gospel writers—Matthew and Luke—probably had access to a written collection of Jesus' sayings, called Q, and other sources that scholars have labeled M and L. None of these documents survives. Other Gospels from early Christianity do survive—a large number of them discovered only during the past century.

There are over 20 of these other Gospels, mostly fragments, which range in date from the 2nd to the 8th centuries A.D. They too, like the New Testament Gospels, had a variety of sources for their stories about Jesus. They used previously existing written accounts—including, in most cases, the New Testament Gospels themselves. They also borrowed extensively from the legendary traditions that continued to be circulated and made up about Jesus through the centuries. There are, very roughly speaking, two kinds of Gospels found among these noncanonical texts: Narrative Gospels are like the Gospels of the New Testament in that they contain accounts of the life and (sometimes) death of Jesus told in narrative form. Sayings Gospels are like the lost source Q, containing principally collections of Jesus' teachings.

To illustrate the first of these categories, we can look at one of the most intriguing of the noncanonical Gospels, one that actually claims to have been written by Jesus' own disciple Simon Peter and is, therefore, called the Gospel of Peter. The Gospel was discovered in a monk's tomb near the end of the 19th century. Even though, unlike the anonymous Gospels of the New Testament, this book actually claims to be written by the disciple of Jesus, it is almost certainly a forgery written sometime during the 2nd century.

Before its discovery, we knew about the account, because it is mentioned by early Church Fathers, who condemned it as heretical. Eusebius was a 4th-century author who is known as the "Father of Church History." His 10-volume book, called *Ecclesiastical History*, provides us with a good deal of information about Christianity in the first four centuries. According to Eusebius, the Gospel of Peter was read by one of the churches ruled over by the 2nd-century bishop of Antioch, Serapion. Once Serapion was warned that the book contained heretical teachings, he examined it himself and forbade its use. We presume that what we now have in hand is this long-lost Gospel. Unfortunately, the part that was discovered is only a fragment of the original. It contains an account of Jesus' trial, crucifixion, and resurrection, but the fragment begins in the middle of a sentence and breaks off in the middle of a sentence.

The part of this Gospel that survives is in many ways like the passion accounts of the New Testament. Jesus is put on trial before Pilate. He is condemned to death. There is an account of his crucifixion. Three days later, he is raised from the dead. What is more striking, though, are the differences from the New Testament accounts. Here "the Jews" are held to be even more liable for Jesus' death than in the New Testament Gospels. They know full well that they have sinned against God in condemning Jesus, but they still urge Pilate to have Jesus killed and they actually do the dirty work themselves—then regret it, fearing that now God will destroy them and their city. Jesus does not appear actually to suffer in this account (v. 10: "he was silent as if he felt no pain"); this may have been what led to Serapion's condemnation of the book as heretical, because it implies that Jesus was not fully human. There is a fantastic description of Jesus emerging from the tomb—supported by angels as tall as the sky, himself towering above them, with the cross itself coming forth from the tomb behind. A voice asks whether he has preached to those who have already died, and the cross replies, "Yes."

These striking features make it appear that the Gospel of Peter was written in the 2nd century A.D. Christians had begun to hold the Jews completely accountable for Jesus' death at this time. Some Christians at the time also maintained that Jesus, as fully divine, could not have really suffered. The legendary details surrounding the resurrection appear to be later additions to the stories about Jesus. Whether the writer of this account had full access to the earlier Gospels of the New Testament and used those accounts to construct this one remains a question that is answered differently by different scholars. There are no lengthy verbatim agreements between Peter and the four canonical Gospels.

A second type of Gospel preserved from ancient Christianity is a "sayings" Gospel, a kind of document that principally records Jesus' sayings, rather than his deeds or his death and resurrection. Perhaps the most brilliant illustration of this kind of text is the now-famous Gospel of Thomas, one of the most remarkable discoveries of the 20th century. The Gospel was discovered in the 1940s by an Egyptian Bedouin, named Mohammed Ali, near his small village Nag Hammadi in upper Egypt. The discovery was a complete accident; Mohammed Ali and his brothers were digging for fertilizer and happened on an earthenware jar containing 13 ancient leather-bound books. These books contained anthologies of texts—52 documents altogether, all written in Coptic, an ancient Egyptian language, although they appear to be Coptic translations of Greek originals. The leather-bound books were manufactured in the mid-4th century (as shown by dated scraps of paper used to strengthen the bindings). The texts contained in the books are much older, though. Most of them are known to have been in existence at least two centuries earlier. The most famous of these 52 texts is the Gospel of Thomas, but the entire collection is highly significant, because it appears to have been the library of a group of Gnostic Christians.

> **Gnostics believed that there was a radical disjuncture between the worlds of matter and spirit: matter was inherently evil; spirit was good.**

Gnosticism was a prominent form of Christianity in Egypt in the 2nd century A.D. We had previously known about the Gnostics almost exclusively from the writings of their opponents, the Christian Church Fathers. The discovery near Nag Hammadi provided our first major collection of texts written by and for Gnostics themselves. An examination of the writings of the fathers and the primary texts shows some of the major components of Gnostic thought.

Gnostics believed that there was a radical disjuncture between the worlds of matter and spirit: matter was inherently evil; spirit was good. Some people in the world were pure matter. These people were like all other animals— destined for annihilation. But other people (i.e., the Gnostics themselves) had a spark of the divine within them, which had become entrapped in this world of matter. They had become entrapped because of the nefarious workings of the creator of this world, who was not the true God but an ignorant and far less powerful being, intent on bringing harm to the divine realm. The goal of the Gnostic religion was to escape from the material trappings of this world to allow the divine spark to return to its original spiritual home. Escape could come only by acquiring the knowledge necessary for salvation. These people are called *Gnostics*, because the Greek word for knowledge is *gnosis*. The only way to acquire this knowledge, though, was for a divine emissary to come down from the spiritual realm to instruct you on what you had to know. Christ, for these people, represented the divine being who came to earth to teach the truth that could lead to salvation. Salvation came to those who understood the secret meanings of his words.

In the judgment of most scholars, the Gospel of Thomas was a Gospel written for Gnostics. It consists of 114 sayings of Jesus—no narrative at all. The point of this Gospel is that those who learn the secret teachings of Jesus will have eternal life (v. 1). It is not by believing in his death that one finds salvation, but by understanding his words. A number of the sayings in this Gospel are like those of the New Testament. For example, here, too, one finds the parable of the mustard seed and the saying "If a blind man leads a blind man, they both fall into a pit" (saying 34). Other sayings convey the Gnostic understanding of the world as a realm that must be escaped if one is to find true life. The body is likened to a set of clothes that must be removed—even trampled on—if one is to be saved (saying 37). Moreover, salvation is not something that will come in the future in the Kingdom of God but in the reuniting of the person with the divine realm from which it came (sayings 3, 11, 29, 113).

The author of this book calls himself Didymus Judas Thomas; he was believed in parts of the ancient church to be the actual brother of Jesus. Needless to say, scholars today are unified in considering the book to be forged in Thomas's name. The question of where the author acquired his sayings continues to be debated. The most dominant view among scholars today is that he did *not* acquire them from the Gospels of the New Testament but from oral traditions that he had heard. If he had acquired the sayings from the New Testament, it would be hard to explain why he left so many out and why the ones he included are always worded so differently.

These then, in conclusion, are two of the noncanonical Gospels, books that allegedly record the sayings and deeds of Jesus but that did not make it into the New Testament. The Gospel of Peter is a legendary account of Jesus' death and resurrection. The Gospel of Thomas is a collection of Jesus' sayings, some of which sound very much like the Jesus of the Synoptic Gospels, while others show clear evidence of Gnostic understanding of the world. The legendary nature of these accounts should alert us to a fact that will begin to be significant in the next lecture; namely, that Christians made up traditions about Jesus. Not everything we read about Jesus in a written account from antiquity can be taken as referring to the historical Jesus himself. We saw this even with respect to the New Testament Gospels themselves. They, too, contain stories that appear to have been changed, or even created, by Christians trying to convince others that Jesus really was the Son of God. In the next part of this course, we are going to move from considering the Gospels as portrayals of Jesus to asking how we can use these ancient accounts to reconstruct what Jesus himself actually did say and do. That is to say, how can we get behind the legendary traditions about Jesus to discover the man himself? ■

Essential Reading

"The Gospel of Peter," in Ehrman, *The New Testament and Other Early Christian Writings*, pp. 124–26.

"The Gospel of Thomas," in Ehrman, *The New Testament and Other Early Christian Writings*, pp. 116–23.

Ehrman, *The New Testament: A Historical Introduction*, chap. 12.

Supplemental Reading

Pagels, *The Gnostic Gospels.*

Questions to Consider

1. In what ways do the Gospels of Peter and Thomas seem to be like, and in what ways unlike, the Gospels of the New Testament?

2. Summarize the beliefs of the Gnostics. Given what you know about them, which of the New Testament Gospels would seem to you to be most useful to Gnostic Christians? Are there religions in America today that have beliefs similar to those of the Gnostics?

3. Given the legendary accounts that sprang up about Jesus, how do you suppose one can separate pious fiction from historical fact in the earliest Christian Gospels?

Noncanonical Gospels
Lecture 9—Transcript

We have now completed our examination of the New Testament Gospels of Matthew, Mark, Luke, and John. It would be a mistake to think that these were the only accounts of Jesus' words and deeds produced by the early Christians. We have seen, for example, that two of the Gospels, Matthew and Luke, probably had access to a written collection of Jesus' sayings, called "Q," along with other sources that scholars have labeled "M" and "L." None of these documents survives.

But there are other Gospels from early Christianity that do survive, a large number of them discovered only during the past century. While these other Gospels are, for the most part, much later in date and more legendary in character than the New Testament Gospels, they nonetheless are significant for scholars of the New Testament. Historians differ on how to enumerate these other Gospels, but most would agree that there are at least 20 of them, more or less, depending on how one counts some surviving fragments of manuscripts that have been dug up by archaeologists, especially in Egypt. These other Gospels range in date from the 2nd to the 8th century A.D. They, like the New Testament Gospels, had a variety of sources for their stories about Jesus. They used previously existing written accounts, including, in most cases, the New Testament Gospels themselves. They also borrowed extensively from the legendary traditions that continued to be circulated, and even to be made up about Jesus, down through the centuries.

There are, very roughly speaking, two kinds of Gospels found among these non-canonical texts: narrative Gospels and sayings Gospels. Narrative Gospels are like the Gospels of the New Testament in that they contain accounts of the life, and sometimes the death, of Jesus, told in narrative form. Sayings Gospels are like the lost source, "Q," containing principally collections of Jesus' teachings. In this lecture, I want to talk about each of these categories of Gospel by giving an illustration of each one. For the narrative Gospel, I want to use the Gospel of Peter, a Gospel discovered in the 19th century, a narrative of Jesus' trial, death, and resurrection. And for the sayings Gospels, I want to use the Gospel of Thomas, discovered in the 1940s, a Gospel that contains 114 sayings of Jesus.

The Gospel of Peter is one of the most interesting among our non-canonical Gospels. It was discovered at the end of the 19th century in the tomb of a monk in Egypt. Even though this Gospel, unlike the anonymous Gospels of the New Testament, claims to have been written by Jesus' own disciple, Peter—Simon Peter—it's almost certainly a forgery written sometime during the 2nd century. It wouldn't be appropriate, of course, to call the New Testament Gospels forgeries because they don't claim to be written by Matthew, Mark, Luke, and John. This book, though, does claim to be written by Simon Peter, and since it wasn't, it appears to have been forged. Before the discovery of this book, we had actually known about it from other others of the early church who sometimes mention it and condemn its teachings as heretical. In particular, we know about the book from the writings of the 4th century church father known as Eusebius. Eusebius is sometimes called "the father of church History." In the early 4th century, Eusebius produced a 10-volume work, called the *Ecclesiastical History* or the *Church History*, which gives an account of Christianity from the days of Jesus on up to his own day. This is an extremely valuable piece of information because it covers the first three centuries of Christianity in narrative form, and Eusebius had some very good sources of information, so that scholars interested in these early centuries of Christianity typically turn to Eusebius as the primary source.

Within this 10-volume account, Eusebius mentions the Gospel of Peter at one particular point. He is telling a story about a bishop in the 2nd century. A bishop of the city of Antioch in Syria, a bishop who was named Serapion. Evidently, Serapion knew of the Gospel of the Peter as a book that was being read in some of the churches that were under his authority. Initially, Serapion approved the reading of this Gospel, since it was allegedly written by Peter. Someone warned Serapion, though, that the book, in fact, contained heretical teachings, and so he decided to examine it himself. And when he did so, he came to think, also, that the book could be dangerous, that it may contain a heretical theology, and so he forbade its use.

Eusebius described this event; unfortunately, you see, this doesn't quote extensively from this Gospel that Serapion had forbade. The reason that's unfortunate is because the Gospel of Peter that we have discovered is only a fragment of the Gospel. And none of the fragments that we have now is quoted by Eusebius, so that we assume that, in fact, Eusebius is talking about this particular book, but it is not absolutely certain. The Gospel of Peter that we have before us is a Gospel that begins in the middle of a sentence and ends in a middle of sentence. In other words, it is just a fragment that was discovered in this monk's tomb. It begins—I am quoting, by the way, from the Gospel of Peter itself in an English translation. It's available in a number of different places. This is a collection of texts of early Christianity that I edited, the New Testament and other early Christian writings which gives all of these early non-canonical text, as well at the canonical ones from the first century of Christianity. The Gospel of Peter begins as follows: "None of the Jews washed his hand; neither did Herod or any of his judges, as they did not wish to wash. Pilate got up, and then Herod the King ordered the Lord to be taken away." It begins in the middle of a sentence, obviously beginning with the account of Pilate, right after Pilate has washed his hands, as he does in Matthew's Gospel. We are told that none of the Jews washed their hands; nor did Herod. The account also ends in the middle of a sentence. At the very end of the text it says, "we"—this is after Jesus has been raised from the dead—"We, the 12 disciples of the Lord, wept and were much grief-stricken. But I, Simon Peter, and Andrew my brother, took our nets and went to the sea; and with us was Levi, the son of Alphaeus, whom the Lord..." There it ends.

In between these two sentences, the fragmentary beginning and the fragmentary ending, is an account of Jesus' trial, his crucifixion, and then his resurrection. In many ways this account is very similar to what you get in the accounts of the New Testament. The basics are the same; you have Herod, you have Pilate, you have the Jews, you have Jesus, you have a guard posted at the tomb, you have people experiencing Jesus' resurrection. What is particularly striking about this account, though, are the things that are found in this account that are not found in the New Testament, differences of emphases and differences of content.

This account is striking for several reasons. First, because in this account, the Jewish people are held to be even more liable for Jesus' death than they are in the New Testament Gospels. In this account, the Jews know full well that they have sinned against God by condemning Jesus. Not only do they urge Pilate to have Jesus killed, in this account, the Jews actually do the dirty work themselves. They later regret it, fearing that now God will destroy them and their city. Verse 15: "It was dark at noon; the Jews were worried and anguished," the text says, "indeed they had fulfilled everything; they brought their sins to full fruition on their heads." Later on, in Verse 25, "the Jews, the elders and the priests, knowing what evil they did to themselves by killing Jesus, began to beat their breasts saying, 'Woe on the account of our sins, the judgment and the end of Jerusalem are at hand.'" In this account, interestingly, it is not Pilate who orders Jesus to be crucified, it is Herod, the King of the Jews, who orders Jesus to be crucified. This account heightens the corruptibility of the Jews in Jesus' death. That is one distinctive feature.

The second distinctive feature, in this account, Jesus does not appear actually to suffer. Most striking is when he is on the cross, Verse 10: "They brought forth two criminals, and they crucified the Lord between them; he was silent as if he felt no pain." Silent, as if he felt no pain. We know of Christians in the 2nd century who believed that Jesus himself was fully divine. Because he was fully divine, he wasn't really human; since he wasn't really human, he couldn't really suffer and die. So that in this account, Jesus doesn't feel any pain; it sounds like maybe this is that kind of understanding of Jesus, that kind of Christology, in which Jesus isn't fully human.

The third distinctive account is a narration of the resurrection of Jesus itself. As I indicated in an earlier lecture, the Gospels of the New Testament don't narrate what happens when Jesus emerges from the tomb. This account does. We are told that after Jesus had died and been buried, he is placed in a tomb. They sat a guard by the tomb, as they do in the Gospel of Matthew. While the guard is watching, two beings descend from heaven. They are called "two young men," descend from heaven. The stone in front of the tomb rolls away by itself automatically. The two figures then enter into the tomb and then emerge from the tomb supporting a third figure. The two youths have their heads reach up to heaven. The third figure they are supporting, obviously Jesus, his head reaches up above the heavens. Behind them, then, emerges a cross; a voice comes from Heaven saying, "Have you preached to those that are sleeping?" and obediently a voice was heard from the cross, "Yes." This is a remarkable account of Jesus' resurrection itself.

These striking features of the Gospel of Peter make it appear that the book was written sometime during the 2nd century. During the 2nd century,

Christians had begun to hold Jews completely accountable for Jesus' death. During the 2nd century, there are Christians who are maintaining that Jesus, as fully divine, could not have suffered. During the 2nd century, legendary details surrounding the resurrection had started to circulate. One of the leading questions, then, about this book is, if it was written in the 2nd century, did it have access to the earlier Gospels, Matthew, Mark, Luke and John? It is a plausible theory that this account had read earlier Gospels and had recorded its narrative in light of what it had read. Especially, there are close connections with the Gospel of Matthew. On the other hand, it is striking that, in the Gospel of Peter, there are no lengthy verbatim agreements, word-for-word agreements, between this account and the earlier accounts, which may suggest that, instead of actually haven't read these earlier accounts, the author of the Gospel of Peter had heard oral traditions similar to those found in the earlier Gospels, and had then written his own account based on the oral traditions he had heard. Scholars debate whether the Gospel of Peter was independent of the other Gospels or not. That, then, is a brief overview of one narrative Gospel account, the Gospel of Peter.

A second type of Gospel preserved from ancient Christianity is a sayings Gospel, a kind of document that principally records Jesus' teachings, rather than his deeds, or his death, or his resurrection. A brilliant illustration of this kind of text is the now-famous Gospel of Thomas, one of the most remarkable discoveries of the 20th century. The Gospel of Thomas was discovered in the 1940s by an Egyptian Bedouin whose name, remarkably enough and memorably enough, was Muhammad Ali. Muhammad Ali was a Bedouin living in Egypt. He lived in a small village named Nag Hammadi in Upper Egypt. His discovery of the Gospel of Thomas was by no means intentional; it was a complete accident. Muhammad Ali and his brothers were out digging for fertilizer in the wilderness, and they just happened upon an earthenware jar that contained 13 ancient leather-bound books. Eventually, the news of the discovery got out to antiquity dealers, and from antiquity dealers, scholars learned about it, and then were able to piece together these books. The books, the 13 leather-bound books, contain anthologies of text. Altogether, there are 52 different texts represented in this collection found within this earthenware jar that scholars have now called the Nag Hammadi Library, because of its place of discovery.

These 52 documents of the Nag Hammadi Library are all written in Coptic, an ancient Egyptian language, which represents translations of these texts into Coptic from their original Greek. In other words, scholars and linguists are pretty sure that the texts they found in these books were originally written in Greek, but they have been translated into Coptic. The leather-bound books within which these texts were found, the 13 leather-bound books, were themselves produced in the mid-4th century A.D. We know when they were produced because the people who made these volumes strengthened the bindings of the books by using scrap paper, and some of the scrap paper actually has dates written on them, so that we can tell when the books were made. The texts within the books, of course, are much older than when the books were made, just as you might have a bible sitting on your desk that was made in 1990, but the books in the bible were, of course, written a long time before that. These books were written, these books were produced, in the 4th century, but the texts in them are much older. In fact, we know about these texts from at least two centuries earlier. These texts are quoted by church fathers from the 2nd century. The most famous of these 52 texts is the Gospel of Thomas. The entire collection, though, is itself significant, because it appears to have been the library of a group of Gnostic Christians, possibly Gnostic Christians who were living in the area, possibly in some way connected with a monastery that is nearby.

If these books were hidden in the 4th century, soon after their production, there might be an interesting circumstance that would explain it. If you recall, in an earlier lecture, I mentioned that Athanasius, the Bishop of Alexandria in the year 367, published a letter for the churches under his authority, which indicated which books should be read as scripture. That was in the year 367. It appears that these books were hidden, possibly by someone in the monastery, soon after that. Is it because these books had been proscribed? Possibly. That would explain why they were hidden out in the wilderness, possibly by somebody who thought that the theological tide may change, and he might be able to go back and get these books. In other words, maybe he liked these books and wanted to keep them in his scriptures, but he knew that they had been forbidden. That would explain why the books hadn't been destroyed but had been hidden. These books, then, represent a library of a group of Gnostic Christians.

I want to take a few minutes to talk about what Gnosticism was like, because Gnosticism was the prominent form of Christianity in Egypt in the 2nd century. We had known about Gnosticism before this discovery, principally from the writings of the church followers who oppose it. The discovery near Nag Hammadi, though, has provided us with our first major collection of texts written by and for Gnostics themselves. Reading through these texts and seeing what the church fathers have said can show us what the major components of Gnostic thought were. So I need to lay this out to help us understand the Gospel of Thomas. This will be a very brief overview of early Christian Gnosticism.

Gnostics believed that there was a radical disjuncture between the worlds of matter and spirit. Matter, for the Gnostics, was inherently evil; spirit was good. These are people who are highly religious people, many of whom consider themselves Christian, but who have a radical dualism between matter and spirit. There are some people in the world, according to Gnostics, who are comprised of pure matter. These are people who are animals, like other animals. Like other animals, when these people comprised of matter die, they are annihilated. That's it, end of story, just as you swat a mosquito and it is done for, people who are pure matter, when they are swatted, they are done for. There are other people, though, especially the Gnostics themselves, who have a spark of the divine within them, a spark that has been entrapped in the world of matter, a little element of spirit. Because they had become entrapped, the system of the Gnostics was to teach these peoples how to escape. Their entrapment had come because of the nefarious workings of the creator god, who was not the true God. The god who created this world was, in fact, not the true God; he was an ignorant and far less powerful being who was intent on bringing harm to the divine realm. In fact, this creator god had created the world precisely in order to trap elements of the divine within it, as a prison. The goal of the Gnostic religion, then, was to escape from the material trappings of this world, to allow the divine spark within to transcend matter, and to return to its original spiritual home. Gnostics were divine sparks seeking escape. Escape could come only by acquiring the knowledge that was necessary for salvation. That is why these people are called Gnostics, because the Greek word for knowledge is *gnosis*. The only way to acquire knowledge necessary for salvation is by having somebody from divine realm come down, someone from the spiritual world come into the material world to instruct the Gnostics on what they had to know in order to escape. For Gnostic Christians, the one who brought this divine knowledge was Christ himself, a divine being who came to earth to teach the truth that could lead to salvation. Salvation, then, came to those who understood the secret meanings of Jesus' words.

Scholars have debated what the Gospel of Thomas is all about ever since its discovery. Most scholars continue to think that Thomas was a Gospel written for Gnostics. It's not a Gospel that explains the Gnostic system. Part of the problem with gnosticism is that we have texts written by Gnostics, but usually they presuppose the gnostic system, instead of spelling out the gnostic system. Just like if you pick up the newspaper, and you read an account of a baseball game last night. The story about the baseball game won't explain the rules of baseball, it will assume you know the rules of baseball. If you are smart enough, you can reconstruct a lot of the rules, but it doesn't give you the rules. Well, that's how these Gnostic texts are; they don't tell you the system, they presuppose the system.

It appears that the Gospel of Thomas is a book that presupposes the system. This book consists of 114 sayings of Jesus. There is no narrative at all in the Gospel of Thomas. Most sayings simply begin by saying, "And Jesus said," and then you have a saying. The point of this Gospel is that those who learn the secret teachings of Jesus will have eternal life. As the Gospel of Thomas itself says, at the very beginning, "Whoever finds the interpretation of these sayings will not experience death." In this Gospel, salvation does not come to people who believe in Jesus' death and resurrection. Jesus' death and resurrection are never mentioned in this book. The way a person has eternal life isn't by believing in Jesus; it is by understanding the meaning of his secret teachings.

A number of the sayings in this Gospel are like those of the New Testament. Let me read you a couple of examples; these will sound much like we find in the New Testament itself. For example, Saying number 34. The numbers are numbers that scholars have given these things. The manuscript itself doesn't enumerate the sayings, these are modern enumeration. Saying 34: "Jesus said, 'If a blind man leads a blind man, they both will fall into a pit.'" Sounds like something from the Synoptic Gospels. Or Saying number 54:

"Jesus said, 'Blessed are the poor, for yours is the kingdom of Heaven.'" Sounds like the Synoptic Gospels. Saying 73: "The harvest is great but the laborers are few; beseech the Lord, therefore, to send out laborers to the harvest." These sayings sound like what you might expect in the Gospels of the New Testament.

There are other sayings, though, in the Gospel of Thomas that appear to convey the Gnostic understanding of the world as a realm that must be escaped in order to find true life. The body, in this book, is likened to a set of clothes that must be removed, even trampled upon, if one is to be saved. For example, Saying number 37: "The disciple said, 'When will you become revealed to us and when will we see you?' Jesus said, 'When you disrobe without being ashamed and take up your garments and place them under your feet like little children and tread on them; then you will see the son of the living One, and you will not be afraid.'" Take off your clothes and trample on them, that's when you will be saved. What does that mean? Well, if you understand this within the Gnostic system, that the body has to be escaped in order to obtain salvation, then the clothes are an image for the body that you need to transcend; the spirit needs to escape.

Salvation, in this document, is not something that comes in the future with the coming of the kingdom of God; instead, salvation, according to this document, comes when the spirit that is within a person is reunited with the divine realm whence it came. For example, Saying number 3: "Jesus said, 'If those who lead you say to you, 'See the kingdom is in the sky,' well then the birds of the sky will precede you. If they say to you, 'It's in the sea,' then the fish will precede you. Rather the kingdom is inside of you and it is outside of you.'" Okay, so the kingdom isn't a place that you can go to in the sky or the sea; it's within you, but it's also outside of you.

How can it be both? Well, you have a divine spark within, but you come from a divine realm that's without. When you come to know yourselves, then you will become known, and you will realize that you are the sons of the living Father; so you need to know, you need to have "gnosis," knowledge. But if you don't know yourselves, you dwell in poverty, and it is you who are that poverty. You are poverty because you're part of the material world. Or consider Saying number 29, "Jesus said, 'If the flesh came into being because of spirit, it's a wonder.'" Well, it would be amazing if the material world came in order because of the spirit, but if the spirit came into being because of the body, it's a wonder of wonders. Well, that's virtually impossible to imagine; it is impossible to imagine. "Indeed I am amazed at how this great wealth has made its home in this poverty," how the spirit has become entrapped in matter is a matter of marvel. This book, then, presupposes that people need to escape the entrapments of their bodies, that salvation isn't coming in the future with the coming kingdom of God. Salvation comes when people acquire the knowledge necessary to escape their entrapment.

The author of this book calls himself (at the very outset) Didamus Judas Thomas. The beginning is, "These are the secret sayings which the living Jesus spoke, which Didamus Judas Thomas wrote down." The word *Didamus* is a Greek word which means twin. *Thomas* is an Aramaic word which means twin. Judas is evidently Jude in the New Testament, the brother of Jesus. We know from some early traditions in Christianity, especially Syriac Christianity, that there were people who thought that Jesus had a twin brother. Born, of course, not of a virgin, as Jesus was, but probably born of Joseph and Mary; but none the less a twin. That person is the one claiming to write these sayings of Jesus. Nonetheless, most scholars are absolutely convinced that Jesus' own brother did not write this book, that, in fact, it is forged in Thomas' name. It continues to be debated, though, where this author, whoever he really was, actually got his sayings. The dominant view amongst scholars today was that this author did not acquire these sayings from the Gospels of the New Testament, which are lacking in most of these sayings, but that he learned them from the oral tradition, just as the authors of the New Testaments had heard their stories from their oral traditions.

Now let me wrap up the lecture. The Gospel of Peter and the Gospel of Thomas are two of our non-canonical Gospels. Peter is a legendary account of Jesus' death and resurrection. Thomas is a collection of Jesus' sayings, some of which sound like the synoptic Gospels, others of them don't. The legendary nature of these accounts, Thomas and Peter, should alert you to a fact that will begin to be significant in the next lecture; namely, that Christians made up traditions about Jesus. Not every word written in an ancient source actually goes back to Jesus. But this applies also to the New

Testament Gospels, which appear to contain stories that have been changed or even created by Christians. In the next part of our course, we are going to move beyond these books as literary texts to go to the historical questions of asking what did Jesus himself really say and do?

The Historical Jesus—Sources and Problems
Lecture 10

There is not much evidence for Jesus' life and teachings outside of the New Testament Gospels.

To this point in our study of the Gospels, both canonical and noncanonical, our overall purpose has been to appreciate each work as a piece of literature with a distinct portrayal of Jesus. We have not, however, begun to ask the more historical question: What can we say about Jesus himself, what he actually said and did? As we move beyond looking at the Gospels as literature into examining how they can be used as historical sources for the life of Jesus, we face another issue: Given that different Gospels portray Jesus differently and that all the Gospels embody traditions that have been more or less altered in the course of their transmission, how can we get behind the portrayals of Jesus in these accounts to see what the man himself was really like? That will be the goal of the next three lectures: to consider our accounts not as literary products designed to convey a particular view of Jesus but as historical sources useful for the task of historical reconstruction.

One place to begin any attempt to reconstruct the life of Jesus is by asking if there are sources *outside* the Gospels that might be useful. It might be useful, for example, to see not only what believers said about him, but also what unbelievers said; to see not only how his friends understood him, but also how his enemies did. For the purposes of our study, we might divide our ancient sources into three groups—pagan (authors who were neither Jewish nor Christian), Jewish, and Christian. Because our concerns are strictly historical, we can probably restrict our search to sources written within 100 years of Jesus' death (that is, from 30 A.D. up to 130 A.D.).

Unfortunately, surviving pagan sources are of virtually no help in trying to reconstruct the life and teachings of Jesus. Given the effect that Jesus has had on history ever since his death, one might expect that his life made an enormous impact on the society of his day—like a comet striking the earth. But if the historical record is any indication, Jesus scarcely made any impact at all—less like a comet striking the earth than a stone being tossed into the ocean. From the 1st century A.D., we have hundreds of documents written by all kinds of pagan authors for all kinds of reasons. Among all these surviving sources, Jesus is never mentioned at all. He is not mentioned by any of the philosophers, poets, historians, or scientists; he's not named in any private letters or public inscriptions. We have no birth records, trial reports, or death certificates—we have no reference of any kind whatsoever even to Jesus' name.

Our earliest recorded references to Jesus in pagan sources come from the early 2nd century. There are, in fact, only two certain references from within our prescribed time limits (30–130 A.D.). The Roman governor of the province of Bythinia-Pontus (in modern-day Turkey), Pliny the Younger, in a letter written to his emperor, Trajan (112 A.D.), mentions a group of Christians who are followers of "Christ, whom they worship as a God" (Letter 10 to the Emperor Trajan). The Roman historian Tacitus gives a lengthier reference in his history of Rome, *The Annals* (115 A.D.), in his discussion of the torching of the city of Rome by the emperor Nero in the year 64 A.D. Here he mentions the Christians as the hatred of the human race and says that they were followers of "Christ" who, he notes, was crucified under the procurator of Judea, Pontius Pilate, when Tiberius was the emperor. There are no other certain references to Jesus in any pagan author within a century of his death.

The surviving Jewish sources (e.g., the Dead Sea Scrolls) are also of little use in reconstructing the life of Jesus.Not nearly as many Jewish sources survive. The main source for the history of Palestine in this period is Flavius Josephus. Josephus was a Jewish aristocrat who, during the revolt against Rome in 66–70 A.D., served as general of the Jewish troops in the northern part of Israel, Galilee. When he and his troops were surrounded, he agreed to a suicide pact in which lots would be drawn to see who would kill whom, until the final two would take their own lives. He drew one of the final two lots but persuaded his remaining companion to surrender. Later in the war, he was used by the Romans as an interpreter to convince other Jews to surrender, and after the war, he was rewarded for his efforts by being appointed a court historian in Rome under Emperor Vespasian. He produced a lengthy account of the Jewish Wars and, about 20 years later, a 20-volume work on the history of the Jews from Adam and Eve onward to his own time, called the *Jewish Antiquities*.

Jesus is never mentioned in the *Jewish Wars*, but he makes two tantalizingly brief appearances in the *Antiquities*. The briefer of the two references indicates that he was called by some the messiah and that he had a brother named James. The longer reference (Book XVIII of *Antiquities*) gives considerably more detail, indicating that Jesus was known to be a wise man who did spectacular deeds and had a following among both Jews and Greeks. This reference also says that Jesus was brought up on charges by the Jewish leaders, appeared before Pontius Pilate, and was crucified and that his followers formed a community that continued to thrive. This manuscript was probably reproduced in the Middle Ages by a Christian scribe who may have added to it. At least this reference confirms the existence of Jesus and coincides basically with the Gospel accounts of him. It obviously is of little use if we want to know any of the details of what Jesus said and did.

Even in the New Testament, the life of Jesus is scarcely mentioned outside of the Gospels. ... The total information would fit on a three-by-five-inch index card.

The surviving Christian sources provide us with much more information. Unfortunately, as we have already seen, the Gospels outside the New Testament are too late to be of much use to us and are full of legendary materials (cf., Peter and Thomas). Even in the New Testament, the life of Jesus is scarcely mentioned outside of the Gospels (e.g., by the apostle Paul, who is far more concerned about faith in Jesus' death and resurrection than in the details of his life). The total information would fit on a three-by-five-inch index card. That means, then, that if we want to know about what Jesus said and did, our only sources are Matthew, Mark, Luke, and John (and possibly Thomas).

As we have already seen, these sources are also problematic if we want to use them to reconstruct what Jesus said and did. They were written between 35 to 65 years after the events they narrate. The authors were not eyewitnesses and they appear to have acquired their stories from oral traditions that had been in circulation for decades. These traditions were evidently changed— sometimes a little, sometimes a lot—in the course of their transmission (as we saw in the case of John and Mark on the day of Jesus' death). Sometimes even *these* authors changed the traditions they inherited (as we saw in the case of Matthew and Luke's modifications of Matthew). The evidence for these changes is the fact that the Gospels contain accounts that appear to be irreconcilable in places.

If these are our only historical sources—and they appear to be relatively late, biased, altered, and inconsistent with one another—how can we possibly use them to reconstruct what Jesus was really like? In fact, most historians of early Christianity would agree that although we cannot use these accounts uncritically as historical sources, we can use them critically, following some rigid historical guidelines. The next lecture contains some detail on what these methods involve, but a quick overview appears below.

Scholars have devised three major criteria for examining the Gospels as historical sources for the life of Jesus. In some ways, it helps to think of the historian as a prosecuting attorney who bears the burden of proof in examining his witnesses (sources) to prove his case. The first criterion used is called "independent attestation." Having multiple witnesses who independently agree in their accounts is stronger evidence than having only one witness. Traditions ascribed to Jesus in more than one independent source are more likely to be historically accurate.

The second criterion is called "dissimilarity." A witness's testimony is particularly valuable when it works against his own vested interest (e.g., when he testifies under oath that he did see his best friend commit the crime). So too, traditions ascribed to Jesus that do not seem to advance the vested interests of the Christians who were telling or writing the stories are particularly to be valued as historically accurate.

The final criterion is "contextual credibility." A witness's testimony will be discounted if it does not coincide with what are otherwise known to be the facts of the case. Traditions ascribed to Jesus cannot be accepted as historically accurate if they cannot be situated credibly into what we know to be the context of Judaism in 1st-century A.D. Palestine. ■

Essential Reading

Ehrman, *Jesus: Apocalyptic Prophet.*

————, *The New Testament: A Historical Introduction*, chap. 13.

Meier, *A Marginal Jew*, vol. 1.

Supplemental Reading

Tatum, *In Quest of Jesus.*

Questions to Consider

1. Summarize what we can know about Jesus from sources outside the New Testament Gospels. Why do you suppose this information is so sparse?

2. Summarize why scholars have seen the Gospels as problematic historical sources. In your opinion, does their value as historical documents affect their importance as religious books of faith?

3. Explain the problems in the Gospels that make each of the three historical criteria (independent attestation, dissimilarity, and contextual credibility) necessary. Can you discern the logic that requires each of these criteria, given the nature of our sources?

The Historical Jesus—Sources and Problems
Lecture 10—Transcript

To this point in our study of the Gospels, both canonical and non-canonical, our overarching purpose has been to appreciate each work as a piece of literature with a distinct portrayal of Jesus. We've not yet begun to ask, though, the historical question, "What can we say about Jesus himself, what he actually said and did?" As we move beyond looking at the Gospels as literature, into examining how they can be historical sources for the life of Jesus, the overarching issue is this: given the circumstance that different Gospels portray Jesus differently, and that all of the Gospels embody traditions that have been more or less altered in the course of their transmission, how can we get behind these portrayals of Jesus in these accounts to see what the man, Jesus himself, was really like? That would be the goal of the next three lectures, to consider our accounts, not as literary products designed to convey a particular view of Jesus, but as historical sources useful for the task of historical reconstruction.

One place to begin any attempt to reconstruct the life of Jesus is by asking whether there are sources outside of the Gospels that might be useful for the task. It might be useful, for example, to see not only what believers said about Jesus, but also what unbelievers said. To see not only how his friends understood him, but also how his enemies did. And so we will begin our discussion of the historical Jesus by talking about sources outside of the Gospels, to see how they might enlighten us with respect to the things Jesus said and did. For the purposes of our study, I will be dividing our ancient sources into three major groups: pagan sources, that is, sources written by those who are neither Jews nor Christians, pagan sources; Jewish sources; and Christian sources outside of our Gospels.

And so we begin with pagan sources. For these sources, and for the others as well, since we are interested in the historical Jesus, we will probably be safe in restricting ourselves to sources that were written within 100 years of his death; and so we will be considering sources that were produced sometime between the year 30 A.D. and the year 130 A.D. And so, pagan sources. Unfortunately, our surviving pagan sources are virtually no use for us as we try to reconstruct the life of the historical Jesus. I one time had a student at

Rutgers University who wanted to do a senior thesis on the question of how non-Jews/non-Christians portrayed Jesus. His idea was that he would go to the library and look up some old books and uncover some things that people had said that nobody has discovered in these ancient sources. I had to tell him that he could do that as a project if he wanted to, but that it would be a very short term paper, indeed, because, in fact, there is virtually nothing that survived from pagan sources that is of any use for us in reconstructing what Jesus said and did. This comes as a surprise to many people today, given the fact that Jesus has made such a huge impact on history ever since his death. You might expect that his life made an enormous impact on the society of his day, like a comet striking the earth. But if our historical record is of any indication, Jesus, in fact, made scarcely any impact at all on society in his day. Less like a comet striking the earth than a stone being tossed into the ocean. From the 1st century A.D., we have hundreds of documents written by all kinds of writers for all sorts of reasons. Among all of these surviving sources from pagan authors, Jesus is never mentioned at all. He is not named by any of the philosophers, poets, historians, or scientists of his day. He is not mentioned in any private letters or any public inscriptions. Not only do we have no birth records, trial reports, or death certificates, we have no reference of any kind whatsoever, even to Jesus' name, in any of these pagan sources.

Our earliest recorded references to Jesus in pagan sources come from the early 2nd century A.D. There are, in fact, only two certain references within our prescribed time limits from A.D. 30 to 130. The first reference comes to us from the writings of a man named Pliny the Younger, who was the nephew of the person known as Pliny the Elder. Pliny the Elder was a famous scientist, a natural scientist, who was in the vicinity when Mount Vesuvius exploded in the year 79, and, as a scientist, he went to explore the explosion of Vesuvius and got too close and expired. His young nephew, Pliny the Younger, had actually seen this explosion as well and recorded the event in his diaries. Some 30 years later (25 or 30 years later), Pliny the Younger had become an important administrator in the Roman provinces. Pliny, in fact, had been appointed as a governor of the province known as Bethenia Pontus, which is in modern-day Turkey. Pliny wrote a number of letters to the Roman emperor Trajan discussing matters within his province, and in one of these letters, letter number 10, he mentions the Christians as a pestiferous group in his province. He says, in this letter, that these Christians got together early in the morning to worship Christ as a god, that they sang songs together, they ate meals together, but that, so far as he could tell, they weren't doing anything that was particularly threatening to society. He was writing this letter to the emperor because he wanted to know what do about these Christians because he knew, in other places, the Christians had been put on trial for crimes against the state, and he wanted to know what he should do about them. His reference in this letter number 10 to the Emperor Trajan is the only reference to Jesus that he has in any of his writings, and all he says about him is that the Christians worshiped him as a god. That's the extent of the reference, but it's the first reference to Jesus in any pagan source from the ancient world, written about the year 112 A.D.

A few years later, we get a second reference to Jesus, this time in the writings of the Roman historian Tacitus, who gives a somewhat lengthier reference in his history of Rome, known as "The Annals," written about 115 A.D. In The Annals, Tacitus discusses the burning of Rome under the Emperor Nero in the year 64. So he is recounting events that took place 50 years before he's writing. And in his account of the burning of Roman in the year 64, he mentions that Nero, who had torched the city himself in order to be able to implement his own architectural design for the city, had been found to be at fault by the population at large and so decided to find a scapegoat, namely the Christians. He rounded up Christians and had them executed for committing acts of arson by burning the city, even though he himself was the one guilty. Tacitus, talking about this event, described who these Christians were and gives us a little more information then Pliny had. He says that these people, these Christians, were the hatred of the human race, and that they were the followers of Christ, whom he notes, was crucified under the procurator of Judea, Pontius Pilate, when Tiberius was the emperor. It is useful to know that this much information was available to a prominent Roman historian about Jesus. The information that Tacitus gives us confirms what we know about from our other sources: that Jesus was in Judea; that he was crucified as an enemy of the state; that this was while Pontus Pilate was the governor of Judea, during the realm of Tiberius. Unfortunately, though, that's all Tacitus tells us. There are no other certain references to Jesus in any pagan author within a century of his death. Just these two very brief references.

What about Jewish sources? Are there Jewish accounts of what Jesus was like? You would expect that, since Jesus himself was a Jew living in Palestine, that there would be references to him in Jewish works from his time. Unfortunately, we don't have an abundance of Jewish writings from the 1st century in Palestine. We have some, of course. We have the Dead Sea Scrolls; Jesus is never mentioned there. And we have a few other remains Jesus is never mentioned in. We have writings from Jews outside of Palestine from the 1st century, including the writings of the famous Jewish philosopher Philo who lived in Alexandria, who would have been living later in the 1st century, about the time of the Apostle Paul. Philo also never mentions Jesus.

We do have one Jewish source, though, from the 1st century, from Palestine, who does mention Jesus, and it is useful to consider these references. This is the Jewish author known as Flavius Josephus, who, in fact, is the main source of our knowledge of Palestine during this period. Let me say a few things about who Flavius Josephus was. Josephus was a Jewish aristocrat who was born about the year 37; was raised in aristocratic circle; was himself, in fact, a priest.

When the Jewish revolt broke out against Rome in 66 A.D., Josephus was chosen to serve as a general of the Jewish troops in the northern part of Israel, Galilee. We know about what happened during his service as a general over the troops because of what Josephus himself tells us later in his own autobiography. The Romans marched into Palestine to quell this revolt. Galilee was quickly taken. Josephus and his own troops were surrounded and, according to Josephus himself, he and his troops agreed to a suicide pact in which lots would be drawn to see who would kill whom until the final two soldiers remained, and then those two would take their own lives. As it turns out, Josephus drew one of the final two lots. Then when everybody else had been killed, he persuaded his remaining companion to surrender with him to the Romans, which he did. Later in the war, Josephus was used by the Romans as an interpreter to try and convince the Jews who were holed up inside Jerusalem to surrender.

After the war, he was rewarded for his efforts by being appointed a court historian in Rome, where the Roman emperor Vespasian gave him a place to stay and gave him an annual income, allowing him to work as a historian there. In the remaining years of his life, then, Josephus produced a number of important literary works. The first book he produced was a multi-volume account of the Jewish wars themselves, narrating the events that led to the tragedy and to its outcome. About 20 years later, near the end of the 1st century, Josephus produced a 20-volume work on the history of the Jewish people, starting with Adam and Eve and going up to his own time. This is the work called "The Antiquities of the Jews." Jesus is never mentioned in Josephus' work, "The Jewish Wars." He does, though, make two tantalizingly brief appearances in the Antiquities. The shorter of the two references indicates that Jesus was called "the Messiah" by some people, and that he had a brother named James. It's a historian's fact that Josephus is telling about James, and he calls James "the brother of Jesus, of whom some call the Messiah," and that's all he says.

The second reference is somewhat longer and considerably more detailed and controversial. In this longer reference, in book 18 of the Antiquities, Josephus says that Jesus was a wise man—in fact, maybe more than a man. That he did spectacular deeds; that he was known to have a following among both Jews and Greeks; that at the end of his life he was brought up on charges before the Jewish leaders; that he appeared, then, before Pontius Pilate, who ordered him crucified. Josephus goes on to say, then, that his followers continued to thrive to his own day because, according to this account, Jesus had been raised from the dead. Scholars have long debated what to make of this reference to Jesus in Josephus because there are parts of this reference which indicate that Josephus himself believed in Jesus, even though we know that Josephus did not; he remained a non-Christian Jew 'til the day of his death. He says, specifically, that Jesus was more than a man. At one point he calls him the Messiah. He says that he was raised from the dead. Scholars have long known that these writings of Josephus were, in fact, copied in the Middle Ages, not by Jews, who considered Josephus to have been a turncoat, but by Christian scribes. The common idea amongst scholars now is that whatever Christian scribe produced this manuscript we have of Josephus, in which he appears to profess belief in Jesus, was probably produced by a Christian scribe who beefed up a bit his reference to Jesus.

When you take out the Christian references to Jesus in this account of Josephus, then, we are left, though, with some good basic historical information. We know, then, from this account that Jesus existed; that he lived in Judea; that he had a big following; he was known to do great deeds; that the Jewish leaders put him before Pontius Pilate, who then had him crucified. This conforms with the basic information we get in the Gospel accounts. But, obviously, this kind of information is of little use for us if we want to have any kind detailed knowledge about what Jesus actual said and did. It is enough to confirm his basic existence and the outline of the Gospel stories, but not much more. These are the only Jewish references to Jesus within the first 100 years of his death.

Our Christian sources, obviously, provide us with a good deal more information than the pagan and Jewish sources do. Unfortunately, as we have already seen, the Gospels outside of the New Testament, by and large, are too late to be of much use for us in trying to reconstruct what Jesus really said and did. We have over 20 of these Gospels. The earliest ones are the two that we have looked at, the Gospel of Peter and the Gospel of Thomas. It may be that these two sources are independent of our canonical Gospels. It may be, that is, that they acquire their traditions of Jesus from the oral tradition rather than reading the Gospel. If that's the case, then that would be useful for us because that would mean there would be independent testimony about what Jesus said and did. The other Gospels we have, though, the other surviving non-canonical Gospels, give us even less information, and it is not clear at all that they were independent. What about, though, books within the New Testament outside of the Gospels? Can they be of any use for us in trying to reconstruct what Jesus said and did? Well, of course, there are 23 other books. Unfortunately, these 23 other books scarcely say anything about what Jesus said and did while he was alive. This comes as a shock to many people who read the New Testament for the first time. You read Matthew; it's about Jesus. Mark, Luke, and John—they are all stories of Jesus. Once you hit the Book of Acts, though, Jesus' life is scarcely ever mentioned.

The author who has the most books attributed to him in the New Testament is the Apostle Paul, whom as I have pointed out has 13 letters that he allegedly wrote. How much does Paul tell us about Jesus? With my undergraduate students, I give them an assignment every year in which they are to make a list of everything the Apostle Paul tells us about Jesus. It is a useful exercise because Paul, in fact, tells us more about Jesus than any of the other authors, outside of the Gospels, in the New Testament. My students, though, are surprised to find that to make a list of everything that Paul tells us about Jesus' life, the things he said and did from the time he was born to the time he died, to make a list like that, they don't even need a 3-by-5 card. I can give you the list of everything that Paul said about Jesus. Paul tells us that Jesus was born of a woman, Galatians 4:4. Well, that's not a particularly useful datum, since one wonders what the option might be. But Paul nevertheless says this: "Jesus was born of a woman." Secondly, he tells us that Jesus was born as a Jew. Again, Galatians Chapter 4:4. So Jesus was Jewish. Paul tells us, third, that Jesus had brothers. He mentions Jesus' brothers in 1st Corinthians Chapter 9, Verse 5. Moreover, he tells us that one of Jesus' brothers was named James, Galatians Chapter 1. Paul tells us that Jesus ministered principally to Jews, that his ministry is principally to Jews, Romans Chapter 15, Verse 8. Paul tells us that Jesus delivered a couple of teachings during his ministry.

Paul, in fact, quotes two teachings of Jesus explicitly. First, that Christians should not get divorced. And second, that Christians ought to pay their preachers. He quotes these two traditions going back to Jesus. Paul appears to know that Jesus was betrayed by Judas Iscariot. Paul doesn't mention Judas Iscariot, but he does say that Jesus was betrayed, 1 Corinthians Chapter 11. Moreover, Paul does know that Jesus had the Last Supper, and he knows what Jesus said at the Last Supper. Again, 1 Corinthians Chapter 11. In addition, Paul knows that Jesus got crucified. He doesn't mentioned Pontius Pilate, but he does know that Jesus got crucified. That's all that Paul tells us about the life of Jesus. If you simply had Paul as the source for your life of Jesus, if you didn't have the Gospels and all you had was Paul, just imagine, for a second, what you wouldn't know about Jesus. You would know nothing about his birth or about his mother, being born in Bethlehem, nothing about her being a virgin. You would know nothing about Jesus having done any miracles, ever casting out demons, ever telling a parable, preaching about the coming kingdom of God. You wouldn't know about the temptation. You wouldn't know about the baptism. You wouldn't know about the transfiguration. You can go on and on and on. Paul simply doesn't mention these things, and yet Paul tells us more than the other authors outside of the Gospels in the New Testament.

Let me give a brief summary, then, of what we learned about Jesus from other sources. We learned virtually nothing from pagan verses from Pliny and Tacitus. We learned a little bit more from Josephus, enough, at least, to know that Jesus lived and that he had a following, that he had great teachings, he did great deeds, and that he was killed under Pontius Pilate. And then we have sources like Paul that tell a few pieces of information, but not very much. Otherwise we have non-canonical Gospels that are highly legendary and late. What this means is that if we want to know about what Jesus said and did during his life, we are restricted to the four Gospels of Matthew, Mark, Luke, and John, and possibly the Gospel of Thomas. Let me emphasize that we restrict our study of the historical Jesus to these sources, not for any theological reasons, because they happen to be in the canon, or we think that they are the ones that are inspired or the ones that should be trusted. It's not a theological reason at all; it's because these are the only sources we have. There are many scholars who have written many books about the historical Jesus. I want to stress that the sources I've detailed are the only sources that are available to them. If anybody writes a tradition of Jesus or discusses something that Jesus said or did that's not found in one of these sources, then that author simply made it up. These are the only sources that are available to us.

Unfortunately, the sources within the New Testament among the Gospels themselves are highly problematic as historical sources. I am not saying that they're problematic theologically or religiously. I am not dealing with the question of their value for religious communities of faith. I am talking about their value for historians who want to know what Jesus really said and did. Recall that these books, especially the four Gospels of the New Testament, but also Thomas, were written years after the events that they narrate. The earliest account is 35 years later. The latest account, John, is 65 years later. Thomas was probably 90 years later. These authors were evidently not eyewitnesses of the events that they narrate. They appear to have acquired their stories from oral traditions that had been in circulation for decades among the Christians. While these traditions were in circulation, they were evidently changed. Sometimes they were changed a little, sometimes were changed a lot, in the course of transmission. We've seen this in specific cases throughout our lectures already. For example, when did Jesus die? John and

Mark have a different account of this. Why? Because somebody has changed the tradition.

The evidence, then, for these changes is actually found within the sources themselves. The Gospels appear to contain accounts that are irreconcilable in places. If these are our only sources, and they appear to be our only sources, then we have a large task in front of us. These sources are relatively late, they are biased, they are altered, and they are inconsistent with one another. How can we use sources such as these to reconstruct what Jesus himself was really like? Well, in point of fact, most historians would agree that we can't use these sources uncritically if we want to determine what Jesus said and did. Instead, we have to use them with a critical eye, developing some rigid historical guidelines for trying to utilize the sources to get behind the portrayals of Jesus, to understand the historical man himself. In the next lecture, I am going to be outlining, in greater detail, what methods scholars have devised for using these sources. I want to say, at this point, that I don't think we should completely throw up our hands in despair and say, "Well, then, we can't know anything about the historical Jesus." I think we can know things about the historical Jesus, but we have to be very careful, methodologically, how we get there. I will be outlining, in greater details, what these methods are in the next lecture; here I want to give them very briefly for you, so that we can be starting to think about the proper method in reconstructing the historical Jesus.

The three major criteria that scholars have devised for examining the Gospels are as follows, and I should say all three of these try to imagine the historian as a kind of prosecuting attorney in a court of law, where the burden of proof is on the prosecuting attorney who is examining his witnesses in order to prove his case. Bearing that in mind, these are the three criteria. First, a criterion that is usually called the criterion of independent attestation. Independent attestation. In a court of law, having multiple witnesses who independently agree in their accounts of what happens is stronger evidence than having only one witness. So, too, with traditions ascribed to Jesus. Those that are ascribed to Jesus in more than one independent source are more likely to be historically accurate than those found in only one source.

Second criterion, sometimes called the criterion of dissimilarity. The criterion of dissimilarity. In a court of law, a witnesses' testimony is particularly valuable when it works against his own vested interest. For example, when a witness testifies, under oath, that he did see his best friend commit a crime. So, too, traditions ascribed to Jesus that do not seem to advance the vested interest of the Christians who were telling or writing the stories about him are particularly to be valued as historically accurate. If you had traditions that seemed to work against the vested interest of the Christians who are preserving the traditions, then those are to be particularly valued as historically accurate. Those are traditions that are dissimilar to what the Christians might have wanted to say about Jesus. Third and final criterion, in a court of law, a witness' testimony will be discounted if it does not coincide with what is otherwise known to be the facts of the case. So, too, traditions ascribed to Jesus cannot be accepted as historically accurate if they cannot be situated credibly into what we know otherwise to be the context of Judaism in 1st century Palestine. The criterion of contextual credibility.

In conclusion, we have now moved from understanding the Gospels as literary texts to examining them for what they can tell us about the historical Jesus himself. There is not much evidence for Jesus' life and teachings outside of the New Testament Gospels. For example, among such pagan sources as Pliny and Tacitus, or even a Jewish source like Josephus. And even the earliest Gospels are problematic as historical sources. Only by following rigorous historical criteria can we move beyond the literary portrayals of Jesus in the Gospels to a historical reconstruction of what he was really like. In the next lecture, I will talk further about these criteria and show how they can be applied.

Scholars have developed three major criteria for establishing what Jesus really said and did based on the surviving sources. The criteria of independent attestation, dissimilarity, and contextual credibility.

The criterion of independent attestation maintains that traditions about Jesus preserved in more than one independent source are more likely to be historically accurate. The logic behind this criterion is that if two sources independently attest to a saying or deed of Jesus, then neither one of them could have made it up. It is important to stress that the sources must be independent. A saying found in both Matthew and Luke is not independently attested, because both Matthew and Luke would probably have gotten it from Q (e.g., the "Lord's Prayer" or the Beatitudes). But a saying found in Mark and John, or in Thomas and Luke, would be independently attested, because John did not use Mark and Thomas, in all likelihood, did not use Luke.

It is also important to emphasize that independently attested traditions are not automatically authentic—they are more *likely* to be authentic. Some examples can be cited to illustrate the criterion. Stories of Jesus associating with John the Baptist are found in Mark, Q, and John (Mark 1; Matthew 3/Luke 3; John 1). Jesus is said to have brothers in Mark (6:3), John (7:3), Paul (1 Cor. 9:5), and Josephus; moreover, both Josephus and Paul (Gal. 1:19) indicate that one of these brothers was named James. Jesus tells parables in which he likens the Kingdom of God to seeds in Mark, Q, and the Gospel of Thomas. Jesus is said to have been put on trial before Pontius Pilate, then crucified in Mark, John, the Gospel of Peter, Josephus, and Tacitus.

In conclusion, I emphasize that this criterion can be used only to indicate which traditions are more likely to be historically accurate. The criterion cannot be used to show what is inaccurate. Just because the "Lord's Prayer" comes only from Q does not mean Jesus did not actually teach it to his disciples. Just because the Parable of the Good Samaritan appears only in Luke does not mean that Jesus could not have said it.

The criterion of dissimilarity maintains that traditions ascribed to Jesus that do not seem to advance the vested interests of the Christians who were telling them are also to be valued as historically accurate. The logic behind this criterion is that we know that Christians were altering, and sometimes even inventing, stories about Jesus. They did so to make their own points about him, that is, because of their own vested interests in telling the stories. If a story does *not* advance the vested interests of the Christians telling it, then it is not a story that they would have made up. Such stories survive in the tradition precisely because they really happened.

This criterion can be used only to indicate which traditions are more likely to be historically accurate. The criterion cannot be used to show what is inaccurate.

Again, some examples of how the criterion can actually work will help to clarify it. Jesus' followers probably would not have invented the tradition that he came from Nazareth, because Nazareth was a tiny, insignificant place that no one had heard of and that had no connection with the coming messiah. If they were to "make up" a place for Jesus to be born, it would probably be Bethlehem (the home of King David) or Jerusalem (the city of God). The tradition of Jesus as a carpenter (or at least a man who worked with his hands) is another example, because this occupation had low social status. Jesus' followers probably would not have made up the idea that he was baptized by John, because that might suggest that he was spiritually inferior to John—the disciple baptized by the master. Jesus' followers probably would not have made up the story that he was betrayed by one of his own followers, because that would suggest that he could not control those who were close to him. Finally, the crucifixion is another example. The Jews would not have expected their messiah to be crucified as a criminal.

This criterion poses some difficulties. First, as should be obvious from the examples, the criterion can be used only to establish traditions that are more *probable*. It, and the other criteria, can never provide any certainty. This criterion is particularly problematic, because we don't have a full account of early Christianity and we don't know completely what the Christians' vested interests were. Moreover, like the preceding criterion of independent attestation, this criterion can only be used in a positive way to argue *for* a tradition. The fact that a tradition does not pass the criterion does not necessarily mean that it didn't happen (for example, when Jesus predicts that he has to die in Jerusalem, surely he could have seen the handwriting on the wall), even though the nature of the tradition may give us pause (for example, his prediction that he would rise in three days, which was exactly what his later followers said had happened). The best-case scenario is when a tradition happens to pass *both* these criteria. For any tradition to be credible, it also needs to pass the third.

The criterion of contextual credibility maintains that traditions ascribed to Jesus cannot be accepted as historically accurate if they cannot be situated credibly into the context of Judaism in 1st-century Palestine. The logic of this criterion should be self-evident: Because Jesus was a 1st-century Palestinian Jew, what he said and did must make sense in the context of 1st-century Palestinian Judaism. Unlike the other criteria, this one is used to argue *against* certain traditions as historically implausible. For example, the Gospel of Thomas contains sayings that make perfect sense in the context of 2nd-century Gnosticism but sound completely unlike what a 1st-century Jew in Palestine would have said. These sayings likely do not go back to Jesus. Another example of lack of context is the discussion between Jesus and Nicodemus in John 3.

Because this final criterion is so important, we will linger for a couple of minutes on a specific aspect of 1st-century Judaism. In an earlier lecture, I noted some of the important features of Judaism in the 1st century, especially its distinctive emphasis on monotheism, the covenant God made with Israel, and the Law he gave. I must also emphasize in particular one perspective that we now know to have been particularly prominent among Jews, commonly known as Jewish apocalypticism. Its relevance for understanding Jesus' own context will appear clear when I remind you of its major tenets. Apocalypticists held to a dualistic view of the world, which was made up of forces of good and evil, and everyone and everything took one side or the other. Moreover, the present age was controlled by the forces of evil, who were determined to punish anyone who took the side of the good. Apocalypticists were pessimistic about the possibilities of improving life in this evil age. The forces of evil were gaining in ascendancy and could not be overcome through human effort. But God would eventually assert himself and overthrow these forces of evil. A judgment day was coming, and it would affect the entire world, including both the living and the dead. Once God had overcome the forces of evil, he would establish his utopian kingdom here on earth, where his people would live forever. This divine intervention was imminent. How soon? As one 1st-century Jew told his own disciples, "Truly I tell you, this generation will not pass away before all these things take place." Indeed, he said, "some of you standing here will not taste death before they see that the Kingdom of God has come in power."

These, of course, are the words of Jesus. In the next lecture, I will argue that Jesus was a Jewish apocalypticist, who, like many of his compatriots, believed that God was soon going to intervene in the course of history and overthrow the forces of evil to bring in a good kingdom on earth, a kingdom ruled by God through his messiah. ∎

Essential Reading

Ehrman, *Jesus: Apocalyptic Prophet.*

———, *The New Testament: A Historical Introduction*, chap. 13.

Meier, *A Marginal Jew*, vol. 1.

Supplemental Reading

Tatum, *In Quest of Jesus.*

Questions to Consider

1. What do you see as the strengths and weaknesses of each of the criteria used to establish historically authentic material from the life of Jesus?

2. Are there other criteria that you can imagine being applied to the traditions about Jesus to establish their historical accuracy?

The Historical Jesus—Solutions and Methods
Lecture 11—Transcript

In the last lecture, we began to move beyond looking at the Gospels as literary portrayals of Jesus to see what we could learn about the man who stands behind the Gospels, the historical Jesus himself. I want to stress a particularly important point, that it is impossible to reconstruct the past without having sources. Everyone who claims to know something about Jesus has a source, or else they made it up, in which case, there is no reason for us to pay attention to them if we are interested in doing history. We, in fact, have very few sources for the life of Jesus. In fact, the four Gospels of the New Testament are our best, and virtually our only, sources in addition with a few things, possibly in the Gospel of Thomas and a few brief references to Jesus outside of the New Testament.

In the last lecture, we saw why the sources we have are so problematic. The Gospels may be useful as documents of faith, they've certainly been valuable historically by believers in the Christian church, but for historians who want to know what actually happened in the past, they are problematic. And so, scholars have devised methods that are to be used in examining these sources to reconstruct what historical events that lie behind them. In this lecture, I want to explain further why these criteria are needed and to illustrate how they can be used to establish reliable information about the historical Jesus. There are, of course, a lot of books written about Jesus by popular authors, but also by scholars who have invested a good part of their lives in understanding what he said and did. When you read these books about Jesus, you should pay particular attention to what the methods are that scholars have used. A lot of books don't talk about method, apparently on the assumption that if an author simply tells you what he or she happens to think about Jesus, you will take their word for it. But, in fact, everybody has a method, and it is important to know what a person's methods are, especially when coming to such a difficult area of research as the historical Jesus. It is important for people to know what the methods are and to lay them out carefully, and so I want to discuss, again, the three criteria that we will use in trying to establish what Jesus himself actually said and did.

The first criterion that we have talked about is the criterion of independent attestation. This criterion maintains that traditions about Jesus that are preserved in more than one independent source are more likely to be historically accurate than traditions found in only source. Let me explain the logic behind the criterion. The logic is that if two sources independently attest to a saying or deed of Jesus, then neither one of them could have made it up, meaning that the tradition must antedate both of the sources that attest to the tradition; they got it independently from somewhere else. It's important to stress that the sources must be independent of one another for this criterion to work. The sources must be independent. If there is a saying, for example, that is found in both Matthew and Luke, that saying is not independently attested, since Matthew and Luke both would have gotten it from the source that scholars have called "Q." That is why it is important for people to come to some conclusions about whether they think "Q" actually existed or not, because if it did exist, then any saying found in Matthew and Luke is not independently attested. For example, in both Matthew and Luke, Jesus gives his disciples the Lord's Prayer.

Well, this isn't independently attested if, in fact, it came from "Q." So, too, the Beatitudes; you find one form in Matthew, another form in Luke, but basically they are the same sayings. Given the fact they probably got this from "Q," this tradition is not independently attested. On the other hand, if you find a saying both in Mark and John, or in Thomas and Luke, such sayings would be independently attested because John evidently did not use Mark, and Thomas, in all likelihood, did not use Luke. When we are talking about the Gospels, occasionally I would say that it looks like this Gospel was dependent upon that Gospel, but Thomas probably was not dependent on the Synoptics, and now you can see why. It is important to know what sources were dependent on others, so that we know which sources are independent for reconstructing the life of the historical Jesus.

I also want to emphasize that independently attested traditions are not automatically authentic. This criterion merely says that independently attested traditions are more likely to be authentic. Let me give you some examples so as to illustrate the criterion. I'll give you several examples. First, we have stories of Jesus associating with John the Baptist in Mark, in "Q," and in John. Well, what conclusion would you draw? Well, since it is found in three sources that were completely independent of one another, then it is likely that Jesus really did associate with John the Baptist. In all three accounts, in fact, it appears that his association with John the Baptist was at the very beginning of his ministry. Conclusion, Jesus was associated with John at the beginning of his ministry.

Second example, Jesus is said to have brothers in Mark 6:3, John 7:3, Paul, 1 Corinthians 9:5, and Josephus. Moreover, both Josephus and Paul indicate that one of these brothers was named James. What conclusion would we draw? Well, Jesus probably had brothers and one of them was named James.

Third example, Jesus tells parables in which he likens the kingdom of God to seeds in Mark, in "Q," and in Thomas. Conclusion, Jesus probably told parables like that. Fourth example, Jesus is said to have been put on trial before Pontius Pilate and then crucified in Mark, in John, the Gospel of Peter, Josephus, and Tacitus. Conclusion, well, all of that probably happened. In conclusion to this criterion, I should say that it can be used to indicate which traditions are more likely historically accurate. But—an important but—this criterion of independent attestation cannot be used to show which traditions are inaccurate. In other words, just because the Lord's Prayer comes from "Q," and we don't have it in any other source, just because it comes only from "Q" does not mean that Jesus did not teach it to his disciples. He may well have. You simply can't show that he did on the basis of this criterion.

And so, too, with a good number of other traditions. For example, the famous parable of the Good Samaritan is found only in Luke's Gospel; in other words, it comes from the sources that scholars have called "L." The fact that it comes only from "L," though, doesn't mean that Jesus really didn't give the parable. It means you can't show that he gave this parable using the criterion of independent attestation.

The second criterion is called by scholars the criterion of dissimilarity. This is easily the most difficult and controversial of our criteria. It sounds somewhat backwards to people who hear about it for the first time. It maintains, as we have seen, that traditions that are ascribed to Jesus that do not seem to advance the vested interest to the Christians who were telling or writing the stories about him, are particularly to be valued as historically accurate. In

171

other words, traditions that are dissimilar to what the Christians would have wanted to say about Jesus are the ones that are probably accurate. If this does sounds backwards, it might be useful to think about the logic that lies behind the criteria. The logic is that, as we have seen, Christians were altering, sometimes even inventing, stories about Jesus. Anyone who doesn't think that Christians were inventing stories about Jesus would have to say that the Gospel of Peter is right, that Jesus emerged from his tomb with his head reaching up as high as a skyscraper, and that a cross emerged behind him, talking to the clouds. Or would have to agree that all of the sayings in the Gospel of Thomas are actual sayings that Jesus himself said; I don't know anybody who thinks that. Since that's the case, it means that people were making up stories about Jesus. His own followers were.

Well, if people are making up stories about Jesus, then they appear to be making them up in light of their own vested interests. So, for example, the Gospel of John changes the story about when Jesus died because he wants to show that Jesus really was the Passover Lamb, the one who died when the lambs in the temple were killed. In other words, John has changed the story in light of his vested interest. What about stories that do not advance Christian vested interest? Well, those would not be stories that were made up by the Christians. Such stories survive in our tradition precisely because they are stories that actually happened. This criterion will not give us everything that Jesus actually said and did, but it will give us some things that are fairly certain that Jesus actually said and did.

As with the other criteria, the best way to explain this one is by giving several examples, which I will now do. First, we have traditions that are multiply attested, looking at the other criteria. We have some traditions that Jesus came from the village of Nazareth. Not only is this tradition multiply attested, it also is not the kind of tradition that a Christian would have been likely to have made up. Why not? Well, Nazareth was a tiny, insignificant place that no one had ever heard of and that no one had ever made any connection with, with regard to the Messiah. Josephus, as I mentioned, was our primary source for Palestine in the 1st century. He was the general of the Jewish troops in Galilee where Nazareth is located, the northern part of Israel. In all of his many volumes of writings, Josephus mentions many towns and villages throughout Palestine. He never even mentions Nazareth. It was that insignificant. It's never mentioned in the Hebrew Bible. In fact, it's never mentioned in any source prior to the New Testament. If Christians wanted to make up a tradition about where Jesus was from, they surely would have made up the tradition that came from some place like Bethlehem, the home of King David, or Jerusalem, the city of God. They wouldn't have made up the idea that he came from a little one-horse town like Nazareth. Conclusion, Jesus probably came from Nazareth; that's why it is in the tradition.

A second example, in our earliest surviving Gospel, Mark, Jesus is said to have been, it's usually translated, a carpenter. It is not quite clear how to translate the Greek word that occurs in English translation as a carpenter. The Greek word is *tectone*. It is usually used as people who were those who worked with their hands. Manual laborers, construction workers, this could have been a carpenter. It is also a term a used for stonemasons and other people who work with their hands. Now why would anybody make up the tradition that Jesus was a construction worker, a *tectone*? Well, there is no mileage that Christians get out of this. There is no vested interest that is being advanced by this idea. In fact, the later Gospels actually changed the story in Mark to say not that Jesus himself was the *tectone*, but that he was the son of the *tectone*. That shows some bit of embarrassment about the tradition because it doesn't advance the Christian interest. Conclusion, well, the reason Mark says that Jesus was a *tectone* wasn't to advance his own purposes, so probably Jesus really was a *tectone* before becoming an itinerant preacher. Although Jesus probably was some kind of construction worker, whether it was a carpenter or stonemason or something else.

Third example, Jesus' followers probably would not have made up the idea that Jesus was baptized by John the Baptist. Early Christians understood that baptism was a ritual performed by somebody who was spiritually superior to somebody who is their spiritual inferior. The preacher baptizes the follower, not the other way around. Why would a Christian make up the idea that Jesus was baptized by someone else? Wouldn't that suggest, at least to the uninitiated, that Jesus was inferior to John? Moreover, why is John baptizing people? According to the earlier accounts, he is baptizing them for the remission of sins; in other words, when people's sins are forgiven. They are being baptized by John as evidence that God has forgiven them of their sins. Would Christians make up the idea that Jesus is being baptized for the remission of his sins? Seems unlikely. It is interesting that in Matthew's Gospel, we have a story that is found only in Matthew, that when Jesus comes to be baptized by John, John tries to prevent him. He says to Jesus, "I am the one who should be baptized by you." And Jesus says, "No, let's do this to fulfill all righteousness." In other words, Matthew's Gospel evidences some embarrassment by the Christians over the tradition that Jesus was baptized by John. It doesn't appear, then, to be the kind of tradition that Christians themselves would have invented because it might suggest to people that Jesus was spiritually inferior to John. The disciple being baptized by the master. Therefore, since they wouldn't have made it up, this is a tradition that actually probably happened.

Fourth example, Jesus' followers would probably not have made up the story that he was betrayed by one of his own followers, Judas Iscariot. This tradition is multiply attested. It's in John; it's in Mark. It may be alluded to, as I have pointed out, by Paul in 1 Corinthians Chapter 11, where he says that in the night in which he was betrayed, and then goes ahead and gives the narration of Jesus' institution of the Lord's Supper. Paul may allude to it. It is multiply attested, but is also not the kind of tradition that a Christian would have wanted to invent because it suggests that Jesus was unable to control even those who were close to him, his own followers. I don't mean to say that it really means this, but I am saying that's how people would have easily interpreted this tradition. And so Christians wouldn't make up the idea that one of his own betrayed him. Well then, why do we have this tradition attested in so many of our sources? Well, Christians wouldn't have made it up, so it is something that probably happened.

Fifth, final example, probably the best attested reference to Jesus' life is the reference to his crucifixion, which, as I have pointed out, is multiply attested over the map. It's also a tradition that would not have been made up by Christians for reasons we have already seen in the course. Jews, prior to Christianity, did not expect a messiah who would be crucified. There was no tradition in any surviving Jewish source that we have prior to the New Testament that indicated that the Messiah would suffer and die. The Messiah was to be a figure of grandeur and power. Jesus was known to have been a crucified criminal; that's not a tradition people would have made up if they wanted to say that Jesus was the Messiah because that's not what anybody expected the Messiah to be. In fact, the Apostle Paul in 1 Corinthians Chapter 2 says that the idea of Jesus' being a crucified Messiah was the major stumbling block for Jews in the Christian mission to convert Jews. It was a huge obstacle. Christians had to convince Jews that, in fact, the Messiah was supposed to be crucified. Since they had to go out of their way to convince Jews of this, it is not the sort of thing that came easily to them; they wouldn't have invented it themselves. They had to explain away a tradition that they knew was true. Conclusion, Jesus really was crucified under Pontius Pilate.

This, then, is the criterion of dissimilarity. It says that traditions that are dissimilar to the vested interest of the Christians are traditions that are probably historically authentic. It's a criterion that poses a number of difficulties, and we should be quite clear about what these difficulties are. As should be clear from the preceding examples, this criterion can only be used to establish traditions that are probable. It and the other criteria can never provide us with any certainty about what happened in the past, only probability. That, of course, is all history is, a set of probabilities. History isn't like the natural sciences, where you, through repeated experimentation, demonstrate what's probably going to happen the next time you conduct the experiment. With history, the experiment is done once, and it's over with. You can't repeat the experiment, which means that you can only establish probabilities of what happened in the past. This criterion of dissimilarity can simply give us some probabilities. It cannot give us any certainty. Moreover, the criterion is problematic because we don't have a full account of the early Christians. We don't know what all early Christians believed, thought, wanted, desired. We don't know what the earliest Christians' vested interests were in toto. This criterion is based on the premise that we have some idea what the Christians' vested interests were, but, again, we are only dealing with probabilities. Moreover, like the preceding criterion of independent attestation, this criterion is best used in a positive way to argue for a tradition. It is not as easy to use this criterion to argue against a tradition. In other words, the fact that a tradition does not pass this criterion does not necessarily mean that it didn't happen.

Let me give you an example. In the Gospels, Jesus predicts that he goes to Jerusalem to die. That prediction cannot pass the criterion of dissimilarity because that exactly is what the Christians said, that Jesus had to go to

Jerusalem and die. That's their whole theology. Because it doesn't pass the criterion, though, doesn't mean it didn't happen. Jesus may well have seen the handwriting on the wall, knowing that he was going to his death. I mean, that is historically possible, but you can't show that he knew that using this criterion.

In other cases, the nature of a tradition may give us some pause. Sometimes there are traditions in the Gospels that are so much like what the Christians were saying about Jesus that they are highly problematic. For example, in the Gospel in Mark, three times Jesus predicts that he is going to be raised from the dead. Well, that's what Christians were saying about him; of course they would want Jesus to know about it in advance, and so it is very hard to know that Jesus actually said that about himself. It doesn't pass the criterion of dissimilarity. Of course, it is historically possible that Jesus said something like that, but the criterion, at least, should cast some doubt on that kind of prediction. The best-case scenario we have is when a tradition happens to pass both of the criterions that I have laid out already, when it passes both independent attestation and dissimilarity. But for any tradition to be fully credible, it also needs to pass our third criterion, the criterion of contextual credibility.

This criterion maintains that traditions ascribed to Jesus cannot be accepted as historically accurate if they cannot be situated credibly into what we know about the context of Judaism in 1st century Palestine. If we cannot locate a tradition plausibly in 1st century Palestine, then it simply can't be accepted as historical. The logic is self-evident. Jesus was a 1st century Palestine Jew, so what he said and did must make sense in the context of 1st century Palestine Judaism. Now let me be clear that this criterion is used, unlike the other two, this criterion is used to argue against certain traditions, to show that some traditions are not historically plausible.

Give you a couple of examples. We looked at a number of sayings in the Gospel of Thomas that make perfect sense in the context of 2nd-century Gnosticism. These sayings, though, don't make very good sense on the lips of a 1st century Palestine Jew. These more Gnostic sayings in the Gospel of Thomas, then, probably do not go back to Jesus. Give you a second example, I mentioned in the lecture on the Gospel of John this interesting saying of

Jesus, one of his most famous sayings in John Chapter 3, where Jesus is talking to Nicodemus, and he tells this leader of the Jews, this Rabbi living in Jerusalem, "You must be born again." Nicodemus replies, "How can I possibly crawl back into my mother's womb and be born a second time?" Jesus responds by saying, "Unless you are born of water and spirit, you will never inherit the kingdom of heaven." And Jesus goes on to say that one must experience a birth that is from heaven if one wants to enter into the kingdom of heaven.

This conversation of Jesus and Nicodemus advances on the basis of an ambiguity in the Greek word that Jesus uses when he says you must be born again. The Greek word is *onothan*. You must be born *onothan*. The ambiguity is that the word *onothan* means two different things. *Onothan* can mean a second time. It can also mean from above. In the Gospel of John, it always means from above. Nicodemus misunderstands Jesus to mean a second time. He thinks he has to crawl back into his mother's womb and be born a second time, when Jesus means you have to have a heavenly birth. The conversation proceeds on the basis of a misunderstanding of a Greek word that's ambiguous, but the same word in Greek that's ambiguous is not ambiguous in Aramaic. The Aramaic word for from above does not also mean a second time. Jesus, though, is speaking to a rabbi in Jerusalem; they would have been speaking Aramaic. This conversation would not have proceeded as it is narrated in John Chapter 3. The criterion of contextual credibility eliminates that tradition.

Since context is so important for understanding the historical Jesus because of this criteria, I want to end this lecture by emphasizing a particular aspect of Jesus' own context in 1st century Palestine. It is the aspect of the context that previously I've called Jewish apocalypticism. Recall the major tenets of an apocalyptic view of what we are going to be talking about in the next lecture, about Jesus himself. Jewish Apocalypticists were prominent in Jesus' day. We know that the Essenes of the Dead Sea Scroll community were apocalyptic, many Pharisee were apocalyptic, and, in fact, many Jews, common Jews, held to apocalyptic views. These views involved a dualistic view of the world. They were forces of good and evil in the world, in everyone, and everybody took a side, either on the side of good, or the side of evil. This modern age that we live in now, according to the apocalyptic view, is controlled by the forces of evil, who were bound and determined to punish anyone who took the side of the good. Jewish apocalypticists in Jesus' day were pessimistic about the possibilities of improving life in the present evil age.

The forces of evil were gaining in ascendancy, and though they would be overcome eventually by God, they could not be overcome by human effort. People were pessimistic about the possibility of life, here and now. God, though, would intervene in the course of history. He would assert himself and overthrow the forces of evil. Apocalypticists believed that a judgment day was coming and that it would affect the entire world, including both those who are alive and those who are dead. Once God overcame the forces of evil, he would establish his utopian kingdom here on Earth, where his people would live forever. Jewish apocalypticists thought that this divine intervention, in the course of history, was imminent. How soon was it? Well, as one 1st century Jew told his own disciples, "Truly I tell you this generation will not pass away before all of these things take place." As he said, "Some of you standing here will not taste death before you see that the kingdom of God has come in power." These are the words of Jesus—as least, as recorded in our earliest surviving Gospel, the Gospel of Mark. In the next lecture, I am going to argue that Jesus was, in fact, himself a Jewish apocalypticist, who, like many of his compatriots, believed that God was soon going to intervene in the course of history and overthrow the forces of evil in order to bring in a good kingdom on Earth, a kingdom ruled by God through his Messiah.

In conclusion, scholars have developed three major criteria for establishing what Jesus really said and did based on the surviving sources. The criteria of independent attestation, dissimilarity, and contextual credibility. Anyone who doesn't approve of these criteria has to come up with criteria of their own. You simply can't read our sources uncritically to get back to the historical Jesus. You have to read them critically, which means developing criteria. It's especially important for us to locate Jesus in his own historical context, because Jesus was not wrapped up in the capitalistic ideology of 20th century America or in some other form of modern ideology. Jesus was wrapped up in the apocalyptic ideology of the 1st century Palestine.

Jesus the Apocalyptic Prophet
Lecture 12

Jesus is best understood as a 1ˢᵗ-century Jewish apocalypticist. … Jesus urged the people of Israel to repent before it was too late.

We have seen that the Gospels are our best sources for reconstructing the life of the historical Jesus, but they cannot be used uncritically. The criteria of independent attestation, dissimilarity, and contextual credibility can assist us, though, in working to get behind the Gospels to the historical events they narrate. Because of time constraints, I won't be able to explain how every tradition I discuss in this lecture passes one or more of these criteria, but full explanations can be found in the readings I've suggested. It is important to stress that the historical context of Jesus involves a particularly influential ideology known as Jewish apocalypticism. In this lecture, I'll explain why many contemporary scholars have understood Jesus as an apocalypticist and show how an apocalyptic perspective can elucidate his words and deeds.

The idea that Jesus was an apocalypticist, expecting the imminent end of history as we know it through a decisive intervention by God, is not new among recent scholars. It was first argued convincingly at the beginning of the century by Albert Schweitzer, the great humanitarian and medical missionary in the Belgian Congo, in his classic text *The Quest of the Historical Jesus* (1906). Most scholars in Germany and America have subscribed to this view for most of the 20ᵗʰ century, although the idea has come under attack in more recent years.

The reasons for holding this view are compelling. It is suggested by the fact that Jesus began his ministry by associating with John the Baptist, an apocalyptic preacher of repentance, rather than some other Jewish leader of his day (e.g., a Pharisee or a Sadducee). We learn some about John in Josephus but mostly in the New Testament. He preached that God's judgment of a sinful world was at hand. The idea is corroborated by the fact that Jesus' followers, even after his death, believed that they were living at the end of time, that God's judgment was near. Paul, whose writings come first chronologically, conveys this idea.

The idea is also confirmed by the fact that the earliest sources (namely, Mark and Q) are filled with sayings of Jesus that anticipate the imminent end of this age, the coming judgment, and the appearance of God's Kingdom (e.g. Mark 8:38; 13:24–27, 30; Luke 17:24–30; 12:39). Interestingly, this emphasis is muted in later sources. As we have seen, the Gospel of Luke changes Jesus' predictions in Mark that the end is imminent. In the still later Gospel of John, Jesus does not preach at all about the coming Kingdom. And in the still later Gospel of Thomas, Jesus is shown arguing *against* an apocalyptic understanding of salvation. There appears to be a clear trend here: the later the tradition, the less apocalyptic it is. How might one explain the trend? When the earlier expectations of an imminent end did not materialize, were Christians forced to modify their understanding? If so, this would suggest that the expectation of an imminent end was most fervent at the earliest stages—that is, during the life of Jesus himself.

As a preacher of repentance, Jesus taught that the Kingdom of God was near. His first words in Mark's Gospel are a fair summary of his teaching: "The time has been fulfilled, the kingdom of God is near; repent and believe in the good news" (Mark 1:15). Jesus taught that a real Kingdom was coming to earth, one that stood in contrast with the evil kingdoms run by the pagan rulers of earth. This kingdom would be ruled by none other than God, through his human emissary, the messiah. The judgment would be brought by a cosmic judge from heaven, whom Jesus called the Son of Man, probably in reference to a prediction found in the Jewish Scriptures (Dan. 7:13–14) about the end of the present age (Mark 8:38; 14:62). Although in some other Gospel passages, Jesus refers to himself as the "Son of Man," he did not appear to be referring to himself in these sayings (cf., Mark 8:38). The Son of Man would bring cosmic destruction (Mark 13:26–27). This judgment would fall on all people and institutions. Even the Jewish Temple, the seat of the Jewish religion, would be destroyed (Mark 13:1–2). Jesus' prediction of this destruction is attested by multiple sources.

The coming judgment would involve a complete reversal of the present order, in accordance with apocalyptic logic. The first shall be last and the last, first

(Mark 10:30). Those who suffer now will be blessed then (Luke 6:20–23). And people needed to prepare for the coming of the judgment. They should repent of wrongdoing (Mark 1:15). They should give up their power and their wealth, to become like small children and slaves (Mark 10:13–15, 23–30, 42–44). They should give up everything they have for the sake of this coming kingdom (Matthew 13:45–46).

Jesus maintained that other Jewish leaders of his day had misunderstood God's will. Pharisees were wrong in thinking that God was concerned with the letter of the law instead of its spirit. "Sabbath was made for people, not people for the Sabbath" (Mark 2:27–28). Sadducees were wrong in thinking that God was ultimately concerned about the sacrifices in the Jewish temple. "I desire mercy, and not sacrifice" (Matthew 12:7). What God wanted was for people to follow the very heart of his Law, the Torah, as summed up in the two commands to love God above all else (Deut 6:4–6) and to love one's neighbor as oneself (Lev. 19:18). Jesus thought that the entire Law was comprised of these two dictates. Those who lived lives of love would enter into God's kingdom, which was soon to appear with the coming of the Son of Man.

The appearance of this kingdom was imminent (Mark 9:1; 13:30; 14:62). There are two ways to explain the urgency in Jesus' message. He was trying to get the people of Israel to repent before the cosmic judge from heaven arrived, destroying all those—even among the Jews—who stood opposed to God. Those who implemented the ethics of the coming Kingdom would get a foretaste on earth of this apocalyptic realm.

Understanding Jesus as an apocalypticist also explains many of the things that he is known to have done. It explains why he was baptized by John. He associated with John, rather than with one of the many other Jewish teachers and leaders (e.g., among the Pharisees, Sadducees, and Essenes), because he subscribed to John's own apocalyptic message: "The ax is already laid at the root of the trees; therefore every tree that does not produce good fruit will be cut down and cast into the fire" (Luke 3:9). It explains why he went up to Jerusalem during the Passover feast. He wanted to bring his message of hope to the heart of Jerusalem, to announce to his fellow Jews gathered together in hopes of God's deliverance that it was soon to come, but that they must repent in preparation. It explains why he "cleansed" the Temple. He was demonstrating that the coming judge would overthrow all the institutions of power—even the Temple and its sacrificial cult; only those who adhered to Jesus' forewarning would be safe.

It also explains why Jesus was seen to be such a nuisance that he had to be destroyed. Jesus must have attracted crowds during this tumultuous time in Jerusalem. According to the Gospels, he spent a week in the city before the feast, preaching to those who came to worship in the Temple. He offended powerful leaders by his actions in the Temple and his dire predictions against it. The leaders were naturally concerned about riots among the people. We know from Josephus of other disastrous riots occurring during Passover during the 1st century.

> **[Pilate] did to Jesus what he did to two other troublemakers that same morning. He ordered Jesus to be crucified at once. In this case, though, there was a major difference that neither the Jewish leaders nor Pilate could have anticipated.**

We also know from Josephus of other prophets who were predicting the end of the age and were arrested as troublemakers. Jesus, then, was arrested as a troublemaker and handed over to the Roman governor, Pilate. Pilate was concerned with keeping the peace during the incendiary time of the Passover Feast. After a very brief trial, Pilate decided to solve the potential problems caused by Jesus, whom he must have seen as a fanatical religious doomsday preacher, quickly and efficiently. And so, he did to Jesus what he did to two other troublemakers that same morning—and may have done to several others during the course of that week. He ordered Jesus to be crucified at once. In this case, though, there was a major difference that neither the Jewish leaders nor Pilate could have anticipated. In this case, three days after his death, the crucified man was believed to have been restored to life. And that is the beginning of Christianity. ∎

Essential Reading

Ehrman, *Jesus: Apocalyptic Prophet*, chaps. 9–13.

————, *The New Testament: A Historical Introduction*, chap. 15.

Sanders, *The Historical Figure of Jesus*.

Supplemental Reading

Meier, *A Marginal Jew*, vol. 2.

Schweitzer, *Quest of the Historical Jesus*.

Vermes, *Jesus the Jew*.

Questions to Consider

1. What evidence strikes you as most convincing that Jesus was an apocalyptic prophet, anticipating the end of society as we know it through an intervention of God? How does this view differ from what you've previously understood about Jesus?

2. Does understanding Jesus as an apocalypticist have any bearing on the relevance of Christianity in the modern world?

Jesus—The Apocalyptic Prophet
Lecture 12—Transcript

To this point, we have seen that the Gospels of the New Testament are our best sources for reconstructing the life of the historical Jesus. But even these sources cannot be used uncritically. The criteria of independent attestation, dissimilarity, and contextual credibility can assist us in working to get behind the Gospels, to the historical events that they narrate. Unfortunately, because of time constraints, I won't been able to discuss how every tradition that I want to bring up in this lecture passes one or more of these criteria. You can find fuller explanations of these criteria and their application, though, in some of the readings that I have suggested that go along in combination with this course. It is important to stress, in particular, at the outset of this lecture, that the historical context of Jesus involves a particularly influential ideology known as Jewish apocalypticism. In this lecture, I'll explain why many contemporary scholars have understood Jesus as an apocalypticist, and show how an apocalyptic perspective can elucidate the words and deeds of Jesus that can be established as historically plausible.

The idea that Jesus was an apocalypticist, expecting the imminent end of the age as we know it through a decisive intervention of God, is not a new idea among recent scholars. It was first argued convincingly at the beginning of the century by Albert Schweitzer, the great humanitarian and medical missionary in the Belgian Congo. In his classic text, *The Quest of the Historical Jesus*, that he wrote in 1906, after he already had a Ph.D. in philosophy and was lecturing in philosophy, and while he was going to medical school in preparation for his missionary work, he wrote this classic book, *The Quest of the Historical Jesus*. This was an extremely influential book, a very clever (in the good sense), witty, penetrating analysis of the study of Jesus from the 18th century up to Schweitzer's own day, in which Schweitzer portrayed Jesus, for the first time, in a popular publication, as an apocalypticist.

The view proved convincing to many people. In fact, it's the view, in broad outline, that Jesus was an apocalypticist that has been ascribed to by the vast majority of scholars in Germany and in America for most of the 20th century. Nobody any longer agrees with Schweitzer's particular recollection of Jesus' mission, his teaching, and his deeds; but most scholars have, since his writing, thought that Jesus, in some sense, was an apocalypticist. This view has come under attack in recent years by many popular publications. In this lecture, I want to show why the reasons for holding to the view that Jesus was an apocalypticist continue to be compelling.

The idea that Jesus was an apocalypticist is first suggested by the fact that Jesus began his ministry by associating with John the Baptist, an apocalyptic preacher of repentance, rather than with some other Jewish leader of his day. Jesus, of course, could have associated with anybody that he chose, but he chose not to associate with Pharisaic leaders; he didn't associate with Sadducees; there's no record of him associating with Essenes; he was not a member of the Fourth Philosophy. With whom did Jesus decide to associate? With John the Baptist. We learn about John the Baptist from the writings of Josephus, but especially from the New Testament. In the New Testament, our earliest source of the Gospels, probably our earliest source, "Q," we learn something about John the Baptist's preaching. John declared to his audience, "The ax is laid at the root of the tree. Every tree that does not bear fruit will be cut down and cast into the fire." He goes on to urge his followers to repent of their sins. This is an image of judgment. God's judgment was soon coming upon those who did not bear good fruit. The ax already being laid at the root of the tree, suggests imminence. God's act of judgment against a sinful world was imminent. This was John's proclamation, and it is worth noting that Jesus associated with John rather than with somebody else at the very outset of his ministry. As we saw in a previous lecture, this association is supported by the criteria of both independent anastation and dissimilarity, as well, of course, as contextual credibility. This suggests that when Jesus started his ministry, at least, he was an apocalypticist. He was a follower of an apocalyptic preacher, John the Baptist.

The idea that Jesus himself was an apocalypticist is corroborated by the fact that his followers, even after his death, believed that they were living at the end of time, that, in fact, God's judgment was near. This appears to have been the belief of Jesus' earliest followers, as we can tell from the writings of the New Testament themselves. The earliest writings of the New Testament were not the Gospels; the earliest writings of the New Testament are the writings of Paul, and Paul's writings are filled with apocalyptic expectations that the end of the age is near. Jesus begins by associating with an apocalyptic prophet. In the aftermath of Jesus' ministry, we have apocalyptic Christian communities springing up.

What is between John the Baptist and the early Christian church? It is the life of Jesus. Jesus provides the continuity between the apocalyptic beginning and the apocalyptic ending. That suggests that Jesus' ministry itself was apocalyptic. This point of view is confirmed by the fact that the earliest sources we have, for example, Mark and "Q," are filled with sayings of Jesus that anticipate the imminent end of the age, the coming judgment, and the appearance of God's kingdom. For example, Mark Chapter 8, Verse 38, Jesus says, "Whoever is ashamed of me and of my words in this adulterous and sinful generation, of that person will the Son of Man be ashamed, when he comes in the clouds of heaven in the presence of the holy angels." Jesus refers to a coming cosmic judge from heaven, that he calls the Son of Man who will be judging the Earth, judging people on the basis of how they react to Jesus. Jesus later says in Mark Chapter 13, Verses 24 and following: "In those days after that great affliction, the sun will turn dark, the moon will no longer give its light. The stars will be falling from the heavens. The powers that are in the heavens shall be shaken and then the Son of Man will appear coming on the clouds with power and glory. And then he, the Son of Man, will send forth his angels and they will gather up the elect from the four winds—from one corner of the Earth, to a corner of the heaven. There is going to be a cosmic disaster—a catastrophe that happens in the heavens. The Son of Man is going to appear, the elect will be gathered up, they will then be brought into the kingdom."

This kind of saying in which the imminent end of the age is anticipated with a coming judgment and the appearance of God's kingdom is found throughout our earliest sources. Mark and "Q," for example, but also "M" and "L." Interestingly, this emphasis begins to be muted in our later sources. We have seen already, for example, that the Gospel of Luke changes Jesus predictions in Mark that the end is imminent. Luke, writing 10 or 15 years after Mark, changes his predictions of the imminent end. The Gospel of John, as we have already seen, does not have Jesus proclaim the coming kingdom. Jesus, instead, talks about himself, of the eternal life that he can bring; no longer does he have an apocalyptic message of the coming end. The Gospel of

Thomas, later still, argues against an apocalyptic understanding of salvation, as we saw in our study of Thomas. There appears to be a very clear trend here: the later the tradition, the less apocalyptic it is.

How might one explain this trend? Is it that when the earlier expectations of an imminent end did not materialize, Christians had to modify their understanding? If so, this would suggest that it was at the earliest stages, that is, during the life of Jesus himself, that the expectation of an imminent judgment of the world was most fervent. And so, I think that Jesus was probably an apocalypticist. As a preacher of repentance, Jesus taught that the kingdom of God was near. I think that the first words recorded on Jesus' lips from the Gospel of Mark, our earliest serving Gospel, are a fair summary of his teaching. As Jesus says in Mark Chapter 1, Verse 15, "The time has been fulfilled, the kingdom of God is at hand, repent and believe in the good news." Jesus appears to have taught that a kingdom of God was soon to appear. The idea that the time has been fulfilled is an apocalyptic image. This age has a certain amount of allotted time to it, this age of evil. After this age of evil, though, a good kingdom will come. The time has now been fulfilled; the end of the age is here; people need to repent and prepare for the coming kingdom of God. I think that Jesus taught that a real kingdom was coming to Earth, a kingdom that stood in stark contrast with the evil kingdoms that are currently run by the pagan rulers now. This future kingdom would be ruled by none other than God, through his human emissary, the Messiah. Jesus did teach that there would be a future messiah, who would rule God's kingdom.

How, though, would the kingdom come? Jesus appears to have thought that there would be sent from heaven a cosmic judge of the Earth, one whom, as we just saw, Jesus called the Son of Man. I take this to be a reference to a prophecy found in the Hebrew Bible, the book of Daniel, Chapter 7, Verses 13 and 14. In Daniel, Chapter 7, a prophet has a vision of the sequence of kingdoms that are going to take over the Earth. Four kingdoms appear that are represented as beasts coming up out of the sea. Each of these beasts is hideous and terrible and wreaks great havoc on the Earth. After the appearance of the fourth beast, though, the visionary sees one like a son of man coming on the clouds of Heaven. To this one is given the eternal rule over the Earth. Jesus uses this term "one like a son of man" and transforms it to talk about the Son of Man who is coming on the clouds of heaven. This

Son of Man is going to come at the end of the present age, and he will be bringing judgment. Scholars have long debated what Jesus means by this phrase "Son of Man," in part, because the term Son of Man occurs in three different context in Jesus' teaching. Sometimes, Jesus teaches about the Son of Man as one who is about to suffer. These are clear references to himself, where he says, "the Son of Man must go to Jerusalem and be crucified." Other times, Jesus refers to the present activity of the Son of Man: "Foxes have lairs, birds have nests, but the Son of Man has nowhere to lay his head." Again, a reference to himself. But the references to the Son of Man who is coming in judgment do not appear to be self-references. Mark 8:38, Jesus says, "Whoever is ashamed of me, and of my words in this adulterous and sinful generation, of that one will the Son of Man be ashamed when he comes on the clouds of heaven."

There is nothing in this verse to indicate that Jesus was talking about himself. In fact, if you didn't know that he was talking about himself, you wouldn't assume so. Since Christians are modifying the sayings of Jesus, which kind of saying about the Son of Man is likely to be a kind that Christians would have come up with? Well, it appears likely that Jesus' words would have been modified by Christians so as to make it clear that when he's talking about the Son of Man, he is talking about himself, precisely because the Christians thought he was the Son of Man. What about the sayings in which Jesus does not clearly seem to be referring to himself? Those are not the kinds of sayings that it looks like Christians would have invented. Conclusion, those sayings are probably the ones that go back directly to Jesus. For this reason, many scholars think that these sayings about the coming Son of Man actually are things that Jesus said, and that he wasn't referring to himself. The Son of Man is coming on the clouds of heaven. This Son of Man would bring cosmic destruction, as we saw from Mark Chapter 13, sayings that, again, I think go all the way back to Jesus.

This judgment would fall on all people and all institutions, including the Jewish temple, the seat of the Jewish religion, which would be destroyed. I think that Jesus probably did predict the destruction of the Jewish temple. One reason for thinking this, probably the best reason for thinking this, is because it is multiply attested throughout our traditions. Jesus predicts this in Mark, he predicts it in John; there are predictions connected with this in the

Gospel of Thomas. Even in the Book of Acts, there are references to Jesus' prediction of the coming destruction of the temple. It is multiply attested all across the map. As we will see in a minute, it is precisely that prediction of Jesus that ends up getting him in trouble.

The coming judgment would involve a complete reversal of the present order. The logic of apocalypticism is that evil powers are now in control, so that people who side with the evil powers are those who have succeeded and prospered. When the new age comes, God is going to overthrow the forces of evil. When that happens, those who are successful, powerful, and prosperous now will be taken down, and those who are poor and oppressed will be lifted up. So, when Jesus says in Mark Chapter 10, Verse 30, "The first shall be last, and the last first," he's not uttering simply a clever one-liner. He actually means this in an apocalyptic sense. Those who are last now, who are low and downtrodden, will be exalted. Those who are exalted now, will be taken down. Those who suffer now will be blessed then. That's why, in the Beatitudes, Jesus can say, "Blessed are you poor." Why are the poor blessed? It's precisely because when the kingdom comes, their fortunes are going to be reversed. Jesus can say, "Blessed are you who hunger and thirst." Well, why are people that are hungry and thirsty blessed? Because when the kingdom comes, the whole matter is going to be reversed.

Because the kingdom is coming in power with the appearance of the Son of Man, people need to prepare for its coming in the present. They should repent of their wrongdoing, as you saw in Mark Chapter 1, Verse 15: "They should give up their power and their wealth to become like small children and slaves." Jesus welcomes the children because of such is the kingdom of Heaven. His followers shouldn't be like gentile lords; they should be "like slaves serving others" Mark Chapter 10. Why? Because in the coming kingdom, all these values are going to be reversed. Those who are exalted now will be the debased then.

Jesus' followers should give up everything they have for the sake of this coming kingdom. Jesus likens the coming kingdom to a merchant who is in search of a great pearl. When he finds the pearl that he desires, he sells everything he has in order to purchase the pearl. That seems like a ridiculous thing to do, if you sell everything you have to buy a pearl, what do you have? All you got is the pearl. What good does the pearl do you if you have nothing else? It seems absurd, but for Jesus that's exactly how people should value the coming kingdom. It maybe ridiculous, but people should give up everything in view of this coming end.

Jesus maintained that other Jewish leaders of his day had misunderstood God's will. There were a number of controversies between Jesus and other Jewish teachers of his day. Jesus appears to have thought that the Pharisees were wrong in thinking that God was concerned with keeping the Law to the Nth degree. Instead, for Jesus, God was more concerned that people keep the spirit of the Law, or as he puts it in one place, with respect to the Law of the Sabbath, "Sabbath was made for people, not people for the Sabbath." In other words, devising laws so that you can keep the Sabbath isn't really the point. The Sabbath is made for human beings; humans, therefore, themselves, are the lords of the Sabbath. Jesus disagreed with the Sadducees. He thought the Sadducees were wrong in thinking that God was ultimately concerned about sacrifices in the Jewish temple. Yes, of course, God had commanded Jews to sacrifice to him, but as the scripture says, "I desire mercy, not sacrifice," as is quoted in the "M" source, Matthew Chapter 12, Verse 7.

What ultimately mattered to God was that people lived lives that were pleasing to him. What God ultimately wanted was for people to follow the very heart of his Law, the Torah, which for Jesus, as for other Jewish teachers of his day, could be summed up in two principal commandments. The commandment of Deuteronomy Chapter 6: "You should love the Lord your God with all your heart, with all your soul, and with all your strength." And the commandment of the Leviticus Chapter 19, Verse 18: "You should love your neighbor as yourself." Jesus, of course, didn't invent these sayings himself; these were sayings that he draws from the Hebrew Scriptures. Jesus appears to have thought that the very heart of the law was comprised of these two commandments. That is, if people did these two things, loving God and loving their neighbor with their entire hearts, they would enter into the kingdom, which was soon to arrive.

Jesus, in fact, thought that the kingdom was soon to arrive. As he says in Mark Chapter 9, Verse 1: "Some of you standing here won't taste death before you see that the kingdom of God has come in power." Mark Chapter

13, Verse 30: "This generation will not pass away before all these things take place." Mark 14:62: "You will see the Son of Man coming on the clouds of heaven." It is attested in our earliest sources that Jesus thought the end was imminent. This can explain the urgency of Jesus' message. Jesus was trying to get the people of Israel to repent before the cosmic judge from heaven arrived, destroying all those, even among the Jews, who stood opposed to God.

This, I think, is the heart and soul of Jesus' message, that the coming kingdom was soon to arrive with the appearance of the Son of Man. People should begin implementing the ethics of the kingdom in the present. When they began implementing the ethics of the kingdom in the present by loving their neighbor and loving God above all else, they would begin to experience the kingdom in the present. Jesus taught that his followers would have a kind of a foretaste of the kingdom in the here and now if they followed his teaching. In the kingdom there would be no more hatred; Jesus' followers have only love. In the kingdom there would be no more wars; Jesus' followers should work for peace. In the kingdom there would be no oppression; Jesus' followers should work for justice. Those who implement the ideals of the kingdom will begin experiencing the kingdom in a minor, small way now. When the kingdom arrives, then, they will experience it in a big way with the coming of the Son of Man. The kingdom of heaven is like a little mustard seed, just a little inauspicious beginning with Jesus' followers in the present, but it grows into a huge plant; it covers the whole Earth, when the Son of Man arrives.

Understanding Jesus is an apocalypticist explains not only the things that he appears to have taught; also, it explains the things that he appears to have done. It explains, for example, why he was baptized by John. Well, he associated with John rather than with some other Jewish leader because he did subscribe to John's apocalyptic message, that the end was coming soon, and people needed to repent in preparation for it. Jesus' apocalypticism explains why he went to Jerusalem during the Passover feast. He didn't go to Jerusalem for Passover simply to celebrate the festival that so many other Jews had done. He went to bring his message of hope to the heart of Jerusalem, to announce to his fellow Jews gathered together in hopes of God's deliverance that it was soon to come, but that they needed to repent in

191

preparation for its coming. Jesus' apocalyptic views explain why he cleansed the temple. This is a multiply attested tradition that is found in a number of our sources, that when Jesus arrived in Jerusalem for the Passover feast, he entered into the temple and turned over tables and drove out those who were selling sacrificial animals and exchanging money. But why was Jesus doing this; was he opposed to the temple, per se? That's hard to imagine, that Jesus would be opposed to the temple; God had instituted the temple in the Torah. Jesus, though, is enacting violence against the temple. Recent scholars have come to realize that what Jesus is doing is enacting a parable. He has predicting that the temple is going to be destroyed, and he goes into the temple and enacts a destruction, showing that the imminent end was soon to appear, and that the temple would be wiped out in the coming of the Son of Man.

Understanding Jesus as an apocalypticist can explain why Jesus was crucified. When Jesus arrived in Jerusalem, he had spent most of his time up in Galilee, apparently, visiting rural places, villages, small areas. He makes a final trip to the capital city Jerusalem, and it appears that he did attract some crowds during this tumultuous time in Jerusalem. The Passover feast was a time when the size of Jerusalem would swell many times over as people came to celebrate this past deliverance of the people of God in the days of Moses during the Exodus. They would celebrate this annually; people would come from all over the world and swell the size of the Jerusalem. Jesus appears to have attracted crowds by his preaching after he had cleansed the temple. He appears to have offended the powerful leaders there by cleansing the temple. The people in charge of the temple, of course, were the Sadducees, who were comprised principally of priests, who were also the aristocrats among the Jews who had the ear of the Roman governor. They were the liaisons with the governing forces. The leaders of the Jews, the Sadducees, may well have been concerned about riots among the people.

We know from the Jewish historian Josephus of other disastrous riots that occurred during the Passover feasts in the 1st century. This was the one time of the year that the Roman governor would come into Jerusalem with troops; normally he resided in Caesarea. For Passover, he would come into Jerusalem with troops because of the possibility of riots, and many times riots did emerge. We also know from Josephus of other prophets in the 1st century who were predicting the end of the age, and they were arrested as troublemakers and prosecuted. Jesus himself was arrested as a troublemaker and handed over to the Roman governor Pilate. It was Pilate's major concern as a governor of Judea to keep the peace, especially during the incendiary time of the Passover feast. It appears that, after a very brief trial, that may not have taken more than a couple of minutes, Pilate decided to solve the potential problems caused by Jesus; in other words, the problems that he might go out again and preach this coming destruction by God and get people's hopes up and possibly cause a riot against the Romans. In order simply to solve the problem, Pilate did with Jesus what he must have done with lots of other people that he considered to be religious fanatics in his day. With other doomsday preachers, with other revolutionaries, he simply ordered him to be crucified. He did the same thing with two other troublemakers the same morning.

In the Roman provinces, there was no such thing as what we might think of as "due process." No chance of appeal, no long wait for a capital punishment to be executed. Jesus was taken off, and he was crucified that very morning. Neither Pilate nor the Jewish leaders, of course, could have anticipated what was going to happen next. Three days after Jesus' crucifixion, his followers came to say that he was restored to life; and that was the beginning of Christianity.

In conclusion, we have seen, in this lecture, that Jesus is best understood as a 1st century Jewish apocalypticist. He taught that societies he knew would be soon destroyed with the arrival of the cosmic judge from heaven, the Son of Man. Jesus urged the people of Israel to repent before it was too late. Many of his actions reflected this apocalyptic message. It was also, in the end, what led him to be executed as a rebel rouser. Rather than to risk a riot, the Jewish authorities turned Jesus over to the ruling governor, who ordered him to be crucified. In our next lecture, we'll move to consider what happened next as Christianity emerged into the Greco-Roman world following the death of Jesus, as recounted in the only history of the church that we have from the period, the Book of Acts.

The Acts of the Apostles
Lecture 13

This is our earliest account of Church history, the earliest account we have of the events that transpired after Jesus' death as Christianity spread throughout the Roman Empire.

To this point, we have been considering the Gospels of the New Testament and the life of the historical Jesus; it is now time to move on to Christianity as it developed after Jesus' death. The earliest account we have about the ancient Christian movement is the Book of Acts, which comes from the pen of Luke, author of the third Gospel. We don't know what his real name was, of course. Like the Gospel, the Book of Acts is anonymous. As we have seen, there was an early Christian tradition that Luke was the traveling companion of the apostle Paul. The four "we" passages indicate that the author was close to Paul. Because the Acts cover the spread of Christianity among the Gentiles, the author may have been a Gentile. There was one such Gentile physician named Luke, but many scholars question the validity of that tradition. On the other hand, the author may have had access to other sources. One thing is clear, no matter who wrote the Acts, Paul is the hero of this narrative, the man most responsible for the spread of Christianity throughout the Roman world.

The book's title is a bit of a misnomer. The apostles do not figure prominently in it. The main players are the apostle Peter (chapters 1–12) and the newly converted apostle Paul (chapters 13–28). In another sense, the real player is the Holy Spirit, who is seen directing all the action from behind the scenes.

The Book of Acts is chiefly concerned with the spread of the Christian church after the death of Jesus. Its overall structure and many of its themes are set up in the opening episode (1:1–11). The disciples meet with Jesus after his resurrection, and he instructs them that the end of all things is not yet at hand. They are anxious for the Kingdom of Israel to be restored. They will soon be empowered by the Holy Spirit to be Jesus' witnesses. They are to spread the good news of his death and resurrection throughout the world "in Jerusalem and all Judea, in Samaria, and unto the ends of the earth" (1:8).

The rest of the narrative describes how the apostles came to be empowered by the Holy Spirit and began to multiply by converting nonbelievers—first Jews, then Gentiles—to faith in Jesus, despite numerous obstacles. On the Day of Pentecost, 50 days after Passover, the Holy Spirit descends upon them and enables them to preach the Gospel in foreign tongues (2:5–13) and to do great miracles to validate their message (3:1–10). Masses of people convert at their preaching, many thousands in Jerusalem alone (2:41; 4:4; 5:14). The apostles organize communities of believers who gather together for worship and fellowship and who share all their goods in common (2:43–47). The Jewish leaders try to silence the apostles, to no avail (5:5–22). The Jewish leaders eventually drive the apostles out of Jerusalem. Rather than slowing them down, this accelerates their mission, as they take the gospel to other lands.

The most significant convert is a former persecutor of the Christians, the pharisaically trained and highly influential Saul, also known as Paul. On the way to persecute Christians in the city of Damascus, Paul has a vision of Jesus and becomes an ardent believer (chap. 9). Paul becomes a great missionary to the Gentiles, going on three missionary journeys throughout Syria, Asia Minor (modern-day Turkey), Macedonia, and Achaia (modern-day Greece). A major conflict emerges in the Christian churches over whether Gentiles (non-Jews) should be required to convert to Judaism (viz., by being circumcised if they are men) before joining the Christian church. At an important conference (chap. 15), Paul's view is endorsed; that is, that salvation comes to all people and circumcision is not necessary. Paul arouses significant opposition among Jews and at their instigation is eventually arrested as a troublemaker (chap. 21). The rest of the narrative (chaps. 21–28) show Paul on trial on various occasions— defending himself as someone who has

Perry–Castañeda Library, University of Texas at Austin.

After his conversion to Christianity, Paul became the faith's best-known missionary.

never renounced Judaism or created any problems for the state; his Roman judges are invariably convinced, but they refuse to release him for fear of the Jewish reaction. Paul is eventually sent to Rome to stand trial before the emperor. The book ends with him in Rome, under house arrest, preaching to everyone who will come to hear him.

Scholars have long recognized reasons for doubting the historical accuracy of aspects of this narrative. In several places, the same event is narrated more than once, and internal inconsistencies appear (e.g., Paul's conversion in chaps. 9, 22, and 26: did the bystanders hear the voice but see nothing, or did they hear nothing but see a bright light? Were they left standing or knocked to the ground?). Even more telling, we have the writings of Paul himself, and he often tells a different story from what we find in Acts.

> **The most significant convert is a former persecutor of the Christians ... Paul. On the way to persecute Christians in the city of Damascus, Paul has a vision of Jesus and becomes an ardent believer.**

After Paul converted, did he go right to Jerusalem to meet with the apostles (Acts 9) or did he intentionally stay away for three years (Gal. 1)? Was the conference to determine whether Gentiles should be circumcised Paul's third trip there (Acts 15) or his second (Gal. 1)? At this conference, was there widespread agreement (Acts 15) or did Paul have to twist some arms (Gal. 2)? Did Paul think that God had overlooked pagan acts of idolatry because they were committed in ignorance (Acts 17) or did he think that God was wrathful in his judgment against such acts because pagans were fully aware of what they were doing (Romans 1)? For almost every point of comparison, one can find discrepancies between the accounts of Acts and Paul's own writings.

It would be a mistake, though, to discount Acts for this reason. Just as the Gospels are not an attempt to give a disinterested historical sketch of Jesus' life for modern-day scholars, so too Acts is not an attempt to give a disinterested historical sketch of the life of the early Church. Like the

Gospels, Acts attempts to explain the significance of what happened in early Christianity, not to provide some kind of data-driven report.

The Book of Acts paints the earliest history of Christianity in theological hues. To understand the author's point, we must see what his particular slant on the narrative was. (Notably, many of themes can already be found in the author's first volume.) There are many literary parallels between Luke and Acts. The proclamation of this gospel was made possible by the power of God, through the Holy Spirit. The early Christian evangelists and missionaries were not acting on their own but were empowered from on high. For that reason, their proclamation could not be stopped or even hindered (cf., 5:33–39). This proclamation came first to the Jewish people, many of whom accepted it, but most rejected it. Note that nothing in this proclamation stands contrary to the Jewish religion itself. The rejection of God's salvation by the Jews led to its acceptance by the Gentiles.

The spread of salvation did not happen only geographically (throughout the world) but also ethnically (among all people—Jews, Samaritans, and Gentiles). Gentiles, therefore, did not need to be circumcised to receive it. For the author of Acts—in opposition to other early Christians—a Gentile did not have to become a Jew to be a Christian. Moreover, this spread of the church was according to the plan of God. This means that, for this author, God never intended for the end to come right away, even though earlier believers had thought so (based, as we've seen, on the teachings of Jesus himself) (see Acts 1:6–8). The believers who formed the Christian church were in complete internal harmony with one another—there were no major conflicts that could not be resolved easily and harmoniously. Ultimately, it was God who was behind the scene, directing every event that led to the ultimate triumph of Christianity.

These are theological views, not historical data. Historians who want to know what actually happened during the early years of Christianity must approach this text critically, applying rigorous criteria to its narrative, much as they do to the Gospels to uncover the words and teachings of the historical Jesus.

In conclusion, Acts is the first historical sketch we have of the early Christian movement. It traces the spread of the Christian church from Jew to Gentile, from Jerusalem to the ends of the earth. The major players at the beginning of the narrative are the apostles (especially Peter), but the focus of attention soon shifts to the most significant convert of the Church, the apostle Paul, who is largely responsible for the Christian missions. This book continues many of the themes we found in the Gospel of Luke; it stresses the theological point that the powerful hand of God was at work behind early Christianity, bringing success to its missionaries and peace and harmony among its innumerable converts. The book is not concerned with providing accurate data for modern historians who are interested in the brute facts of the early Christian movement. The book's characters are historical figures, the most significant of whom is the apostle Paul, whose story takes up two-thirds of the book's narrative. In our next lecture, we will turn to Paul himself, to learn about the person that most scholars would agree was the most important figure in the history of Christianity outside of Jesus. ■

Essential Reading

The Book of Acts.

Brown, *Introduction to the New Testament*, chap. 10.

Ehrman, *The New Testament: A Historical Introduction,* chap. 9.

Supplemental Reading

Powell, *What Are They Saying About Acts?*

Questions to Consider

1. If there are reasons for doubting the historical accuracy of Acts, how do you suppose scholars could use it as a historical source for reconstructing the early days of the Christian movement?

2. Discuss the ways that the Book of Acts continues the themes and theological perspectives found in the Gospel of Luke.

The Acts of the Apostles
Lecture 13—Transcript

Now that we are half-way through our course on the New Testament it is time to move beyond our discussion of Jesus and the Gospels. It has been appropriate to spend half of our course on the first four books of the New Testament, because in terms of total bulk, they make up more than half of the New Testament itself. But there are 23 other books that we need to consider. In this lecture we are going to consider the fifth book of the New Testament, the Book of Acts, which picks up the story after Jesus' death and resurrection and begins to narrate an account of the spread of Christianity by Jesus' apostles after his death.

This is our earliest account of Church history, the earliest account we have of the events that transpired after Jesus' death as Christianity spread throughout the Roman Empire. The account comes from the same author who wrote our third Gospel, traditionally called Luke. It is somewhat unfortunate that the third Gospel and the Book of Acts have been separated within our canon by the Gospel of John. The sequence of our Gospels, in our English Bibles at least, was determined to some extent by the Greek manuscripts of the New Testament, even though in the Greek manuscript there are different sequences for our Gospels. In most of the manuscripts we have the Gospel of John is last, probably because most people thought the Gospel of John was the last book to have been written among the Gospels. But the unfortunate result of that is that Acts is separated from its companion volume, the Book of Luke.

We don't know, of course, who the author of this book was—like the Gospel, the Book of Acts is anonymous. There was, though, an early Christian tradition that said that both Luke and Acts were written by a traveling companion of the Apostle Paul. There is, in fact, some evidence to suggest that the Book of Acts was written by one of Paul's traveling companions. This would be a significant conclusion to draw precisely because Paul is the main character of the Book of Acts, and so one if his traveling companions wrote this narrative, you would expect it to have particular credence as an historical document.

The evidence comes in four passages in the Book of Acts, where the author stops talking in the third person about what Paul and other people were doing and begins to talk in the first person about we were doing—four passages in the Book of Acts that are called the "we" passages. Who is this person who is accompanying Paul on some of his journeys who discusses himself as one of his companions? Well, one of the principal concerns of the Book of Acts, of course, as I have indicated in an earlier lecture, is the spread of Christianity outside of the realm of Judaism to the realm of the Gentiles. Christianity is taken outside of Judaism. It becomes a religion of Gentiles. Well, so the companion of Paul would be somebody who is interested in Gentiles, possible he himself is a Gentile.

What Gentile companions of Paul do we know about? In Paul's own letters he mentions several of his traveling companions, one of them is a person named Luke, that Paul in the Book of Colossians calls the beloved physician. The tradition, then, is that it was this person, the beloved physician Luke, who is Paul's traveling companion, who produced the Book of Acts. There is some evidence for it, in these four "we" passages. Unfortunately, Luke himself is never mentioned in the Book of Acts. The author doesn't say that he was Luke. Moreover these "we" passages are not completely convincing as evidence that a traveling companion of Paul wrote this book. When you look at these "we" passages, for example in chapter 16 of the Book of Acts, they begin very abruptly, almost right in the middle of a sentence, and they end very abruptly right in the middle of a sentence. In other words, the author doesn't say, and then I joined up with Paul and we did this, that, or the other thing. Suddenly, in the middle of the narrative, the author starts saying "we".

Some scholars suspect that what is going on is that the author has had available to him some sources, much as he had sources available for the Gospels, and that he has incorporated these sources in his narrative of Paul's activities, and that one of these sources may have been some kind of travel diary or travel log by one of Paul's companions that is simply incorporated wholesale into the narrative. That would explain why suddenly he begins to say "we", because that is where this new source picks up, so that on four occasions he would have been using this travel log as one of his sources. If that's the case, then, in fact, these "we" passages don't indicate that the entire thing was written by one of Paul's traveling companions. There is nothing in the text, again, to suggest that it happened to be somebody named Luke, and nothing about the document that suggests it happened to be written by a physician.

One thing is correct, though, about this early Christian tradition that the book was written by one of Paul's traveling companions, namely, that Paul himself is the clear hero of this narrative. Paul is the man who is most responsible for the spread of Christianity throughout the Roman world, even though Paul himself was not one of Jesus' own disciples. The book is called the Acts, sometimes called the Acts of the Apostles. This title for the book is probably a bit of a misnomer. The apostles, as an whole or as a group, simple don't figure prominently in this book. They are mentioned at the outset, the 11 apostles, and then there is an election to replace Judas, who has died, so there are 12 apostles. But the 12 don't figure prominently in the book. The main players in this book are Peter, in chapters 1 through 12, and then Paul in chapters 13 through 28. In another sense though, for this author the real player is the Holy Spirit, who is seen directing all of the action behind the scenes.

Since this is a narrative of the spread of Christianity, I would like to introduce the book by discussing the flow of the narrative—what actually happens in the course of the book. In terms of its overarching structure and many of its themes, we have a very nice introduction to what's going to happen in the opening episode of the book—chapter 1, verses 1 through 11. In this opening episode we are told that Jesus has been raised from the dead and that he meets with his apostles before ascending into heaven. They've been staying in Jerusalem. Jesus meets with them after he has been raised from the dead, and he tells them that they need to wait because they are going to be baptized with the Holy Spirit. The disciples want to know: Lord, is this the time that you will now restore the kingdom to Israel. In other words, is the Kingdom of God going to come now. And Jesus replies, It's not up to you to know the times or the seasons when the kingdom will come, instead you need to wait to receive power from on high. The Holy Spirit is going to come upon you, and—chapter 1, verse 8—"you will be my witnesses in Jerusalem, in all Judea and Samaria, and to the ends of the earth." This is a kind of outline for what happens in the Book of Acts. The apostles are going to receive empowerment from the Spirit, and they are going to be

Jesus' witnesses spreading his good news, first in Jerusalem, then Judea, then Samaria, and then to the ends of the earth to the Gentile lands. When Jesus says this, then, they are looking upon him and he is lifted up, he ascends into heaven, a cloud takes him from their sight. Two men appear, these may be angels, who say, "Men of Galilee, why do you stand looking up toward heaven? This Jesus, who has been taken up from you into heaven, will come back again in the same way as you saw him go." So Jesus is going to return, but it is not going to happen right away.

Well, as is predicted in these early verses of the Book of Acts, the narrative goes on to describe the events. Fifty days later, on the Day of Pentecost—the Day of Pentecost is named Pentecost because the word pente, five, for 50 days—this is a festival that takes place 50 days after the Passover. Jesus was killed during the Passover, 50 days later during the festival of Pentecost, the Holy Spirit does come upon the apostles. They are gathered together, the Spirit descends about them, they see flames—looks like tongues of fire over their heads—they begin speaking foreign languages that they don't know. People who are gathered in Jerusalem, Jews from all over the world who are gathered together, hear the Gospel preached in their own languages, the Spirit empowers the apostles to preach the message in languages of these other people and many people then convert. This is the beginning then of the Christian church.

The apostles go about preaching their message and converting thousands of people. Masses of people convert at their preaching because of their empowerment through the Spirit. Chapter 2, verse 41—3,000 people convert at one time. Chapter 4, verse 4—5,000 more people convert. Chapter 5, verse 14—many more people convert, thousands upon thousands of people converting in Jerusalem. These people are not just disparate converts who then go off on their own way. The apostles organized the communities of believers, who then gathered together for worship and fellowship. Moreover, these communities in Jerusalem all share their goods in common. They sell what they own, they contribute to a common pool, and then they live communally together—chapter 2, verses 43 to 47. The Jewish leaders in Jerusalem, according to this account, don't much like the fact that the Christians are having such success. They thought that they had gotten rid of the problem by having Jesus executed. But, in fact, Jesus' apostles attract more crowds obviously then even Jesus did, and so in this narrative we are told that the Jewish leaders try to silence the apostles. They imprison them, they order them to silence, but nothing can stop them. Eventually, the Jewish leaders drive the apostles out of Jerusalem thinking that that will slow down the progress of their mission. But, in fact, rather than slowing it down, this accelerates the Christian mission because now the apostles are forced to take their message to other lands.

Among all of the early converts in this book, the most significant is a former persecutor of the Christians. The Pharisaically trained and highly influential Saul, who is also known as Paul. People sometimes mistakenly think that Saul was this person's name and then when he converted he became Paul. That's not quite right, his Hebrew name is Saul, his Greek name is Paul—just two different languages. This fellow Saul was a persecutor of the Christians. He was a Pharisee himself. On one of his trips outside of Jerusalem to persecute the Christians, he was going to the city Damascus and, according to Chapter 9 of the Book of Acts, he has a vision of Jesus himself and becomes an ardent believer. Paul then becomes a great missionary to the Gentiles, going on three missionary journeys in this book. A good deal of this book has to do with Paul's missionary journeys to Syria; Asia Minor, which is modern-day Turkey; Macedonia; and Achaia, modern-day Greece. A major conflict emerges within the Christian churches as a result of Paul's missions to the Gentiles over whether Gentiles, that is non-Jews, should be required to convert to Judaism if they are to be followers of Jesus. Most specifically, the question is do Gentile men have to be circumcised and thereby join the Jewish religion before coming members of the Christian church. Paul is converting people—Gentiles—to be Christians without being Jews. Other people are saying that of course this is a Jewish religion. Jesus is the Jewish Messiah sent from the Jewish God in fulfillment of the Jewish Law and so anybody who belongs to this religion has to be Jewish. And so there is a controversy. The controversy is resolved in chapter 15 of this book when Paul and his companion, Barnabas, go to Jerusalem to confer with the apostles about the matter. There is a major conference there and everybody at the conference agrees to endorse Paul's view that salvation comes to all people whether they are circumcised or not, that circumcision is not necessary for salvation. There was great rejoicing among the Gentile believers at the conclusion of this conference.

Paul rouses significant opposition among Jews in his mission, Jews in the very cities to which he goes. In addition to converting people, he has people that he makes irate, they persecute him in a variety of ways, driving him out of town, sometimes actually flogging him or stoning him. Eventually, at the instigation of his Jewish opponents, Paul is arrested as a troublemaker in Jerusalem, in chapter 21, and the rest of the narrative, chapters 21 through 28, shows Paul on trial on various occasions defending himself as someone who has never renounced Judaism or created any problems for the state. Paul's Roman judges are invariable convinced by his defense, but they refuse to release him for fear of the Jewish reaction. At the end of the book, Paul is sent to Rome to stand trial before the emperor. The book concludes then with him in Rome under house arrest, preaching the Gospel to everyone who will come near him.

So the Book of Acts begins with Jesus saying that the apostles need to take the Gospel, spread the good news from Jerusalem to the ends of the earth. And the book ends then with Paul preaching the Gospel in the heart of the empire, the city of Rome itself, the capital city, so that now Jesus' injunction has been fulfilled by the end of the book. Since this is the only surviving account of early Christianity that we have from the period, we might ask how accurate it is as a historical document. Scholars, in fact, have had reasons for questioning the historical accuracy of the Book of Acts. There is a range of opinions on this among scholars. There are some scholars who think that Acts is highly reliable, there are some who think that Acts is completely untrustworthy, and most people somewhere probably in the middle.

There are good reason, though, for doubting a number of the details of Acts' account, and I am going to look at two kinds of evidence. The first I am going to do very briefly, it has to do with internal inconsistencies of the narrative. If you have a historical source, of course you would hope that the source would be consistent with itself, that would show some basic concern at least for reliability. Acts narrates in several instances the same event twice or three times. When it does so, often inconsistencies emerge. I will just give you one example. In Acts we have the conversion of Paul narrated in chapter 9. Paul narrates the events leading up to his conversion himself on two other occasions, once in chapter 22 and once in chapter 26. Unfortunately, these three accounts have minor inconsistencies between them that make you question whether the author is really striving to give a disinterested account of what really happened. You can read these accounts for yourself and just do a comparison. This is sort of a classic instance of inconsistency.

Paul is traveling with some companions. Well, his companions—the way it works is Paul sees this bright light, he falls to the ground, he hears a voice saying Saul, Saul, why are you persecuting me, and he has this conversation with Jesus, he is blinded by the light, but then he comes to realize that Jesus has been raised from the dead. Well, he had some companions with him, did his companions hear the voice of Jesus, but not see him, or did they see this light, that was Jesus, but hear nothing? Well, it depends which of the accounts you are reading, it is just the opposite between chapter 9 and chapter 22. Were these companions left standing because they didn't see anything, or were they knocked to the ground with Paul. Well, it depends if you are reading chapter 9 or chapter 24—minor little inconsistencies that might suggest that the author is not principally concerned with giving a completely accurate account of what really happened.

More important, though, is that there are inconsistencies between this account and other accounts that we have of the same events. Luckily we have a number of writings by Paul himself in the New Testament. Paul sometimes talks about his own life, Acts talks about his life, and so we can compare the two. It is striking that whenever you compare what Paul says about himself and what Acts says about himself, they seem to differ. Let me just give you a couple of examples. Right after Paul's conversion in the Book of Acts, he is in Damascus, he's been converted, when he leaves Damascus, where does he immediately go? He goes to Jerusalem to talk to the apostles—Acts chapter 9. That's striking, because Paul also talks about what happened to him after he converted in Galatians chapter 1, and in Galatians 1, Paul is completely insistent that when he came to believe in Jesus, "I did not go Jerusalem to consult with those who are apostles before me." Paul makes a big point that he didn't go to Jerusalem for three years. Now Paul has his own reason for insisting on this. His own reasons are that he doesn't want anybody to think that he got his Gospel message from the apostles, he got it straight from God in a revelation from Jesus. He proves that by pointing out to people in Galatians, "I didn't even go to Jerusalem right away", but in Acts that's exactly what he does. Well that would be a kind of inconsistency.

There is this conference, in Acts chapter 15, which is meant to decide whether Gentiles have to be circumcised. According to Acts, this is Paul's third trip to Jerusalem. Paul is insistent in Galatians chapters 1 and 2 that it's his second trip. He doesn't want people to think that he has been going back and forth to Jerusalem a lot. At this conference, was there a wide spread agreement among everybody who was there, that in fact Gentile don't have to be circumcised, that is what Acts 15 indicates. Paul seems to indicate that he had to twist some arms in a back room, Galatians chapter 2, to get the apostles to agree.

These are the kinds of inconsistencies you find between Paul and the Book of Acts. Another one that has struck scholars over the years is the content of Paul's preaching, the content of Paul's proclamation to Gentiles. We have sermons in the Book of Acts where Paul tries to convert pagans to believe. And Paul himself refers to what he preached. It's interesting to compare the two. In Acts chapter 17, Paul is preaching to a group of philosophers on the Areopagus in Athens. And Paul tells these people, these philosophers, that God has overlooked the ignorance of idolatry. Paul says that people committed idolatry because they didn't know any better, and since they didn't know any better, God has overlooked it, but now they have a chance to realize that they have been wrong and to turn to God. In Romans chapter 1, Paul also talks about idolatry. In Romans 1 it is very clear that Paul does not think that it is an act of ignorance. People who commit idolatry, who worship idols, according to Romans 1, don't do so out of ignorance, they do so out of willfulness. They know precisely that there is only one God. They worship idols because they reject the one God, and because this is an act of the will and knowledge, God condemns people who do this. It is just the opposite message that Paul gives in Acts chapter 17. Now it may be that Paul simply changed his message depending on his audience, or he may, maybe you could conclude that in Acts 17 he is preaching what he doesn't really think. I suppose that's possible. It is also possible that Acts has one perspective on Paul, and Paul has a different perspective on Paul.

How accurate is the Book of Acts? Well as I have said there is a spectrum of opinion. In my opinion, the Book of Acts is about as accurate on Paul as the Book of Luke is on Jesus. There are some historically accurate material here, but there has also been changes as this author has attempted to provide a narration of the events. I think it would be a mistake though to discount the Book of Acts for this reason. Just as the Gospels are not trying to give a disinterested historical sketch of Jesus' life for modern-day scholars, so too, Acts is not trying to give a disinterested historical sketch of the early church. Like the Gospels, it is trying to explain the significance of what happened in early Christianity. It is not trying to provide some kind of data-driven dry report. Acts in fact is a literary text with theological motifs.

The literary character of Acts can be seen in a number of ways. This author is, in fact, someone who is skilled in writing literature. It is interesting, for example, to compare Luke and Acts—the narratives of Jesus and the early church—because there are a number of similarities that the authors obviously put in there intentionally. Jesus, in the Book of Luke, is baptized and he receives the Spirit. In the Book of Acts, the believers in Jesus are baptized, they receive the Spirit. After Jesus receives the Spirit in the book of Luke, he is empowered to do miracles, and so he heals the sick, he casts out demons, he raises the dead. In the Book of Acts, the apostles of Jesus after they received the Spirit can do miracle, they heal the sick, they casts out demons, they raise the dead. In the Book of Luke, Jesus is opposed by the Jewish authorities. In the Book of Acts, his followers are opposed by the Jewish authorities. In the book of Luke, because he is rejected by the Jews, Jesus' message goes to the Gentiles. In Acts, because the apostles are rejected by the Jews, their message goes to the Gentiles. There is literary artistry going on here in the parallels between Luke and Acts. This literary character in the Book of Acts needs to be taken seriously because it shows that this book is not trying simply to give the raw facts of history, but is trying to paint the history of early Christianity in theological hues.

I want to spend the rest of this lecture just detailing some of the theological emphases that one finds in the Book of Acts, understanding that this is intending to be a theological account. This author wants to emphasize that the proclamation of the Gospel of Jesus was made possible by the power of God. This is a major theological point of his. It is because the Holy Spirit of God has come upon the church that the mission is made possible. The early Christian evangelists and missionaries are not acting on their own. They are empowered from on high. For that reason, according to this author, the Christian mission cannot be stopped. This is another overarching motif.

207

People try to shut down this mission, especially the Jewish leaders, but they can't do it because God is behind it. At one place early in the narrative of Acts, chapter 5, one of the Jewish leaders stands up and says that we shouldn't oppose this movement, because if it is not from God, then it will fail, but if it is from God and we oppose it, then we will be opposing God. That's the theme of this book, that in fact if you oppose the Christian mission, you are opposing God.

The proclamation in this book comes first to the Jewish people, many of whom accept it and convert, but most of whom reject it. This author wants to emphasize though that there is nothing in the proclamation that stands contrary to the Jewish religion itself. The rejection of this message, though, by the Jews, leads to its acceptance by the Gentiles. The mission then spreads, not just geographically as it moves out from Jerusalem into Judea and Samaria and on into Gentile lands, it also spreads in what we might say ethnically, from Jews to Samaritans, who were thought to be sort of half Jews, Gentiles. The Gentiles who accept this message do not need to be circumcised in order to receive it. A Gentile does not have to be a Jew in order to be a Christian. That's an important point for this book, because there are a lot of early Christians, of course, who thought completely otherwise. The spread of the church, for this author, is going according to the plan of God. One implication of that is that, according to this author, God never intended the end to come right away. The message is deapocalypticized a bit. The end wasn't supposed to come right away because the church first had to be formed. Behind it all, of course, for this author is God himself. These are theological views, not historical data.

Historians who want to know what actually happen during the early years of Christianity therefore need to approach the text of Acts critically. They have to apply criteria to this text, much as we apply criteria to the Gospels to figure out what really happened. It is best to understand this book as a kind of theologically driven narrative of the spread of early Christianity. So in conclusion, this Book of Acts is our first historical sketch of the early Christian movement that traces the spread of the church from Jew to Gentile. It's main players are Peter at the beginning, and Paul throughout most of the narrative. The book continues many of themes that we found in the Gospel of Luke. In particular, the book is far less concerned to provide historically accurate data for modern historians who are interested in the brute facts of the early Christian movement than it is to give a theological sketch of what this movement was all about. But the characters is this book are all historical figures, the most significant of whom is the Apostle Paul. In our next lecture we will turn to Paul himself to learn about this person, that most scholars would agree is the most important figure in early Christianity outside of Jesus.

Paul—The Man, the Mission, and the *Modus Operandi*
Lecture 14

It is safe to say that Paul was the most significant early convert to Christianity—one who moved from being the greatest persecutor of the faith to being its greatest apostle.

In the last lecture, we saw that the hero of the Book of Acts was the apostle Paul, who more than anyone was responsible for the spread of the Christian movement from its small beginnings in Jerusalem out into the wider Roman world. Most historians would agree with Luke that apart from Jesus, Paul was the most important figure in the history of early Christianity. We now move into a study of Paul himself, based on the letters that happen to survive in the New Testament. These are the *only* works that survive from Paul's hand. In this lecture, we will consider some of the difficulties associated with trying to understand the writings of Paul, then provide some biographical background on his life. The study of Paul is complicated by several difficulties.

As we have already seen, one of the principle sources for knowing about Paul is the Book of Acts, which must be treated critically. In places where Paul and Acts both speak about the same event, discrepancies emerge. Sometimes these are minor (where he was and when and with whom); sometimes, major (what his proclamation to the Gentiles entailed). Moreover, Acts provides some information about Paul that is not corroborated in his letters and must, therefore, be taken gingerly (e.g., that he was a Roman citizen and that he came from Tarsus in the region of Cilicia). How did he proceed on his mission? Acts says he started in the synagogue; in his own writing, Paul does not reflect this.

There are other examples of discrepancies between Acts and Paul's own letters, as well. Some of the writings that appear under Paul's name were probably not written by him. There are a number of Pauline writings outside of the New Testament that are clearly forgeries, as we will see more fully in a later lecture (e.g., "Third" Corinthians). Even in the New Testament, there are "Pauline" books whose authorship is debated. Most scholars, for example, are convinced that Paul did not write the books of 1 and 2 Timothy and Titus (called the "Pastoral" epistles, because they deal with how these pastors should oversee their churches). Scholars continue to dispute whether Paul wrote three other books that claim him as an author: Colossians, Ephesians, and 2 Thessalonians. These books, therefore, are designated the Deutero-Pauline epistles; that is, epistles that have a secondary standing in the Pauline canon. The seven remaining letters—Romans, 1 and 2 Corinthians, Galatians, Philippians, 1 Thessalonians, and Philemon—are designated the "undisputed" Pauline epistles, because virtually everyone agrees that Paul wrote them. Any study of Paul is best served to restrict itself to the letters he is known to have produced.

All of Paul's letters were "occasional" in nature. These are not systematic treatises on set topics, but letters written to address actual concerns that arose in Paul's churches. We should not expect these letters to cover every topic of importance to Paul. For example, Paul mentions the "Lord's Supper" in only one passage, 1 Cor. 11, because the Corinthians were not observing it correctly; if they had been, we never would have known that Paul found its observance to be important.

A careful study of Paul's letters, with an eye to the Book of Acts for corroboration, reveals several important pieces of biographical information on Paul, which can serve as the backdrop for our study. Paul was born and raised a Jew, committed to the traditions of Pharisaism; he was steeped in and deeply attached to the Law of Moses as given by God (Gal. 1:13–14; Phil. 3:4–6). In fact, Paul is the only surviving Pharisaic author from before the destruction of the Temple in Jerusalem. He seems to have been raised outside of Palestine and evidently did not know Jesus. He spoke and wrote Greek and appears not to have understood the Semitic languages of the region.

For some reason, when he learned about the early Christian movement as an adult, he found it blasphemous and dangerous (Gal. 1:13). He may have shared a traditional view that the messiah was to be a figure of grandeur and power and found that the proclamation that the messiah was a crucified criminal—one who was, therefore, cursed by God (Deut. 27:26;

cf., Gal. 3:13)—to be utterly blasphemous. He may have found the Christian claim that salvation came to non-Jews apart from Jewish Law to be completely offensive.

He actively persecuted the Christians (Gal. 1:13). He had some kind of visionary experience of Jesus that changed his life (Gal. 1:15–16; 1 Cor. 15:8). Even though Acts describes the event in some detail (Acts 9, 22, 26), Paul is more elusive. It appears, though, that he had some kind of vision of Jesus (Gal. 1:16; 1 Cor. 15:8). This experience completely transformed his understanding of Jesus. Paul's thought process seems to have worked backward from his conviction that Jesus really was raised from the dead, based on Paul's own vision of him. Rather than being a dead criminal, Jesus was the living Savior. Because God had showered such favor on Jesus after his death, his death must not have been an accident or a mere miscarriage of justice, but the plan of God. Rather than the one who was cursed by God, Jesus was the one man more than any other who was ultimately blessed by God. Because Jesus, as God's blessed one, could not have borne the curse of death for anything he had done, he must have borne it for others. That is to say, Jesus' death was a sacrifice for the sins of others. A person's sins can, therefore, be removed if he or she will accept that sacrifice by faith, or trust in Christ's death for salvation.

Having a right standing before God must come through Christ's death and resurrection, and nothing else. For this reason, the Jewish Law cannot be the way to attain a right standing before God; Jesus' death is the only way. Rather than continuing on as a Pharisee, urging Jews to keep the Law more perfectly and Gentiles to start keeping the Law through being circumcised, Paul came to promote faith in Christ as the way of salvation. There could be no other way: Salvation comes to all people, Jew and Gentile, through the death of Jesus. Thus, Paul became the leading proponent of the view that Gentiles, along with Jews, could belong to the people of God. As a result, he became an influential missionary, taking the message of Christ principally to the Gentiles.

Not only did Paul change his views about Jesus and the way to salvation, he also came to see the significance of Jesus' resurrection for the history of the world. As a Pharisee, Paul already believed in an apocalyptic form of Judaism. Apocalypticists believed that there would be a resurrection of dead bodies at the end of the age, when all would come to face judgment. Jesus, though, had already been raised. This shows that the end has already begun. Paul refers to Jesus as the "first-fruits" of the resurrection (e.g., 1 Cor. 15:23). He anticipated that the full resurrection would occur soon, within his lifetime (cf., 1 Thess. 4:13–18). That explains, in part, the urgency of his mission to spread the Gospel throughout the world before the end arrived.

Paul's missionary work resulted from his new-found conviction that only faith in Christ's death could bring salvation and that people need to prepare for an immediate end of all things. Paul worked in major urban areas through Asia Minor, Macedonia, and Achaia (modern-day Turkey and Greece) to establish communities of Christians. The Book of Acts suggests that he used local synagogues as bases of operation, but Paul himself doesn't say so. Nor does Paul ever say that he engaged in open-air evangelism or tent revivals. It appears that Paul met people to preach to by going into a new city, opening up a business, and using it as a point of contact.

Convinced that the end of all things was at hand, Paul engaged in an urgent mission to get people to believe in Christ before it was too late.

Throughout his letters, Paul gives several hints concerning what he said to potential converts. Because his audience consisted of pagans, he first had to convince them that their worship was pointless, because the pagan gods didn't really exist (1 Thess. 1:9–10). Moreover, the one true God had sent his son into the world to die for the wrongdoing of which everyone was guilty. The truth of this message was proven by the resurrection of Jesus from the dead. For people to have a right standing before God, therefore, and to be saved when the imminent day of judgment arrived, they needed to believe in the one true God and trust the death of his son, Jesus. For Paul, this was the fulfillment of the Jewish Law. It was not necessary, though, to follow the Jewish Law to achieve salvation.

Paul's conversion appears to have been based on some vision of Jesus after his death, a vision that completely altered Paul's understanding of Jesus, the plan of God, the way of salvation, and the role of the Law that God had given to his people Israel. Convinced that the end of all things was at hand, Paul engaged in an urgent mission to get people to believe in Christ before it was too late. The undisputed writings from Paul's hand are letters that he wrote to some of the churches he established after he had moved on to other areas for further missionary work. Problems inevitably arose in these communities after Paul, their founder, had left them, and he wrote to help them deal with these problems. These letters are the earliest Christian writings we have, produced mostly in the 50s, 16 or 20 years before the first Gospel. Starting with the next lecture, we'll begin to look at some of these letters to unpack further the teachings of the most significant figure in the history of early Christianity. ■

Essential Reading

Brown, *Introduction to the New Testament*, chap.16.

Ehrman, *The New Testament: A Historical Introduction*, chap. 18.

Supplemental Reading

Fitsmyer, *Pauline Theology*.

Keck, *Paul and His Letters*.

Roetzel, *The Letters of Paul*.

Questions to Consider

1. From what we've seen so far, in what ways did Paul's belief in the resurrection confirm what he already thought and in what ways did it alter what he thought? To what extent can it be said that Paul "changed his mind"?

2. Paul indicates that a Gentile does not have to become a Jew to be a Christian, but he does not press this further to say that a Jew should *stop* being a Jew to be a Christian. What do people in the modern world think about this? Is it possible to be both Jewish and Christian?

Paul—The Man, the Mission, and the *Modus Operandi*
Lecture 14—Transcript

In the last lecture we saw that the hero of the Book of Acts was the Apostle Paul, who, more than anyone, was responsible for the spread of the Christian movement from its small beginnings in Jerusalem, out into the wider Roman world. Most historians would agree with Luke that apart from Jesus, Paul was the most important figure in early Christianity. We can now move into a study of Paul himself, based on the letters that happen to survive in the New Testament. These are the only writings that we have from Paul's hand. There are other writings that we will see later in the course that claim to be written by Paul, but they are forgeries. The New Testament books attributed to Paul are the only ones that Paul himself actually wrote.

In this lecture we'll be considering some of the difficulties associated with trying to understand the writings of Paul, and then we will look at some biographical background on his life. The study of Paul is complicated by several difficulties. First, as we have already seen, one of the principal sources for knowing about Paul is the Book of Acts, which must be treated critically. We can't simply trust that when Acts says something about Paul it is historically accurate because Acts' account is governed by theological concerns. We have seen that in places, Paul and Acts talk about the same events. Invariably when they do so, discrepancies either large or small emerge. Some of the small discrepancies may seem insignificant—where Paul was and when and with whom. But sometimes the discrepancies are major—what did his proclamation to the Gentiles entail. Moreover, the Book of Acts provides some information about Paul that's not corroborated in his letters that must, therefore, be taken gingerly. For example, most people who know anything about Paul think that he was a Roman citizen. Well, not everybody living in the empire of course was a citizen of Roman, it was privilege to be a Roman citizen. Paul himself never says anything about being a Roman citizen, that's found only in the Book of Acts. Well, was he a Roman citizen? It's hard to know. Acts would have had reasons of its own for wanting to elevate the status of Paul, and so one could imagine Acts saying that he was a citizen, even if the author didn't know. The Book of Acts is the only place where we find that Paul came from the city of Tarsus in the region of Cilicia. He is frequently known as Paul of Tarsus. Did he really come from Tarsus? It is hard to say. He himself, never mentions Tarsus in any of his letters.

It matters whether one takes Acts as historically reliable or not. How did Paul proceed on his mission? Well, according to the Book of Acts, the way Paul engaged in his missionary activities was by going into a city and using the synagogue as a base of operation. As a Jew he'd go into the synagogue, he'd convert some Jews, the Jewish leaders would get upset with him, they'd kick him out, and then he'd go to the Gentiles. City after city after city he begins in the synagogue—Paul himself doesn't indicate so. Well, is Acts accurate about this then?

What did Paul preach? Did Paul preach to the Gentiles that it was okay that they had committed idolatry because they were ignorant, they didn't know any better? That's what Acts says. Paul, though, indicates that he condemned pagan idolatry as a willful act. What was Paul's view of himself as a Jew? In the Book of Acts, Paul never does anything against the Jewish Law. This is a major motif of the book. Paul himself though says that he acted as a Jew when he was among the Jews, but he acted as a Greek when he was among the Greeks. Was Paul always keeping the Jewish Law after he became a Christian? Well it depends, if you read Acts or Paul. The first problem then in the study of Paul is what to do with Acts. I think that when you use the Book of Acts, you have to use it critically, with a critical eye recognizing it's own theological agenda.

Second problem with studying Paul is that some of the writings that appear under Paul's name were probably not written by him. I have already pointed out that there are a number of Pauline writings outside of the New Testament that are clear forgeries. As we will see in a later lecture, for example, there is a third letter to the Corinthians that is not in the New Testament. Well, this was forged in the 2nd century. But even within the New Testament there are Pauline books, books who claim Paul as their author, whose authorship is debated. As we will see, most scholars are convinced that Paul did not write the books of 1 and 2 Timothy and Titus. These three books are called the Pastoral epistles because they deal with problems that pastors are facing in their churches and Paul as the head pastor is writing them a letter to tell them how to deal with the problems. The question is, is this really Paul. Most scholars are convinced on a number of grounds that we'll examine in a later lecture, that Paul didn't write the Pastoral epistles.

Scholars debate the authorship of three other books that claim Paul as the author—Colossians, Ephesians, and 2 Thessalonians. These books are designated by scholars as the Deutero-Pauline epistles, that is, they are epistles that have a secondary standing in the Pauline canon because their authorship is disputed. Again, we'll see reasons for these disputes in a later lecture. At this stage, it is simply important to emphasize that the seven remaining letters are typically designated the undisputed Pauline epistles. Virtually no competent scholar disputes that Paul wrote the letters of Romans, 1 and 2 Corinthians, Galatians, Philippians, 1 Thessalonians, and Philemon. These seven letters—the undisputed Pauline epistles—are unanimously agreed to have gone back to Paul. Any study of Paul, therefore, is best served to restrict itself to the letters that he has known to have produced. You can't very well talk about Paul's theology and quote a letter that he didn't write. And so it is important to stick to the seven undisputed letters.

So the first problem of studying Paul is what to do with the Book of Acts. The second problem has to do with the letters that claim to be written by him, but were not.

The third problem with studying the Apostle Paul is that all of Paul's letter are occasional in nature. By that I don't mean that Paul occasionally wrote letters, I mean that he wrote letters for particular occasions. These letters that come from Paul's pen are not systematic treatises on set topics. They are actual letters written to address actual concerns that have arisen in Paul's churches. Paul will establish a church, go somewhere else, he will hear of problems, and he will write his letter back to the churches to explain what they should do about the problems. That probably means that there are lots of things that are important to Paul, that never show up in the letters because there never were problems in his churches. We shouldn't then expect these letters to cover ever topic of significance to Paul—they'll only cover issues that had arisen in the churches that were problematic.

I'll just give you one example. Paul only mentions the Lord's Supper one time in the surviving letters, even if you count the disputed epistles. The

Lord's Supper occurs only once, 1 Corinthians, chapter 11. When you read 1 Corinthians 11, it's clear Paul thought that the correct conduct at the Lord's Supper was extremely important, that in fact because people weren't conducting themselves properly at this meal, this periodic meal in the communities, some people had gotten sick as a result and some people had died as judgment against their activities, and so Paul tells them they have to conduct themselves in a certain way. It is clearly a very important issue. But it occurs only once in his letters. If this had not been a problem in the church of Corinth, we wouldn't even know that Paul followed any rules at all at the Lord's Supper, or that he thought that the Lord's Supper was important at all. It's only because we have this in 1 Corinthians, chapter 11. And so the third problem in studying Paul's letter is that all of these books are occasional in nature.

A careful study of Paul's letters with an eye to the Book of Acts for corroboration reveals several important pieces of biographical information on Paul, which can serve as a kind of backdrop to our study of his writings. And so here what I want to do is go through some basic biographical information so that we know who Paul was and what happen to him to lead him to become a Christian and then to develop his theology.

From Paul's letter we learn that Paul was born and raised a Jew who was committed to the traditions of Pharisaism. Paul refers to his background in Galatians chapter 1 and Philippians chapter 3, where he clearly states that he was born and raised a Jew and that he had been raised as Pharisee. That, by the way, is an interesting datum. I mentioned in an earlier lecture the four major group of Jews that we know about—Pharisees, Sadducees, Essenes, and the Fourth Philosophy. Among the Pharisees we don't have any authors who were themselves Pharisees living before the destruction of the temple in the year 70, except ironically for the Apostle Paul. Paul is the only Pharisaic author that we have writing before the destruction of the temple. Of course, when he's writing he is no longer just a Jewish Pharisee, he is a Jewish Pharisee who has become a believer in Jesus. But scholars have had to appeal to Paul for what Pharisaism might have been like, since he is the only author who survives. In any event, we know enough about the Pharisees to say that they were very concerned about following the Law of God and had developed traditions, oral traditions, to help them keep the written Law of Moses. Paul, then, was thoroughly steeped both in the Torah and in these world traditions.

It appears that Paul was raised outside of Palestine and that he did not know Jesus himself. As I indicated, Paul doesn't say that he was born in Tarsus, but he may well have been born in Tarsus, which was a large metropolitan area, or some place like it. The reason for thinking he was raised outside of Palestine is because Paul gives very little indication that he understands any Semitic languages. He speaks and writes Greek, without evident knowledge of Hebrew or even Aramaic, which is the language in Palestine. Therefore, it appears that he didn't know Jesus himself and makes no claims to have known Jesus when Jesus was alive.

For some reason, Paul learned about the early Christian movement wherever he was, and he found it blasphemous and dangerous. It's usually assumed that Paul learned about the early Christian movement when he himself was mature adult, but that it was soon after the Christian movement had started. There are a number of reasons for dating it this way, but this would mean that Paul was roughly the age of Jesus. Paul heard about Christianity and found it dangerous. We don't know what about Christianity he found to be blasphemous or dangerous. He doesn't tell us what it was that he found to be problematic, but it's possible to read his writings and come up with some hypothesis about it.

It may be, this strikes me as highly plausible, it may be that Paul had a thoroughly traditional view of what the Messiah was suppose to be—a figure of grandeur and power who would overthrow God's enemies to bring in God's kingdom. When he heard that some Jews were saying that Jesus was the Messiah, he may have found this to be outright blasphemous. Because who is Jesus? He wasn't a figure of grandeur and power whom God had blessed by allowing him to bring in the kingdom. Jesus was a man who was crucified. He was a lowly criminal who was crushed by the state. This is not at all what God said the Messiah was going to be like in the Hebrew Scriptures. As I have pointed out, there were no Jews prior to Christianity, who thought the Messiah was going to suffer and die. So to say that someone was a Messiah even though he had been crucified was ridiculous. Even worse than that, for Paul—there are indications of this from the Book of Galatians, chapter 3—even more problematic for Paul was the circumstance that Jesus died by being nailed to a cross. The reason that was a problem is because of a passage on the Torah. In the book of Deuteronomy, chapter 27, Moses says, as Paul attributed Deuteronomy to Moses, Moses says, "Cursed is the one who hangs on a tree." Well, how is one crucified? By being nailed to wood, nailed to a tree. Whoever is nailed to a tree is under God's curse. Christians, though, are saying that this one that God has cursed is the Messiah. That seemed completely ridiculous to Paul, even blasphemous. That may be why he persecuted the Christian church.

It may also be that the concomitant claim of the Christians that salvation came not just to Jews, but to Gentiles, who didn't have to become Jews, was also found to be offensive. Christians before Paul were saying that Gentiles did not have to be circumcised, so that the salvation of God to the Jews is going to non-Jews? Most Jews would not have found this to be particularly acceptable, even offensive, and Paul seems to have been in that category. These may be the two reasons that Paul decided to persecute the Christians, as he himself indicates he did in Galatians, chapter 1, verse 13, he actively persecuted the Christian church. We don't know exactly what this entailed, but it may have involved some violence.

In the midst of his persecuting activities, Paul evidently had some kind of visionary experience of Jesus that changed his life. The Book of Acts describes the event in some detail as we saw in Acts, chapters 9, 22, and 26. Paul himself is much more elusive when it comes to describing the event, he doesn't say exactly what happened to him. He mentions it in a couple of occasions, in Galatians, chapter 1, Paul says that God was pleased to reveal his Son to me. God was pleased to reveal his Son to me. It is not clear whether that means that he actually had a vision of Jesus, or if God enlightened him about the truth of Jesus, or something else. But in 1 Corinthians, chapter 15, verse 8, Paul in the context, he is describing Jesus being raised from the dead and appearing to several people—to Cephas, to the Twelve, to the apostles, and to James his own brother—and he says to last of all, he appeared to me, as one untimely born.

Paul claims that he had some kind of visionary experience of Jesus. We aren't sure exactly what that visionary experience involved. We are sure, though, that this experience completely transformed Paul's understanding of Jesus. Having seen Jesus after his death, convinced Paul that he had been completely wrong about Jesus and wrong to persecute the Christian church, and it moved him from being the greatest persecutor of the church to being it's greatest apostle.

I want to explain how Paul's thought processes appeared to have worked as a way of setting up how his own distinctive theology developed—how Paul moved from being a persecutor of Christians to being an apostle for the Christians. The way his thought processes work, I think, were somewhat in reverse, arguing from the experience of the resurrection of Jesus that he had to a theology about Jesus. So that he doesn't start about some ideas about Jesus, he starts with an experience that he had. And the way I think the thought processes work, is as follows.

Since Paul became convinced that Jesus was raised from the dead, because he had some vision of Jesus, he was convinced that God had showered favor on Jesus after Jesus' death. That must mean, though, that the death of Jesus itself was not an accident or a miscarriage of justice. Since God honored Jesus after his death, the death itself must have been planned by God, otherwise God wouldn't have honored Jesus in his death. So, rather than one who was cursed by God, Jesus was the one man, more than any other, who is ultimately blessed by God. Since Jesus as God's blessed one, could not have borne the curse for anything that he himself had done, he must have borne it for others. In other words, Paul thought that by being nailed to the cross, Jesus was under a curse—accursed is anyone who hangs on a tree. Since God blessed Jesus by raising him from the dead, it is clear that he stands under God's blessing, not under God's curse. Why then does he bear the curse? It must not be for anything that he himself has done. He must have borne the curse for others. That is to say, in using this kind of logic, Jesus' death must have been a sacrifice, not for his own sins, not for anything that he did, but for the sins of others.

Paul, then, reasons that a person's sins can be removed if they accept this sacrifice that Jesus paid. They accept this sacrifice by faith, that is, by trusting in Christ's death for salvation. Having a right standing before God must therefore come through Christ's death and resurrection and through nothing else. It is only through Jesus' death and resurrection that a person can be made right with God. For that reason, the Jewish Law cannot be the way to attain a right standing before God, because Jesus' death is way to have a right standing before God. You see how this is all working. He is reasoning back from the resurrection. The resurrection says something about the importance of the death. The death says something very important about salvation, the way of salvation now says something important about the Jewish Law. Salvation comes not by Law, but through Jesus' death.

Rather than continuing on as Pharisee, urging people to keep the Law more perfectly, urging Gentiles if they want to join the community to be circumcised, Paul came to promote faith in Christ as the way of salvation. There could in fact be no other way. Salvation comes to all people, Jew and Gentile, through the death of Jesus. Thus Paul becomes the leading proponent of the view that Gentiles, along with Jews, could belong to the people of God, and, in fact, could belong to the people of God without becoming Jews, without being circumcised. As a result, Paul became an influential missionary taking the message of Christ principally to the Gentiles.

So okay, you see what I have just done is I have tried to develop for you Paul's distinctive theology, showing you that Paul's view that salvation comes by faith in Christ, not by doing the works of the Law, results from his belief in Jesus' resurrection. Not only did Paul change his views about Jesus and his views about how one has salvation as a result of the resurrection, he also came to see the significance of Jesus' resurrection for the history of the entire world.

As a Pharisee, Paul evidently had already believed in some kind of apocalyptic Judaism. It appears that most Pharisees were apocalypticists. Apocalypticists believed that at the end of the age there would be a resurrection of the dead. Remember the logic in apocalyptic thought that we are living in an evil age that is going to come to an end, and at the end of this age, God would intervene and everybody would face judgment—those who are alive and those who are dead. Those who were dead would be raised from the dead. When, then, does a resurrection from the dead occur for apocalyptic Jews? It comes at the end of this age immediately before the kingdom of God arrives.

Paul, because of his visionary experience, came to think that Jesus was raised from the dead. That showed Paul that the end had already begun. The end had already begun. That's why Paul sometimes refers to Jesus as the first fruits of the resurrection. This is an agricultural image, the first fruits of the resurrection. When it is harvest season, the farmer goes out, they bring in the crops, and they have a party that night to celebrate the first fruit. Well when do they get the rest of the harvest? The next day. Jesus is the first fruits of the resurrection. That means that the rest of the harvest, the rest of the resurrection, is going to come right away. It's not going to be 2,000 or 3,000 years later. Paul thought that the end had already begun. He anticipated that the full resurrection of the dead would occur soon, probably within his own lifetime, as he indicates in 1 Thessalonians, chapter 4, verses 13 through 18. He appears to have expected to have been alive when Jesus returned and all people are raised from the dead. This explains in part the urgency of Paul's mission to spread his gospel throughout the world. He thought the end was coming soon and people needed to repent soon or else they wouldn't be prepared for this coming end. Salvation depended on the urgency of his mission.

And so Paul began a mission. His missionary work resulted from his new-found conviction that only faith in Christ's death could bring salvation and that people needed to repent to prepare for an imminent end of all things. Paul worked in major urban areas trying to spread this message through Asia Minor, Macedonia, and Achaia—modern-day Turkey and Greece—establishing communities of Christians wherever he went. As I have indicated, the Book of Acts suggested that he used local synagogues as his base of operation. Paul himself doesn't say so, and Paul also doesn't say that he ever engaged in some kind of open air evangelism or tent revivals. It doesn't appear that he went into open places and just began preaching openly. And so what Paul himself talks about, especially in books like 1 Thessalonians and 1 Corinthians, is that he worked among the people that he converted, working day and night, he said, 1 Thessalonians, chapter 2, verse 9. I think he probably means he actually worked. What most scholars now tend to think is that Paul would go into a town or city and set up a business—possibly a Christian leather goods shop, he worked in leather according to the Book of Acts—and that he would use this as a way of making contact with people who came in to do business with him. And when he would meet people then, he would talk to them about his message.

He gives several hints throughout his letters what his message was. One of the clearest hints is in 1 Thessalonians, chapter 1, verses 9 and 10 where he reminds his audience that he convinced them to turn from idols to worship the living and true God and to await his Son from heaven, who would deliver us from the wrath to come. In order words, Paul had to convince these pagans who are polytheists that their gods were ineffectual, they were dead. Worshiping idols was pointless, because idols were simply lumps of stone or wood, but there was a living God who's opposed to the idols, and Jesus was his Son, and Jesus was the one who was going to deliver people from the wrath of God that is going to strike the world. In other words, Paul taught an apocalyptic message of the coming end, a day of judgment that was soon to arrive that one could be saved from only by having faith in Jesus. Moreover, he taught that this salvation would come to these former pagans simply be believing in this God and in the death and resurrection of his Son. He saw this as the fulfillment of Judaism. He saw this as the Jewish God who had sent his Son in fulfillment of his Jewish scriptures, but those who accepted this message, didn't have to follow the Jewish Law because the salvation came to all people, Jew and Gentile, not just simply to Jews.

It is hard to say why Paul was so successful in his mission. It is hard to know what it was about his personality that convinced people that he was right, to give up their former gods to worship this God. But it is clear that he had considerably success. He established communities in major urban areas in the various places he visited in Asia Minor, Macedonia, and Achaia.

In conclusion to this lecture, it is safe to say that Paul was the most significant early convert to Christianity—one who moved from being the greatest persecutor of the faith to being its greatest apostle. Paul's conversion appears to have been based on some vision of Jesus after his death, a vision that completely altered Paul's understanding of Jesus, the plan of God, the way of salvation, and the rule of the Jewish Law that God had given in salvation. Convinced that the end of all things was at hand, Paul engaged in an urgent mission trying to get people to believe in Christ before it was too late. The undisputed letters from Paul's hand that we have represent letters that he wrote to some of the churches that he had established after he left them to move on to other areas for further missionary work. Problems inevitably arose in these communities after Paul, their founder, had left them. And Paul wrote to them to help them deal with these problems. These letters are the earliest Christians writings that we have. They are earlier than the Gospels. They were produced some time in the 50s, 50s A.D.—15 or 20 years before the first Gospel was written. Starting with the next lecture, we will begin to look at some of these letters to unpack further the teachings of this most significant figure in the history of early Christianity.

Paul and the Crises of His Churches—
First Corinthians
Lecture 15

Paul's theological belief in Christ's death and resurrection has clear ethical implications for the life of believers.

The surviving Pauline letters are addressed, for the most part, to churches established by Paul in Asia Minor, Macedonia, and Achaia. They were written by the apostle to his converts to help them deal with problems that had arisen in their communities since his departure. The letter of 1 Corinthians is a fairly representative example of these Pauline epistles. We know both from Paul's letters and Acts that Paul spent a good deal of time in Corinth trying to establish a community of Christians there. The city is located on the isthmus dividing the northern and southern parts of modern-day Greece; Paul went there after establishing a church in nearby Thessalonica. According to Acts, Paul spent 18 months in Corinth, converting people and teaching those he had converted. Acts indicates that he began his work in the synagogue and converted mainly Jews (18:4–11), but 1 Corinthians suggests that the community was made up of former pagans (12:2).

Paul's message to them, as he himself indicates in the letter, was similar to what we saw in the previous lecture (see 1 Cor. 15:3–5): Pagan idols are dead; there is only one true God. Christ, his son, died for the sins of the world, in accordance with the prophecies of the Jewish Scriptures. (Because the Hebrew Scriptures did not prophecy the suffering and death of the messiah, we are not sure what passages Paul is adducing to make this point.) God raised Christ from the dead, again as a fulfillment of Scriptures. Large numbers of people saw him alive afterwards, including the apostles, 500 people at one time, and Paul himself. Those who want a right standing before God must believe in Christ; those who do so will be given an entirely new life.

After Paul and his co-workers had converted a large number of people, organized their church, and taught them the rudiments of the faith, they left for other missionary areas to start all over again.

After his departure, Paul learned of significant problems that had arisen in the Corinthian Church. Some of the members had written a letter to him asking his opinion about some pressing theological and practical matters (see 1 Cor. 7:1). He was also visited by several members of the congregation ("Chloe's people") who gave him the lowdown on the church, and the news was not good (1 Cor. 1:11). 1 Corinthians itself provides a sense of the magnitude of the problems. There were major divisions in the church at Corinth. Different church leaders were claiming to be more spiritually knowledgeable and powerful than others and were creating factions in the church (chaps. 1–4), claiming to follow Paul or other leaders. Some members of the church took others to court (chap. 6).

There were disputes about important ethical issues. Some were claiming that sex was wrong, even in the confines of marriage (chap. 7). Others hotly debated whether meat that had come from pagan sacrifices could be eaten in good conscience by Christians (chaps. 8–10). There were instances of flagrant immorality. Some men in the church were visiting prostitutes and seemed proud of it (chap. 6). One man was sleeping with his stepmother (chap. 5).

And finally there were problems in the worship services. There were abuses of the communal meal; some members were gorging themselves and getting drunk while others had nothing to eat or drink (chap. 11). There was chaos during worship as people tried to demonstrate their spiritual superiority over one another by disruptively "speaking in tongues" (i.e., speaking in foreign languages they didn't know, under the inspiration of the spirit) (chaps. 12–14).

Even though Paul dealt with these problems one by one, his response to the Corinthian situation doesn't fully make sense until the very end of the letter, where he deals with the one major problem that has generated all the others: some of the Corinthians don't appear to understand the nature of the future resurrection. Paul had taught them that Christ had been raised from the dead and that by believing in him, people could be given a new life through a right standing with God. For Paul, this meant that believers would be saved when Jesus returned and all people were raised from the dead for reward or punishment, in eternal bodies that couldn't die, like the resurrected body of Jesus. Paul, in other words, taught an apocalyptic view of the faith.

Some of the Corinthians had taken this teaching a step further and in a different direction. For them, the new life available now in Christ was *already* a glorified resurrected existence. Life in the present was an exalted kind of existence above the mundane concerns and realities of life. Bodily existence didn't really matter, because the body had been transcended by those who were related to Christ. True believers had thus already begun to experience the full effects of salvation. And those who were truly spiritual were the ones who had most fully transcended this material world and its mundane concerns and realities. Some historians have seen this Corinthian view as a forerunner of Gnosticism, with its belief that this material world was evil but that it could not ultimately affect the divine spark within that had already acquired the knowledge of salvation.

Paul saw this as the key to all the other problems, and he deals with it last, in his famous chapter on the resurrection, 1 Corinthians 15. Paul begins by establishing common ground with the Corinthians: They began to believe in Christ when they put their faith in his death and resurrection (15:3–4). But Jesus' resurrection was not merely a spiritual resurrection: It was a physical one. He was actually seen, bodily, after he arose (15:5–8). This is the key point of the chapter. This means that the Christians' resurrection—if it's going to be like Christ's—is also going to be a *physical* resurrection. Because it's going to be a physical resurrection, it obviously hasn't happened yet. Christians are *not* already experiencing the full benefits of salvation; these will come only at the end, when Christ returns, raises the dead, and brings immortality to those who are living. Paul's teaching here reflects what he says in other passages of his letters, including the intriguing words of 1 Thess. 4:13–18, used by some conservative groups still today to refer to the coming "rapture" (even though the term does not occur in the passage).

Each of the problems the Corinthians have is related in some sense to their failure to understand the nature of this future resurrection. For example:

The divisions in the church have occurred because some leaders have tried to "prove" their superiority, that they have heavenly wisdom and power. Paul doesn't take a side in the dispute—because all sides have erred in thinking that full spiritual wisdom and power have already come in this age. In fact, God has shown that power and wisdom have no role in salvation; paradoxically, God now works through what appears to be weak and foolish (as seen in the cross of Jesus, the make-up of the Corinthians' congregation; and Paul's own ministry itself (1 Cor. 1:18–2:5). The immoral activities of some of the members are the result of their belief that they have transcended the physical realities of this world. For them, because the body is irrelevant (in that it's been transcended), people can do whatever they want with their bodies (such as using prostitutes with impunity). For Paul, though, the fact that God will raise the body from the dead shows that God is concerned about what people do with their bodies.

In short, the numerous problems that emerged in the Corinthian church—church divisions, rampant immorality, chaotic church organization—are all related in one way or another to a fundamental misunderstanding of the nature of salvation. The resurrection of Christians, for Paul, is a future event with serious implications for the present. To adhere to the will of God, Christians must understand the nature of life in the present. This is not an age—even for believers—of glory and grandeur; it is an age of weakness and suffering. Not until Christ returns will Christians enjoy the full benefits of salvation. In the meantime, they must lead humble and moral lives, working for harmony together and setting a good example for those who are outside the community. ∎

Essential Reading

1 Corinthians.

Brown, *Introduction to the New Testament,* chap. 22.

Ehrman, *The New Testament: A Historical Introduction*, chap. 20.

Roetzel, *Paul and His Letters*.

1. How does Paul's belief in the future, bodily resurrection of believers relate to forms of Christianity that are prevalent in our world? Is it any longer a central conviction of most Christians? If not, why not?

2. Try to explain how each of the problems that Paul discusses in 1 Corinthians can be tied into a different understanding of the nature of the resurrection.

Paul and the Crises of His Churches— First Corinthians

Lecture 15—Transcript

In the previous lecture we learned some significant things about Paul's life. Paul had converted from being a persecutor of the Christians to being a Christian missionary. His belief in Jesus' resurrection based on some kind of visionary experience led him to work out a theology of Jesus' death, which he came to see as a sacrifice for the sins of the world and the only means by which a person might have a right standing before God. Paul took this message out into the world, establishing churches in major urban areas in Asia Minor, Macedonia, and Achaia. The surviving Pauline letters are addressed, for the most part, to these church, written by the Apostle back to his converts to help them deal with problems that had arisen in their communities after his departure. Unfortunately, we don't have time in these lectures to consider each of these letters in depth. In this lecture, though, I would like to deal with the letter of 1 Corinthians as a fairly representative example.

First Corinthian was not the first of these letters to have been written. Probably the first letter that Paul wrote that survives is 1 Thessalonians, which I will refer to in the course of this lecture. First Corinthians was probably written several years after that, probably in the 50s of the Common Era and, again, this would have been 10, 15, 20 years before the Gospels themselves were produced.

First some background information about the church in Corinth that Paul is addressing in the letter. We know both from Paul's letters and the Book of Acts that Paul had spent a good deal of time in Corinth trying to establish a community of Christians there. The city is located on the isthmus dividing the northern and southern parts of modern-day Greece. Paul had gone there after establishing a church in nearby Thessalonica. According to the Book of Acts, Paul spent 18 months in Corinth converting people and teaching those he had converted. Paul doesn't himself refer to the length of time he had spent there, but there are indications in the letter that he had gotten to know this community rather well and had spent considerable time teaching them in the rudiments of the faith. And so the idea that he had spent a year and a half there is completely plausible.

Acts indicates that Paul began his work in this community in the synagogue, that he converted a large number of Jews to faith in Jesus, and then when he had been kicked out of the synagogue he began to teach Gentiles, former pagans whom he then converted. The Book of 1 Corinthians itself, though, suggests that Paul's converts weren't Jews at all, but that they were former pagans. As Paul himself says in chapter 12, verse 2 of this book, "You know that when you were pagans, you were enticed and led away to idols that could not speak." He's addressing his converts and he indicates that they formerly had been pagans. And so it is hard to know whether the Acts narrative is accurate or not, that he had converted Jews as well.

Paul's message to his converts is alluded to in this letter. It is similar to what we had seen in the previous lecture as to Paul's basic message when trying to convert pagans. At one point in this letter, near its end in chapter 15, Paul summarizes what it was that he had preached to these people. He says—this is chapter 15, verses 3 to 5—I handed on to you, he says, as of first importance, what I in turn had received—and now he is going to say what it is that he had told them—that Christ died for our sins in accordance with the Scriptures and that he was buried. That he was raised on the third day in accordance with the Scriptures and that he appeared to Cephas, then to the Twelve, then he appeared to more than 500 brothers and sisters at one time, most of whom are still alive, though some have died. Then he appeared to James, then to all apostles, last of all as to one untimely born, he appeared also to me.

Paul's message, then, is about the death and resurrection of Jesus. He indicates that his message included the teaching that Christ died according to the Scriptures, which must mean that Christ's death, in Paul's preaching, was a fulfillment of prophecy in the Hebrew Bible. When Paul mentions the Scriptures of course, he's not talking about the New Testament, because the New Testament hadn't been written yet. So when he says it was in accordance with the Scriptures, he means that it was in accordance with the prophecies of the Hebrew Bible. Christ died in accordance with the Scriptures. Moreover, there is proof because, Paul says, he was buried.

Secondly, Paul says that Christ was raised from the dead. Again he says that was in accordance with the Scriptures, Hebrew Bible, and again there is proof because Jesus appeared to Cephas, to the Twelve, to the Apostles, and Paul himself. And Paul interestingly says that he appeared to 500 brothers and sisters at one time, many of whom are still alive. In the Gospels of the New Testament, of course, we have accounts of Jesus appearing to various people after his resurrection. We have no account of him appearing to 500 people at once. Paul's version in 1 Corinthians 15 is the only reference we have to this. His indication that many of them are still alive may be that he is telling these people, if you don't believe me just go and ask them, because there are plenty of people who saw Jesus.

This then is the core of Paul's message that he preach to these former pagans—Christ's death and resurrection. It is interesting to speculate on what Paul means when he says that the death and resurrection of Jesus were according to the Scriptures. I assume this meant that when Paul was with them he actually adduced scriptural proof for his message about Jesus' death and resurrection being a fulfillment. We wish we knew which passages Paul would have looked at to indicate that the Messiah was suppose to die and be raised from dead, since as I have indicated in the Hebrew Bible, whenever there is talk about a future Messiah, there is no talk about him dying and being raised.

There are passages in the Hebrew Bible though that do talk about a righteous man of God who suffers. Sometimes this person is called the servant of God, as in Isaiah, chapter 53. Sometimes it's simply a righteous man as in Psalm 22. In no incidences is this person called the Messiah. But the early Christians who knew that Jesus had died, who believed that Jesus was the Messiah, attached these passages to the events of his life and death. In other words, they interpreted what happened to Jesus in light of passages in the Hebrew Bible that talk about the suffering and death and the vindication of God's righteous one. They attached Psalm 22, Isaiah 53 to Jesus and interpreted Jesus in light of those passages, even though the passages don't talk directly about the Messiah. It may be that those are the passages that Paul was referring to when he was in Corinth trying to convince these people that Jesus fulfilled Scripture.

Now why would Paul be referring to the fulfillment of the Hebrew Bible in order to convince people who weren't even Jews in order to convert them? My hunch is that Paul converted people in part by convincing them that Jesus' death and resurrection were miraculous, obviously the resurrection would be miraculous, but especially miraculous because they fulfilled what God had predicted would happen. If you can show, well long ago this was predicted and in fact it came to pass, that might be a proof that would convince people that in fact Jesus is a fulfillment of the prophecies of the Hebrew God. This may convert them from worshiping their own pagan idols to worshiping the God of the Jews and Jesus as his son.

Paul's message then to the Corinthian is probably comparable to what he preached to other people in other places. He principally converted pagans and so he convinced them that their pagan idols were dead. There's only one true God. He tried to convince them that Christ, God's son, died for sins of the world in accordance with the prophecies of the Jewish Scriptures, that God raised him from the dead in fulfillment of the Scriptures, and that those who want a right standing with this God must believe in Christ. Those who do so will be given an entirely new life.

After Paul and his co-workers had converted a large number of people, organized their church, and taught them the rudiments of the faith, they left for other missionary areas to start all over again. That's the background to this letter. In his absence, Paul evidently learned of significant problems that had arisen in the Corinthian church after he left. He had two sources of information for his knowledge of these problems as he indicates in the letter. First, some of the members of the community had written to him asking his opinion about some pressing theological and practical matters. He indicates in 1 Corinthians 7:1, he says, "Now concerning the matters about which you have written," which indicates that they have written a letter asking him some questions. So that's one source of information—a letter that came from the community.

Secondly, he's been visited by several members of the congregation who have given the low down on the church. Evidently the news wasn't good. He refers to these members who have visited him in chapter 1, verse 11, where he says that, "I have heard from Chloe's people." Chloe's people. Chloe is a feminine name evidently referring to a woman in the congregation who has people—it is normally interpreted that this refers to some slaves of a woman in the congregation—who have come to where Paul is now in Ephesus and reported what's going on in the community. First Corinthians itself provides a sense of the magnitude of the problems that have been experienced in this community as reported both in the letter that Paul received and from the report from Chloe's people.

And I will go through some of the major problems. As indicated in this letter, there are four basic areas. First, there are major divisions that had occurred within the Corinthian community. There are splits within this community, major divisions. Evidently, according to chapters 1 through 4, different church leaders had created factions within the community claiming to be more spiritually knowledgeable and powerful than others, thereby creating factions, divisions. Some of these church leaders claimed to be followers of Paul himself, some claim to be followers of Paul's successor in the community, Appolos. Some claim to be followers of the Apostle Cephas. Some claim to be followers particularly of Christ, in other words, they don't have some human follower they have Christ as their leader. These individuals are claiming as a source of their authority, other figures in the Christian community, and they are claiming that they themselves have superior spiritual knowledge and power.

The divisions in the church are evident in a number of ways. Most strikingly we learn from chapter 6 that some members of this community are actually taking others to court, civil court, over some matters or other. We aren't sure exactly over what, but that's how divisive the community has become. So first problem, there are major divisions in the church.

The second problem, there are disputes about important ethical issues. Disputes about important ethical issues. There are some members of this community that are claiming that sex is wrong, even within the confines of marriage. There are others who are hotly debating other topics, which may not seem quite as pressing to us. One of the other hot topics in Corinth was over whether a person should be free to eat meat that had been previously sacrificed to a pagan idol. This is the problem dealt with in chapters 8 through 10. The situation is that in most pagan cities when meat was put up for sale, it had been meat that had been previously offered in an idol's temple. You simply didn't have a butcher shop. The butcher was in fact a priest, who sacrificed an animal as an act of reverence to the gods, but then they would sell the meat. Well, is it legitimate for us to eat this meat that has been sacrificed to an idol or not? Some Corinthian were saying well sure it is fine to eat this meat because in fact these idols don't exist, the idols are just a lump of wood or stone. And so since they don't exist, you can eat anything offered to them, because that's fine. Others were saying, no in fact if you eat this meat you are participating in idolatry. This was a hot issue, apparently as hot of an issue as to whether it is ever appropriate to have sex.

Third, in addition to major divisions and ethical issues, there were instances in this community of flagrant immorality. Flagrant immorality. We learn from chapter 6 that there are men in the congregation of Corinth who have been visiting prostitutes and apparently have bragged about it in church. In chapter 5 we learn that there is one man in this community who is actually sleeping with his stepmother. Paul takes these instances of immorality quite seriously as we'll see.

Fourth and finally, there are problems in the worship services in this community. Various kinds of problems in the worship services. For example, there are abuses of the communal meal, as I mentioned in the previous lecture. They would have a Lord's Supper, a periodic meal, probably a weekly affair in which they would—it wasn't like a Eucharist service that people might have today in a Christian church, it was more like pot luck supper, where people would bring food and they would commemorate Jesus' last meal with his disciples. Well, in Corinth problems have emerged because some people are coming early and gorging themselves and getting drunk, other people are coming late and they have nothing to eat or drink. Well this is indicating problems within the worship community.

Within the worship services themselves, apparently a good deal of chaos had broken out. I mentioned that you would have these church leaders who were trying to demonstrate their spiritual superior to others. Apparently one of the ways that spiritual superior is being manifest is in the worship services. The Corinthian believed, as we will see in our next lecture more fully, the Corinthian believed that each person in the community had received some kind of spiritual gift from God, including the ability for some of them to speak in foreign languages that they didn't know as an act of revelation from God. They could speak in tongues. Other people could interpret these unknown languages that were being spoken. In order to demonstrate their superior over one another, evidently some of the Christians leaders were speaking in tongues in a completely chaotic way—interrupting each other, speaking out over one another, trying to speak in tongues for the entire service—chaos has erupted in these worship services. These then are four major areas of problem within the church: major divisions, important ethical issues, flagrant immorality, and chaos during the worship services.

The letter of 1 Corinthians is designed to deal with each of these problems. Paul deals with the problems one by one, but his response doesn't really make sense until you get to the very end of the letter where he deals with the major problem that has generated all the others. In other words, when you read through 1 Corinthians, you can just outline it very easily because it deals with one problem after the other. He deals with divisions in the church, he deals with the man living with his stepmother, people taking each other to court, people visiting prostitutes, people eating meat offered to idols, etc. You just go through the letter and each of these problems is dealt with.

It is not until the end though that you realize what the big problem is. The big problem is that some of the Corinthians don't appear to understand the nature of the future resurrection of the dead. Now this may not sound like the problem that would tie together all the others, but in fact it does and that's why Paul saves it for the end—chapter 15. And we will talk about chapter 15 at some length in the rest of this lecture.

Let me set up the discussion by showing why this is the big problem. Paul had taught the Corinthians that Christ had been raised from the dead and that believing him people would have a new life through right standing before God. For Paul this meant that believers would be saved when Jesus returned from heaven and all people then were raised from the dead, either for reward or punishment. When they were raised from the dead they would have eternal bodies that couldn't die, they would have a resurrected body, like Jesus himself did, that's how people would enter into God's eternal kingdom, their bodies would be transformed at the future resurrection. In other words, Paul taught an apocalyptic view of the faith.

Some of the Corinthians had taken Paul's teaching a step further and in a different direction. For these Corinthians, not all of them maybe, but some of them, the new life that was available in Christ was already a glorified resurrected existence. For them, life in the present was a kind of exalted existence above the mundane concerns and realities of life. For these people, since they had already had an experience of a new life in Christ, they had already been saved. Their bodily existence, therefore, didn't really matter, since the body had been transcended by those who were closely related to Christ. For these people, true believers had already begun to experience the full effects of salvation. Those who were truly spiritual were the ones who were most fully transcended from this material realm. Those who were most spiritual had gone out of their bodies in a sense, transcended their bodies and were experiencing the full benefits of salvation in the here and now.

Some historians have seen this Corinthian view as a kind if forerunner of Gnosticism that we mentioned previously with its belief that the material world was evil, but that it could not ultimately affect the divine spark within that had already acquired the knowledge of salvation. This is a disputed point whether these Corinthians are sort of forerunners of what you are going to get with Gnostics. In any event, Paul saw this particular point of view that people had, that they had already experienced the full benefits of salvation, as the key to all the other problems, which is why he deals with it last in his famous chapter on the resurrection—1 Corinthians 15.

And so now I want to talk a little about this chapter and show how Paul deals with this big problem. As I have already read to you, Paul begins this chapter by establishing common ground with the Corinthians about what he taught them when they converted. He taught them that Christ died according to Scriptures and that Christ had been raised according to the Scriptures. His death was proved by the fact that he was buried. He resurrection was proved by the fact that people saw him including Cephas, the Twelve, the other apostles, and Paul himself.

Jesus' resurrection, for Paul, was not merely a spiritual resurrection of Jesus' soul. Jesus' resurrection was a physical resurrection. This is the key point to the chapter. Jesus' body was actually seen after he arose from the dead. People experienced it somehow. This means though that if Christians are also going to be raised from the dead as Christ was, that their resurrection will not just be a spiritual resurrection, it will be a physical resurrection. Since Jesus is the first fruits of the resurrection, then everybody will be raised like him, which means they will be raised physically. But since that means Christians are going to be raised physically, it obviously hasn't happen yet. Paul is disputing the interpretation of some of the Corinthians who say they have already been raised from the dead, already been given an exalted existence; in fact, it hasn't happened yet. Christians are not experiencing the full benefits of salvation. The full benefits of salvation will come only at the end, when Christ returns and raises the dead and brings immortality to those who are living.

Paul's teaching here reflects what he says in other passages of his letters, including the intriguing words of 1 Thessalonians, chapter 4, verses 13 through 18. This has become an important passage for some modern Christians especially evangelical Christians who are firm believers that there is going to be a rapture at the end of time. The doctrine of the rapture is that Christ will return from heaven, and those who are living will be transported up into heaven, and then that those who have died already will also be taken up into the clouds, and that there will then be this kind of reunion up in the sky.

The term rapture doesn't occur in 1 Thessalonians. In fact, the term doesn't occur anywhere in the New Testament, but the passage is based on this passage in 1 Thessalonians, chapter 4, where Paul says that we believe that Jesus died and raised again; so too, through Jesus, God will bring with him those who have died. Then he says that we declared to you by a word of the Lord, that we who are alive, who are left until the return of the Lord, will not precede those who have fallen asleep. The Lord himself will descend from heaven with the sound of the cry of command, the archangel's call and God's trumpet, and the dead in Christ will rise first, then we who are alive will be caught up in the clouds together to meet the Lord in the air. This is a view, then, that Christ is coming down from heaven, those who are alive will go up to meet him, those who are dead will go up to meet him, and people then will live up in the air. Paul seems to be assuming something quite similar in 1 Corinthians—that there's going to be a return of Jesus and at that point there's going to be resurrection of the dead. It's going to be physical resurrection, and since it is a physical resurrection, it's going to be a future resurrection. It hasn't happen yet. I've said that this is the main problem the Corinthians have that they don't understand this. I want to show you why their failure to understand this has led to the various problems that they've had. I can't go through all the problems in the short time that's left to me, but I do want to show how a couple of the problems relate directly to this big issue.

There have been divisions in the Christian church in Corinth. Why? Because leaders have tried to prove their superiority. They have superior spiritual wisdom and power. These are the people who think they have already experienced the full benefits of salvation and are manifesting it now. When Paul deals with the disputes in the congregation in chapters 1 through 4, he doesn't take a side. He doesn't say well some people side with Cephas, and some with apostles, and some with me. Well the people that sided with me are the ones that are right. He cuts through all of the disputes by saying that everybody who is taking a side is flat out wrong. Why? Because people who are spiritually superior don't understand this is not an age of power and wisdom. God in this evil age works through weakness and foolishness. The idea that God would save the world through a crucified man is ridiculous and foolish. Those who claimed wisdom and power are working against the Gospel rather than for the Gospel. This age now is an age of weakness so that people who are involved in these divisions simply don't understand the true Gospel.

So, too, the immoral activities of some members of the congregation are due to their belief that they have transcended the physical realities of this world. Why are these people behaving in such obviously immoral ways? For Paul it's because they think that the body is of no importance to salvation. They think they have transcended their bodies and already begun to experience salvation. For Paul, though, salvation is going to take place in the body. For these people, since the body doesn't matter—this is their line—since the body doesn't matter, then it doesn't matter what you do with your body. So you can sleep with your stepmother, you can visit the prostitute, you can get drunk at the Lord's table, you can do whatever you want with your body because it doesn't matter for salvation. For Paul, though, the body does matter for salvation, because salvation is going to come in the body at the future resurrection. The fact that God will raise bodies from the dead shows that God is concerned with what people do with their bodies.

You can examine all of the problems in 1 Corinthians and see them in light of this over arching thesis of Paul—that there is a future physical resurrection and that should affect how we behave in the present as individuals with ethics and within the church community as a whole. In short, the numerous problems that have emerged in the Corinthian church—church divisions, rampant immorality, chaotic church organization—are all related in one way or another to a fundamental misunderstanding of the nature of salvation. The resurrection of Christians for Paul is a future event with serious implications for the present. This is not an age, even for believers, of glory and grandeur, it's an age of weakness and suffering. Not until Christ returns will Christians enjoy the full benefits of salvation. In the meantime, Christians must lead humble and moral lives working for harmony together and setting a good example for those who are outside the community. One way to summarize this teaching is to say that Paul's theological belief in Christ's death and resurrection has clear ethical implications for the life of believers. In the next lecture, we'll turn to a closer examination of the kinds of ethical norms then found throughout Paul's letters.

Pauline Ethics
Lecture 16

> Paul had become convinced that it was Christ's death, not the Jewish Law, that put a person into a right relationship with God. He therefore argued that keeping the Law had no bearing on one's salvation.

The problem of Christian ethics was a very real one for Paul, because some of his enemies accused him of advocating lawless behavior. The charge was rooted in Paul's theology of salvation by faith in Christ, apart from the Law. Paul argued that keeping the Jewish Law had no bearing on one's salvation. His opponents took that to mean that Paul urged lawlessness (Rom. 3:8).

Paul did not see it this way and spent a good deal of effort trying to explain both how salvation came apart from keeping God's Law and yet how salvation involved keeping God's Law. It was true that doing what God had commanded in the Law would not be enough to put one in a right standing before God (Rom. 3:20; Gal. 2:15–16). But for Paul, one who had a right standing before God would nonetheless follow the Law (Rom. 13:8–10). This is very clear in his letter to the Galatians.

Paul based many of his moral judgments on the view (which as a Jew no doubt struck him as uncontroversial) that the Law of Moses—in its ethical requirements—should be followed. It is quite true that for Paul, a person did not have to become a Jew to be saved. This is why he was opposed to Gentiles taking up Jewish ways—by being circumcised and keeping kosher, for example (Gal. 5:2–3). In fact, he argued in the angry letter to the Galatians that anyone who did so was in danger of losing their salvation, because doing so would imply that Christ's death was not sufficient for salvation but that keeping the Law was also required (Gal. 5:4).

But Paul nonetheless taught that the *ethical* requirements of the Law should be followed (e.g., the commands not to murder or commit adultery and the command to love your neighbor as yourself). This has caused a good deal of confusion for Paul's interpreters over the years. Paul never explains clearly why he thinks some laws are not to be followed (circumcision) but others are (don't commit adultery). It appears that there was some kind of "common sense" distinction for him between laws meant just for Jews to preserve their Jewish identity (ceremonial laws) and laws meant for everyone who wanted to worship the God of Israel (ethical laws).

The one law from Scripture that Paul particularly stressed was Leviticus 19:18: "You shall love your neighbor as yourself." In both Galatians and Romans, Paul claims that believers in Christ must follow this rule of love, because by doing so they would "fulfill the Law" (Gal. 5:14). In 1 Corinthians, in particular, he applies the "love commandment" to show how people ought to behave; one of the most famous passages of the New Testament is 1 Corinthians 13—the "love" chapter. What most readers overlook is the context of the passage: It comes right in the middle of Paul's discussion of how spiritual gifts are to be used in the church. This context is significant for our understanding of the chapter.

> **The one law from Scripture that Paul particularly stressed was Leviticus 19:18: "You shall love your neighbor as yourself."**

Paul believed that Christians were living in an interim period between the beginning of the end of all things, with the resurrection of Jesus, and the culmination of the end, with his return in judgment. In this interim period, God provided believers in Christ with the Holy Spirit, as a kind of foreshadowing of what it would be like in the future kingdom. The Spirit was received by a person at baptism and endowed the person with a gift that was to assist the community in its life together, here during this interim period before the end. Different people had different gifts (the Greek term is *charismata*; hence, these are called "charismatic" communities): Some were leaders, others were administrators, others were teachers, others were healers. Some could speak God's word through prophecies from on high, others spoke God's word in unknown tongues, and yet others could interpret these tongues (1 Cor. 12:1–11). These gifts, in Paul's view, were for the good of the whole community. The Corinthians who believed themselves most spiritual maintained that they were especially endowed with the ability to speak in tongues, a most spectacular gift, and were disrupting the worship services by trying to prove it. A good bit of chaos resulted. In 1 Corinthians 12–14, Paul deals with the problem and lays down some rules: Only two or three should speak in tongues at any service, in turns; only if an interpreter is present; and so on. But in the midst of the discussion, he deals with what is really wrong with the situation in Corinth. Those trying to exalt themselves through manifesting this gift fail to understand that the gifts are given for the sake of the community and are to be practiced out of love for others, not the desire to elevate oneself. And so, he speaks his famous words of 1 Cor. 13:1–13: "If I speak in the tongues of men and of angels, but have not love, I am a clanging gong or a crashing cymbal…" His mention of tongues, prophecies, and knowledge relate directly to the problems of the Corinthian Church.

For Paul, the love commandment was flexible; it could be applied to new situations to determine how believers should live. It applied to obvious problems of personal relationships—such as whether you should defraud your brother or sister (1 Thess. 4). It also applied to less obvious problems of communal relationships—such as whether you should eat meat that had been sacrificed to a pagan deity (1 Cor. 8). His solution to this is very interesting, but can be related to the "love" commandment.

Paul did have other criteria of behavior, including some rooted directly in his apocalyptic theology. Paul's apocalyptic expectation of the end had a radical impact on such areas as his views of marriage and slavery. Because the end was near, one should not change one's social standing (1 Cor. 7). Slaves should not seek to be set free. People who were single should not get married. A person married to an unbeliever should not seek to be divorced.

Even though Paul taught that salvation came apart from the Law, he did not urge lawless behavior. In fact, Paul insisted on the morality of his congregations and applied a number of criteria to ethical situations to determine what the proper mode of behavior was. The ethical injunctions of Scripture were to be followed—especially the command to love one another as oneself. The apocalyptic realities of this world were to affect how one lived one's life. Paul's ethics are ultimately rooted in his understanding of God's act of salvation in Christ. In the next lecture, we will look at Paul's fullest exposition of his doctrine of salvation, as found in his letter to the Romans. ■

Essential Reading

1 Corinthians.

Galatians.

Ehrman, *The New Testament: A Historical Introduction*, chap. 20.

Supplemental Reading

Furnish, *The Love Commandment in the New Testament*.

Schrage, *New Testament Ethics for Today*.

Questions to Consider

1. Paul placed a huge emphasis on the love commandment, to "love one's neighbor as oneself." Can you think of ethical issues in the modern world that are difficult to resolve simply on the basis of this commandment? What other ethical criteria can be adduced to direct behavior today?

2. How do you imagine Paul's ethical stands would have been affected if he realized that the end of the age was not imminent, but that the world would go on existing for thousands of years?

Pauline Ethics
Lecture 16—Transcript

We saw in the last lecture that Paul's belief in the death of Jesus for salvation had clear ethical implications for how believers ought to live. The Corinthians were confronted with a number of ethical problems. Rather than simply give his opinion about how each of these problems should be handled, Paul based his response on a theological understanding of the nature of the future resurrection of the dead. That is say, Paul did not simply deal with these issues off the cuff. He had clear criteria that he used to help him to resolve them. Unfortunately as clear as Paul's ethical criteria may have been to him, they are often hidden to us behind his words.

In this lecture, I will discuss some of the criteria that appear to be implicit in many of Paul's writings, criteria that he used to judge what constituted ethical behavior and what did not. The problem of Christian ethics was a very real one for Paul, since some of his enemies accused him of advocating lawless behavior. The charge was rooted in Paul's theology of salvation by faith in Christ apart from the Law.

Paul had become convinced that it was Christ's death, not the Jewish Law, that put a person into a right relationship with God. He therefore argued that keeping the Law had no bearing on one's salvation. Paul's opponents took that to mean that Paul urged lawlessness. If salvation comes completely apart from the Law that God had given, which includes by the way the Ten Commandments, if salvation comes apart from the Law, then doesn't that mean that a person can break the Law and still have salvation? If so, doesn't Paul in fact urge people to break the Law? Doesn't he urge people to do what God had commanded them not to do? We know that this is what Paul's enemies had charged him with, because he himself refers to the charges. For example, Romans, chapter 3, verse 8, should we do evil that good might come as some have falsely accused us of saying, he writes. Paul himself, of course, did not see it that way. He did not think that because salvation came apart from the Law that one should behave lawlessly. In fact, Paul spent a good deal of effort trying to explain both how salvation did come apart from keeping God's Law and yet how salvation involved keeping God's Law.

It's true that for Paul doing what God had commanded in the Law would not put a person into a right standing before God. As Paul himself says in Galatians, chapter 2, verses 15 and 16, referring in part to his own past, we ourselves, he says, are Jews by birth and we are not Gentile sinners. Yet we know that a person is justified or made right with God, not by following the works of the Law, but through faith in Jesus Christ. And we have come to believe in Christ Jesus so that we might be justified by faith in Christ and not by doing works of the Law, because no one will be justified by works of the Law, justified or made right with God by works of the Law. Paul is unequivocal on the point. Doing the works of the Jewish Law, doing the things that the Law demands, will not put a person into a right standing before God.

Nowhere is Paul's view on this point seen more clearly than in his letter to the Galatians. I want to take a brief excursus to explain what the letter of Galatians is about because it is such a central letter for understanding Paul. Galatians is a letter that was written to the churches of Galatia, which is in central Asia Minor, modern-day Turkey. Paul had establishes some churches in this region. We aren't sure which cities he is actually writing to in this region of Galatia. What we are sure about is that Paul establishes these churches in Galatia on one of his missionary journeys. He taught these people as he taught everyone that they could be made right with God by faith in Christ, that they didn't have to become Jews in order to be right with the God of the Jews.

After Paul left these communities, other Christian missionaries came in who taught the people whom Paul had converted, that to be full members of the people of God, they had to join the Jewish people. Their argument is the one that I have outlined previously, namely that since salvation came from the God of the Jews, by sending the Jewish Messiah to the Jewish people in fulfillment of the Jewish Law, that for anybody to accept this salvation they had to be Jewish. For men that meant they had to circumcised if they were Gentiles. For men and women it meant that they had to keep kosher food laws and other laws laid out in the Scriptures.

When Paul found out that other missionaries had come into Galatia advocating this point of view he was furious. The letter of Galatians is written in order to correct the situation as Paul saw it. This letter is written in white hot anger. Of all of Paul's letter, it's the only one that does not begin by Paul thanking God for the congregation. Paul is incensed. For Paul, for a Gentile man to be circumcised and for Gentiles to keep kosher food laws after they have had faith in Christ is not simply to do things they don't need to do—not to do additional things that are unnecessary—for Paul, anybody who does these things in fact has compromised the very core of his Gospel message. If someone thinks they need to be circumcised or keep kosher food laws, they in fact have claimed that Christ's death is not sufficient for salvation. So they are not simply doing something additional that's unnecessary, in fact they are compromising the entire Gospel. For Paul, this meant that anybody who did such things was in danger of falling from God's grace. They were in danger of losing their salvation. Paul is explicit on this point throughout the letter to the Galatians where he says that you who want to be justified by following the Law have cut yourselves off from Christ, you have fallen from grace.

At points in this letter, Paul even turns sarcastic. Later on he says that—he's referring to the operation of circumcision, which by all accounts was not a pleasant operation for adults—Paul says that, I wish that those there who are unsettling you, urging you to be circumcised, would castrate themselves. In other words, when they perform the operation on themselves, he hopes that the knife slips.

Paul was insistent that keeping the Law was not necessary for salvation, that anybody who thought they did have to keep Law was in danger of losing their salvation. At the same time, Paul taught that people who have salvation, who have been justified, who have been right with God, should follow the ethical requirements of the Law, for example, the commands not to murder and to commit adultery, the command to love one's neighbor as one's self. This has created a certain amount of confusion for Paul's interpreters over the years. How can, on the one hand, he say, "don't follow the Law, because if you do, then you have fallen from grace," and, on the other hand, how he can tell people, "you have to follow the ethical laws of the Old Testament?" Paul never explains clearly why he thinks some laws are not to be followed, like the law of circumcision, but other laws are to be followed, like the law not to commit adultery. He doesn't explain why he has these two different categories in his head. It may be, scholars debate this, it may be that Paul had some kind of common sense distinction in his head between laws that were meant to make Jews Jewish, that were meant to allow Jews to preserve their distinctiveness as the Jewish people, and other laws that were meant for everybody who wanted to worship the God of Israel so that laws about circumcision, kosher food laws, keeping the Sabbath, keeping other festivals, these laws found in the Torah would be for Jews, but other laws such as most of the Ten Commandments—don't commit adultery, don't murder, don't bear false witness—would be commandments for everybody. The first criterion of ethical behavior for Paul then involves the ethical laws of the Hebrew Bible that Paul seems to accept unproblematically as important for Christians to follow. When God tells people how to behave in ethical ways in the Hebrew Bible, Paul simply assumes that one can follow these laws and that is a criterion then for ethical behavior.

The one law from Scripture that Paul particularly stressed was one that was important to Jesus as well. Leviticus, chapter 19, verse 18: "You shall love your neighbor as yourself." This law of love can be seen as an overarching ethical criterion for Paul, the love commandment. In both the letter to the Galatians and the letter to the Romans, Paul claims that believers in Christ must follow this rule of love, because when they do so, they will fulfill the Law—Galatians, chapter 5, verse 14. It is a very interesting idea that Paul tells people to love one another because in so doing they will fulfil the Law, after Paul has said that the Law doesn't matter for salvation. Nonetheless, this is one of the ironies of Paul's letters. People are to love one another so as to fulfill the Law.

Some scholars have seen the love commandment as being the very core of Paul's ethics. And to some extent that's true. Paul does base a number of his ethical judgments on this commandment to love one's neighbor as one's self. There are other ethical criteria that he uses that we will see near the end of the lecture. So I don't think it is quite correct to say that all of Paul's ethics are related to the love commandment, but certainly a number of Paul's ethical injunctions are related to the love commandment. In 1 Corinthians, in particular, Paul applies the love commandment in order to show people how they ought to behave.

One of the most famous passages of the New Testament is 1 Corinthians, chapter 13, which is sometimes called the love chapter. People are familiar with this chapter because it is the most popular passage of Scripture to be read at weddings. It is striking though that in fact this love chapter—1 Corinthians 13—in its own context has nothing to do with marriage or marital love or sexual love. I'll read the passage and then I'll try and explain what it means in its own context. By common consent, this is the most beautiful passage in the Pauline Epistles. It is so well constructed, some scholars have wondered whether Paul is adopting somebody else's writing here because it is so unlike most of the other passages in Paul's letters.

"If I speak in the tongues of mortals and of angels, but do not have love, I am a noisy gong or a clanging cymbal. If I have prophetic powers and understand all mysteries and all knowledge, and if I have all faith, so as to remove mountains, but don't have love, I am nothing. If I give away all my possessions, and if I hand over my body so that I may boast, but don't have love, I gain nothing. Love is patient, love is kind, love is not envious or boastful or arrogant or rude. It does not insist on its own way. It is not irritable or resentful. It does not rejoice in wrongdoing, but rejoices in the truth. It bears all things, believes all things, hopes all things, endures all things. Love never ends, but as for prophecies they'll come to an end. As for tongues they'll cease. As for knowledge it will come to an end. For we know only in part and we prophecy only in part. But when the complete comes the partial will come to an end. When I was a child, I spoke like a child, I thought like a child, I reasoned like a child. When I became an adult, I put an end to childish ways. For now we see in a mirror dimly, but then we will see face to face. Now I know only in part, then I will know fully even as I have been fully known. And now faith, hope, and love abide, these three. And the greatest of these is love."

Well, it is a terrific passage, the question is what did Paul mean by it. As I've indicated, he is not referring to marriage or wedding ceremonies. It's important to situate this passage on love in its own context. First Corinthians 13, of course, occurs between 1 Corinthians 12 and 1 Corinthians 14. The passages 1 Corinthians 12 and 14 are dealing with a particular problem that had arisen within the Corinthian community. It has do with what we referred to in the last lecture of the chaos that had ensued in the worship services of this community.

I need to set up what is going on in these worship services by explaining a little bit of the background. Paul's churches and Paul himself believed that they were living in an interim period between the beginning of the end of all things, which began with the resurrection of Jesus himself, and the culmination of the end that would occur with Jesus' returned in judgment. There is a short interim between the time Jesus was raised and the time he is going to come back. In this interim period, God had provided believers in Christ with the Holy Spirit as a kind of foreshadowing of what life would be like in the future kingdom. The Spirit was received by a person at baptism, an adult in this early period of Christianity would be baptized when they became a Christian and at that point the person would receive the Spirit. The Spirit endowed cach person with a gift that was to assist the community in its life together here during this interim period before the end. Different persons had different gifts. The Greek word for gifts is charismata. So these are called charismatic communities, communities that are run by spiritual gifts.

The gifts were various, some people were given the gift of leadership, others were administrators, others were teachers, some were healers, some could do miracles, some could speak God's word through prophecy from on high. Others spoke God's word by speaking in foreign tongues, unknown tongues. Yet others could interpret these tongues. Paul lays out his understanding of these spiritual gifts in 1 Corinthians 12:1–11, insisting that these gifts were given for the sake of the community so that people within the community could build one another up, therefore life in the community in the interim between Jesus' resurrection and his return. The Corinthians who believed themselves most spiritual maintained that they were especially endowed with the most spectacular gifts. In particular, some of these Corinthians were trying to lead the community by convincing them that they were spiritually superior to others, believed that they were particularly endowed with the gift of tongues. Speaking in tongues. And so during their worship services they would often disrupt these services by trying to prove that they had this most exotic of gifts. As a result, as I indicated in the last lecture, a good bit of chaos had come about.

Paul, in 1 Corinthians 12 through 14, tries to deal with this problem of people exercising the gift of tongues and prophecy and some of the other more spectacular gifts in inappropriate ways. He deals with the problem by laying down some rules. He says, for example, only two or three people should speak tongues at any given service, and when they do speak in tongues they should do so only if an interpreter is present.

In the midst of this discussion of spiritual gifts, Paul deals with what is really wrong with the situation in Corinth. Those who are trying to exalt themselves through the manifestation of this spiritual gift, or these spiritual gifts, have failed to understand that the gifts are given for the sake of the community. They are to practiced out of love for others, not out of the desire to elevate oneself as being spiritually superior, and so that's why he emphasizes in chapter 12 that these gifts are for the unity of the church. God has given knowledge, he's given prophecy, he's given tongues, he's given leadership, he has given all of these gifts for the sake of the community. After laying out these principles is when Paul then launches into his discourse on love in chapter 13. Knowing that makes sense of how Paul begins the chapter, otherwise it's hard to understand when you hear this at a wedding ceremony, it's hard to understand why Paul is talking about the things he talking about in the first few verses. You have to understand it within the context of spiritual gifts.

He begins by saying, as we just heard, if I speak in the tongues of mortals and of angels, but don't have love, I am a noisy gong or a clanging cymbal. In other words, if I have this gift of tongues, but I don't manifest it through love of others, then it is pointless. So, too, in verse 2, if I have prophetic powers, if I have the gift of prophecy; if I understand all mysteries and all knowledge, if I have the gift of knowledge; if I have the gift of faith so as to even move mountains but I don't have love, I'm nothing. These gifts are worthless if they are not manifested through love. If I give away all my possession, hand over my body that I might boast but don't have love, I gain nothing. This chapter is about how people are to manifest the gifts that they have been given by the Spirit within the community by showing love for others.

And so at the end of this thing, after Paul goes on and describes what true love is—it's patient, it's kind, it's not envious, boastful, arrogant, or rude—he appears to be describing problems within the community where you have Christian leaders who aren't patient, kind, who are boastful, arrogant, and rude. He's trying to correct the problems in the community. After he goes through these characteristics of love, he then returns to the question of spiritual gifts at the end of the chapter. He says prophecies will come to an end. Well, why is he saying that, because prophecies are a temporary gift for the sake of the interim. Love, though, is going to go on forever. Tongues will cease. Knowledge will come to an end. We prophecy in part, we know in part, but when the complete comes the partial will be done away with. What is the complete that is coming? There is going to be a kingdom that comes, for Paul. Jesus is going to return to earth, and partial knowledge will be done away with, people will know in full. I look now in a mirror dimly, I can barely kind of see the truth of the situation in the present. But then, I will see face to face, I will see exactly how things really are. And so there are three major gifts—faith, hope and love—but by far the greatest of these is love. And so then Paul continues on in chapter 14, again to show how people ought to manifest their gifts in the church.

This love commandment in other words is being used to explain how people ought to conduct themselves within the community. Paul understood this criterion of love to be a very flexible one. It could be made to apply to a variety of situations that believers found themselves in. In fact, when you read through Paul's letters it is quite clear that he applies this love commandment in a variety of contexts in a range of situations. For example, sometimes this is done rather obscurely, sometimes it's done quite clearly. For example, 1 Thessalonians, chapter 4, there is a very elusive reference to a situation going on in the Thessalonian church, where Paul says that a brother or sister should not defraud another. It is not quite clear what the situation is, but there seems to be some kind of sexual impropriety going on within the Thessalonian community. And Paul is telling whoever is doing this, and the reason Paul doesn't come out and say what the problem is, is presumably the people reading the letter know full well what the problem is, because it is their problem, and so Paul doesn't have to tell everybody else what the problem is. But he does say that out of love for one another, you shouldn't defraud a brother or sister. Well okay, so this can apply to instances of sexual impropriety.

It can apply to a wide range of situations as is clear in 1 Corinthians. I mentioned in the lecture on 1 Corinthians that one of the problems in the community had to do with eating meat that had been offered to idols. Some people in the Corinthian community thought that it was okay to eat meat that had been sacrificed to idols because these idols don't really exist. Other people thought that you shouldn't eat this meat because to do so was to participate in pagan idolatry. Paul's response to this situation is very interesting because he agrees with the people who say that idols aren't anything, the other gods don't really exist. And so eating meat sacrificed to idols is not really committing a sacrilege. He agrees with them in terms of what they think about the situation; he disagrees with them about the ethical corollary. They think therefore it's okay to eat the meat. Paul says no, it's not okay to eat the meat. But why not, if in fact this meat has just an offer to some idol that doesn't exist, why not eat the meat?

The reason you can't eat the meat, according to Paul in 1 Corinthians 8, is because other people think that these really do exist as other gods. These other Christians who think that the gods really do exist and that to eat this meat involves idolatry, will see you eat the meat and then themselves will be led to eat the meat even though they think it's wrong. Now they are incorrect, because it's not wrong, but it is what they think. So if you eat the meat, you will lead them to do something that they think is wrong, and you will cause them to sin because they will be doing something that they think is wrong. It's a kind of a convoluted argument, but the basic point is that if you love your neighbor within the Christian community you won't do anything that will lead them astray, even if their going astray is based on their own false knowledge. It is far more important that you love others than you eat meat. And so, Paul says, it's better just to be a vegetarian, if it comes to that. So far we have seen two of Paul's criteria for ethical behavior: the ethical injunctions of Scripture, broadly and more specifically secondly the command to love one's neighbor as oneself—Leviticus chapter 19, verse 18.

Paul did have other criteria of behavior, the other one that I want to talk about in this lecture very briefly involves more directly Paul's apocalyptic theology. As we have seen, Paul had an apocalyptic expectation that Jesus was soon to return from heaven in judgment on the earth. Paul appears to have believed that he himself would be alive when this happened. For Paul, the end was very near. This theological view that the end was near had implications for Paul's views of ethics. There was a kind of apocalyptic criterion for ethical behavior. In particular, Paul argued that since the end was near, one should not change one's social standing. One should not change one's social standing. In Paul's world, of course, there was slavery. In large urban areas a large proportion of the population was enslaved. In the city of Rome, possibly up to one-third of the population in Paul's day was comprised of slaves.

Should slaves attempt to be set free from their slavery? Well you would think yeah, that would be a good cause that Christian probably ought to work to free slaves from their slavery. Paul says, though, that since the end is near, slaves should not seek to be set free. Why worry about your social standing when the end is coming soon anyway? Some people are wondering whether they should get married. Paul insisted that people who were single, should remain single, since the end was near. If you get married, you'll need to be concerned about the needs of your spouse, and you won't be able to devote yourself fully to the coming kingdom and pressing the urgent mission to get other people to convert. And so if you are single, you should remain single, if you can. Paul does make a concession, though, that if you are in a relationship and unable to restrain yourself sexually, then it is better to go ahead and get married. Whereas Paul says it is better to marry than to burn, but since the end is near, it is better not to. Similarly, if a person is married, even if they are married to unbeliever, Paul says they shouldn't get divorce. Why? No point changing your social standing, when in fact the end is imminent.

In conclusion, even though Paul taught that salvation came apart from the Law, he did not urge lawless behavior. In fact, Paul insisted on the morality of his congregations and applied a number of criteria to ethical situations in order to determine what the proper mode of behavior was. The ethical injunctions of Scripture were to be followed first. Second, the command to love one another as one's self was to be applied to a variety of situations. And third, the apocalyptic realities of this world were to affect how one lived one's life. And so, ultimately Paul's ethics were rooted in his understanding of God's act of salvation in Christ. In the next lecture we will look at Paul's fullest exposition of his doctrine of salvation as found in the letter to the Romans.

Paul's Letter to the Romans
Lecture 17

By all counts, Romans has a unique position among the Pauline epistles. The letter indicates that Paul was *not* the founder of the church in Rome and that he had never even visited it.

The letter does not appear, at least on the surface, to be directed to any problems found in the Roman church; when it does deal with ethical or theological issues, it does so abstractly—not in direct response to a situation in the congregation. Instead of addressing the needs of the Roman church per se, Paul uses the letter to explain at great length his understanding of the Christian gospel, emphasizing in particular his view that salvation comes to all people—Jew and Gentile equally—through faith in Christ, apart from doing the works of the Law. His reasons for developing his views at such length to a church he had never visited are never stated, but may be inferred from some of the things he says in the course of the letter. Paul indicates that he is about to travel to Jerusalem and he is concerned about his reception among "Jewish-Christians" there, who are suspicious of his "Law-free" gospel (15:25–31). He may be developing his views about the relationship of Jews and Gentiles in Christ as a trial run for his trip. Paul also indicates that he will be starting a mission to the West and suggests that he would like to use the Roman church as a base of operations (1:10–15). Given the misperceptions that some people in the Roman community have about his gospel (e.g., 3:8), he may be using the letter to assure his readers that his mission is worthy of their support.

Whatever the precise reason for the letter, it's clear that Romans provides the most systematic exposition of Paul's understanding of God's work of salvation through Christ. We have already seen some of the basic features of Paul's understanding of the importance of Christ as the way to salvation. In Romans, we find the clearest development of Paul's theological reflections.

A close reading of Romans indicates that Paul has different ways of conceptualizing how God used Christ's death to bring salvation; that is to say, Paul has different conceptual "models" for salvation. The model Paul most commonly uses understands salvation in legal or judicial terms. The judicial model imagines salvation to be comparable to a legal procedure. God is likened to a cosmic lawgiver, who has given his Laws for people to follow (all people, not just Jews). God is also the judge who enacts punishment for the violation of his laws; unfortunately, everyone has broken them, in one way or another (i.e., they've committed acts of transgression, or sins, against God's Law). As a result, everyone falls under the judgment of the court, and the penalty for breaking God's Laws is death. But according to this model, Christ is one who does not deserve death, because he has not violated any of God's Laws. Christ's death, then, is not to pay a penalty that he owes but to pay the penalty for others. God shows that he accepts the payment of this penalty by raising Jesus from the dead. Humans can avail themselves of this payment of their debt simply by trusting that God will find Christ's death adequate; the only alternative is to pay the penalty themselves. Those who trustingly accept Christ's death as a payment for their sins (i.e., who have "faith" in Christ's death) are treated as if they are "not guilty" by the court (even though, in fact, they're completely guilty); that is, they are "justified" (put into a right standing with God).

Paul has different ways of conceptualizing how God used Christ's death to bring salvation; that is to say, Paul has different conceptual "models" for salvation.

This model is commonly called Paul's "doctrine of justification by faith apart from the Law." The term "justification" in Greek comes from the same root as the word "rightness." It refers to the act of God in which he puts someone into a "right" relationship with himself. According to this model, the human problem of sin cannot be solved by trying to keep the Jewish Law. Both Jews and Gentiles have violated the law in one way or another, even religious Jews who do their best. All stand under the same penalty of death and, therefore, all must be saved from death in the same way. The Law can't bring about salvation because the Law is what brings condemnation. Paul says that God is righteous and that people can be made "right" with God by faith. Paul then launches into the human dilemma, that is, the sinful nature of mankind (whether Jew, Christian, or pagan). Thus, everyone is under the power of sin (3:9) and, therefore, under God's condemnation. But God has a solution (3:21–26). He has acted on mankind's behalf by having Christ die for them in an act of unmerited favor. Jesus' sacrifice is an atonement for sin and proof of God's righteousness. Paul sees this notion of justification by faith apart from the Law to be taught by the Law itself, particularly in the stories of the father of the Jews, Abraham, who was "justified" by God on the basis of his faith well before he had been circumcised (Romans 4, quoting Gen. 15:6).

We can see from the Letter to the Romans that Paul does not always think of salvation in judicial terms. Consider, for example, what Paul says about "sin." Clearly, for Paul "sin" is more than an act of disobedience to God. Sin is in the world (5:13); sin rules people (5:21); people can serve sin (6:6); people can be enslaved to sin (6:17); people can die to sin (6:11); and people can be freed from sin (6:18). Rather than an act of disobedience, sin is conceived in an apocalyptic way, as a kind of demonic power that is in the world and trying to enslave people to do its will. Paul speaks of "death" in similar ways—as an evil force opposed to God that can enslave his people. Thus, Paul sometimes conceives of the act of salvation not in legal but in apocalyptic terms. We can call this mode of conceptualization Paul's "participationist" view of salvation. The participationist view contains many surface similarities to the judicial: The problem is thought of as "sin"; sin leads to death; and the solution to the human problem is Christ's death and resurrection. But the meanings of these terms and the way the model works are completely different.

In this model, sin is a cosmic power that enslaves people. Everyone is enslaved to this power, and no one can escape. Christ, though, escaped this power. Evidence is provided by the resurrection. Because Christ defeated the power of death, he must also have defeated the concomitant power of sin. People can escape the power of sin by participating in Christ's victory, which occurs by being united with Christ in his death. This happens when a person is baptized. Therefore, those who have been baptized into Christ have escaped the nefarious powers of sin and death and are freed for eternal life.

It may be useful to compare and contrast these two conceptual models of salvation (i.e., judicial and participationist). In one, sin is an act of disobedience; in the other, it is an evil cosmic power. In one, the human problem is the penalty of death that comes through violation of God's Law; in the other, the problem is enslavement to an alien power. In one, the divine solution is for Christ to pay the penalty that humans owe; in the other, the solution is for Christ to break the enslaving power of death to bring liberation. In one, salvation comes by means of a trusting acceptance that Christ's death has paid the penalty; in the other, it comes by participating in Christ's victory by being united with him in baptism.

Paul did not see these models as being at odds with one another. He never explicitly lays out his models or explains their similarities or differences. Rather, the models are presupposed throughout the letter and Paul's other writings. The models appear to interact closely with one another in Paul's mind. Why is everyone guilty before God? Because they have all sinned through acts of transgression (the judicial model; 3:23). Why has everyone sinned? Because all are under the alien power of sin (the participationist model; 3:9). Why is everyone under the alien power of sin? Because the first man, Adam, committed an act of disobedience (judicial model) that allowed the power of sin to enter the world (participationist model; 5:12). And so on.

As Paul himself saw, both models have profound implications for understanding the nature of Judaism—because both insist that it is only by Christ's death and resurrection that God brings salvation. Paul then needs to deal with the question of whether God has "changed the rules" or, even worse, whether he has rescinded his eternal covenant with Israel. In Romans 9–1, Paul deals with these thorny issues and argues that God is faithful and has not gone back on his promises—even though his own people have rejected him when they rejected the messiah. Still, bringing the Gentiles into the people of God is all part of the divine plan for all people—Jew and Gentile—to be saved. ■

Essential Reading

Romans.

Brown, *Introduction to the New Testament*, chap. 24.

Ehrman, *The New Testament: A Historical Introduction*, chap. 21.

Supplemental Reading

Donfried, *The Romans Debate*.

Roetzel, *The Letters of Paul*.

Wedderburn, *The Reasons for Romans*.

Questions to Consider

1. Summarize the judicial and participationist models of salvation. Are there points at which these models appear to be at odds with one another?

2. What other conceptual models can you imagine as a way of presenting the importance of Christ's death for salvation? How, for example, would a model look that was based on viewing Christ's death as a "purchase" of people? Or a "reconciliation" between warring factions?

Paul's Letter to the Romans
Lecture 17—Transcript

To this point in our study of Paul's letters we have seen how he addressed ethical and theological problems of his churches. First Corinthians represents Paul's response to a highly troubled situation that emerged in the church in Corinth after he left to engage in missionary activities elsewhere. The other letters as well represent Paul's attempts to make sure that the churches he founded remained true to the Gospel that he preached and the ethical implications that arose out of it.

The one major exception is Paul's letter to the Romans. By all counts Romans has a unique position among the Pauline Epistles. The letter itself indicates that Paul not only was not the founder of the church in Rome, but that he had never even visited it. Chapter 1, verses 10 through 15, Paul writes to these people and tells them that he is eager to visit them even though he hasn't done so yet and in fact has been prevented from doing so, but he wants to come to them to share with them his Gospel message.

Paul did not found this church. We are not sure how the church in Rome was established. There have been various theories that have been put out over the years. In the Book of Acts on the day of Pentecost, among the Jews who are present to hear the Apostles speaking in foreign tongues are Jews who are from Rome. Is it possible that visitors to Jerusalem became converted to Christianity and then took the religion back to Rome and started a community there? That is certainly possible. It is also possible that other Christian missionaries from Jerusalem or elsewhere visited Rome and established the community there. In any event, it is certain that Paul did not establish this community, and our first direct evidence of there being any community of Christians there at all is in fact Paul's own letter to the Romans. Paul had never visited this church, he had not founded the church, which makes this letter quite unlike any of the other letter in the Pauline corpus. This is not a letter directed to Paul's churches or one of Paul's churches in order to solve its problems. In fact, the letter does not appear at least on the surface to be directed to any problems of the church in Rome at all. When it does deal with ethical or theological issues, the letter does so abstractly, not in direct response to a situation that Paul appears to know about from the church.

Instead of addressing the needs of the Roman community per se, Paul uses this letter to explain at great length his understanding of the Christian Gospel, emphasizing in particular his view that salvation comes to all people— Jew and Gentile equally—through faith in Christ, apart from doing works of the Law.

One continual question amongst scholars has to do with why Paul wrote the letter if it's not being directed to one of his own churches. Why does Paul develop his views of salvation by faith through Christ to a community that he has never visited? It is not completely clear why Paul does this, but there are a couple of possible reasons that one can infer from the letter itself. Paul indicates in this letter near the ending of it, that he is about to travel to Jerusalem. He has taken up a collection for the Jewish Christians in Jerusalem during a time of crises there. There was a drought and there were financial problems being experienced by the Christians in Jerusalem and so Paul has taken up a collection among his Gentile communities to help meet the needs of the Christians in Jerusalem. Paul appears to be expecting that he will be confronted with Jewish Christians there in Jerusalem who may be suspicious of his Gospel which says that a person is made right with God apart from becoming a Jew, apart from following the Jewish Law. It is possible that he is writing the letter to the Romans in part in order to allow him to develop his views about the relationship of Jews and Gentiles in Christ as a kind of trial run for his trip to Jerusalem. That's a possibility.

In addition, Paul indicates that he is soon going to start a Christian mission to the West, and he suggest in this letter that he would like to use the Roman church as a base of operation—chapter 1, verses 10 through 15. He moreover indicates in the letter that there are people in the Roman community who have some misperceptions about his teachings. For example, in the last lecture I mentioned Romans, chapter 3, verse 8, where Paul says that some people claim that he thinks we should do evil so that good might come. In other words, that Paul's gospel apart from the Law leads to lawlessness. Paul may be writing this letter in order to correct the misperceptions about him and to assure his readers in Rome that he stands for the same Gospel that they stand for, precisely so that they might support him in his mission to the West. That, too, is a possibility for why he writes this letter.

In any event, it is clear that this letter is quite different from the others. While the other letters that Paul wrote are directed to needs within his own communities, in Romans, Paul is not directing his counsel to any of his communities, instead he is writing a systematic exposition of his understanding of the Gospel to a community he has never visited. He wants to explain his view of God's work of salvation through Christ, either as a dry run for what is going to happen to him in Jerusalem or possibly even more likely in order to acquire support of this community for his westward mission.

We have already seen some of the basic features of Paul's understanding of the importance of Christ as the way to salvation in earlier lectures. In Romans, we will find the clearest development of Paul's theological reflection. A close reading of Romans indicates that Paul has different ways of conceptualizing how God used Christ's death to bring about salvation. That is to say, Paul has different conceptual models for how salvation works. I should emphasize that these are models for understanding salvation. Paul has ways of talking about how the death of Christ brought about a right standing before God. These are models that he uses, they aren't the thing themselves.

We're going to talk in this lecture about two of Paul's major models that you find in the letter to the Romans. The reason I am laying things out this way is because Paul says things in Romans that would be confusing unless you understood that he has different conceptual models that work at the same time. The first model that Paul appears to use is one in which he tries to understand salvation in the legal or judicial terms. Legal or judicial terms. This judicial model of salvation imagines God's activities to be comparable to a legal procedure. It works like this. According to this way of conceptualizing things, God is likened to a cosmic lawgiver who has given his laws for people to follow—all people, not just Jews. All people are governed by God's laws. The Jews, of course, have their Law found in the Torah of Moses. But all people know the right thing to do. All people have laws that God has given that they need to follow. So, God is a lawgiver.

Under this model, God is also the judge who enacts punishment for the violation of his laws. Unfortunately, everyone has broken these laws in one way or another. That is to say, that everyone has committed an act or more likely many acts of transgression against God or sins. As a result, everyone falls under the judgment of the court, and the penalty for breaking these laws of God is death. But, according to this model, Christ is one who does not deserve death because he himself has not violated any of God's laws. Christ's death then is not to pay a penalty that he himself owes. Instead, Christ's death pays the penalty owed by others. In this model, God shows that he accepts the payment of the penalty that Jesus has made for others by raising Jesus from the dead. The logic is that once the death penalty has been paid, it no longer needs to be continued to be inflicted and so God raises Jesus from the dead to show that payment has been accepted.

Human beings can avail themselves of this payment of their debt simply by trusting that God will find Christ's death adequate. The only alternative is for a person to pay the penalty of death him or herself. Those who trustingly accept Christ's death as a payment for their sins, that is those who have faith in Christ's death, are treated as if they are not guilty by the court, even though in fact they are completely guilty. That is, they are justified. They are put into a right standing before God.

This model of salvation is commonly called Paul's doctrine of justification by faith or, more fully, Paul's doctrine of justification by faith apart from the Law. The term justification comes from a Greek word, which has the same root as the term rightness. Rightness. It refers to the act of God, in which God puts a person into a right relationship with himself, so to be justified is to be put into a right relationship with God. According to this model then, the human problem of sin cannot be solved by trying to keep the Jewish Law. Both Jews and Gentiles have violated the Law in one way or another, even religious Jews who do their best. All people stand under the same penalty of death because they have broken the Law and therefore all must be saved from death in the same way. The Law can't bring about salvation because it's the Law that brings condemnation. Because it is by violating the Law that one gets condemned.

The letter to the Romans provides an exposition of this understanding of Paul's doctrine of justification by faith. I want to take just a minute to show how this doctrine gets played out in the early chapters of Romans, Romans chapters 1 through 3. The letter begins, as most of Paul's letter do, by Paul introducing himself and indicating to whom he is writing. He begins with Paul, a servant of Jesus Christ, called to be an Apostle. He goes on to indicate that he is writing to God's beloved who are in Rome. At an early part of this letter, after saying how much he wants to visit these Christians, Paul launches into the subject of the letter, which is his own Gospel message. Chapter 1, verses 16 and 17, Paul sets out the thesis of this book where he says, I am not ashamed of the Gospel, it is the power of God for salvation to everyone who has faith, to the Jews first and also to the Greek. For in it, the righteousness of God is revealed from faith to faith. For as it is written, the one who is righteous by faith will live.

Let me take just a second to unpack this. Paul says that he is not ashamed of the Gospel, the Gospel being a word for good news—the good news of God's salvation. Why is he not ashamed of this gospel, because it provides God's power for salvation to everyone who has faith, to the Jews first and also the Greek. Why to the Jews first? Well, because the message of salvation first came to the Jews because it is in fulfillment of the Jewish Scriptures. But it also goes to those who are non-Jews or, as Paul call them here, the Greek. For the Gospel reveals God's righteousness, his upright way of dealing with people. His upright way of dealing with people is from beginning to end on the basis of faith. For as it is written, the one who is righteous by faith will live. In other words, a person will have eternal life if they are made right with God through their faith. That's the thesis of the Book of Romans, where Paul is going to go on then to show that in fact a person is made right with God through faith, not by works of the Law.

The beginning chapters of this book lay out the human problem that makes God's provision of salvation necessary. In the next verse, verse 18 of chapter 1, Paul launches into the human dilemma. It's the dilemma that all people have violated God's law—not just Jews who have broken the Torah, but also Gentiles who don't have the Torah. Chapter 1, verse 18, the wrath of God is revealed from heaven against all ungodliness and wickedness of those who by their wickedness and suppress the truth. Paul goes on to talk about pagans who know that there is only one God, the Creator, but nonetheless chose not to worship God, but instead to worship idols. By committing rank acts of idolatry, pagans are given over to all sorts of immoral acts, which further estrange them from God Chapter 1, then, deals with pagan immorality, pagan sin, pagan disobedience to God.

Chapter 2 turns to the Jews, who have also broken God's law even though they knew better. They have the Torah and yet they violate the Torah. By the time that Paul's is done with chapters 1 and 2 there is nobody left—the pagans are sinners before God and God's wrath is revealed against them; and the Jews, even though they have the Law, are no better off because they also have sinned. Paul sums it up at the beginning of chapter 3 then by saying that everybody stands under God's condemnation, whether they have the Torah or not. All people, he says, chapter 3, verse 9, are under the power of sin. Verse 20, no human being, he says, will be made right in God's sight by deeds of the Law, because through the Law comes the knowledge of sin. All people stand under God's condemnation.

And then Paul begins to discuss God's solution to this human dilemma. This is a packed passage, chapter 3 of Romans, verses 21 through 26, where Paul shows that even though everybody has violated God's law, God has acted on their behalf by having Christ die for them so that they could be made right with him. Paul says all have sinned and fallen short of the glory of God, but now they are justified, that is, made right with God on the basis of his grace. His unmerited favor as a gift through the redemption that is provided by Christ Jesus, whom God put forward as a sacrifice of atonement by his blood. Jesus dies as a way of bringing atonement his is a sacrifice for the sake of others. God did this to show that he is right because in his divine forbearance, he passed over sins previously committed. It was to prove at the present time that he himself is righteous—he is upright—and he makes right the one who has faith in Jesus. A person is made right with God by having faith in Jesus because Jesus has died to pay the penalty of sins.

Paul goes on then, most interestingly in chapter 4 of Romans, to show that this understanding, that a person is justified by God apart from the Law, Paul goes on to show that this doctrine of justification by faith is actually taught by the Law itself. This is an interesting irony that Paul wants to claim that being made right with God apart from the Law is a doctrine taught by the Law. It may seem like a peculiar argument, but it is the one that he wants to maintain. Chapter 3, verse 31, do we overthrow the Law by this faith? By no means. On the contrary, we uphold the Law. Well, how does Paul think that he upholds the Law by saying the Law is of no use for salvation?

Paul turns to a passage in the Book of Genesis, the first book of the Torah, in which the father of the Jews is discussed, Abraham—Abraham, the first person, according to Paul, to be made right with God. How is Abraham made right with God? Abraham believed in God and that was counted to him as righteousness. Abraham is made right by God by believing, not by doing anything. Abraham, of course, is the father of the Jews. It was to Abraham that God gave the law of circumcision, that all of his descendents should be circumcised. But Paul asks, when Genesis says that Abraham believed God and reckoned him as righteousness, was that before or after Abraham was circumcised. Well, in fact, that verse—Abraham believed God and it was reckoned him as righteousness—is found in Genesis, chapter 15. It is not until Genesis, chapter 17, that Abraham is circumcised, receives the law of circumcision, so that being made right with God occurs before the act of circumcision, which means that the act of circumcision has nothing to do with being made right with God. In other words, Paul wants to use the Torah, the Law itself, especially the Book of Genesis, to show that being made right with God is not a matter of following law, it's a matter of having faith. This then is Paul's doctrine of justification by faith. This is his judicial or legal way of understanding salvation.

But Paul understands salvation in other ways as well, he has other models to unpack what it means to say that Christ's death brings about salvation. You can see from the letter of Romans itself that Paul does not always think about salvation in judicial terms. This can be seen most clearly by what Paul says about sin. Clearly for Paul, sin is not only an act of disobedience to God. Notice the following things that Paul says. Paul says, sin was in the world. Sin is in the world, chapter 5, verse 13. Sin rules people, 5:21. People can serve sin, 6:6. People can be enslaved to sin, 6:17. People can die to sin, 6:11. People can be freed from sin, 6:18. In these passages the term sin isn't referring to an act of disobedience. In these passages, sin is being understood in an apocalyptic way as a kind of demonic power that is in the world trying to enslaved people to do its will. Sin here is a demonic power. Paul speaks of death also as a kind of demonic power. An evil force that's opposed to

God that can enslave people. Thus Paul sometimes conceives of the act of salvation, not in legal or judicial terms, but also in apocalyptic terms.

We might call this mode of conceptualization, Paul's participationist view of salvation. This participationist model contains many surface similarities to the judicial model. In this model as well, the problem humans have is called sin. In this model as well, sin leads to death, and in this model, the solution to the human problem is Christ's death and resurrection. But the meaning of these terms and the way the model works is completely different from the way the judicial model does. In the participationist model, sin is a cosmic power that enslaves people. Everyone, according to this way of thinking of things, everyone is enslaved to the power of sin and no one has the power to escape. Christ, though, did escape this power. How does Paul know that Christ escaped the power of sin? Because Paul knows through his own experience that Jesus was raised from the dead. Since Jesus was raised from the dead, that shows that he defeated the power of death. If he defeated the power of death, he must have defeated the other power, the other powers in the world including the power of sin. So Christ has defeated the powers aligned against God.

In this model, people can themselves escape the power of sin by participating in Christ's own victory. How does a person participate in Christ's victory? It's by being united with Christ in his own death. This happens when a person is baptized. Romans, chapter 6, Paul says that a person is unified with Christ in his death when the person is baptized. When you are unified with Christ in his death, then you participate in his victory over death and the other powers, including the powers of sin. So, those who have been baptized into Christ have escaped the nefarious powers of sin and death and are freed for eternal life. That's the participationist model.

It might be useful for us to compare and contrast the two models. In one model, sin is thought of as an act of disobedience. In the other, it's an evil cosmic power. In one model, the human problem is a penalty of death that comes from violating God's law. In the other, the problem is an enslavement to an alien power. In one, the divine solution is for Christ to pay the penalty that human's owe. In the other, the solution is for Christ to break the enslaving power of death to bring liberation. In one, salvation comes by a trusting acceptance that Christ's death has paid the penalty. In the other, it comes by participating in Christ's victory by being united with him in baptism.

Paul did not see these two models as being at odds with one another. He nowhere explicitly lays out the models or explains their similarities or differences for us. Instead they are presupposed throughout the letter to the Romans and throughout his other writing. But it is important to think about these two models when you read this book and Paul's others letters, because otherwise what Paul says sometimes won't make sense because it will be talking about sin in different ways, or death in different ways, or the meaning of Jesus' death in different ways.

These models seem to interact closely though with one another in Paul's mind. You can see the close interaction of the two models by seeing the various things that Paul says. Why is everyone guilty before God for Paul? Well, it is because they have committed acts of transgression. That's the judicial model, Romans 3:23. But why has everybody done that, why has everybody committed acts of transgression, because everybody is under the alien power of sin. That's the participationist model, chapter 3, verse 9. But why is everybody under the alien power of sin? Well, it's because the first man, Adam, committed an act of disobedience—the judicial model, chapter 5. By Adam committing an act of disobedience, that allowed the power of sin to come into the world—the participationist model. And so it goes, the two models are closely intertwined throughout the letter.

As Paul himself saw, both of these models have profound implications for understanding the nature of Judaism, since both models insist that it's only through Christ's death and resurrection that God brings about salvation. For that reason, Paul has to deal with the question of whether God has changed the rules, or, even worse, whether he has rescinded his eternal covenant that he made with Israel. Has god now started giving a different way of salvation than he had for the Jews in the Hebrew Bible?

Romans, chapters 9 through 11, represents Paul's attempt to deal with those thorny issues of the relationship of God's salvation through Christ with the historic existence of the people of Israel. Paul insist that in fact God remains faithful and true to his covenant. He has not gone back on his promises, even though his own people have rejected him when they rejected the Messiah. Still, God had planned all along to bring Gentiles into the people of God. That is part of God's plan for all people, Jew and Gentile, to be saved. In the end, God will be faithful to his promises to Israel and will bring them, too, into the kingdom.

In conclusion, the letter to the Romans is unique in that it is not directed to the needs of one of Paul's own congregations, but is the Apostle's exposition of his own understanding of the Gospel, written in order to garner support for his mission by the large and influential church in Rome. Throughout the exposition, Paul applies two modes of conceptualization to the salvation that comes in Christ. The judicial model and the participationist model. His overarching point is that all people, Jew or Gentile, need God's salvation and that the salvation comes only through Christ's death, not by works of the Law. This, though, is not contrary to the Jewish religion. The Jews for Paul remain God's chosen vehicle for bringing salvation into the world— salvation that is now available to Gentiles as well on equal terms. Even though the salvation comes apart from the works of the Law, that does not mean that those who believe in Jesus can live lawlessly. One might well ask after looking at this exposition, how Paul's emphasis on the saving work of Christ's death relates to the teaching of Jesus himself, that people need to repent and keep the Jewish Law in view of the coming Son of Man. Is this sophisticated theology of Paul's at all like the simple preaching of Jesus? That will be the question that I will address in our next lecture.

Paul, Jesus, and James
Lecture 18

> On the one hand, there are broad ranging similarities between Jesus
> and Paul that you would expect from two 1st century apocalyptic Jews.
> On the other hand, there are also a number of striking differences
> between the two.

ow that we have nearly completed our study of Jesus and Paul, the
two most important figures of early Christianity, it might be useful
to take a step back and compare what we've discovered. That will
be the goal of this lecture. We will compare and contrast the teachings of
these two men, to see whether they are completely compatible—as most
people who haven't given the matter a good deal of thought probably
assume—or whether, instead, they stand at odds with one another in some of
their key ideas. After making that comparison, we'll compare Paul's writings
with one other book of the New Testament, the epistle of James, which has
been thought by some, since the 16th century, to stand in direct opposition to
Paul's teaching of justification by faith apart from works. The overarching
question that these comparisons—indeed, that this entire course—is trying
to answer is whether early Christianity was one solid monolith or extremely
diverse, whether it was one thing or lots of things, whether there was, in fact,
one early Christianity or several early Christianities.

It is interesting to compare the fundamental teachings of Jesus and Paul
on a point-by-point basis. We are presupposing that we have reconstructed
what the historical Jesus taught. As you might expect, there are a number of
striking similarities. Both men were 1st-century Jews who, like most Jews,
believed in the one God, the creator of all, who had made a covenant with
the people Israel and given them his Law. Both were apocalypticists, who
thought the end of history was imminent, to be brought in a cataclysmic
judgment by a cosmic judge from heaven. Both taught that people needed
to prepare for this coming climax of history. Both taught that keeping the
letter of the Law would have no effect on one's standing before God and
that the Law could be summed up in the command to love one's neighbor
as oneself.

There are also a number of striking differences between the two. The historical Jesus (i.e., the man himself, not the Jesus as portrayed in one or the other of the Gospels) taught that the cosmic judge coming from heaven was someone that he called the Son of Man, and this Son of Man was not Jesus himself. Paul taught that the cosmic judge was Jesus. Jesus taught that to escape judgment, a person must keep the central teachings of the Jewish Law, as he himself interpreted them. Paul never mentioned Jesus' interpretations of the Law and insisted that keeping the Law would never bring salvation; the only way to be saved was to trust Jesus' death and resurrection. Jesus saw his own importance as lying in his proclamation of the coming end and his interpretation of the Law. Paul saw Jesus' importance as lying exclusively in his death and resurrection for sins.

A passage from Matthew (25:31–46) will help us explore these differences. Jesus speaks of the cosmic judge ("the Son of Man") in a passage that probably goes back to the historical Jesus. Salvation comes by loving others and doing good things (cf., Leviticus 19:18), not through Jesus or belief in him. In both Romans 3 and Galatians 3, Paul says just the opposite: Justification is through faith in Christ, not through works of the Law. How does one account for these differences? The traditional view of the difference is that Jesus was teaching *before* his death and resurrection and Paul was teaching *afterwards* and that Jesus could not have emphasized his death and resurrection before they occurred.

Some interpreters question this view. Why would Jesus teach people that they could enter God's Kingdom by keeping his Law if it simply wasn't true? An alternative view is that Paul represents a significant development of Jesus' teachings, that he altered the basic message in light of his experience of Jesus' resurrection, making Jesus' death, rather than his proclamation, the key point of the message. According to this view, Paul transformed the religion *of* Jesus into a religion *about* Jesus. Many scholars today think this view is too simplistic and that perhaps Paul is not quite the innovator that earlier scholars thought he was. It is striking in this connection that Paul rarely talks about the religion that Jesus himself propounded and rarely mentions anything that Jesus said or did. Are the two men talking about the same religion?

This raises the interesting point of whether Paul actually knew what Jesus had said and done during his life. It's important to remember that Paul was living and writing before the Gospels were produced. We shouldn't assume, therefore, that he knew what was going to be written in them. If we were to read just Paul's letters, how much information about Jesus' life would we be able to learn from them? That is, how much do we know that Paul knew about Jesus? There's not a lot of information there. The following list is fairly complete:

1. Jesus was born of a woman (Gal. 4:4).
2. He was born Jewish (Gal. 4:4).
3. He was reputedly from the line of King David (Rom 1:3).
4. He had brothers, one of whom was named James (1 Cor. 5:9; Gal. 1:19).
5. His ministry was among Jews (Rom 15:8).
6. He had 12 disciples (1 Cor. 15:5).
7. He had a last meal with his disciples, in which he instituted the Lord's Supper (1 Cor. 11:23–25).
8. He was betrayed (1 Cor. 11:23).
9. He was crucified (1 Cor. 2:2).
10. He taught that his followers should not be divorced (1 Cor. 7:11) and that they should pay their ministers (1 Cor. 9:14).

Think of the things about Jesus we wouldn't know if this were all the material we had. How does one account for the paucity of this material? Maybe Paul knew a good deal more about Jesus but, given the occasional nature of his letters, had no reason to provide more information. He did know some of Jesus' disciples, after all. On the other hand, Paul constantly reminds his readers what he taught them: Why didn't he ever remind them what Jesus taught? On rare occasions, he does cite Jesus as an authority for his views; if he know more about what Jesus said, why would he not cite him more often? Maybe Paul knew a good deal more about Jesus, but considered that information irrelevant for his own mission. He does say, after all, to the Corinthians, "I knew nothing when I was among you except Christ, and him crucified" (i.e., he didn't "know" or "teach" anything other than the importance of Jesus' death). Could Paul have had a view precisely opposite that of the Gospel of Thomas, for whom only the words of Jesus, not his death and resurrection, were what mattered for salvation? Maybe Paul did not know much more than he mentioned. Could it be that the death and resurrection of Jesus were of such earth-shattering importance to Paul that he didn't even inquire into what Jesus said and did while he was alive? Scholars continue to debate this question, and there does not appear to be any clear-cut answer.

It may also be fruitful to compare Paul, not just with the one who came before him, Jesus, but also with one who came after him, James. The epistle of James is commonly attributed to Jesus' own brother. The author does claim to be someone named James, but he does not claim to be a personal relation to Jesus. James was a common name in the ancient world. We aren't sure, therefore, who wrote the letter, except to say that unlike Jesus' brother James, who would have been a lower-class Aramaic-speaking peasant, this epistle is written by a well-educated Greek-speaking Christian.

We have seen a good deal of diversity in early Christianity. The different Gospels have different portrayals of Jesus and there appear to be discrepancies among them.

The book consists of a number of moral exhortations for its readers to behave in ways appropriate to their faith. Many of the exhortations sound very similar to Jesus' own teachings, for example, from the Sermon on the Mount. One passage in particular has given readers pause over the years, James 2:14-26. The passage seems to stand in stark contrast to what Paul teaches, for example, in the Book of Romans. James indicates that a person "is justified by works, not by faith alone." Contrast Rom. 3:28: "a person is justified by faith apart from the works of the Law." Interestingly, just as Paul in Romans uses the father of the Jews, Abraham, as proof that justification comes by faith alone (Rom. 4:2, 22), James uses him to show that a person is justified only by doing works (2:21). Both even quote the same verse from the Old Testament, Gen. 15:6, to support their views: "And Abraham believed God and it was counted to him as righteousness."

How does one explain these differences? Some people would argue that James has heard the teaching of Paul, that a person is justified only by faith in Christ apart from doing what the Law demands, and wants to provide a corrective. In addition to faith, one must lead a life that is ethical. Other people would point out that this perspective is not so far off from what Paul taught, because he did require his converts to follow strict codes of conduct. Again, though, interpreters continue to debate whether these two authors stand at odds with one another.

We have seen a good deal of diversity in early Christianity. The different Gospels have different portrayals of Jesus and there appear to be discrepancies among them. Jesus himself preached a message that was altered before being written into the Gospels. In his own proclamation, Jesus saw the imminent intervention of God in the affairs of the world, through the appearance of the Son of Man in judgment. Paul's message appears to be different, based on his view that salvation comes, not through faithful obedience to the Law of God, but through faith in Jesus' death and resurrection. As we continue our discussions of the New Testament, we will see even more diversity. Some of this diversity can be found in books that claim Paul as their author but that seem to present a different understanding of the Gospel than his. That will be the subject of our next lecture. ■

Essential Reading

Brown, *Introduction to the New Testament*, chap. 34.

Ehrman, *The New Testament: A Historical Introduction*, chap 22.

Furnish, *Jesus According to Paul*.

Supplemental Reading

Wenham, *Paul and Jesus*.

1. Consider each of the possible explanations in this lecture for why Paul does not mention more about Jesus' life; work out a list of arguments both for and against each explanation. When you look at them closely, which view strikes you as the most plausible? Can you think of other options?

2. If Paul and Jesus represent different understandings of salvation, can they really be said to have subscribed to the same religion? Put differently, is it historically right to say that Jesus was a Christian?

Paul, Jesus, and James
Lecture 18—Transcript

Now that we have nearly completed our study of Jesus and Paul, the two most important figures of early Christianity, it might be useful to take a step back and to compare what we have discovered. That will be the goal of the present lecture—to compare and contrast the teachings these two men to see whether they are completely compatible, as most people who haven't given a good deal of though to the matter probably assume, or whether instead they stand at odds with one another in some of their key ideas.

After making that comparison, we'll compare Paul's writings with one other book of the New Testament, the Epistle of James, which since the 16th century has been thought by some to stand in direct opposition to Paul's teaching of justification by faith apart from works. The overarching question that these comparisons, indeed that this entire course is trying to answer is whether early Christianity was one solid monolith or was extremely diverse. Whether it was one thing or lots of things. Whether there was in fact one early Christianity or several early Christianities. It's interesting to compare the fundamental teachings of Jesus and Paul on a point-by-point basis.

It is important to recall as we engage in this kind of comparison that when we talk about the historical Jesus, we are not referring to Jesus just as he is portrayed in one or another of the Gospels. I am presupposing for this comparison that we have reconstructed what the historical Jesus himself actually taught, of course that's done on the basis of the surviving Gospels, but is applying the various criteria to these Gospels that we've already explored.

What did the historical Jesus teach in comparison with what the historical Paul taught? As you might expect, there are a number of similarities between Jesus' and Paul's teaching. After all, both men were 1st century Jews, who like most Jews believed in the one God, the creator of all, who had made a covenant with his people of Israel and given them his Law. Both men were apocalypticists who thought that the end of history was imminent to be brought in a cataclysmic judgment by a cosmic judge from heaven. Both men taught that people needed to prepare for this coming climax of history. Both taught that keeping the letter of the Law would have no effect on one's standing before God and that the Law could be summed up in the commandment to love one's neighbor as one's self. And so, on the one hand, there are broad ranging similarities between Jesus and Paul that you would expect from two 1st century apocalyptic Jews.

On the other hand, there are also a number of striking differences between the two. The historical Jesus, that is the man himself, not the Jesus portrayed in one or other of the Gospels, the historical Jesus taught that the cosmic judge coming from heaven was someone that he called the Son of Man. As we saw in an earlier lecture, Jesus did not appear to be talking about himself, but as some other divine-like figure coming from heaven on the clouds. Paul, on the other hand, thought that the coming judge was Jesus himself.

Jesus taught that to escape judgment a person must keep the central teachings of the Jewish Law as he, Jesus himself, interpreted them. Paul interestingly enough never mentioned Jesus' interpretation of the Law, and Paul was quite insistent that keeping the Law would never bring salvation. The only way to be saved for Paul was to trust Jesus' death and resurrection. Jesus taught that people who repented and kept the Law would enter into the kingdom. Paul taught that repentance and keeping the Law would never allow someone into the kingdom. Salvation came only through Christ's death and resurrection. Jesus saw his own importance as lying in his proclamation of the coming in and his interpretation of the Law. Paul saw Jesus' importance as lying exclusively in his death and his resurrection for sins.

One of the ways to see this difference between Jesus and Paul on such central issues as how one attains salvation, how one enters into the kingdom, how one understands Jesus himself, is by comparing a couple of passages, one that relates to the historical Jesus and one that relates to Paul himself. I want to talk about a passage from the Gospel of Matthew, which is found in only one of our sources, going back to the "M" source. But it's a passage that I think can with some confidence be traced back to the historical Jesus himself, for reasons that I will explain in a moment.

This passage is the famous parable of the sheep and the goats found in Matthew 25, verses 31 and following. Jesus says, "When the Son of Man comes in his glory and all the angels with him, then he will sit on the thrown of his glory." So Jesus is talking about the cosmic judge whose coming in judgment on the earth does not seem to be referring to himself. He continues,

> All the nations will be gathered before him and he will separateeople one from another as a shepherd separates the sheep from the goats. He will put the sheep at his right hand and the goats at the left. Then the king will say to those at his right hand, come you who are blessed by my father, inherit the kingdom prepared for you from the foundation of the world, for I was hungry and you gave me food, I was thirsty and you gave me something to drink, I was a stranger and you welcomed me, I was naked and you gave me clothing, I was sick and you took care of me, I was in prison and you visited me. Then the righteous will answer him, Lord when was it that we saw you hungry and gave you food, or thirsty and gave you something to drink, and when was it that we saw you a stranger and welcomed you or naked and gave you clothing, and when was it that we saw you sick or in prison and visited you? And the king will answer them, truly I tell you as you did it to one of the least of these who are members of my family, you did it to me. Then he will turn to those at his left hand, You that are accursed depart from me into the eternal fire prepared for the devil and his angels, for I was hungry and you gave me no food, I was thirsty and you gave me nothing to drink, I was a stranger and you did not welcome me, naked and you did not give me clothing, sick and in prison and you did not visit me. And then they also will answer, Lord when was it that we saw you hungry, or thirsty, or a stranger, or naked, or sick, or in prison and did not take care of you. Then he will answer them, truly I tell you just as you did not do it to one of the least of these, you did not do it to me. And these will go into eternal punishment and they, the righteous, into eternal life.

It is a very interesting passage that I think must go back to the historical Jesus. How is it that people inherit eternal life, according to this passage? It's by doing good things for others. It is by manifesting the commandment of love. You shall love your neighbor as yourself. By loving others even others they don't know, people inherit eternal life. Salvation, in this passage, comes by following the Law of commandment found in Leviticus, chapter 19, verse 18. It does not explicitly come to people, salvation does not come to people by believing in Jesus. In fact in this passage, the sheep who enter into the eternal kingdom, don't even know Jesus. They don't even recognize Jesus, let alone believe in him. It seems unlikely that Christians would have invented a passage which says that eternal life comes to those who do good things without believing in Jesus, that's the reason for thinking that the passage must go back to the historical Jesus himself.

How though does this teaching about salvation on the basis of doing good works relate to what Paul has to say? As we've seen from the Book of Romans, Chapter 3, Paul is also quite explicit. No human being will be justified in his sight by doing deeds prescribed by the Law, for through the Law comes the knowledge of sin. Or as Paul says, in the letter to the Galatians, Chapter 3, even more clearly, he says we ourselves are Jews, not Gentile sinners, we know that a person is justified not by doing the works of the Law, but through faith. Therefore, we have come to believe in Christ, so that we might be justified by faith in Christ, not by doing the works of the Law, because no one will be justified by works of the Law.

These seem to be very different teachings on how one attains salvation. How does one account for the differences between them? The traditional view is that the difference between Jesus and Paul on salvation is due to the fact that Jesus was teaching prior to his death and resurrection and that Paul was teaching afterwards. So that Paul could emphasize that it's the death and resurrection of Jesus that brings salvation, whereas Jesus obviously couldn't emphasize that because he hadn't died or been raised yet.

Some interpreters, though, question this view. Why would Jesus teach people that they could enter into God's kingdom by keeping God's Law, if it weren't true? For Paul, if a person could be good enough to enter into the kingdom, as he says in the letter to the Galatians, then Christ died in vain. In other words, there'd be no reason for Christ to have died if in fact a person could enter into the kingdom simply by being good enough. Paul doesn't think it is possible; Jesus does seem to think it is possible, at least in some of these materials that appear to go back to him. An alternative view, then, is that Paul represents a significant development of Jesus' own teaching. That, in fact, he altered the basic message of Jesus in light of his own experience of Jesus' resurrection. That because of his experience of Jesus resurrection, his visionary experience, whatever it involved, Paul decided that the death of Jesus was the point, the death of Jesus was according to the plan of God. That it's the only way that one can receive salvation, rather than Jesus' proclamation, rather than doing the good things prescribed by the Law.

According to this point of view, that's been supported by scholars for well over a century, Paul transformed the religion of Jesus into a religion about Jesus. Paul transformed the religion of Jesus, the religion Jesus had, to a religion about Jesus. Many scholars today think that this way of putting things is probably a little bit too simple, in part because any transformation that took place of Jesus' religion, took place before Paul came on the scene. Paul should not be seen as a major innovator when it comes to early Christianity, because Paul himself indicates that he received his Gospel message from others—in the passage that we read earlier from 1 Corinthians, Chapter 15 where Paul indicates what he preached to the Corinthians in order to convert them, he says, 1 Corinthians 15, verse 3, I handed on to you as a first importance, that which I in turn had received, that Christ died for our sins in accordance with the Scriptures. Paul himself had received a Christian message before he started to proclaim it so that the transformation of Jesus' teaching probably happened before Paul developed his own theology.

Yet we are stuck with the differences between Jesus and Paul. Jesus appeared to proclaim that a person could be made right with God by doing what God demanded—repenting, loving one's neighbor as much as one's self. Paul insisted that a person could never be right with God by doing these things. This raises the question: Do Paul and Jesus represent the same religion. This raises a corollary question, which is whether Paul actually knew about the religion that Jesus himself propounded. Did Paul know what Jesus himself taught or what Jesus himself did?

I want to explore this question next. It's a question that hasn't occurred to a lot of people because they simply assume that Paul must have known everything about Jesus. After all, we can pick up our New Testaments and read about what Jesus said and did, surely Paul living close to the time also knew. It's important to recall, though, that Paul's letters were being written before the Gospel accounts—10, 15, 20 years before the Gospels were written—which means that Paul hadn't read the Gospels. Did he know what was going to be in the Gospels?

It is a very interesting question. How would one go about deciding how much Paul knew about Jesus? I don't think that we can simply assume that he knew everything that we know or that we think we know. What kind of evidence exists for Paul's knowledge about Jesus' life, his words, his deeds? As I indicated in an earlier lecture, Paul doesn't tell us very much about Jesus' life. He indicates that Jesus was born of a woman, that he was Jewish, he gives an indication that he at one point thinks Jesus came from the line of David—Romans, chapter 1, verse 3. He knows that Jesus had brothers, one of whom was named James. He knows that Jesus' ministry was principally among Jews, that he had 12 disciples. He knows that he had a last meal with his disciples in which he instituted the Lord's Supper. Paul seems to know that Jesus was betrayed. He certainly knows that he was crucified. And, as I have indicated, he repeats two of Jesus' teachings attributing them to Jesus, namely that his followers should not get divorced, but that they should pay their ministers. That is all Paul gives us in terms of what Jesus said and did between the time of his birth and the time of his death. He doesn't indicate that he knows anything else, he doesn't know anything about the virgin birth, the birth in Bethlehem, the baptism, the temptation, the transfiguration, casting out demons, telling parables, preaching about the coming kingdom, on and on and on.

How does one account for the paucity of this material? How does one explain the fact that Paul doesn't tell us anything more than he tells us about Jesus? Well, it's a very interesting question, and it's one that could have different answers to it. I want to lay out three possible ways of answering the question, each of these ways strike me as somewhat problematic, but I think that they are the three major options. One option: Maybe Paul knew a good deal more about Jesus then he lets on, but given the occasional nature of his letters, Paul had no reason to provide us with more information. In other words, it may be that he knew lots about what Jesus said and did, that he had a full inventory of knowledge, but that he had no occasion to mention it.

One reason for thinking that Paul might have known far more he lets on is that, according to Paul himself, he knew some of Jesus' disciples. Remember in Galatians he insist that he didn't go to Jerusalem right away to consult with the apostles, but he does say in Galatians, chapter 1, that after three years, he went to Jerusalem and consulted with Cephas, who is thought by most people to be Peter. Cephas is an Aramaic word which means rock. Petros— Peter—is a Greek word that means rock. This is actually a nickname. It'd be, like it's comparable to the modern Rocky. His real name was Simon. If Cephas is in fact Peter the disciple, then Paul met with Cephas, Peter, in Jerusalem and he did know the brother of Jesus, James. He spent some time with them—two weeks according to Galatians. If he knew these people, then presumably they told him something about what Jesus said and did while he was living. So, in fact, he must have known a good deal more, but just didn't say more because the occasion never demanded it.

There are problems, though, with this solution. Throughout Paul's letters, Paul constantly reminds his readers what he himself taught them while he was with them. If Paul taught his converts the things that Jesus had said and the things that Jesus had done, why doesn't he ever remind them of that if he is constantly reminding them of what he himself taught them? Now some people have thought that Paul couldn't have possibly have established churches without teaching people what Jesus had said and done, but I am not sure that's true. If Paul's belief was based on Jesus' death and resurrection and the idea that Jesus was coming back soon as the judge of the earth, Paul might well have taught people that, might well have taught people about Jesus' death and resurrection and his imminent return and might well have taught that Jesus is a fulfillment of the Hebrew Scripture, which talked about his death, resurrection, and return. That doesn't necessarily mean that he taught them the things that Jesus said and did, especially the things Jesus said and did in the Gospels. If he did teach them these things, it is odd that he never reminds them that he taught them those things as he does remind them of other things that he himself taught.

Moreover, on rare occasions, Paul does cite something about Jesus as we have seen. For example, the teachings of Jesus at the Last Supper. Paul reminds the Corinthians of what Jesus taught at the Lord's Supper. So he's not disinclined to tell people what Jesus taught on occasion. Why doesn't he do it then more often if he has more information at his disposal? For example, in Romans, chapter 13, Paul tells his readers in Rome that they ought to pay their taxes. Why doesn't he say, you should pay your taxes because remember Jesus himself said render under Caesar the things that are Caesar's? Why doesn't he quote Jesus if he wants to urge people to do something that he knows Jesus himself urged them to do? Well, when he says that you should love your neighbor as yourself to fulfill the Law, why doesn't he say because that's what Jesus himself said? Remember, our Lord said, you should love your neighbor as yourself. Why doesn't Paul say these things if in fact he knew more about Jesus? Well, that's the problem with the first option, that Paul did know more but simply didn't say more, because this information about Jesus was irrelevant.

A second option—Paul knew a good deal more about Jesus, according to this option, but that he considered the facts about Jesus' life to be irrelevant for his own mission. He knew more, but he considered this information about Jesus to be irrelevant. This is closely related, of course, to the first option. It's worth noting that in the first letter to the Corinthians, Paul says to them, "I knew nothing among you except Christ and him crucified." In other words, the only thing Paul taught among the Corinthians was about Jesus' crucifixion. That might suggest that the teachings and actions of Jesus were irrelevant to Paul. The problem with that option, of course, is that Paul does occasionally mention the teachings of Jesus and a few of the other data from Jesus' life. And so if he thought that they were completely irrelevant, why does he bring them up on occasion?

A third option is that Paul may not have known much more than he mentions about Jesus. It may be that Paul thought that the death and resurrection of Jesus were of such earth shattering importance that he didn't even inquire into what Jesus said and did while he was alive. People object to this point of view because, as we know, Paul did meet with some of the disciples in Jerusalem, surely they weren't talking about the weather when they got together. On the other hand, it's not clear that they were getting together in order to talk about the life of Jesus. Paul indicates that the reason they were talking together was to discuss the Gentile mission. It may well be that they didn't go over the facts of Jesus life to get them straight before Paul returned to the mission field.

285

In the long run I'm afraid we really don't know the answer to why Paul doesn't say more about Jesus. It is clear that he doesn't give us a lot of information, and it is clear that whatever you make of it, his gospel message is different from the message proclaimed by Jesus. Some people think that this difference is an irreconcilable discrepancy; that Paul, in fact, represents a different religion from that of Jesus. That's a fairly radical conclusion, but you can see the compelling force behind it—that Paul, in fact, says things that Jesus seems to have disagreed with and vice versa. Other people think that Paul developed the teaching of Jesus after his death and resurrection, so that there is basic continuity between the two. In any event, I think it is clear that Paul and Jesus are saying different things, whether or not they are irreconcilable.

It may be fruitful at this point to compare Paul not just with the one who came before him, Jesus, but with someone who came after him, James. The epistle of James in the New Testament is commonly attributed to Jesus' own brother, James. The author of this book does claim to be someone named James. He begins the book by naming himself, James. This person, though, does not claim to be James the brother of Jesus. He doesn't claim to be a personal relation to Jesus. I should point out that the name James is quite common in the ancient world. We aren't sure for that reason who actually wrote the letter, except I should point out that Jesus' brother James would have been a lower class Aramaic-speaking peasant. This epistle is written by a well-educated Greek-speaking Christian. It's possible that it is written by Jesus' brother, but it seems somewhat unlikely, since it is being written by somebody who is highly literate in Greek, whereas Jesus' brother would have been a lower class pleasant in Palestine who spoke Aramaic.

The book consists of a number of moral exhortations for its readers to behave in ways that are appropriate to their faith. Many of these exhortations sound very similar to Jesus' own teaching, for example in the Sermon on the Mount. We won't be able to look at the entire book of James, I want to focus in on a particular passage that has struck readers over the years, because the passage seems to stand in stark contrast with what Paul himself teaches, for example, in the Book of Romans and the Book of Galatians. In the 16th century, Martin Luther thought that this passage stood at odds with Paul so much that this book in fact did not proclaim the Gospel. Martin Luther didn't much like the Epistle of James, he called it a right strawy epistle, and when he translated the Bible into German, he included the book of James at the end as one of the books in his appendix, taking it out of the canonical order.

The passage in question is James, chapter 2, verses 14 through 26. It's a very interesting passage, because in it James indicates that a person is justified by works, not by faith. As James says, what good is it my brothers and sisters if you say you have faith, but you don't have works, can your faith save you. If a brother or sister is naked and lacks daily food and one of you says go in peace, be warm, be filled, yet you don't supply their bodily needs, what good is that? So faith by itself, if it has no works, is dead. He goes on to show that works, that faith without works is dead by appealing to Abraham. Was not our ancestor Abraham justified by works, when he offered up his son Isaac on the alter? He concludes, you see that a person is justified by works, not by faith alone. For just as the body without the spirit is dead, so faith without works is also dead. It's very interesting because whereas Paul uses Abraham to show that a person is justified by faith, apart from works of the Law, James uses Abraham to show that a person is justified by works and not by faith. Are these two in contradiction to one another?

People have different opinions on the question. One can understand why it looks like they are contradictory. Other people have pointed out that the contradiction may simply be on the surface. That James when he says a person is justified by works means that a person has to do good things in order to demonstrate they really have faith. That doesn't seem to be so far off from what Paul said, when Paul indicates that if somebody really has faith in Christ, they will live in ethical ways. Not that a person is justified by doing works of the Law, but once a person is justified, one will do the ethical requirements of the Law. It may be, in other words, that the contradiction between James and Paul is simply on the surface and that they don't fundamentally stand at odds with each other. It's possible.

In conclusion, I should stress that we've seen in this course a good deal of diversity of early Christianity. The different Gospels have different portrayals of Jesus, there even appear to be discrepancies among them. Jesus himself preached a message that was altered prior to being put into the Gospels. In his proclamation, Jesus proclaimed the imminent intervention of God in the affairs of the world, through the appearance of the Son of Man and judgment. People need to prepare for this by keeping the Law. Paul appears to have proclaimed a different message, based on his view that salvation comes not through faithful obedience to the Law, but through faith in Jesus' death and resurrection. As we continue our discussion of the New Testament, we are going to see even more diversity. Strikingly enough, some of this diversity can be found in books that claim Paul as their author but that appear to present a different understanding of the Gospel from his. That will be the subject of our next lecture.

The Deutero-Pauline Epistles
Lecture 19

The New Testament epistles that claim to be written by Paul but that in the judgment of a majority of modern scholars probably were not.

We are now moving into a different, but equally disputed, area of scholarship—the New Testament epistles that claim to be written by Paul but that, in the judgment of most modern scholars, probably were not. The first group of these letters, the so-called Deutero- (or secondary-) Pauline epistles, are so named because, as disputed epistles, they have a secondary standing in the Pauline corpus. We need to start by discussing the issue of pseudonymity in the ancient world. The term *pseudonym* simply means "false name." A pseudonymous writing is one that is written under a name other than the author's. Sometimes this simply involves the use of a *pen name*, as when Samuel Clemens wrote under the name Mark Twain or Mary Ann Evans wrote as George Eliot. Sometimes, though, it involves a deliberate act of deception or forgery, in which an author for one reason or another claims to be someone else, as happened some years ago when journals forged under the name of Adolf Hitler turned up.

Forgery was a relatively common practice in the ancient world. There were no copyright laws in antiquity and, because books could not be mass produced, it was difficult for most people to compare a book in hand with other books by the same author to see whether they were basically similar in vocabulary and style. Most people couldn't read. Taking Athens in the 5th century B.C. as an example, the literacy rate was, at most, only to 10 to 15 percent. We know that forgery was common because the ancients talked about it. One famous author from the 2nd century A.D., the Roman physician Galen, actually found a forgery in his name at a local bookshop and wrote a book on how to recognize books actually written by Galen! Sometimes forgers were caught in the act, as happened with a Christian who forged a *third* letter of Paul to the Corinthians and, according to 3rd-century Church Father Tertullian, was found out.

Why did people forge writings in the name of famous authors? Sometimes there was a profit motive. If a new library was paying gold on the head for original works of important authors, you'd be amazed how many original works began to turn up. In the philosophical schools, there was a completely different reason. Some students felt that all they thought and understood was directly the result of their studying under their revered teachers. When writing their own treatises, then, they would sign their teachers' names as an act of gratitude and modesty. Probably the most common reason for forgery, though, was to get an audience for your writing. If you wanted your philosophical views heard and wrote a treatise using your own name (Marcus Aristides, or whatever), no one might read it, but if you signed it Plato, you might have a chance. This final motive is not necessarily wicked. It may well be that forgers thought that what they wrote would have been completely approved by the author they ascribed it to. If he only had a chance to address the issue, this is what he himself would have said. This seems to be the case in the forged 3 Corinthians.

Forgers used a variety of techniques to hide the traces of their deceit. Simply to claim to be someone carried a lot of weight, especially for religious texts, in which you naturally wouldn't expect an author to fib. The main trick was to make sure that nothing in the writing would tip one's hand. Forgers would typically try to imitate the style of the author they were claiming to be, use his vocabulary, and imitate some of his better known turns of phrase. The forgers also added elements of verisimilitude, such as off-the-cuff

Forgers used a variety of techniques to hide the traces of their deceit.

remarks that make it sound as if something has just occurred to the alleged author or even an emphatic insistence that he really is the author. One of the most interesting instances of the latter occurs in a Christian book of the 4th century, called the *Apostolic Constitutions*. The book claims to be written by Jesus' apostles immediately after the resurrection (even though it reflects knowledge of much later Christianity); in it, the author warns readers *not* to read books that falsely claim to be written by the apostles!

We know that there were a number of forgeries in Paul's name. Third Corinthians, mentioned above, is one obvious example. There is also forged correspondence between Paul and the most famous Roman philosopher of his day, Seneca, an advisor to the emperor Nero, in which Seneca praises Paul for being one of the greatest minds of his day. The question, then, is not whether Christians would have forged documents in Paul's name; it's whether any of these pseudonymous works made into the New Testament. The canon was determined long after the works were written.

Many scholars continue to be persuaded that the Deutero-Pauline epistles of 2 Thessalonians, Colossians, and Ephesians are all pseudonymous. As with all pseudonymous writings, the debates center on whether the books are so unlike the books that are known to come from the hand of an author—for example in vocabulary, writing style, and theological perspective—that they could not have been written by him. With respect to 2 Thessalonians, many scholars continue to think that its emphasis that the end of the age is *not* imminent (2 Thess. 2:2–13) does not sound like Paul's eschatology, as seen in 1 Thessalonians, where he warns that the end-time could arrive at any moment, like a thief in the night (1 Thess. 4:13–5:10). With respect to Colossians, most scholars find that its emphasis that Christians have not only died with Christ but have already been raised with him to experience an exalted, glorified existence (2:12; 3:1) contradicts what he says in 1 Corinthians, where he argues precisely *against* such a view. These two books are particularly debated among scholars. You can read further about these debates in the readings I've suggested.

With Ephesians, there is less debate. Most critical scholars are fairly persuaded that Paul did not write it. The overall purpose of this letter is to remind Gentile readers that even though they were formerly alienated from God and his people Israel, they have now been made one through the work of Christ—one with the Jews through Christ's work of reconciliation and one with God through Christ's work of redemption. The first half of the letter explains how Jew and Gentile have been united and how both have been made one with God, all through Christ. The second half contains numerous exhortations to live in ways that manifest this unity. As you'll see by reading this letter, it is a powerful and eloquent statement of the meaning of Christ's work and the need to live moral lives in light of it. At the same time, the question remains: Did Paul write it?

The first reason for thinking that Ephesians is pseudonymous is its distinctive vocabulary. This short book of only six chapters uses a total of 116 words not found in any of Paul's undisputed letters—an inordinate number when compared with other books. Corroborating evidence is found in the style of the author's Greek writing—usually a matter of unconscious habit. Whereas Paul tends to write very short choppy sentences in Greek, this author writes very long, convoluted sentences (it's hard to tell this just from the English) that are not characteristic of Paul's known writings. Most significant, though, is the substance of what this author says. This is a complicated criterion, because the author often says things that sound very much like Paul—as you would expect from someone who wants his readers to think he is Paul. But what this author says about himself is curious. Paul was proud of his Jewish upbringing and claimed that he knew the Law could not bring salvation precisely because he himself had stringently followed it: "According to the righteousness found in the Law, I was blameless" (Phil. 3:6). Not so this author, who admits that he had previously lived an immoral life as a pagan, "in the passions of the flesh, following its desires and senses." What he says about Christians is even more curious. Paul insisted to the Corinthians that they had not yet been resurrected with Christ, spiritually raised to a new existence in heaven, but that's precisely what the author of this book does claim: "God has raised us up with Christ and seated us with him in the heavenly places" (2:5-6). For Paul, Christians have not been exalted to a new, glorified existence, but for this author, they have. It's a fundamental difference. In fact, the view advanced here in Ephesians appears to be closely related to the one that Paul attacks in Corinthians. Was Ephesians written by Paul, then? There is still debate, but most critical scholars think not. If it was not written by Paul, then it was likely written by a follower after Paul's death.

We have seen, very briefly, several of the reasons that scholars doubt the Pauline authorship of 2 Thessalonians, Colossians, and Ephesians. These judgments are principally based on questions of vocabulary, writing style, and theology. It's possible, of course, that Paul simply adopted a different vocabulary, writing style, and theology when writing these letters. In that case, then, one could say that they were written by Paul but by a different Paul than the one who wrote the undisputed letters. As we'll see in the next lecture, the differences in the Pastoral epistles of 1 and 2 Timothy and Titus are even more stark. ■

Essential Reading

2 Thessalonians, Colossians, Ephesians.

Brown, *Introduction to the New Testament*, chaps. 25–28.

Ehrman, *The New Testament: A Historical Introduction*, chap. 23.

Supplemental Reading

Beker, *The Heirs of Paul*.

Roetzel, *The Letters of Paul*.

Questions to Consider

1. It is possible to distinguish between the authorship and the authority of a work. In your view, would the fact that a book was pseudonymous necessarily compromise its authority? That is to say, could it still convey true, important, or normative teaching? Why or why not?

2. As an exercise in determining whether Paul wrote one of the Deutero-Paulines, do a (very) detailed comparison of 1 Thess. 4:13–5:10 and 2 Thess. 2:1–12 to see if you think the same author could have written both. Are any of the differences particularly stark? Then do the same exercise with Rom. 6:4 and Col. 2:12.

Erratum: Professor Ehrman refers to Philippians 2:3. The correct reference should be Philippians 3:6.

The Deutero-Pauline Epistles
Lecture 19—Transcript

To this point in our discussion of the Apostle Paul, we have had to be selective in our reflections on the undisputed Pauline epistles, focusing most of our attention on the two longest of them—1 Corinthians and Romans. But at least we've gotten an idea of Paul's basic Gospel message and of how he applied it to different situations that were confronting him from within his churches. We have also compared and contrasted this message with the preaching of Jesus himself. We are now moving into a different, but equally disputed area of scholarship—the New Testament epistles that claim to be written by Paul but that in the judgment of a majority of modern scholars probably were not.

In this lecture we will look at the first group of these letters, the so called Deutero- or secondary-Pauline epistles, so named because as disputed epistles they have a secondary standing in the Pauline corpus. First, I need to set the context for this discussion by looking at the issue of pseudonymity in the ancient world. The term pseudonym simply means false name. A pseudonymous writing is one that is written under the name of a person that is not the author. Sometimes this simply involves the use of a pen name such as when Samuel Clemens wrote under the name Mark Twain, or when Mary Ann Evans wrote as George Elliott. Sometimes though, a pseudonym involves a deliberate act of deception, forgery, where an author for one reason or another claims to be someone that he is not or that she is not. This happened some years ago when the so-called Hitler diaries showed up. These were books that were claiming to be diaries that Hitler himself had kept during the Second World War, and for several days after their discovery they fooled the world until experts examined them and showed beyond any doubt at all that in fact they were forgeries and so then the books were relegated to the trash heaps of historical curiosities.

Forgery occurs in the modern world; it also occurred in the ancient world. In fact, it was a relatively common practice in antiquity. In antiquity there were no copyright laws that made it illegal for somebody to forge a document in somebody else's name. Moreover, since books could not be massed produced, it was difficult for most people to detect a forgery, because to detect a forgery, one would need to compare a book in hand with other books by the same author to see whether it was basically similar in vocabulary and style. And most people in antiquity couldn't read in any event. The most recent and reliable studies of literacy in antiquity suggest that at the best of times, at most 10 to 15 percent of the population could read, by best of times I mean Athens in the 5th century.

Around the time of the New Testament, probably far fewer people could read, especially in areas like Palestine and Asia Minor, with higher literacy rates of course in the urban areas. So probably in the time period of the New Testament, maybe 10 percent of the general population could read. So that in antiquity, reading a book for the most part meant hearing somebody else read it to you, which was a common form of recreation back in the days before there was television and movies.

We know that in antiquity forgery was common because the ancients themselves talk about it. One famous author from the 2nd century A.D., the Roman physician Galen, actually found a forgery in his name at a local book shop. He was walking down the street and looked through the window of a bookstore and there was this book claiming to be written by Galen. Well he knew full well he hadn't written that book, and so Galen produced a book in which he described how one can recognize books written by Galen. This was not an unusual occurrence for people to forge books in other people's names.

Sometimes forgers were actually caught in the act. One of the most famous instances of Christian forgery occurred in the 2nd century A.D. Near the end of the 2nd century, the church father Tertullian describes an incident in which somebody had forged a letter in the name of the Apostle Paul. This person though was caught red-handed in the act. He said then once his forging act had been discovered, he said that he had done it out of love of Paul. But nonetheless, it was a forgery and everybody knew it.

Why did people forge writings in the name of famous authors? Well, sometimes in antiquity there was a profit motive. If a new library was paying gold on the head for original works of important authors, you'd be amazed at how many original works began to turn up. When a library started out sometimes they would be looking for original documents and so sometimes these were, the shelves would be stocked with forgeries.

In the philosophical schools there was a completely different reason for people forging documents. Some students within the philosophical schools felt that all that they thought and understood about the world was directly the result of their having studied under their own revered teacher. When writing their own treaties then, these students would typically sign their teacher's name as an act of gratitude and modesty. We know this particularly within the neo-Pythagorean schools of thought. Well in this case then, there is no profit motive, it is simply as an act of a kind of modesty, saying well, this is what my teacher has taught me.

Third, probably the most common reason for forgery, was to get an audience for your writing. Suppose you have a philosophical point of view that you want to get across, you want people to understand your view of the world, but you are a nobody. Your name is Marcus Aristides and nobody has heard of you. Well you write your philosophical treatise, but at the end you sign it Plato on the assumption that if you sign it Marcus Aristides nobody will read it, but if you sign it Plato, everybody will read it and thereby you will get a chance for your views to be heard. This final motive is not necessary wicked. It may well be that forgers thought that what they wrote would be of good use for people to read. Moreover, in most instances, it's probable that whoever is forging a document in somebody else's name, genuinely thought that this is what the person would have said if they had had the chance to say it. We have this instance from the 2nd century of a letter forged in the name of Paul where the forger was caught in the act. He said as I've indicated that he did it for the love of Paul. He may well have thought that if Paul had had a chance to address the issues that he himself is addressing in this letter, that this is what Paul would have said.

Forgers used a variety of techniques to hide the traces of their deceit. Simply claiming to be somebody carried a lot of weight in most texts, especially in religious texts in which you wouldn't expect an author to fib about it. If you read a text which says I, Moses, am writing to you these words, or that says this is the vision which I, Abraham, saw, most readers are simply going to take the author at his word. And so simply claiming to be somebody is a kind of technique.

Secondly, forgers would make sure that what they wrote was basically in the style of the author they were trying to imitate. They wanted to make sure that nothing in the writing would tip their hand, and so forgers would typically try to imitate the style—using the vocabulary, using many of the same catch phrases of the author that they were claiming to be.

And third, they would typically add elements of verisimilitude. For example, off the cuff remarks that make it sound as though something has just occurred to the alleged author. Where an author might say something like, please remember to bring the manuscripts that I left behind in Ephesus to an alleged audience, to an alleged recipient of the letter. One of the ways of putting verisimilitude into a text was for an author to make an emphatic insistence that he himself actually is the author. Sometimes, of course, the author doth protest too much.

One of the ways of throwing an audience off the scent of one's own deceit was by telling the reader not to read documents that had been forged in the name of the author. You wouldn't expect a forger to say don't read documents that are being forged. Well, in fact, this happens somewhat commonly in forged documents. One of the most interesting instances of this is in a Christian book of the 4th century, which is called the Apostolic Constitutions. It's called the Apostolic Constitutions because it is a book which claims to be written by the Apostles of Jesus immediately after the resurrection. We know it wasn't written immediately after the resurrection because it reflects knowledge of later Christianity. Clearly this wasn't written by the Apostles of Jesus, yet within this book these Apostles of Jesus warn their readers not to read books that falsely claim to be written by the Apostles of Jesus. But why would they do this? So that you wouldn't suspect that they themselves are forgers.

We know that there were a number of forgeries in Paul's name. That will be the subject for the next two lectures—pseudonymous writings in Paul's name. We know, whatever you happen to think of the epistles in the New Testament, we know that there were forgeries in Paul's name in antiquity.

I've already mentioned 3 Corinthians, forged sometime in the 2nd century. This is the letter that Tertullian says that a Christian had forged and was caught in the act—3 Corinthians. We also know of a forged correspondence between Paul and the most famous Roman philosopher of his day, Seneca. Seneca was an advisor to the Emperor Nero, was a famous stoic philosopher. We have from later times a correspondence between Paul and Seneca. This is completely forged by a Christian author in which they go back and forth and Seneca praises Paul for being one of the greatest minds of his day. He says that he's shown Paul's letters to the Emperor Nero, Nero is really impressed, he'd really like to have a chance to meet with Paul, and it goes on and on. Well, of course, Seneca had never heard of Paul, but this forgery is set up to show that in fact the greatest philosopher of the 1st century, well one of the greatest philosophers of the 1st century, praises Paul for being one of the greatest philosophers of the 1st century.

One of the most striking proofs that there were early forgeries in Paul's name actually comes from the New Testament itself, from one of the letters attributed to Paul. This letter gives, I think, incontrovertible proof that people early on were forging letters in Paul's name. The reference comes in 2 Thessalonians, chapter 2, verse 2, where the author warns his readers not to be put off in their thinking by a letter allegedly written by him. Now this author claims to be Paul, 2 Thessalonians, claims to be written by Paul. The author says don't be put off by letters allegedly written by me. That proves beyond a doubt that there were forgeries in Paul's name. Some scholars think that 2 Thessalonians itself is pseudonymous. If it is pseudonymous, then in fact this is a forger technique to put off the scent of the deceit. If it is not pseudonymous, if it is authentic, then there really was a letter forged in Paul's name that the Thessalonians had gotten. Either way, it shows that beyond any doubt, that in 1st century you have forgeries in Paul's name that were circulating among the Christian communities. We will be exploring why people might have wanted to forge specifically in Paul's name, near the end of this lecture.

The question then for us is not whether Christian would have forged documents in Paul's name. The only question is whether any of these pseudonymous works happened to make it into the New Testament. Remember, the books of the New Testament were put into the New Testament in the process of canonical formation—2nd, 3rd, 4th centuries, long after the authors had died, when people didn't have the means for determining who the original authors were. It's not implausible that some forged documents made it into the New Testament. The question is whether any did. Many critical scholars continue to be persuaded the Deutero-Pauline epistles of 2 Thessalonians, Colossians, and Ephesians are all pseudonymous.

I am going to deal briefly with 2 Thessalonians and Colossians and then a little more substantively with Ephesians in this lecture. As with all pseudonymous writings, the debates over these three books center on whether the books are so unlike the books that are known to have come from the hand of the author that they could not have been written by him—so unlike Paul's writings for example in vocabulary, in writing style, in theological prospective, that we can't attribute them to him.

Let me briefly tell you what the issues are for 2 Thessalonians and Colossians. With 2 Thessalonians the principal issue has to do with eschatology. Eschatology is a term which means the doctrine or the teaching about the end times. As we've seen, Paul believed that the end of all things was near. He believed that he would be alive when Jesus returned, and he thought that the return of Jesus was going to happen very soon. Nowhere is this taught more clearly than in 1 Thessalonians, which everybody agrees actually was written by Paul, where at the end of the letter Paul indicates that he will be alive when Jesus returns, and he warns his readers that they need to be alert. They need to be ready because this coming of Jesus could happen at any time. As he says it, the day of the Lord will come like a thief in the night. In other words, there will be no preparation for it, it's going to come suddenly. As he says, people will be saying there is peace and security, then sudden destruction will come upon them. It's going to come quickly, suddenly, you need to be alert for it. And so he warns them, let us keep awake and sober, because you don't know when it is going to happen.

That was Paul's teaching in 1 Thessalonians. Second Thessalonians, which also is allegedly written by Paul, which also has many similarities to 1 Thessalonians—it sounds like Paul in places as you would expect of one of Paul's own letters and as you would expect of a forged document. You would expect a forged document to sound like Paul, because the author is trying to imitate Paul. So 2 Thessalonians sounds a lot like Paul, but there are places where 2 Thessalonians does not sound like Paul, especially with regard to its eschatology. Second Thessalonians indicates that the end of the age is not imminent. The letter, in fact, is written in order to disabuse people of thinking that the day of the Lord is upon us—chapter 2, verse 2. This author says let no one deceive you in any way for that day will not come unless the rebellion comes first and the lawless one is revealed and the one destined for destruction. He goes on to describe then that there's going to be a kind of an Anti-Christ who appears, who sets himself up as divine, who enters into the temple of God and declares himself to be God and that only after that has happened will there be the possibility of the coming of the end. In other words, there are things that have to happen first. After those things happen, then the end can come.

That doesn't sound like 1 Thessalonians, which says that the end is imminent, it is going to come like a thief in the night, you need to be awake because you don't know when it's going to hit. That's the reason the scholars have disputed whether 2 Thessalonians was actually written by Paul. It may be that 2 Thessalonians was written by a later follower of Paul who knew that the end wasn't going to come right away and didn't want people to expect it to come right away because it had led to all sorts of problem in the Christian communities. At the end of 2 Thessalonians it becomes clear that one of the problems is that people have quit their jobs and are sponging off of others to live in expectation of the imminent end. Well, this author is trying to show that, in fact, it's not all that imminent. Is that Paul? Well, that really doesn't sound like Paul.

With respect to Colossians, the issue in Colossians isn't so much eschatology in this sense, as the overarching view of salvation. Again the letter sounds a lot like Paul in many respects and so some people still think that Paul wrote the letter, but there are striking differences between Paul and Colossians. Colossians is a book that is intending to counter some misteachings within the Christian communities, some false philosophies. The author wants to emphasize that people already have experienced the benefits of salvation in the present. This author says for example, chapter 2, verse 12, when you were buried with Christ in baptism, you were also raised with him through faith in the power of God who raised him from the dead. You've died with Christ, you've been raised with Christ.

Chapter 3, verse 1—you have been raised with Christ, so seek the things that are above. For this author, Christians have experienced enormous benefits from the salvation. They have died with Christ, they have been raised with Christ, they are already living with Christ in the heavenly places. In some respects that sounds like Paul, but in other respects it doesn't because Paul himself was quite emphatic that people have died with Christ, but they have not yet been raised with Christ. You see this when Paul talks about salvation in both Romans and 1 Corinthians. For example in Romans, Paul says we have died with Christ in baptism, we will be raised with him in the future. The resurrection of believers with Jesus is a future event. Remember in 1 Corinthians that was the entire point. Christians had thought that they had been raised with Christ and had experienced the full benefits of salvation. Paul writes 1 Corinthians to opposed that point of view. The view that he opposes in 1 Corinthians, though, that we have already experienced some kind of resurrected existence, the view he opposes there is the view that seems to be endorsed by the letter to the Colossians. That's the main reason for thinking that Paul didn't write it. Scholars continued to debate these two books, because as I have indicated there are a lot of aspects of them that sound like Paul.

There are fewer debates about the letter to the Ephesians. Most critical scholars are fairly persuaded that Paul did not write Ephesians. There are some who still think he did, of course. But throughout this century, the majority of critical scholars have been fairly convinced that Paul didn't write it. The overarching purpose of this letter is to remind its Gentile readers that even though they were formerly alienated from God and his people of Israel, they've now been made one through the work of Christ. They have been made one with the Jews. These Gentiles have been made one with the Jews through Christ's work of reconciliation, and they have been made one with God through Christ's work of redemption.

The first half of the letter explains how Jew and Gentile have been unified together and how both have been made one with God through Christ. The second half contains moral exhortations urging its readers to live in ways that manifest this unity. Unity with Jews, unity with God. As you see by reading the letter, it in fact is a powerful and eloquent statement of the meaning of Christ's work and the need to lead moral lives in light of it. At the same time the question remains, did Paul write the letter.

The first reason for thinking that Ephesians is pseudonymous is its distinctive vocabulary. This short book of only six chapters has a total of 116 words that are not found in any of Paul's undisputed letters. That's a high proportion of vocabulary in comparison with other letters—116 words found only here. Corroborating evidence is found in the style of the author's Greek. When a person writes usually they incorporate a fairly unconscious style. We try to think what we write. But there are stylistic characteristics when we write that are distinctive to us that aren't really a matter of consciousness, so that some people write really complicated, convoluted grammar, other people write very short choppy kind of sentences. Paul tended to write short, choppy sentences in Greek. This author writes long convoluted sentences in Greek. You can't really see this in the English translations, because English translators of Ephesians have to cut up the sentences because they are so long in Greek, that you just can't do it in English and make sense of them. So you can't get it when you read the English, but in Greek it is pretty clear. Just to give you some comparative data: Galatians and Philippians, two undisputed letters, are about the same length as Ephesians. In each of these letters there is only one sentence that goes on for over 50 words in Galatians and Philippians. In Ephesians, there are nine sentences that go over 50 words. Nine times as many. Throughout Paul's letters, in fact, he hardly ever uses this kind of long style, here he does. These first two reasons for thinking that the book is pseudonymous, they have to be taken into consideration, but they are not completely compelling in themselves.

The most compelling reason for thinking that Paul did not write this letter has to do with the substance of what the author says. Again, this is a complicated criterion, because an author will obviously say things that sound very much like Paul because he is forging a document, if he is forging it in Paul's name, and there are passages here that do sound like Paul on the surface until you get out down into the details. For example, chapter 2, verses 1 through 10, the author begins by saying that you were dead through the trespasses and sins in which you once lived, you were dead. All of us, he says, once lived among the pagans in the passions of our flesh, following the desires of flesh and senses. We were by nature children of wrath. But God out of his great love, with which he loved us, even when we were dead through our trespasses, made us alive together with Christ. And he raised us up with him and seated us with him in the heavenly places in Christ Jesus. For by grace you have been saved through faith, this is not your doing, it is the gift of God. It is not the result of works, so that no one may boast. This sounds like Paul, you were dead, God made you alive through Christ. It's a matter of grace, not through your works, but through faith.

It looks like Paul until you start looking closer at the details. First, what does this author say about himself? He says that he was with everyone else living according to the passions of his desire and flesh. Living like pagans. What does Paul say about himself in his undisputed letters? Philippians, Chapter 2, verse 3, Paul says, before he became a Christian, "With respect to the righteousness that is found in the Law, I was blameless." Blameless before the Law. That doesn't sound like somebody who spent his life living according to the passions of his flesh, following the desires of flesh and senses. Is it the same author, maybe, but it doesn't sound like it. What he says about Christians is even more curious. Remember, Paul insisted to the Corinthians that they had not yet been raised with Christ, spiritually raised to a new existence in heaven, but that's precisely what the author of this book does claim. God has raised us up with Christ and seated us with him, in the heavenly places. Whereas for Paul, Christians have not yet been exalted to a new glorified existence, for this author they have. It's a fundamental difference. Remember, the view that's being advanced here in Ephesians—that we have already experienced the resurrected existence, we are living with Christ in heavenly places—that's the view that Paul attacks in 1 Corinthians. Was Ephesians then written by Paul? Well there still is debate, but most critical scholars think not.

Who then wrote this letter? Well, probably the letter, if it wasn't written by Paul, the letter would have been written by one of his followers in one of his later churches. This would be a follower who is dealing with a problem that had arisen in the churches after Paul's day. In other words, the problem of having a vast majority of Gentiles in the church who were in a sense lording it over Jews in the church, thinking that they were spiritually superior to

Jews in the church, this author is writing a letter saying Jews and Gentiles are one in Christ. You Gentiles should be grateful that you have been allowed to join the people of God with the Jews because Christ has made all of one with God through his work of redemption.

In conclusion, we've seen, briefly, several of the reasons that scholars doubt the Pauline authorship of 2 Thessalonians, Colossians, and Ephesians. These judgments are based on questions of vocabulary, writing style, and theology. It's possible, of course, that Paul himself simply adopted a different vocabulary, a different writing style, and a different theology when writing these letters. That's possible. In that case, though, one could say that they were written by Paul, but by a different Paul from the one who wrote the undisputed letters. As we'll see in the next lecture, the differences are even greater when we come to the Pastoral epistles of 1 and 2 Timothy and Titus—books that the majority of scholars again think were not written by Paul.

The Pastoral Epistles
Lecture 20

We know that there were documents forged in Paul's name in early Christianity. ... It appears that several such documents actually made their way into the New Testament.

We have looked at the three Deutero-Pauline epistles of 2 Thessalonians, Colossians, and Ephesians and the reasons to question their authorship. Remember that the question is not whether Christians in antiquity forged documents in the names of the apostles. We know they did. We have apocalypses allegedly written in the names of Peter and of Paul; Gospels allegedly written by Thomas, Peter, Bartholomew and even Mary Magdalene; and letters forged in the names of various Christians—even Jesus himself. We only question specific cases: Was a particular document written by its alleged author and did this document make its way into the canon of the New Testament? In the Deutero-Paulines, it appears that later disciples of Paul wrote letters in his name, addressing problems that had arisen in their own communities by claiming the authority of their revered teacher.

Something very similar seems to have happened with the three letters of 1 and 2 Timothy and Titus. These letters are called the Pastoral Epistles, because they provide instruction to pastors in how to execute their responsibilities. Most critical scholars are convinced, though, that the author giving these instructions was not Paul.

We will begin our discussion by considering these three letters as a group. It is clear that whoever authored these letters wrote them as a group. Both 1 and 2 Timothy are addressed to the same person and are very similar in terms of style—for example, in the opening words of each letter. Titus looks almost like an abstract of 1 Timothy, virtually a *Readers Digest* version. Each letter is written to a pastor of a large Christian community: Timothy of the church in Ephesus, Titus of the church on the isle of Crete. Each letter deals with slightly different situations, but the major issues are the same. False teachers have begun to create problems for the congregations. The communities are suffering from internal problems of disorganization.

The letters urge the pastors to take charge, to run a tight ship, to keep everyone in line, and above all, to silence those who promote ideas that conflict with the ideas of the author and his pastoral friends. One of the prominent instructions involves the heretical teachings of the author's opponents, whom he describes in harsh tones. He calls them "lovers of themselves, lovers of money, boasters, arrogant, abusive, disobedient to their parents, ungrateful, unholy, inhuman…profligates, brutes, haters of good, treacherous, reckless, swollen with conceit, lovers of pleasure," and so on (2 Tim. 3:2–5). Indeed, they may have been all these things and more, but he never indicates what they teach that he found so offensive. Nor does he indicate why what they teach is wrong. In fact, the pastors are not to have serious discussions with these teachers to work out their differences; they are to bring them into submission (1 Tim. 1:3–5). This seems unlike Paul, who usually marshals his arguments against wrong teaching. There may be some indications that the teachers were Gnostics. They appear to subscribe to what the author refers to as "the contradictions of what is falsely called knowledge" (= *gnosis*) (1 Tim. 6:20) and, like Gnostics, they seem to be particularly enthralled with "myths" and "endless genealogies" of the gods (1 Tim. 1:4). If so, this might indicate that the author is writing in a later period than Paul was, because Gnosticism had probably not taken root in Paul's day.

The author is concerned that these churches appoint proper leaders. In both 1 Timothy and Titus, he gives detailed instructions concerning the qualifications of the bishops and deacons who have charge of the churches' physical and spiritual well being. They are to be seasoned Christians with upright moral lives who know how to control their own households and have good reputations on the outside (e.g., 1 Tim. 3:1–13).

These leaders are all to be men. Women are to have no leadership roles in the church; in fact, they are not even to speak in church. In one of the most infamous passages of the New Testament, the author explains that women are descended from Eve, who was deceived by the serpent in the garden of Eden, ate the forbidden fruit to bring sin into the world, then duped her husband into doing likewise (1 Tim. 2:11–15). His conclusion is that if women are allowed to lead, they will be deceived by the devil, will deceive their husbands, and will lead their husbands into sin and ruin. Women are, therefore, to be silent in church and hope to be saved by bearing children.

There are compelling reasons for thinking that Paul did not write these letters. On the micro-level of the words themselves, the vocabulary of the letters speaks against their authenticity. To illustrate: Suppose someone were to uncover a letter allegedly written by Paul that urged its readers to attend mass every Saturday night, go to confession twice a week, and say three Hail Mary's for every unintentional sin? The vocabulary itself, as well as the concepts they express, developed long after Paul's day. Nothing that striking occurs in the Pastorals, but the vocabulary is strikingly non-Pauline. Of the 848 different words found here, 306 occur nowhere else in the Pauline writings of the New Testament (even counting the Deutero-Paulines). Two-thirds of these non-Pauline words appear in Christian authors of the 2nd century. Perhaps even more striking is that some words are found in the Pastorals and in Paul, but they have taken on different meanings. For example, *faith* no longer refers to "a trusting acceptance of Christ's death for your sins" (i.e., it is no longer a *relational* term); instead, it refers to "the body of teaching that makes up true religion" (i.e., it is a *propositional* term) (Tit.1:13).

More striking are the differences in the historical situation presupposed by these letters, compared to Paul's historical context and the way he responded to it. We have already discussed the issue of Gnosticism in terms of the time of its emergence in the early Christian church. These letters presuppose an established hierarchy of church authority, but there was no such hierarchy in place in Paul's day. In these letters, there is one head of the church (Timothy or Titus) and a group of bishops and deacons serving under him. Contrast that with what is found in Paul's letters. In 1 Corinthians, riddled with so many problems, why didn't Paul write to the pastor of the church to tell him to get his congregation in order? The answer is plain: There was no pastor. Paul's churches of the 50s A.D. were thought of as Spirit-led communities, in which everyone had a gift and a role to play. There weren't leaders with the authority to make ultimate decisions. For Paul, the end was coming right away; in such a short term, there's scarcely any need to organize for the long haul. The situation in the Pastorals appears more like what develops later in the 2nd century, where there is one leader over the church, a group of elders who serve under him, and a group of deacons in charge of the physical needs of the community. Eventually, of course, this led to the development of a bishop over the bishops and beyond that, to one head bishop, the Bishop of Rome, who later became known as the Pope. That, of course, is a later development, well beyond Paul's day. The Pastorals seem to presuppose some such later situation.

The different situation appears to be reflected in the Pastoral's attitude toward women, as well. They are to have no leadership roles in the churches, not even to speak, let alone serve as bishops and deacons. What about Paul's own churches? It's true that 1 Cor. 14:34–35 sounds a lot like 1 Timothy 2:11–15, namely, that women are not to speak in church. Many scholars believe there are grounds for thinking that 1 Cor. 14:34–35 was not written by Paul but inserted into his letter by a later scribe who wanted the book to sound more like the Pastorals. Variorum text demonstrated this likelihood. In fact, elsewhere, even in 1 Corinthians itself, Paul grants women the right to speak out in church services—for example, as they pray

The Church was becoming more highly organized and women were being pushed into the margins.

and prophesy (1 Corinthians 11). In other places in his letters, Paul affirms women leaders in the church. In Romans 16, for example, he mentions such women missionaries as Prisca and Persis, a woman deacon of the church named Phoebe, and even a woman named Junia whom he calls "foremost among the apostles." Unlike the Pastoral Epistles, Paul's writing endorses the active leadership of women in the Church.

The Church was becoming more highly organized and women were being pushed into the margins. This was a clear trend in early Christian communities. Jesus had a number of women followers, as seen throughout the Gospel traditions (this would have been unusual for a Jewish rabbi); Paul seems to have supported women in the Church. Women's influence in the churches may have been justified on the grounds that churches met in private homes—which was mostly where women's authority resided in the Roman world. As the Church grew, it became more public, and men may have grown uncomfortable with allowing women to exercise authority. By the 2nd century, it appears that women were shut out of authority roles altogether in most Christian circles. The Pastoral Epistles presuppose that later context and tend to indicate that the author wrote these letters in response, fictitiously urging (under the authority of Paul) that the churches build up their internal hierarchies to be equipped to face the challenges of their day. ■

Essential Reading

1 Timothy, 2 Timothy, Titus.

Brown, *Introduction to the New Testament*, chaps. 29–31.

Ehrman, *The New Testament: A Historical Introduction*, chap. 23.

Supplemental Reading

Beker, *Heirs of Paul*.

Roetzel, *The Letters of Paul*.

Questions to Consider

1. In your judgment, would a pseudonymous author necessarily have to consider his writing to be a work of deceit?

2. Read through the Pastoral Epistles on your own and list ways that these books seem to you to be very much like and very much unlike the undisputed letters of Paul.

The Pastoral Epistles
Lecture 20—Transcript

In the last lecture we looked at the three Deutero-Pauline epistles of 2 Thessalonians, Colossians, and Ephesians and saw reasons to question whether Paul wrote them. I should stress that it's not a question of whether Christians in antiquity forged documents in the name of the apostles. We know that they did. We have apocalypses allegedly written in the names of Peter and of Paul; Gospels allegedly written by Thomas and Peter and Bartholomew and even Mary Magdalene; and letters forged in the names of various Christians—even Jesus himself. There is no question that Christians in antiquity forged documents. It's only a question of specific cases. Was a particular document written by it's alleged author. In the case of the Deutero-Paulines, it appears that later disciples of Paul wrote letters in his name, addressing problems that had arisen in their own communities by claming the authority of their revered teacher.

Something very similar appears to have happened with the three letters of 1 and 2 Timothy and Titus. These letters are called the Pastoral epistles because they are addressed to pastors who are instructed how to execute their pastoral responsibilities. The majority of critical scholars are convinced though that the author giving these instructions was not Paul.

It would be useful to begin our discussion by considering these three letters as a group. It's clear that whoever authored these letters, whether it was Paul or someone else, wrote them together. First and 2 Timothy are addressed to the same person and are very similar in terms of style, for example in the opening words of each letter. If you read the opening phrases of 1 Timothy and then the opening phrases of 2 Timothy, you will see that they are virtually identical. Clearly they are being written by the same person. The Book of Titus looks almost like an abstract of 1 Timothy, virtually a Reader's Digest version, so it too obviously comes from the same author. These three books, then, were written as a group.

Each letter is written to a pastor of a large Christian community. Timothy is assumed to be the pastor of the church in the City of Ephesus, which is in Asia Minor. Titus is assumed to be the pastor of the church on the Isle of Crete. Each letter deals with slightly different situations, but the major problems addressed in each letter are the same. First, false teachers have begun to create problems for the congregations and second, the communities are suffering from internal problems of disorganization. The letters then are written to address these problems of false teaching and disorganization.

In the letters, the author urges the pastors of these churches to take charge, to run a tight ship, to keep everyone in line, and above all to silence those who promote ideas that conflict with those of the author and his pastoral friends. One of the prominent instructions that this author addresses involves the heretical teachings of his opponents, whom he describes in harsh tones. It's not crystal clear exactly what it is these false teachers are teaching. It is clear that this author has no love for them. This can be seen for example in the second letter to Timothy where the author describes his opponents—chapter 3, verses 2 and following—where he says that his opponents are lovers of themselves, lovers of money, boasters, arrogant, abusive, disobedient to their parents, ungrateful, unholy, inhuman, implacable, slanderers, profligates, haters of good, and he goes on and on and on. Unfortunately, he doesn't tell us what it is that these people are doing that his made him so irate. This is simply an instance of name calling. He doesn't tell us, though, what it is these people are actually teaching, nor does he indicate why what they teach, in his opinion, is wrong.

Unlike Paul who engaged his opponents in argument, where Paul would actually mount arguments to show what the problem was with the false teachers, this person simply engages in name calling. And he doesn't tell his pastor readers, Timothy and Titus, how to engage these opponents in argument or how to show their congregations that these false teachers aren't teaching correct doctrine. Instead, these pastors are simply to have nothing to do with these false teachers. They are to bring them under submission to themselves.

There are some slight indications within the letters that these false teachers may be Gnostic Christians. In other words, the author doesn't come out and say this is what they believed, this is why they are wrong, and this is how you should argue against them. But a couple of the things that the author says may indicate that the problem is that these teachers are promoting some form of Gnosticism. At the end, for example, of 1 Timothy—1 Timothy chapter 6, verse 20—the author tells his reader, Timothy, guard what has been entrusted to you, avoid the profane chatter and contradictions of what is falsely called knowledge. Falsely called knowledge. The Greek word there for knowledge is gnosis—the word from which Gnosticism comes. So he is to avoid this false Gnosticism, this false gnosis.

There are other indications of the same thing. For example, at the beginning of this letter of 1 Timothy, the author begins by urging his reader not to occupy himself with myths and endless genealogies that promote speculations. Myths and endless genealogies. If you will recall, Gnosticism maintained that the creator of this world was not the true God, but was an evil deity. Gnostics developed entire mythologies that explained how this evil deity came into being so as to create the world. In fact, Gnostics had genealogies of the divine realm, where you have the one true spiritual God at the top, who emanates other spiritual beings who sort of descend from him in pairs. And these Gnostic systems then have entire mythological structures that explain who these various divinities are that descend from the one true God until the very end at the very bottom of the pile is this creator, creator being, this divine God.

Many of the Gnostic writings, in fact, are filled with this kind of myth and speculations about what the divine realm was like. Is this author warning against that kind of myth and genealogy? If so, then this author is opposing some form of Gnosticism, possibly and early form of Gnosticism. If that's the case, then the author probably is writing in a later period than Paul, since Gnosticism as we know about it probably had not taken root yet in Paul's own day.

This author is especially concerned that the churches appoint proper leaders. In both 1 Timothy and Titus, he gives detailed instructions concerning the qualifications of the bishops and the deacons who have charge of the churches' physical and spiritual well-being. And so you get these lists of the qualification, for example in 1 Timothy, chapter 3, where it turns out that these leaders are to be seasoned Christians, not new converts, with upright moral lives. They should be Christians who know how to control their own households, who have a good reputation on the outside—1 Timothy, chapter 3, verses 1 through 13. So for the problems of disorganization, he is concerned that you have proper leadership.

These leaders are all to be men. Women are to have no leadership roles in these churches. In fact, women are not even to be allowed to speak in the churches. And in what is probably the most infamous passage of the entire New Testament, the author explains why women are not supposed to speak in church. This is a passage that is frequently used to show that the Apostle Paul was a misogynist. It is clearly the most misogynist passage of the New Testament—1 Timothy, chapter 2, verses 11 through 15—where the author says, let a woman learn in silence with full submission. I permit no woman to teach or to have authority over a man. She is to keep silent. For Adam was formed first, then Eve. And Adam was not deceived, but the woman was deceived and became a transgressor. Yet she will be saved through childbearing provided that she continue in faith and love and holiness with modesty.

It is a very interesting passage in which the author mounts an argument from an interpretation of the Hebrew Bible, Book of Genesis, to show why women should not be leaders in the church, in fact should not even speak in the church. His logic is that men are to have priority over women because Adam was created first, the man was created first, and that Eve was created second, as a helper for man. Not to lord it over the man, but to be his helper. Moreover, how did sin come into the world? Well, according to the Genesis story, the serpent tempted Eve to eat the fruit, and she was deceived and did so. And then she compelled her husband to eat. So that she is easily deceived by the devil, and she will lead the man astray. That's why women can't teach in church—they'll be deceived and they will lead the men astray. Women, then, are to be silent in the church. They still do have some hope of being saved though, if they bear children and do so in modesty. As I have said, this passage is frequently used to show that Paul was a misogynist. The problem, of course, is whether Paul actually wrote it. We will do more of this in a minute.

There are compelling reasons for thinking that Paul was not the author of the Pastoral epistles. I want to give several of the leading reasons that scholars are fairly unanimous on this point—that Paul did not write these books. As was the case with the Deutero-Pauline epistles, the arguments have to do with such things as vocabulary, writing style, theology, assumed historical situation. First, I want to deal with the vocabulary of these letters, because in this case vocabulary is a strong argument against the authenticity of the books. Before giving the data let me illustrate how the argument works. Suppose you were to, or somebody, was discover a letter that was allegedly written by the Apostle Paul, which urged its readers to attend mass every Saturday night, to go to confession twice a week, and to say three Hail Mary's for every unintentional sin. Well, one would know fairly clearly that this is not a letter written by the Apostle Paul, because the vocabulary in a letter such as that dealing with things like mass, confession, Hail Mary's, the vocabulary itself, as well as the concepts the vocabulary is expressing, developed long after Paul's day. Nothing that striking, of course, occurs in the Pastorals, but the vocabulary is quite non-Pauline.

Scholars who sit around doing things like counting the words in the New Testament—and there were plenty of scholars doing this, even before the days of the computer—in those days people realized that there were 848 different words used in the Pastoral epistles, if you don't count the same word twice, so every word just counts once. There are 848 words that occur in these three letters. Of these 848 words, 306 of them occur nowhere else in the Pauline writings of the New Testament—306 out of 848 words do not occur in the Pauline letters. That's even including the Deutero-Pauline letters in the calculation. In other words, well over a third of the vocabulary is not Paul's. Moreover two-thirds of these non-Pauline words do appear in Christian authors of the 2nd century. You see the point is that these words aren't Pauline, but they are the kind of words that start showing up later in Christianity.

What's even more striking with respect to vocabulary is that there are words that occur in these books that do occur in Paul, but that appear to take on a different meaning in these books. I have time just to give one example, the term faith. We saw that faith is a very important concept for Paul. What does he mean by it? By faith, Paul means the trusting acceptance of Christ's death for salvation. In other words, it's a relational term, a term having to do with how one relates to Jesus' death on a personal level. You trust it. That's what faith is, it's trust in Christ's death. What about the author of the Pastorals? In the Pastoral epistles, the term faith no longer means a trusting acceptance of Christ's death, instead the term faith is a propositional term that refers to the body of teaching that makes up true religion. So you have to stay true to the faith, which means you stay true to the body of teaching that true religion is all about. It's the same word, but it doesn't mean the same thing any more. It's looks like it's a term that has taken on a new meaning later in Christianity that this author then has taken up. Just on the basis of vocabulary then, it's hard to maintain that Paul wrote these letters.

Even more striking, though, than the differences in vocabulary are the differences in the historical situation that's presupposed by these letters, as opposed to historical situation of Paul himself and the way he responded to it. I've already mentioned one aspect of the new historical situation, which is these letters appear to be opposing some sort of Gnosticism. Even more striking, these letter seem to presuppose an established hierarchy of church authority. These letters presuppose a situation in which you've got a hierarchy of church authority within the Christian communities. As you might have surmised from our earlier discussions, during Paul's day there was no hierarchy in the churches in the sense that you get in the Pastoral epistles. In the Pastoral epistles there is one person who is the head of the church—Timothy, the head of the church at Ephesus; Titus, the head of the church in Crete. These are the pastors. Under the pastors there is a group of bishops and a group of deacons who are serving probably the spiritual needs and the physical needs of the church. So we have some kind of church structure, some kind of hierarchy—people who are appointed to offices within the church. Contrast that with what we've found in Paul's letters.

We spent a good deal of time, for example, looking at 1 Corinthians. Corinth is an important case, because we know more about the church in Corinth than any other of Paul's churches because he wrote two very long letters to the church in Corinth. Corinth was riddled with problems of all sorts—ethical, theological, practical. Why didn't Paul write to the pastor of that church to tell him to get his congregation in order? Why did he write to the entire church and try and persuade them to be behave in certain ways? Why didn't he just write to the pastor? Well, because there wasn't a pastor. Paul's churches in the 50s of the Common Era, 50 A.D., Paul's churches were thought of as spirit-led communities in which everyone had a gift and a role to play. There weren't leaders of these churches with the authority to make decisions. Remember Paul believed that the end was coming right away, that he and his churches were living in the interim period between the resurrection of Jesus, which started the end, and the return of Jesus, which would culminate the end, which would bring the end to culmination. They are living in a short interim period in which the spirit had been given to lead the community until the end came. These are charismatic communities which were not organized with a hierarchy to sustain them over the long haul. Paul didn't understand that his churches were going to last for the long haul.

In contrast, the situation in the Pastoral epistles appears to be more like what developed later in the 2nd century where there is one leader over the church, a group of elders who serve under him, a group of deacons then who are in charge of the physical needs of the community. Eventually, of course, this develops even further into a more rigid hierarchy so that in the 2nd century we have Christian authors who are insisting that there can only be one bishop over the church and that everybody has to follow the dictates of the bishop. These bishops were over local churches, and then there developed the idea of there being bishops over entire regions. So you have local bishops and then archbishops. And eventually you've got major cities that have jurisdiction over all the cities throughout a region. Eventually there develops the idea that the bishop of one of the cities, the bishop of Rome, is to be the bishop over all of the churches throughout Christendom and thus develops the idea that there is a Pope, a father, a Pope, who is over all of the churches in Christianity. That, of course, is a later development, well beyond Paul's own day. The Pastoral epistles, though, appear to be presupposing a situation in which the churches are moving toward this idea of hierarchy. In the Pastoral epistles you have one pastor over the church, with deacons and bishops under him. That's much more like what you get in the 2nd century than you get in the days of Paul, in which you have charismatic communities without leaders who are making all of the decisions. And so, in terms of the historical situation, we've seen two aspects that suggest that the letters are later than Paul's day—the attack on what appears to be Gnosticism, and the hierarchy of church authority.

A third way in which the historical situation seems to be different from Paul's day has to do with the attitude toward woman manifested in these letters, an attitude we have talked about already with respect to 1 Timothy, chapter 2, verses 11 through 15. It is striking that in the Pastoral epistles, woman are to have no leadership roles in the churches. They're not even to speak in the churches, let alone be allowed to serve as bishops and deacons in the churches. How does that compare with Paul's own letters?

Well, in fact, as I am going to show in a minute, Paul's letters presuppose that women could have roles of leadership in the church, that women could speak and be involved in various aspects of church life. Not the Pastoral epistles though. The one exception in Paul's own letters is a much disputed passage found in 1 Corinthians in chapter 14. It's a passage that, in fact, does sound a lot like the passage in 1 Timothy, chapter 2, that I've read. This passage in 1 Corinthians 14, though, is highly debated among scholars. I'll read the passage to you, then explain the terms of the debate. First Corinthians, chapter 14, Paul is in the context of speaking about the spiritual gifts in the church. He has been talking about speaking in tongues and prophesying, and he has been telling the people speaking tongues and prophesying how they ought to engage the use of their gifts in the church. And then he launches into a discussion of women, chapter 14, verse 34, where the author says, "Women should be silent in the churches for they are not permitted to speak, but should be subordinate as the Law also says. If there is anything that they desire to know, let them ask their husbands at home, for it is shameful for a woman to speak in church."

Well, this is in an undisputed Pauline letter, 1 Corinthians 14, and it sounds a lot like what the author of the Pastoral epistles said. The problem is that scholars have long suspected that these two verses in 1 Corinthians 14, were not originally in 1 Corinthians 14. As we'll see in the final lecture in this course, we don't have the original copy of 1 Corinthians or any of the books in the New Testament. We have Greek copies of these books that date from hundred of years after the books were originally written and in the intervening years, scribes copied the books by hand and sometimes they changed things and, in fact, in a lot of places they changed things. This passage looks like these two verses, look like verses that a scribe has inserted into 1 Corinthians. Why? Well, for several reasons. For one thing, immediately before these verses Paul is talking about prophesying in the church. Immediately after these verses he is talking about prophesizing in the church. These verses disrupt what he's been saying in the context. They don't look like they fit in the context.

Moreover, some of our manuscripts of 1 Corinthians take these two verses and relocate them after verse 40; put them in a different place. That might suggest that the verses originated as a marginal note that a scribe wrote in the margin of a manuscript and that later scribes sometimes stuck it in, these verses, in after verse 33; another stuck them in in another place. The clincher is that these verses say women should not speak in church. But three chapters earlier, Paul said that women could speak in church. In fact, Paul talks in 1 Corinthians 11 of women praying and prophesying out loud in church. These verses say they can't speak in church. It doesn't look like these verses fit in the context of 1 Corinthians. The conclusions that scholars have drawn, many scholars have drawn, this is a debated issue, but many scholars have drawn the conclusion that these two verses in 1 Corinthians were not originally written by Paul, but were inserted into Paul's letter by somebody who agreed with the kind of theology expressed in 1 Timothy, chapter 2.

It's striking that in other places of Paul's letters, the undisputed letters, Paul not only mentions, but he affirms women leaders in the churches. You can see this most clearly in Romans, chapter 16—undisputed letter, chapter 16 to the Romans—where Paul mentions women missionaries like a woman named Pricilla and Persis, he mentions a woman deacon named Phoebe, and he even mentions a woman name Junia, whom he calls foremost among the apostles. Unlike the Pastoral epistles, the Apostle Paul himself appears to have endorsed the active leadership of women in the church.

We appear then to be in a situation where the church was becoming more highly organized and women were being pushed out into the margins. This appears to have been a clear trend in the early Christian communities. Jesus himself evidently had a number of women followers as you can see in the Gospel traditions themselves. That would have been fairly unusual for a Jewish Rabbi, in fact it would have been highly unusual. Paul, immediately after Jesus, appears to have supported having women in the church,

318

participating. It may be that early on women's influence in the churches was justified on the grounds that churches in the earlier period actually met in private homes rather than in public buildings. It was widely thought in the Greco-Roman world that the home was the place of a woman's authority and that in public, on the outside, is where a man exercised his authority. Since churches met in private places within the homes, it may be that women were given some grounds of authority there early on. But as the church grew, it became far more public rather than private. Since it became a public affair, with the passing of time and the growth of the church, men appear to have grown uncomfortable with the idea of having women exercise authority in the church. By the 2nd century it appears that women were shut out of authoritative roles all together in most Christian circles. The Pastoral epistles appear to be presuppose that later context.

And so there are three aspects of the Pastoral epistles that suggest they're written and a later historical context. First, they appear to be opposing some form of Gnosticism. Second of all, they are affirming a strong hierarchy of church authority, and third of all their understanding of women's role in the churches appears to be a later view from that found in Paul's own writings.

In conclusion, I should stress that we know that there were documents forged in Paul's name in early Christianity—documents such as 3 Corinthians and Paul's alleged correspondence with Seneca. It appears that several such documents actually made their way into the New Testament. The Pastoral epistles—1 and 2 Timothy and Titus—appear to be documents of this sort. These books were evidently written after Paul's death by someone who considered himself to be one of Paul's followers, who penned these accounts in the apostle's name in order to deal with new problems that had come to confront the church. The churches were filled with teachers who proclaimed a version of the Gospel that the author found offensive. Moreover, the churches had become internally disorganized. In part, this internal disorganization was evident by what the author took to be an unwarranted role of leadership taken by women—a role that he was certain the apostle himself would never have approved of and so he wrote these letters in response, fictitiously urging under the authority of Paul that the churches get rid of the heretical teachers and build up their internal structure of hierarchy so as to be equipped to face the challenges of their day.

The Book of Hebrews
and the Rise of Christian Anti-Semitism

Lecture 21

> Most scholars think that [the Epistle of Hebrews] was just that—a sermon, a word of exhortation, a sermon that was delivered by an early Christian preacher to his congregation. As such, this would be the earliest Christian sermon to survive intact.

The Epistle to the Hebrews appears to be misnamed on both counts. It is not an epistle. Ancient letters usually begin by naming the author and indicating the audience (as in Paul's epistles). There is nothing like that here; instead, the author describes the writing as "a word of exhortation" (13:22). Most scholars think that the letter was just that, a sermon delivered by an early Christian preacher to his congregation. As such, it would be the earliest Christian sermon to survive intact. The congregation does not appear to have been made up of Jews, as the later title "to the Hebrews" might lead one to suspect. At one point in the letter, the writer reminds them of what they learned when they first came to believe, including "faith in God, the resurrection from the dead, and eternal punishment" (6:1–2). Presumably Jews would already have subscribed to such beliefs, even before becoming Christian. It appears then that the congregation is made up of Gentiles, former pagans.

The book deals extensively with the relationship of Christianity and Judaism, mounting numerous arguments that Jesus and the religion based on him are superior in every way to anything Judaism has to offer. This may have been what confused later readers into thinking that the book was addressed to Jews—perhaps as a way of showing them that they should convert. The author indicates, however, that he is concerned that members of his congregation should not be tempted to leave the Church and become Jewish. He is writing to head them off, to show them that it would be a huge mistake with eternal consequences for them to forsake Christ for Judaism.

It does not appear that this author was Paul. Paul's name never appears in the book and the writing style is not at all like his. The major topics of discussion (e.g., the Old Testament priesthood and the Jewish sacrificial system) never show up in Paul's writings. Even though a number of names have been proposed as the author of this book over the years, including Paul's companions Barnabas and Apollos and even the woman Priscilla, we really don't know who the author was. As the 3rd-century Church Father from Alexandria, Origen, once said: "As to who the author of this book is, God knows."

The author organizes his sermon around the innumerable ways that Christ is superior to everything in Judaism. For example, he is superior to the Jewish prophets, because they spoke so long ago but he has spoken in recent times, as the perfect reflection of God's own glory (1:1–3). He is superior to Moses, who was one of God's servants. But Christ is God's actual son (3:1–6). He is superior to the Jewish priests (4:14–5:10; 7:1–29). Because they were sinful, they had to offer a sacrifice for their own sins before they could offer one for the sake of the people. Christ, on the other hand, was completely without sin and did not need to make a sacrifice for himself. The sacrifices the Jewish priests made had to be performed repeatedly; Christ's sacrifice of himself was perfect and needed to be offered only once.

Christ is the minister of a superior sanctuary (9:1–28), especially compared to the tabernacles used in Jewish worship. The Jewish priests performed their sacrifices in a temporary sanctuary that was constructed according to a heavenly model. Christ did not sacrifice himself in the replica, but took his sacrifice up to heaven itself, into the real sanctuary, in the presence of God himself.

Christ is the fulfillment of all that the Jewish Scriptures anticipated. This may seem like an ironical claim—that the Jewish Scriptures show that Judaism is no longer valid and a new religion is superior to it. But it's a claim made in slightly different ways by other Christians as well (for example, Matthew and Paul). The author seems to understand Jesus' fulfillment of the Scriptures in two distinct, but related, ways. First, he uses predictions of the Jewish Scriptures to show that God had planned something new that would supplant the Jewish religion. For example: Jer. 31:31–34 indicates that God was going to make a new covenant with the people of Israel, because they had broken the old one (8:7–9). Jesus is that new covenant. The old covenant, based on the Law, is no longer in force.

He also portrays Christ as superior to Judaism to the extent that the reality of a thing is superior to that which foreshadowed it. The Old Testament sanctuary and Law, for example, are both said to be mere "shadows" of the reality of Christ (8:5; 10:1). This imagery of "shadow" versus "reality" reflects philosophical metaphors that go back to Plato, nearly 500 years earlier. Plato insisted that things that appear to be real were only shadows of a greater reality. Physical pleasure, for example, has all the appearance of being a great good, but it is good only in appearance (witness the suffering sometimes brought on by excessive indulgence in pleasure).

The most famous illustration of this idea is in Plato's "Allegory of the Cave." There, prisoners chained together can see shadows on the wall in front of them but not the people behind them who are manipulating puppets in front of a great fire, thereby creating the shadows. The prisoners wrongly assume that the shadows are the things themselves. Were they to be unchained and see for themselves the real situation, though, they would realize how fully they had been deceived by what they had mistaken to be reality (Plato, *Republic*, Book VII). Once one sees reality "as it really is," there is no longer any pleasure in the "shadows." For the author of Hebrews, Christ is the reality foreshadowed in the Hebrew Bible. Once a person has experienced him, there is no turning back.

The Epistle to the Hebrews is probably the strongest statement in the New Testament that the religion of the Jews is no longer valid, that God has transcended it in bringing the Christian religion into the world. In some ways, it marks an early point in the trend

The imagery of foreshadowing versus reality in the New Testament reflects philosophical metaphors that go back to Plato.

Prints and Photographs Division, Library of Congress, LC-US261-1310.

among Christians to discount, and eventually to attack, Judaism. The irony, of course, is that Christianity started out as Jewish in the teachings of the Jewish prophet, Jesus. After his death, though, Christians appeared to be far less concerned with the religion he espoused than with the religion founded on his death and resurrection.

Most Jews, of course, rejected this new religion right from the earliest days of Christianity. For many Jews, it seemed ludicrous to call Jesus the messiah, because he was not a figure of power that had overcome the enemies of the people of Israel. He was a crucified criminal. To insist that God had "changed the rules," by invalidating the Law that he himself had given his people, or that he had rescinded an "eternal" covenant that he had made, was tantamount to calling God a turncoat and a liar. Christians insisted that their religion was "true Judaism" and, because the only way to God was through the death of Jesus, anyone who retained the old Judaism was necessarily damned by the God they claimed to worship.

Christianity started out as Jewish in the teachings of the Jewish prophet, Jesus.

Animosities naturally arose and were exacerbated as Christianity became a primarily Gentile religion—yet one that claimed to represent Judaism as it ought to be. Jews naturally found this offensive—non-Jews who did not even attempt to keep the Jewish Law or join the Jewish people were claiming to be the true people of the God of the Jews, insisting that the Jews themselves had been rejected by their own God. Christians, to validate their beliefs, looked to Scriptures to find examples of when and where God expressed his displeasure with the Jewish people. There were many examples in the Prophets that were adduced for this purpose.

We can see the animosities in later sermons from the early Christians, including one particularly vitriolic homily delivered by a 2nd-century Christian bishop named Melito from the city of Sardis in Asia Minor. In Melito's sermon, preached on an Easter with the Exodus story of the Passover as the background, Israel is maligned and attacked for the way it treated Jesus (as if all Israel were to blame), killing their own Passover lamb. Even more horrific, because Melito considers Jesus to be God, he accuses Israel of deicide: they have murdered the creator of the universe, God himself. (Melito *Easter Homily*, chapters. 95–96). This is the first of many charges that the Jewish people killed God. Such animosity, as it emerged in the 2nd and 3rd centuries, did not have a huge impact on society at large. Most people were neither Jew nor Christian, so the squabbles were ultimately of little moment outside the small circles of Christianity.

All that changed, of course, with the conversion of the Roman emperor Constantine to Christianity in the 4th century A.D. Thereafter, it become quite popular to be Christian, and Christianity, as a result, eventually had the power of the entire empire behind it. At that point, Christian animosity toward Judaism took on a fevered pitch and Christians had the wherewithal, at last, to act out their animosity. Synagogues were burned, property was confiscated, Jews were killed. This was the beginning of one of the most heinous chapters in the history of Christianity, from the anti-Semitism dominant among Christian countries throughout the Middle Ages to the climax in our own time with the unspeakable crimes of the Holocaust.

The Book of Hebrews, of course, does not urge acts of anti-Semitism. It stands only at the beginning of a trajectory of thought that leads to anti-Semitism. In fact, it's clear from the book that it is the *Christians* at the time who have been experiencing persecution—possibly at the hands of Jews, who near the end of the 1st century were far more numerous and powerful than the Christians, but more likely at the hands of local governmental authorities (cf., 10:32–34). This author is urging his hearers not to fall away from the faith in the midst of their suffering, not to turn away into a more protected religion, such as Judaism. Those who neglect the salvation provided by Christ, who return to the outside world after joining the Church, will receive a fearful and eternal punishment (2:1–4; 3:7–18; 10:27–29). ∎

Essential Reading

The Epistle to the Hebrews.

Brown, *Introduction to the New Testament*, chap. 32.

Ehrman, *The New Testament: A Historical Introduction*, chap. 24.

Sandmel, *Anti-Semitism in the New Testament*.

Supplemental Reading

Gager, *The Origins of Anti-Semitism*.

Lindars, *The Theology of the Letter to the Hebrews*.

Ruether, *Faith and Fratricide*.

Questions to Consider

1. Choose several of the important figures we have considered in this course—e.g., Jesus, Matthew, Luke, Paul, the author of Hebrews—and discuss ways in which they can be seen as both Jewish and anti-Jewish. Do you see anything that you would label "anti-Semitism" in the New Testament?

2. We saw in an earlier lecture that pagan religions were mostly tolerant of one another, none of them making "exclusivistic" claims for itself. Christianity seems, though, to be different. Do you think Christianity is *necessarily* exclusivistic (i.e., that it necessarily has to claim that it alone is "true" and "right")? Is it necessarily intolerant? Is there any way an exclusivistic religion could still be tolerant?

The Book of Hebrews
and the Rise of Christian Anti-Semitism
Lecture 21—Transcript

For the past two lectures we have considered books of the New Testament that claim to be written by Paul, but probably were not. In this lecture, we will look at a book that does not claim to be written by Paul, but was included in the New Testament because the Christians of the 3rd and 4th centuries who constructed the canon thought it was—the Epistle to the Hebrews.

The Epistle to the Hebrew appears to be misnamed on both counts. It's not an epistle. Normally, ancient letters begin by naming their author and indicating to whom they are being directed, as in Paul's epistles. There is nothing like that here. Instead, the author describes his writing as a word of exhortation—chapter 13, verse 22. Most scholars think that, in fact, this book was just that—a sermon, a word of exhortation, a sermon that was delivered by an early Christian preacher to his congregation. As such, this would be the earliest Christian sermon to survive intact.

The congregation does not appear to have been made up of Jews, as the title "To the Hebrews" might lead one to suspect. One reason for thinking that the congregation was not Jewish is that the author reminds them what they learned when they first came to believe including such things as faith in God, the resurrection from the dead, and eternal punishment—chapter 6, verses 1 through 2. Presumably Jews would already have subscribed to such beliefs as belief in God, the resurrection, and punishment even before they had become Christian. This makes it appear that congregation is made up of Gentiles, former pagans. And so the Epistle to the Hebrews is misnamed. It's not an epistle; it appears not to be directed toward Jews.

The book does deal extensively with the relationship of Christianity and Judaism, mounting numerous arguments that Jesus and religion based on him are superior in every way to anything Judaism has to offer. This may have been what confused later readers into thinking that the book was addressed to Jews, as a way perhaps of showing them that they should convert. But the author indicates that his concern instead is that members of his congregation not be tempted to leave the church and become Jewish. He's writing to them to head them off at the pass, to show them that it would be a huge mistake with eternal consequences for them to forsake Christ for Judaism.

It does not appear that this author was Paul. Paul's name never appears in the book, and the writing style is not like his at all. Moreover, the major topics of discussion in the book are topics that never show up in Paul's own writings. For example, this author is particularly concerned to compare Jesus to the priesthood found in the Hebrew Bible—Jewish priest such as discussed in the Hebrew Bible—and he is concerned to show that Jesus is superior to the sacrificial system of the Jews. These are not topics of real concern in any of Paul's writings. And so, even though the later Christians who formed the canon included this book in the canon because they thought Paul wrote it, Paul evidently did not.

Well, who then did write this book? A number of names have been proposed over the years as the author of the book, including Paul's companions Barnabas or Appolos. Some have even suggested that a woman wrote the book, Pricilla. The reality is that we really don't know who the author was, or, as the Church Father Origen, a 3rd-century Church Father living in Alexandria, Egypt, once said, as to who the author of this book is, God knows. Well, we certainly don't.

This author organizes his sermon around the innumerable ways that Christ is superior to everything in Judaism. His point, as we are going to see even more later, his point is that he wants to show that Jesus is superior to Judaism so that people in his congregation aren't tempted to leave the church to join Judaism, and so in order to make this case he has to show that Christ is superior to Judaism. And most of his book, then, is design to show aspects of Christ that are superior to everything that Judaism has to offer.

He begins his book, for example, by arguing that Jesus is superior to the Jewish prophets. The Jewish prophets spoke long ago, but Jesus has spoke in recent times. They were spokespersons for God. Jesus, though, for this author is the perfect reflection of God's own glory. When you look upon Jesus, you actually see what God himself looks like. And so Jesus is obviously superior to Jewish prophets. Jesus is superior to Moses. Moses in the Hebrew Bible is described as one of God's servants. Christ, though, is described by the early traditions about Jesus as God's own son. The son is obviously superior to the servants.

This author wants to maintain that Jesus is superior to the Jewish priests. We find this teaching particularly in chapters 4, 5, and 7 in this book, it's a particular emphasis that the author wants to make. Since the priests were human beings who were sinful within Judaism, they had to offer a sacrifice for their own sins before they could offer a sacrifice for the sake of the people. They were humans like everyone else and so they needed sacrifice for their sins. Christ, on the other hand, according to this author, was completely without sin. And so he did not need to make a sacrifice for himself; he's superior, then, to the Jewish priests. Moreover, the sacrifices that priests made in the temple needed to be made repeatedly. A one-time sacrifice wasn't enough because people continually sin, people then need sacrifices that continually go on, and the sacrifices themselves aren't sufficient to cover all sins, only sins committed periodically. Christ, though, had a perfect sacrifice; he had to offer his sacrifice only once. His sacrifice, in fact, was the sacrifice of himself. A perfect sacrifice offered only once, therefore, is superior to the sacrifices of the Jewish priest in the temple.

Moreover, Christ by this author is portrayed as a minister of a superior sanctuary—chapter 9. The Jewish priests performed their sacrifices in a temporary sanctuary that was constructed according to a heavenly model when God gives instructions in the Hebrew Bible of how to construct the sanctuary. First, the tabernacle in the wilderness, which was a kind of a tent sacred structure that they would carry around with them as they wondered in the wilderness, and then eventually the temple itself. These were temporary structures in which sacrifices were brought to God.

Christ, though, is a minister of a superior sanctuary because these temporary sanctuaries were modeled on the sanctuary in heaven, but for this author, Christ took his sacrifice up to heaven itself offering his blood in the presence of God, so that his sanctuary was superior. It was the archetype on which the type of the temple on earth was formulated.

Christ, for this author, is the fulfillment of all that the Jewish Scriptures themselves anticipated. Christ is the fulfillment of all that the Jewish Scriptures anticipated. This may seem like an ironical claim—that the Jewish Scriptures show that Judaism is no longer valid, but that a new religion is superior to it. That's what this author is claiming, that Jewish Scripture shows that Judaism is no longer valid. It seems then like an ironical claim, but in fact it's the claim this author is making and he is not alone in making it.

We've already seen two New Testament authors who make a similar kind of claim—the Gospel of Matthew, which claims that Jesus is a fulfillment of all things in Judaism, and the Apostle Paul, who also sees Jesus as the fulfillment of Judaism. Paul wanted to maintain, for example, that salvation comes to people on the basis of faith, apart from the Law, and he used the Law to prove it. He showed that the Law itself says that salvation comes apart from the Law.

The author of the Hebrews has a similar notion that Jesus fulfills Judaism, thereby making Judaism obsolete, and he wants to insist that the Jewish Scriptures indicate this. This author seems to understand Jesus' fulfillment of the Scriptures in two distinct but related ways. There are two ways for this author that Jesus fulfills Scripture. First, this author uses predictions of the Jewish Scriptures to show that God had planned something new that would supplant the Jewish religion. He uses the Jewish Scriptures themselves to show that God had planned something new that would supplant Judaism.

This is seen most clearly in chapter 8, where the author cites a passage from the Book of Jeremiah—the prophet Jeremiah chapter 31, verses 31 and following—in which God talks about a new covenant or a New Testament that he is going to make with his people. And so he says, as this author quotes, God finds fault with them when he says, "The days are surely coming, says the Lord, when I will establish a new covenant with the house of Israel and with the house of Judah. Not like the covenant that I made with their ancestors on the day when I took them by the hand to lead them out of the land of Egypt. For they did not continue in my covenant, and so I had no concern for them, says the Lord."

Okay, God is going to make a new covenant because the people of Israel broke the old covenant. For, he says, verse 12, "For I will be merciful toward their iniquities and I will remember their sins no more." This new covenant will bring a complete forgiveness of sins. The author resumes, verse 13, in speaking of a new covenant, God has made the first one obsolete. And what is obsolete and growing old, will soon disappear. In other words, for this author, Jesus represents a new covenant that's been given by God.

The old covenant was based on the Law given to Moses on Mount Sinai after the Exodus. But the people of Israel broke that law. Since they broke the covenant, it's no longer in force. God, recognizing this, predicted that he would make a new covenant that would bring forgiveness of sins. This is what he gives in Christ. So that Scriptures themselves indicate that the Jewish Law is going to be done away with, with the coming of Jesus. The Jewish Law is no longer in force. So, the first way that Jesus fulfills Scripture for this author is that he brings to fulfillment that which God predicted in the Hebrew Bible.

There is a second way in which Jesus is shown to be superior to Judaism as a kind of fulfillment of Judaism. For this author, Christ is superior to Judaism to the extent that the reality of a thing is superior to that which foreshadowed it. The reality of a thing is superior to that which foreshadowed it. According to this author, the Old Testament Hebrew Bible sanctuary and the Hebrew Bible Law are both said to be mere shadows of the reality that has come into being through Christ.

This imagery of shadow versus reality reflects philosophical metaphors that go all the way back to Plato, nearly 500 years earlier. Plato insisted that things appearing to be real were only shadows of a greater reality. For example, for Plato physical pleasure has all the appearance of being a great good. That's why people engage in it with such abandon is because it seems like a good thing, physical pleasure. But for Plato, physical pleasure is good only in appearance. It's not the reality of a good, it's only the appearance of a good. Witness the suffering sometimes brought on by excessive indulgence in pleasure, as most of us who are given to excess can amply attest. Is the hangover really worth it, or the guilt, or worse the rehab program? Pleasure might seem like a good, but it's not the real thing itself for Plato.

The most famous illustration of this idea in Plato comes in his famous allegory of the cave, which can be found in his dialogue, The Republic Book 7. Plato imagines a situation in which people are in a cave. You have a line of people who are chained together as prisoners, chained in such a way that their vision can be directed only ahead of them to a wall that is facing them as they sit down. Behind the people at some distance is a great fire. They, of course, don't know a fire is there because all they can see is what's on the wall in front of them. Between their backs and the fire are other people who are carrying little puppets of animate objects and inanimate objects, which the light of the fire is striking these puppet images and casting shadows on the wall in front of the prisoners. These prisoners can only see the shadows on the wall, and they assume that these shadows are the things themselves. When they hear people talking for example, they see shadows of people cast on the wall, they hear talking, they assumed that it's the shadows that are doing the talking. These people are living in a shadow world. There's a reality that's casting images on the wall, but all they see are the images, not the realities.

Plato asks what would happen if somebody were unchained and able to stand up and look behind. Well, first his eyes would be blinded, because the light would be so much stronger that he wouldn't be able to see. But if he withstood the light for long enough, his eyes would adjust and he'd realize that there are people carrying puppets behind him, and he'd realize that everything that he had seen before this were, these were just shadows on the wall.

Plato continues to think what would happen if this person then, finally got up and left the cave. He'd look up in the sky and he'd see the sun and he'd realize that the fire in the cave itself was a kind of a shadow of a greater reality. Once you realize that what you're experiencing is a shadow of a greater reality, there is no longer any pleasure in seeing the shadows. Nobody in that situation then would want to be chained again, simply to see shadows up against the front wall of the cave.

For the author of the Book of Hebrews, Christ is the reality that is foreshadowed in the Hebrew Bible. The Hebrew Bible is like shadows cast on the wall of the cave. Once you've experienced the reality, which in this case is Christ, there's no turning back. The Epistle of Hebrews is probably the strongest statement in the New Testament that religion of the Jews is no longer valid, that God has transcended it in bringing the Christian religion into the world.

In some ways this book marks an early point in the trend among Christians to discount and eventually to attack Judaism. And so I want to spend the rest of this lecture talking about the emergence of anti-Jewish attitudes among Christians.

The entire progress of anti-Judaism in early Christianity is ironic, since Christianity itself started out as Jewish. As we saw in the lectures on Jesus, Jesus himself was completely Jewish. He was born a Jew, he was raised a Jew, he followed Jewish customs, he kept the Jewish Law, he interpreted the Jewish Law as a Jewish Rabbi to his Jewish disciples, teaching the Jewish people that they needed to repent because the Jewish God was going to intervene in history and overthrow the forces of evil. This was a Jewish religion from the get go. The irony is that eventually it became to a completely anti-Jewish religion.

Well how did it happen? After Jesus' death, Christians appeared to be, to have become far less concerned with the religion that Jesus himself espoused than with the religion that was founded on his death and resurrection. As we know, Christianity that developed didn't simply propagate the teachings of Jesus, that the Son of Man was coming on the clouds in judgment of the earth. Christianity changed drastically. We have seen changes most clearly in the case of the Apostle Paul, who built an entire theology around the idea that Jesus' death and resurrection brought salvation. This is not the message of Jesus himself.

Paul's message, though, was also a Jewish message. He understood Jesus as the fulfillment of the Jewish Scriptures. And he himself was Jewish. We have no indication that Paul thought that Jews should stop being Jewish. It's clear that Paul thought that Gentiles didn't need to become Jewish. But Paul never tells Jews to stop keeping the Law. Paul thought that Jew and Gentile were equally made right with God through the death of the son of God, Jesus, the Jewish Messiah. But that didn't mean that Gentiles had to become Jews, on the one hand, but it didn't mean that Jews had to stop being Jews, on the other hand.

This message, though, that it was Jesus' death and resurrection that put people into a right standing before God was rejected by the vast majority of Jews in Paul's day and in later days. As Paul himself at an earlier stage appears to have thought, most Jews thought that it seemed ludicrous to call Jesus the Messiah. The Messiah was supposed to be a figure grandeur and power who overthrew God's enemies to set up God's kingdom. Jesus, though, was a lowly crucified criminal. To call him the Messiah simply didn't make sense to most Jews.

Moreover, most Jews thought that the idea that salvation came through the death and resurrection of Jesus would mean that God had completely changed the rules. God had given his Law to his people telling them how they could live in ways to maintain a relationship with himself. Maintaining a relationship with God meant doing what he commanded in his Law. He had made an eternal covenant with the people of Israel to be their God, so long as they kept his Law. If now salvation came not by the Law, but by believing in the death and resurrection of a crucified criminal, that would be tantamount to calling God a turncoat and a liar. No wonder most Jews found this idea completely blasphemous.

Christians, for their part, insisted that their religion was true Judaism. Christians initially, Christians who themselves were Jewish and then Christians who were Gentile who came to understand what Judaism was about, claimed that their religion was true Judaism and that Jews who rejected Jesus had rejected their own religion, and, therefore, had rejected their own God. These people claim that those who retained the older form of Judaism were necessarily damned by the God that they claimed to worship.

Obviously animosities arose. And these animosities became exacerbated as Christianity became principally a Gentile religion, yet one which claimed to represent Judaism as it ought to be. Jews naturally found these claims to be offensive. Jews would point out that here you have a group of non-Jews who don't even attempt to keep the Jewish Law or to join the Jewish people, who are claming to be the true people of the God of the Jews. That just simply made no sense. Moreover, these non-Jews who don't even keep the Jewish Law are claiming that the Jewish God has rejected the Jewish people.

Part of the animosity that arose became reflected in various ways that Jews and Christians interpreted the Jewish Scriptures. Christians had to search through the Scriptures to find validation for their beliefs. It wasn't difficult to find passages in Scripture which indicated that God was angry with the Jewish people. The Jewish prophets of the Hebrew Bible are filled with passages in which God is angry because his people have gone astray, and it says that he is going to enter into judgment with them. These passages, though, are inside literature written by Jews, for Jews to tell Jews to return to the Jewish God. Christians took these passages and they used them to show that God had rejected his own people, suggesting then that God was going to create a new people.

The debates over the interpretation of Scripture emerged in the 1st, 2nd, and 3rd centuries and became somewhat vitriolic. We can see the animosities in later sermons from the early Christians that have survived. One particularly interesting instance to show how high, how much the animosity had grown is found in a recently discovered sermon by a Church Father named Melito, who was a pastor of a church in Sardis, which is in Asia Minor. This sermon dates from about the year 190 A.D. So we are talking about a century after the Book of Hebrews was written. But this shows how much the animosities have heightened. This is a sermon that Melito delivered during an Easter celebration in which he had read the passage from the Hebrew Bible about the Exodus, and he's using this account of the Passover lamb in Exodus as a way of talking about Jews and Christians.

In particular, this sermon attacks Jews for killing their Passover lamb, which he understands to be Jesus. I'll just read brief excerpts. "Why, oh Israel," says Melito, "did you do this strange injustice? You dishonored the one who had honored you. You held in contempt the one who held you in esteem. You denied the one who publicly acknowledged you. You renounced the one who proclaimed you his own. You killed the one who made you to live. Why did you do this, oh Israel?" By rejecting Jesus, see, they've rejected God. "Therefore hear and tremble, because of him for whom the earth trembled, the one who hung the earth in space is himself hanged. The one who fixed the heavens in place is himself impaled. The one who firmly fixed all things is himself firmly fixed to the tree. The Lord is insulted. God has been murdered. The king of Israel has been destroyed by the hand of Israel."

Because Melito understood that Jesus himself was God, he maintained that the Jews had killed their own God. This is the first instance we have of a charge of deicide leveled against Jews, the charged that they had murdered God.

This kind of rhetoric did not have a huge impact on society at large in Melito's day nor earlier in the time of the writing of the Book of Hebrews. The situation changed drastically only much later. When the emperor Constantine converted to Christianity in the 4th century, Christianity stopped being a very small and persecuted little minority group within the empire to becoming the dominant religious force in the empire. Once that happen in the 4th century, Christians took these earlier kinds of sermons, which displayed animosities toward the Jews and took them quite literally and used them as propaganda as a way of opposing Jews and their religion. After the 4th century, synagogues were burned, Jewish property was confiscated, and Jews were killed.

This then is the beginning of one of the most heinous chapters in the history of Christianity with the anti-Semitism dominant among Christian countries throughout the Middle Ages and the climax in our own time with the unspeakable crimes of the holocaust being the direct result of later Christians taking this earlier kind of rhetoric very seriously, rhetoric that emerged because of differences between Jews and Christians in the early stage.

Of course, the Book of Hebrews doesn't urge acts of anti-Semitism and doesn't urge any acts of violence. In fact, this book is written to Christians, who themselves appear to be suffering persecution, rather than themselves practicing acts of persecution. This author is living in a different situation, where he is trying to get his congregation not to fall way from their faith because they are suffering. He doesn't want them to turn to Judaism. At a later time, though, this kind of book was used by Christians to urge the opposition to Judaism.

In conclusion, we can say that this sermon is written to strengthen a Christian congregation to prevent the members of the congregation from turning from the church to the synagogue. The author wants to argue that Jesus is the fulfillment of the Jewish Scriptures and that he should not be abandoned for Judaism because he is superior to everything in Judaism. The temptation, of course, for Christians to fall away was particularly acute in times of persecution. The question of the official opposition to this young religion will be the subject of our next lecture, which will focus on the Book of 1 Peter.

First Peter and the Persecution of the Early Christians

Lecture 22

This was the message of hope that many Christians continued to cling on to in the face of sporadic persecution.

Throughout the books of the New Testament, one finds numerous references to Christians' suffering. In the last lecture, we saw that the Epistle to the Hebrews was a sermon written to a group of Christians who were experiencing some form of persecution; the author was striving to convince his hearers not to succumb to pressure and leave the church for Judaism In the Synoptic Gospels, Jesus tells his followers that they must take up their crosses if they want to follow him. In the Book of Acts, the early Christian communities are persecuted by the Jewish leadership in Jerusalem. The apostle Paul himself is eventually arrested and put up on charges of disturbing the peace. Nowhere is the theme of Christian suffering more pronounced, though, than in the book of 1 Peter.

This book is addressed to Christians living in Asia Minor (modern-day Turkey); the word for *suffering* occurs more often in this short letter than in any other book of the New Testament—even more than Luke and Acts combined. These people were probably former pagans, who have removed themselves from the daily life of the larger community and adopted a stricter set of moral standards for themselves. There has been some kind of public outcry, apparently by those who feel abandoned by their former friends and companions (4:4). The turmoil may have reached the point of mob violence or governmental intervention. The author speaks of the "fiery ordeal that is taking place among you" (4:12).

The author writes his letter both to console those in the community who are suffering and to urge them to maintain their solidarity with one another. On the one hand, he explains that their suffering is natural and to be expected— they are, after all, followers of Christ, who was himself crucified (4:12–13). He urges them, though, to make sure they suffer for doing what is right, never for doing what is wrong (3:14–17; 4:14–15). They should not behave in a way that offends outsiders but should be ready to explain what it is that makes them different (3:15–17). The author stresses that these Christians have a distinct status as a community that has been set apart from the world to belong to God. Sociologists have long recognized that group solidarity can be created by acts of hatred and persecution, because the group forms bonds of cohesion, realizing that they are "all in it together." Something like that appears to be happening in this letter, as the author assures his readers that they are a people set apart, belonging to God alone (1:3, 2:3, and especially 2:9). Moreover, when he urges them to engage in moral behavior, he may be thinking not only of their own need to follow God's Law but also of the possible repercussions on those outside the community. When outsiders realize how the Christians react to persecution, they too might repent (2:11; 3:13–15).

Scholars continue to debate whether this author was actually the disciple of Jesus, Simon Peter. He certainly claims to be, in the first verse of the book. But as we've seen, all such claims need to be tested. According to the Gospels, Peter was a lower-class Jewish fisherman from Galilee. As such, he would have been uneducated (only the upper classes had the leisure to learn to read) and his native tongue would have been Aramaic. According to Acts, he was known to be illiterate (Acts 4:13). his book, though, is written by a well-educated, rhetorically trained, Greek-speaking Christian. Although it is possible that Peter wrote the book or dictated its contents to someone (perhaps the "Silvanus" mentioned in 5:12), who translated his words into Greek and provided them with a rhetorical flourish, it's also possible that the book is written pseudonymously in Peter's name—as were several other books that have come down to us from the 2nd century (cf., the Gospel of Peter).

As one of the clearest indications that early Christians were persecuted, 1 Peter can serve as a springboard for the larger question of Roman opposition to Christianity in its early days. Many people have a complete misperception of Roman attitudes toward Christians, thinking, for example, that Rome declared Christianity illegal and sent out the troops to round up the Christians, who survived by hiding in the catacombs. That may be suitable for a Hollywood screenplay, but it is simply not true historically. Christianity was not declared "illegal" until nearly two centuries after the writings of Paul—not until A.D. 250 under the fervently pagan emperor Decius. Only then were there any empire-wide persecutions (and there is some question about how extensive the persecution was even at that point). Before then, Christians were occasionally persecuted, as were many other groups, but they did not go into hiding *en mass* and communicate with one another only in private.

Christians had the same rights and responsibilities as anyone else in the Roman Empire. Starting a new religion was not illegal. Christians had the right to worship any God they wanted, even the Jewish God. And no one would have thought it "illegal" even to call Jesus "God." Most people believed that occasionally humans came along who were also divine.

To understand why Christians were occasionally persecuted by Roman authorities, we have to know something about the Roman legal system. Unlike Roman civil law, which was extremely complex and nuanced, Roman criminal law was, by our standards, completely lax and haphazard. Criminal activities were not strictly defined and punishments were not prescribed by law. Neither the Roman emperor nor the Senate passed criminal legislation binding on all the inhabitants of the Roman Empire. The provinces were ruled by governors, chosen from the Roman aristocracy, who were appointed by either the emperor or the Senate. The provincial governors had two major responsibilities: to raise tax revenues and to keep the peace. They were granted nearly absolute authority to achieve these objectives. It was assumed that the governor, on location, would best know how to handle any situation, using whatever means necessary to maintain public order and maximize revenue collection. Using any means necessary meant having the power of life and death. From a Roman administrative point of view, Pontius Pilate was completely justified in condemning Jesus to death as a public nuisance. Making that kind of decision was what he was appointed to do.

> **Christians were themselves persecuted and prosecuted—not because their religion was against some kind of Roman law—but because they were perceived as public nuisances.**

Christians were themselves persecuted and prosecuted—not because their religion was against some kind of Roman law—but because they were perceived as public nuisances. Authorities took care of problems on an ad hoc basis. From both Paul and the Book of Acts, we see that Christian missionary activity sometimes led to public disturbances. Christians would often abandon their own families to join the new community. These splits in the family were often painful to those who were left behind (cf., Matt. 10:34–37). Because the Christians were known to be a closed community, they sometimes came under suspicion as a secret society.   In particular, widely believed slanders were leveled against the Christians. Because they met at night, called one another brother and sister, engaged in "love feasts" (that is, communal meals), practiced a ritual kiss, and actually ate the body and drank the blood of the son of God, they were widely believed to engage in nocturnal orgies involving incest and cannibalism (cf., the words of Fronto, the teacher of the 2nd-century emperor Marcus Aurelius).

Altogether, the early Christians had a considerable "image problem." Consider the two pagan authors who were the first to mention Jesus, whom we discussed earlier. The Roman historian Tacitus labeled the Christians a "pernicious superstition" and says they were the "hatred of the human race." This, he claims, is why Nero could easily make them scapegoats for the burning of Rome for which he was responsible (*Annals* 15). Pliny the Younger, governor of part of the region that 1 Peter itself addresses, called them "obstinate" and "mad" adherents of a "depraved superstition." He was responsible for their persecution when they refused to abandon their Christian ways.

The problem was exacerbated by the fact that Christians refused to participate in the public ceremonies honoring the state and local gods. Because the Christians believed there was only one true God, they couldn't very well participate in the worship of others. This made no sense, though, to pagans. As polytheists, they found the idea that if you worshipped one god you couldn't worship another to be nonsense (it would be the same as saying that you couldn't like one friend if you happened to like another). In addition, it was widely believed that the only thing the gods required was that people perform occasional acts of reverence to them—for example, through public sacrifices—and that any calamities that happened in life were the result of the gods' anger at not being properly acknowledged. Because Christians didn't make these acknowledgements, they found themselves in the hot seat when any disasters hit a village, town, or city.

The earliest Christians were persecuted in a completely ad hoc and random fashion. It appears that persecution usually began at the grassroots level, as either alienated family members or rebuffed friends took umbrage when Christians removed themselves from everyday life. The problems were exacerbated when small or large disasters occurred, because these were easily laid at the feet of the Christians, who steadfastly refused to worship the gods. If any acts of mob violence occurred, Roman governors might step in and round up the Christians. If the Christians continued to flout authority (e.g., by still refusing to worship the gods), they could be punished or executed. The emperors appear to have sanctioned this kind of activity, and why not? If any group caused problems, it had to be dealt with.

It was not for a couple of centuries that Christians grew large enough as a group to begin to worry the Roman administration in any serious way. At that time, in the middle of the 3rd century, serious and systematic persecutions began. ∎

Essential Reading

1 Peter.

Brown, *Introduction to the New Testament*, chap. 33.

Ehrman, *The New Testament: A Historical Introduction*, chap. 25.

Supplemental Reading

Frend, *Martyrdom and Persecution in the Early Church*.

Musurillo, *Acts of the Christian Martyrs*.

Wilken, *The Christians as the Romans Saw Them*.

1. Make a catalogue of the reasons and ways people suffer and consider which of these might be justly considered "religious" suffering.

2. How could early texts that portray Christians as a small, persecuted minority be relevant to the modern context, in which the Christian religion wields such enormous social, economic, and political power? Are there instances in which modern Christians *talk* as if they were still a small, persecuted minority? What is behind this sort of rhetoric?

First Peter and the Persecution
of the Early Christians
Lecture 22—Transcript

Throughout the books of the New Testament one finds numerous references to Christians suffering. In the last lecture, we saw that the Epistle to the Hebrews was a sermon written to a group of Christians who were experiencing some form of persecution. The author was striving to convince his hearers not to succumb to pressure and leave the church for Judaism. In the Synoptic Gospels, Jesus tells his followers that they must take up their crosses if they want to follow him. In the Book of Acts the early Christian communities are persecuted by the Jewish leadership in Jerusalem, and the Apostle Paul himself is eventually arrested and put up on charges of disturbing the peace. Nowhere is the theme of Christian suffering more pronounced than in the Book of 1 Peter.

The book is addressed to Christians living in Asia Minor, modern-day Turkey. The word for suffering occurs more often in this short letter than in any other book of the New Testament. These people appear to have been former pagans who have removed themselves from the daily life of the larger community and adopted a stricter set of moral standards for themselves as Christians. There has been some kind of public outcry apparently by those who feel abandoned by their former friends and companions. First Peter is addressed to these people in order to show them that they should withstand the suffering that they are going through, withstand the persecution and not be surprised that it has happened, as the author himself says in chapter 4. You have already spent enough time in doing what the Gentiles like doing— living in licentiousness, passions, drunkenness, revels, carousing, and lawless idolatry. In other words, this is what you used to do, he says. They are surprised that you no longer join them in the same excesses of dissipation and so they blaspheme, but they will have to give an accounting to him who stands ready to judge the living and the dead.

This author, then, is writing to a Christian community that is experiencing some kind of suffering because their former friends and companions and colleagues have rejected them because the Christians have removed themselves and no longer consort with them. The turmoil may have reached the point of mob violence or governmental intervention. The author, in chapter 4, verse 12, speaks about the fiery ordeal that is taking place among you to test you. He says they shouldn't be surprised at this as though something strange were happening, but you should rejoice in so far as you are sharing Christ's sufferings. This author writes his letter both to console those within the community who are suffering and to urge them to maintain their solidarity with one another. On the one hand, he explains that their suffering is natural and to be expected. They are, after all, followers of Christ who was himself crucified. This is a common motif throughout the New Testament—that those who follow Christ are not destined for glory and power and exaltation, they are destined for suffering, since Christ himself was crucified, then so too will his followers suffer. And so this author tells his readers that they shouldn't be surprised that they are suffering.

He does urge them though to make sure that when they suffer, they suffer for doing what is right, never for doing what is wrong. There are, of course, all sorts of reasons for people suffering. This author does not want his readers to be prosecuted by the law for doing things that are against God's will. In other words, he doesn't want them thrown in jail for committing murder or for stealing, he wants them to suffer, if they must suffer, only for doing what is right. As he says, "Let none of you suffer as a murderer, a thief, a criminal, or even as a mischief maker. Yet if any of you suffers as a Christian, do not consider it a disgrace, but glorify God because you bear this name."

His readers should not behave in ways that offend outsiders. They should instead behave in ways that are appropriate to the Gospel, and they should be ready at every point to explain to those who wonder why they live the way they live. They should explain to such people what it is that makes them different. As he says in chapter 3, "Always be ready to make your defense to anyone who demands from you an accounting for the hope that is within you. Yet do it with gentleness and reference. Keep your conscious clear, so that when you are maligned, those who abuse you for your good conduct in Christ may be put to shame." People should behave in ways that are appropriate to the Gospel, and if anybody wants to know what it is that makes them different they should be willing to make a defense before them.

Throughout this letter the author stresses that they as a community have a distinct status in the world. They are ones who have been set apart from the world. They belong to God. Modern sociologists have long recognized that group solidarity can be created by acts of hatred and persecution perpetrated against a group. Under persecution, a group forms bonds of cohesion as they realize that they are all in it together. Something like that appears to be going on here in this letter of 1 Peter as the author assures his readers that they are a people set apart belonging to God alone. As an example from chapter 2, verse 9, the author informs his readers, you are a chosen race, a royal priesthood, a holy nation, God's own people in order that you may proclaim the mighty acts of him who called you out of darkness into his marvelous light. He's trying to show his readers that they are a group that is distinct from the rest of the world, that has been called together by God. For this reason, he wants them to engage in moral behavior.

He may not be thinking only of the need of Christians to follow God's law because after all it is God's law and people should follow it. When he urges his readers to engage in moral behavior, he may also be thinking of the possible repercussions of that moral behavior on those who are outside the community. In other words, when outsiders realize how the Christians react to their persecution, they too might repent as he says in chapter 2, "Conduct yourself honorably among the Gentiles, so that though they malign you as evil doers, they may see your honorable deeds and glorify God when he comes to judge."

Scholars continue to debate if the author of this book was actually the disciple of Jesus, Simon Peter. The book certainly claims to be written by Peter, as we see from the first verse: Peter, an Apostle of Jesus Christ, to the exiles of the dispersion. The author claims to be Peter. Some scholars consider this though to be a dubious claim. As with all claims of authorship, it has to be tested historically. According to the Gospels of the New Testament, Peter the Apostle of Jesus was a lower class Jewish fisherman from the Galilee. His native tongue would have been Aramaic. If in fact it's right that he were a lower class fisherman, he would have been uneducated. Only the upper classes had the leisure and the money to become educated. According to the Book of Acts, chapter 4, verse 13, this disciple Peter was in fact illiterate. This particular book though is written by a well educated, rhetorically trained, Greek-speaking Christian. Was it Peter? Well it seems unlikely given the circumstance.

Some scholars realizing that an Aramaic-speaking lower class fisherman from Galilee is unlikely to have a produced a book like this, have taken note of the conclusion of the book, in which the author says that he has written his book through Silvanus, whom I consider a faithful brother. He has written a book through Silvanus. This appears to be a reference to a common practice in antiquity to write a book by dictating it to somebody else, who would then write down the words and possibly even edit the words before sending them out. Is it possible that the disciple Peter, didn't actually write the book, but dictated it to Silvanus. That, of course, is a possibility. If that were the case though, perhaps one should probably, perhaps one should say that it wasn't Peter who was the author of this book, but Silvanus himself. If Peter, for example, dictated these words in Aramaic and Silvanus translated it into Greek and then put them into a rhetorical form that was so well educated and refined that perhaps Silvanus should be considered the author of the book.

In any event, there is another possibility, which is that the book is pseudonymous. We know of a number of writings that circulated in Peter's name in the 1st and 2nd centuries. For example, we have already talked about in this course, the Gospel of Peter, which claims to be written by Peter, but wasn't. In addition, we have an apocalypse that claims to be written by Peter, an apocalypse which describes a kind of a tour of heaven and hell that Peter allegedly went on. Virtually everybody recognizes this as well as a forgery. It is possible that the Book of 1 Peter as well was pseudonymous.

As one of the clearest indications that the early Christians were persecuted, 1 Peter can serve as a springboard for us into a larger question of the Roman opposition to Christianity in its early days. I want to spend the rest of this lecture dealing principally with this question of Roman opposition to Christianity, Roman persecution. It's an important topic because many people have a complete misperception of the Roman attitudes toward the Christians—for example, thinking that Rome had declared Christianity illegal and sent out the troops to round up the Christians who survived by hiding in the catacombs. That might be suitable for a Hollywood screenplay, but historically it simply isn't true. Christianity was not declared illegal until nearly two centuries after the writings of Paul. It wasn't until the year 250 A.D. that Christianity was considered illegal, against the law and the empire. This was through a decree by the fervently pagan Emperor Decius—250 A.D. Only then at that point in the middle of the 3rd century was there any empire-wide persecution of the Christians. And even then, at that point in the year 250, there is some question about how extensive the persecution was throughout the empire. Prior to that time, Christians were on occasion persecuted by Roman authorities.

It's important for us though to understand the reasons for this persecution. I should say the Christians weren't the only group that was persecuted in the early part of the empire and that even when it was persecuted, Christianity wasn't forced to go underground. Christians had the same rights and responsibilities as everyone else in the Roman Empire. Starting a new religion was not illegal. Christians had the right to worship any God they wanted, even the Jewish God, if they chose to. Moreover, nobody would have thought that it was illegal to call Jesus God, as Christians began to do at the end of the 1st century and into the 2nd century. There is nothing illegal about this. Most people believe that occasionally there were human beings who were also divine. Why then if it wasn't illegal to start a new religion and there was nothing wrong with calling Jesus divine, why then were Christians persecuted occasionally by the Romans?

To understand early Christian persecution we need to know something more about the Roman legal system. Unlike Roman civil law, which was extremely complex and nuanced, Roman criminal law, at least by our standards, was completely lax and haphazard. The Romans loved to make laws about civil affairs. There were all sorts of laws about inheritance rights, about property rights, about marriage and divorce—all sorts of laws having to do with civil affairs. Criminal law, though, was a completely different matter within the empire. Criminal activities were not strictly defined throughout the empire, and punishments were not prescribed by law. Neither the Roman emperor nor the Roman Senate passed criminal legislation that was binding on all inhabitants of the empire. Again, this seems so peculiar to us because we are used to having federal laws and state laws having to do with criminal activities, but it simply didn't work that way in the Roman Empire.

The provinces of Rome, the areas that they had conquered and then taxed, the provinces were ruled by governors. They were either governed by local aristocrats, who could be client kings, or else they were ruled by members of the Roman aristocracy who were appointed by either the emperor or the Senate, depending on which province it was. The provincial governors in the Roman Empire had two major responsibilities: to raise tax revenues from the province and to keep the peace. These were their two major responsibilities, and they were given free reign in order to meet these responsibilities. The Roman governors, in fact, had nearly absolute authority to achieve their objectives. It was simply assumed by the Romans that a governor who was a competent administrator would, on location, know the best way to handle any particular situation, utilizing whatever means were necessary to maintain public order and to maximize revenue collection. The idea was that the person on the scene will know the best way to execute his duties. And so there weren't national laws that governed criminal activity. The governors can take care of this themselves.

Using any means necessary to achieve their objectives meant that the governors had the power of life and death. We have seen an instance of this already in the Gospel accounts of Jesus' trial before Pontius Pilate. The way Pilate conducted this trial would not have been at all unusual. From a Roman point of view, the way Pilate condemned Jesus to death was perfectly justified. Pilate thought of Jesus as a public nuisance. He had been brought forward to Pilate at the instigation of the local Jewish aristocrats, the leaders of the people in Judea, in Jerusalem. Pilate took their word for it that this person was a nuisance, he had a very short trial, he condemned Jesus to death, and Jesus was immediately taken off and crucified. Under the Roman system there was nothing that we might think of as due process. There was no need for a trial by jury. There was no need for witnesses necessarily, if the governor didn't think there was a need for one. There was no appeal process. There was no long wait for the sentence to be executed. Jesus, then, is immediately taken off and crucified. Pilate probably had trials like this going on almost every day. There was nothing unusual about that. This kind of administrative decision was exactly why Pilate was hired to do the job.

After Jesus, Christians were themselves occasionally persecuted, prosecuted by the governors of the provinces they happened to be in. This, though, was not because the religion was against some kind of Roman law, it was because they, like Jesus before them, were occasionally perceived to be public nuisances. We see this from the New Testament itself—both from Paul, his own letters, and the Book of Acts—where Christian missionary activity in public sometimes leads to public disturbances, riots, mob reactions. Roman governors who want to take care of the problem, or even below the governors, simply the rulers of the various cities and towns that these things take place in, who want to take care of the problem, [do] take care of the problem—not following the laws that are already laid out for them, but simply dealing with these situation on an ad hoc basis.

The problems were exacerbated by the fact that Christians caused disturbances, not just publicly, but also within the sphere of the family. We have solid Christian traditions to suggest that Christians were thought of [as] being opposed to the family units that they were raised in, as opposed to the modern sense of having family values. Christians, in fact, were disruptive in their families, which may have led to more hatred and animosity.

Consider the words of Jesus himself as found in the Gospel of Matthew. Whether or not these words go back to Jesus, for our purposes here they clearly show what the early Christians thought about faith in Jesus. Jesus says in Matthew, chapter 10, verse 34, "Do not think that I have come to bring peace to the earth, I've not come to bring peace, but a sword. I have come to set a man against his father, a daughter against her mother, a daughter-in-law against her mother-in-law, and one's foes will be members of one's own household." Faith in Jesus brought divisiveness to families.

Moreover, because Christians were known to be a closed community, they sometimes came under suspicion by the public at large as being members of a secret society. Christian were suspected of being members of a secret society. You know full well how secret societies today are viewed. Christians in antiquity were viewed no better, in fact somewhat worse. In particular, it appears that there were widely believed slanders leveled against the Christians. It was known that Christians met at night or early in the morning, when it was dark. It was known they called one another brother and sister. They greeted one another with kisses. They engaged in love feasts, as they called their communion meals. It was known that the Christians actually ate the body and drank the blood of the Son of God. Christians, on the basis of these known facts, were widely believed to engage in nocturnal orgies that involved incest and cannibalism. This might seem remarkable to people today who know full well that Christians don't do such things, but you have to consider the context. Pagans are suspicious of these anti-family closed societies that engage in the kinds of activities that they were known to engage in.

Consider the evidence from the 2nd century of a very famous scholar named Fronto, who was in fact the teacher of the Roman Emperor Marcus Aurelius, 2nd century Roman emperor. In one of his writings, Fronto discussed what the Christians were up to. It's a graphic portrayal of how Christians were commonly thought to engage in their ritual meals together. This is what Fronto said about the Christians. "They, the Christians, recognize each other by secret marks and signs. Hardly had they met, when they love each other, throughout the world uniting in the practice of a veritable religion of lusts," he says. "Indiscriminately they call each other brother and sister thus turning even ordinary fornication into incest"—since they are brothers and sisters and since they are suspected of engaging in these love feasts, then they are committing incest. "The notoriety of the stories told of the initiation of the Christians is matched by their ghastly horror," he says.

Now he [Fronto] goes on to describe what the rumor is that that the Christians do during their initiation ceremonies. He says as follows, "A young baby is covered with flour, the object being to deceive the unwary. It is then served before the person to be admitted into their rites. The recruit is urged to inflict blows upon it. They appear to be harmless because of the covering of flour, thus the baby is killed with wounds that remain unseen and concealed. It is the blood of this infant, I shudder to mention it, it is this blood that they lick with thirsty lips. These are the limbs they distribute eagerly. This is the victim by which they seal their covenant. It is by complicity in this crime that they are pledged to mutual silence. These are their rites, more foul than all sacrileges combined." This is what Christians were thought to be doing when they eat the blood and body of the Son of God.

"On a special day" he [Fronto] says, "they gather for a feast with all their children, sisters, mothers, all sexes and ages. They are flushed with a banquet after much feasting and drinking. They begin to burn with incestuous passions. They provoke a dog tied to a lamp stand to leap and bound towards a scrap of food that they have tossed outside the reach of his chain. By this means, the light is overturned and extinguished, and with it common knowledge of their actions. In the shameless dark with unspeakable lust they copulate in random unions, all equally being guilty of incest."

This is what the Christians were believed to be doing during their worship services. No wonder local officials found them to be problematic. Christians had a serious image problem in the first several centuries of the church. Consider what the two pagan authors who mention Jesus say about him. Remember, the Roman historian Tacitus mentioned Jesus in his discussion of Nero's torching of the city of Rome, where Nero used the Christians as scapegoats for the fire in Rome. Why could Nero do this? Because, according to Tacitus, the Christians were a pernicious superstition who were the hatred of the human race. Pliny the Younger, who mentioned the early Christians, says that they are obstinate and mad adherents of a depraved superstition.

The difficulties that the Christians had were probably exacerbated by the fact that Christians refused to participate in the public ceremonies that honored the state and local gods. Since Christians believed there is only one true God, they couldn't very well participate in the worship of other gods. This made no sense to most pagans who thought that since there are lots of gods you should feel free to worship any one of them you chose including the state gods, which had after all made the state great. When Christians refused to do so, this was seen as a political statement against the state since you refuse to worship the state gods. Moreover, since it was widely believed that the only thing the gods really required of people was that they perform occasional acts of reverence to them, for example through public sacrifices, and since it was thought that any calamities that happened in life were because the gods were angry at not being properly acknowledged, when Christians refused to participate in this worship and when disasters hit a village or town, naturally they were the ones who were thought to be at fault. And so Christians were persecuted because they were thought to be the cause of public catastrophes.

The earliest Christians, then, were persecuted probably in a completely ad hoc and random fashion. Normally it appears that persecution began at the grass roots level, as either alienated family members or rebuffed friends took umbrage when Christians removed themselves from everyday life. Their problems were exacerbated when disasters happened. If any acts of mob violence occurred, Roman governors might step in and round up the Christians for good measure. The emperors appeared to have sanctioned this kind of activity, this kind of persecution of Christians that sometimes led to Christians trials and death, because after all if they are Christians they are the ones that are causing the problems.

It was not, though, for a couple of centuries that Christians grew into a group that was large enough to worry the Roman administration as a whole in any serious way. And it was only then, in the middle of the 3rd century, that serious and systematic persecution began.

In conclusion, 1 Peter was written to address a situation that had become all too common for Christians at the end of the 1st century and into the 2nd. Local opposition had arisen, and Christians were subject to harassment and persecution, possibly leading to official intervention against them by local authorities. The author of the book urges his readers to stay strong in their faith and not to yield to pressure. In particular, Christians could remain steadfast when they believed that their suffering would not last long but would come to a triumphant end when God intervened in the course of history to overthrow the powers of evil. This was the message of hope that many Christians continued to cling on to in the face of sporadic persecution. As we will see in the next lecture, that in fact is the theme of the Book of Revelation, written to suffering Christians—they should hold on because the end would arrive soon.

The Book of Revelation
Lecture 23

The Book of Revelation was not written to describe our own future, it wasn't written in the context of 21st century America, but in the context of 1st century Rome.

In the last lecture, we saw that a good deal of the early Christian literature was produced in the context of persecution and suffering. Nowhere is this more obvious than in the final book of the New Testament, the Book of Revelation, also known as the Apocalypse of John. This is a fascinating visionary account of the end of the world, an account that has provided grist for the mills of doomsday prophets ever since, for whom it is by far the most favored book of the New Testament. It is probably also the book that is, and always has been, the most misunderstood.

The basic story line of the book is reasonably clear. After some introductory matters, the book describes a series of disturbing visions given to a prophet named John. After an opening vision of the risen Christ, John is instructed to write letters to each of the seven churches of Asia Minor, detailing their successes and failures and urging them to remain committed to Christ. He is then miraculously transported to heaven, where he is shown the future course of the earth's catastrophic history. He sees God on his thrown and a lamb that has been slain next to it (representing Christ). The lamb is handed a scroll that is sealed with seven seals. As he breaks the seals, one by one, disasters strike the earth: war, famine, plague, suffering, and death. The breaking of the seventh seal leads to another sequence of disasters, as seven angels appear blowing seven trumpets, each blast bringing yet more disasters. The seventh trumpet leads to another sequence of disasters, as seven angels appear with seven huge bowls filled with God's wrath, which are poured one by one upon the earth. Meanwhile, on earth, the great enemy of God has arisen, the satanically inspired anti-Christ, who is responsible for destroying the people of God and leading multitudes away from him. At the end, when God's wrath is used up, there is a final battle. Christ confronts and overthrows the anti-Christ, destroys all his enemies, subjects them to eternal punishment in a lake of fire, and creates a new heaven and a new earth, a utopian world in which his followers will live forever apart from any trace of evil.

The natural tendency of people who read this book is to assume that it is offers an account of what is still to come in our own future. And so it has been understood through the ages. One of the problems, though, is that every generation has assumed that the book predicts what will happen in its own time. So far, every generation has been wrong (even though each new one thinks that it will surely be the one). Our own generation, of course, is no exception. The book was used that way by David Koresh and the Branch Davidians, by Marshall Applewhite and Heaven's Gate, by most mainline evangelical preachers that you can hear any day of the week by turning on your TV, and by scores of serious interpreters of prophecy whose books line the shelves of most Christian bookstores—including second and third editions when the predictions of the first have had to be modified in light of their failure to come true.

> **One of the problems, though, is that every generation has assumed that the book predicts what will happen in its own time.**

Luckily, there is an alternative to this approach, and that is to try to understand the book in light of its own historical context. The term *revelation* derives from a Latin word that is the equivalent of the Greek word *apocalypse*, which means "an unveiling" or "a revealing." The term *apocalypse* is applied to a number of ancient Jewish and Christian books, all of which another claim to unveil or reveal the spiritual truths from above that make sense of the mundane realities we experience down here. These books embody the world view of apocalypticism that we've already discussed on several occasions, although, of course, most people who subscribed to that world view did not write apocalypses.

The Book of Revelation seems so strange and bizarre and unique to most readers today, precisely because this is the only book of its kind from antiquity that people know about and read. In fact, this kind of book was not at all unusual in the ancient world. To understand this book, we need to understand how its literary genre works. Recognizing the genre of any piece of writing is important to its interpretation. Suppose you were to read about a highly sensitive biological project that could leak a new strain of bacteria into the atmosphere and could destroy life as we know it. Your reaction to the piece would depend on whether you found it in a Stephen King novel or on the front page of the *New York Times*. Without understanding the conventions of the genre of a piece of writing, you will misconstrue its intention and meaning.

Because there are numerous works like the Book of Revelation from antiquity—both Jewish and Christian apocalypses—we can compare them to one another to get some idea of the genre. In the most basic terms, these books reported visions or dreams—usually fairly bizarre visions or dreams—of a prophet. These visions were taken to explain the nature of reality, either by showing the true meaning of life here on earth or, as in the case of Revelation, by showing how life here on earth was soon to come to a crashing halt.

There were two major types of apocalypses. In some, a prophet is taken on a guided tour of heaven, to see what ultimate reality looks like and to realize how events taking place on earth reflect, and are therefore determined by, events that take place in heaven. In others, the prophet is shown the future course of history, up to the very end, when the world comes to a screeching halt. Revelation represents a conflation of these two basic types: The prophet is shown the heavenly realm *and* sees the future catastrophic climax of the world's history.

Most apocalypses contain several specific literary features. The majority of them are pseudonymous, written in the famous names of persons from the past. Thus, we have apocalypses attributed to Moses, Abraham, Elijah, and even Adam. By claiming to be one of these famous men of God in the past, the author, of course, ascribes unusual authority to his work. The writer can place himself back in time and make predictions about the future that sound valid because they describe history. The Book of Revelation is virtually unique in not being pseudonymous. It is written by someone who calls himself John. Because this was such a common name in antiquity, it is difficult to know who he was. He does not appear to be John the son of

Zebedee, Jesus' disciple, because at one point, he has a vision of the apostles and doesn't seem to see himself.

Apocalyptic writings contain bizarre symbolic visions. The future is described not in straightforward and prosaic terms but in mystical and metaphorical ones. Often, though, the symbols are transparent when read in light of the book's historical context. Take, for example, the "great whore of Babylon" whom the prophet sees in Revelation 17. This is a prostitute who has committed fornication with the kings of the earth; who is seated on a scarlet beast, bedecked in fine clothes and jewelry; who is drunk with the blood of the martyrs; and who has written on her head, "Babylon, the mother of whores." A strange sight indeed. But this image is not so hard to interpret: The beast is said to have seven heads, which the author explains refers to seven hills on which the woman is seated (v. 8). At the end, we're told that she is the "great city that rules over the kings of the earth" (v. 18). Who then is the great whore of the earth? Which city ruled the world at the end of the 1st century, a city that had persecuted the Christians, a city in fact that was known throughout antiquity as the city built on seven hills?   Any ancient reader would have recognized the city of Rome readily.

Consider the most famous puzzle of Revelation: the great enemy of God, the anti-Christ (Chapter 13), who is given the number of the beast, 666. Who is it? The answer is not so surprising when the text is put in a 1st-century context. By indicating the beast's "number," the author is referring to the common practice from antiquity of calculating the number of a word or name based on the numerical value assigned to each of its letters. Who was the first emperor of Rome to persecute Christians? Nero. Spell Caesar Nero's name in Hebrew letters and add them up. They total 666. Interestingly, a recent book that discusses a newly discovered Greek manuscript has the number as 616, which is the numerical value of an alternate spelling of Nero's name. This may not be as exciting as thinking that the anti-Christ is someone living in our own day or is soon to come. We have had devoted Christian authors over the past 50 years arguing that 666 must refer to Hitler, Mussolini, the Pope, Henry Kissinger, Saddam Hussein, or Ronald Wilson Reagan (6-6-6). But if we're interested in knowing what the author himself meant, it helps to think about his world.

The narratives of apocalypses are characterized by violent repetitions, i.e., repetitions that "violate" any literal chronological sequencing of events. For example, at one point in Revelation, when God's wrath strikes the earth, there are disasters of cosmic proportions: The sun turns dark, the moon turns to blood, the stars fall from heaven, and the sky is rolled back. You would think that we are at the end of all things, but we're only in chapter six. There are 12 more chapters of disaster to occur, with sun, moon, and stars still shining in full force. The repetitions are for effect; they can't be taken as a literal sequence.

Apocalypses are characterized by a triumphant movement from cataclysm to utopia, from horrendous suffering on earth to the restoration of peace and harmony. Suffering in these books can reach unimaginable heights, but the entire course of events is directed by God himself, who is sovereign over his creation and will reward those who remain faithful to him. This makes particular sense if we understand that the books are directed to those who are already suffering in what appears to them to be unimaginable ways. The point of the books is that this suffering is overseen by God, who will soon bring it to an end before setting up his utopian kingdom.

The point of the books is that this suffering is overseen by God, who will soon bring it to an end before setting up his utopian kingdom.

These books stress that the end of all things is imminent. Suffering won't last long, because God will soon bring all history to a resounding climax. In the Book of Revelation, the emphasis is just this point: "Lord Jesus come quickly." The overarching themes of these books, then, are encouragement and admonition. The author of Revelation, as the authors of most apocalypses, was writing to encourage his readers in the midst of their own suffering: God is sovereign and in control; he will soon bring your sufferings to an end. Do not give up hope. In many respects, the point is not to give a precise blueprint of future events or an itemized timetable of when they will occur. It is to give hope to those for whom life in the present was virtually unbearable. God can be trusted to bring all things to a happy end.

By way of a quick conclusion and summary, I can reaffirm that the Book of Revelation was not written as a blueprint for our own future. It was written in the context of 1st-century Rome. In that context, the enemy of God was Rome and its emperor was the anti-Christ; they were responsible for the intense suffering that Christians were experiencing. In that context, an author named John wrote an apocalypse. His work was similar to other apocalypses written before him and others written since, filled with bizarre dreams and strange symbolism, to assure his readers of the final sovereignty of God and of his Christ, who would soon bring their suffering to an end. Christians living in a context of intense suffering need to realize that God is ultimately in control and he, rather than the forces of evil aligned against him, will have the last word. ■

Essential Reading

The Book of Revelation.

Brown, *Introduction to the New Testament*, chap. 37.

Ehrman, *The New Testament: A Historical Introduction*, chap. 27.

Supplemental Reading

Collins, *Crisis and Catharsis*.

Pilch, *What Are They Saying about the Book of Revelation?*

Questions to Consider

1. In what ways is the apocalyptic worldview found in the Book of Revelation similar to and different from the apocalyptic views of Jesus? Of Paul? How does it compare with the emphases of the Fourth Gospel (which later Christians actually attributed to the same author, John)?

2. Many Christians over the centuries have read the Book of Revelation as a blueprint for events that were soon to come and have thus seen it as a source of hope. Is it possible to read the book more historically, as addressed to Christians suffering in the days of Rome and not as a descriptive account of things yet to take place, and still find its message inspired by hope?

Note: For information about another Teaching Company course on apocalyptic writing, please refer to the end of the Bibliography.

The Book of Revelation
Lecture 23—Transcript

In the last lecture we saw that a good deal of the early Christian literature was produced in the context of persecution and suffering. Nowhere is this more obviously true than in the final book of the New Testament, the Book of Revelation, also known as the Apocalypse of John. This is a fascinating visionary account of the end of the world, an account that has provided grist for the mills of doomsday prophets ever since, for whom it is by far the most favorite book of the New Testament. It is probably also the book that is and always has been the least understood.

The basic story line of the book in any event is reasonably clear. After some introductory matters, the book describes a series of disturbing visions given to a prophet named John. After an opening vision of the risen Christ, John is instructed to write letters to each of the seven churches of Asia Minor detailing their successes and failures and urging them to remain committed to Christ. He is then miraculously transported up to heaven where he is shown the future course of the earth's catastrophic history. He sees God himself on a throne and a lamb that's standing next to it, a lamb that has been slain. This lamb, of course, represents Christ.

The lamb is handed a scroll that is sealed with seven seals. As the lamb breaks the seals, one by one, enormous disasters strike the earth. War, famine, plague, massive suffering, and death. The breaking of the seventh seal leads to other sequences of disasters as seven angels appear blowing seven trumpets, each trumpet blast bringing yet more disasters. The seventh trumpet leads to another sequence of disasters as seven angels appear with seven huge bowls filled with God's wrath, which are poured one by one upon the earth. Meanwhile on the earth, there has arisen the great enemy of God—the satanically inspired anti-Christ, responsible for destroying the people of God and leading multitudes away from him. At the end, when God's wrath is used up, there's a final battle in which Christ confronts and overthrows the anti-Christ, destroys all of his enemies, subjects them to eternal punishment in a lake of fire, and creates finally a new heaven and a new earth—a utopian world in which his followers will living forever apart from any trace of evil. That's the narrative scope of the Book of Revelation.

The natural tendency of people who read this book is to assume that it's providing an account of what is still to transpire in our own future. And so it has been understood down through the ages. One of the problems though is that every generation has assumed that the book is referring to what will happen in its own time. And so far, of course, every generation has been wrong, even though each generation thinks that surely it will be the one. Our own generation is no exception.

The Book of Revelation was used this way by David Koresh and the Branch Davidians, by Marshall Applewhite and Heaven's Gate, by most mainline evangelical preachers that you can hear any day of the week by turning on your TV who talk about the Book of Revelation, and by scores of serious interpreters of prophecy whose books line the shelves of most Christian bookstores, including second and third editions when the predictions of the first edition have had to be modified in light of their failure to come true.

Luckily there's an alternative to this approach. It's to try to understand the Book of Revelation in light of its own historical context. Rather than predicting what's going to happen in our future, as if the book were written today, at the end of the 20th century in America, it is to understand the book as it was written in the 1st century in the Roman Empire. That's what we are going to try and do in this lecture, is understand what the book might have meant in its own original context.

The term revelation that gives the book its title, is the Latin equivalent of the Greek word apocalypse, which means an unveiling or a revealing. The term apocalypse is applied to a number of ancient Jewish and Christians books, all of which in one way or another claim to unveil or reveal the spiritual truths from above that make sense of the mundane realities we experience down here below. These books embody the world view of apocalypticism that we have already discussed on several occasions. Apocalypticism: this world view that maintains that there are two fundamental components of reality—good and evil—that history is set up dualistically as this age run by the forces of evil and the age to come run by the forces of good; a world view that was pessimistic about possibilities in life in this world now, because the forces of evil were in control and going to get more and more power and make things worse and worse; a world view that maintained though that God was going to intervene in history, overthrow the forces of evil, and set up his good kingdom on earth; and a world view that maintained that this end of this age was imminent, that it was going to happen very soon. Apocalypses embodied this particular world view.

I should stress though that not everybody who held to an apocalyptic world view wrote an apocalypse. In fact, very view people did. But those who did want to embody an apocalyptic world view into a genre of writing, could and did write apocalypses. The writing of apocalypses was a popular art form in the 1st and 2nd centuries A.D among both Jews and Christians.

The Book of Revelation seems so strange and bizarre and unique to most readers today precisely because it's the only book of its kind that people know about in our own culture. But in fact, this kind of book was not at all unusual in the ancient world. To understand this book, as to understand all books, we need to understand how its literary genre works. Do you see what I am saying—it might seem strange to us, but it is because it's the only book like this that we read. Just as if you were in a different culture, which didn't know anything about science fiction novels, and somebody read a science fiction novel, it would seem extremely peculiar as a piece of writing. But in our culture, of course, it's common because we have lots of science fiction novels. So too in the ancient world they had lots of apocalypses. And so to understand any particular science fiction novel, it makes sense to see how the structure of science fiction novels works. So too with apocalypses. To understand how any particular representation of an apocalypse works, it's important to see how the literary genre works. My basic point is that to understand a literary work you have to know something about it's genre.

Suppose you yourself were to read about a highly sensitive biological project, which would potentially leak a new strain of bacteria into the atmosphere, a strain of bacteria that would destroy life on earth as we know it. Well, if you read this in a Stephen King novel, then you would have one kind of reaction to it. If you read it on the front page of the New York Times, you'd have a different reaction to it. Without understanding the conventions of the genre of the piece of writing—Stephen King novel, the front page of the New York Times—you will misconstrue the intention of the writing and its meaning.

Since there are a number of works like the Book of Revelations from antiquity—Jewish and Christian apocalypses—we can compare them to one another to get some idea of their basic genre. That's what I am going to do here, describe what the basic genre was like as a way of enlightening what happens in the Book of Revelation. In the most basic terms, apocalypses were books that reported visions or dreams—usually fairly bizarre visions or dreams of a prophet which were taken to explain the nature of reality, either by showing the meaning of life here on earth or, as in the case of Revelation, by showing how life here on earth was soon to come to a crashing halt.

There were two major types of apocalypses in antiquity. In some apocalypses, a prophet is taken on a guided tour of heaven to see what ultimate reality looks like and to realize how events taking place on earth are reflecting and therefore to some extent determined by events that take place in heaven. And so in some apocalypses there is a tour of heaven. The second kind of apocalypse involves a prophet being shown the future course of history up to the very end when the world comes to a screeching halt. As you will have seen from the summary of the story line of the book of Revelation that I just gave, Revelation represents a conflation of these two basic types of apocalypse—the prophet is shown the heavenly realm, and he sees the future cataclysmic climax of the world's history.

Most apocalypses contain several specific literary features. It is important to understand these literary features to put Revelation within the context of its own time. First, most apocalypses were written pseudonymously in the name of a famous person from the past. We have apocalypses that are attributed to Moses—Apocalypse of Moses—and Abraham and Elijah and even Adam, as in Adam and Eve. By claiming to be one of these famous men of God in the past, the author of these books would ascribe unusual authority to his work. I mean, who better to know about the future course of the world than Elijah, who was taken into heaven without dying, or Adam the first man, etc.

Sometimes the pseudonymous authorship works in an even more interesting way, especially in the apocalypses that give a detailed description of the course of history. Sometimes the way these detailed descriptions of the course of history work is that an author living in a particular point of time pretends that he's an author living centuries earlier. This pretended author living centuries earlier predicts the course of future events. Of course, when the author himself, the actual author, is writing these things, these are events that have already transpired so he's not making predictions, he's writing things that have already happened. The predictions continue though up to his own day, which is projected as being very near the end of time, and then there are predictions about what will happen next. The reader, of course, doesn't realize that the author himself is writing about history. It sounds like this author is making prediction from the very beginning so that the things that have not yet happened in the readers experience have just as much likelihood of happening as the things that were being predicted. In other words, the pseudonymous authorship allows for the author to predict what's going to happen in his own future, and it sounds like he has been making predictions all along and so that provides some validity to what he has said already.

That way of doing pseudonymous authorship, by the way, is probably what's going on in the Book of Daniel in the Hebrew Bible. Daniel is allegedly a 6th century Jew living in the Babylonian exile, who predicts what's going to happen in the future. He makes a number of predictions that go up to the middle of the 2nd century B.C. And his predictions are fairly accurate, especially as you get closer to the middle of the 2nd century B.C. And then he predicts things that are going to happen next. The trick though is that this book was probably written in the middle of the 2nd century B.C. so that the earlier predictions in fact are talking about things that have already happened, that's at least the scholarly consensus of the dating of the Book of Daniel.

The first characteristic of apocalypses is that they tend to be pseudonymous. Having said all that, I should point out that it looks like the Book of Revelation is fairly unique in not being pseudonymous. The Book of Revelation, unlike most other apocalypses, appears to be written by the person it claims to be written by, somebody who calls himself John. We don't know who this John was. The name John was common in antiquity. This John does not appear to be calling himself John the son of Zebedee, Jesus' own disciple. The reason for thinking that he is probably not calling himself John the son of Zebedee is because at one point in the narrative, this author has a vision. It looks like he's having a vision of the Twelve Apostles, and he gives no indication that he is seeing himself. So he doesn't seem to be claiming to be one of the

Twelve. We don't know who the author was. The first feature of apocalypses, they tend to be pseudonymous.

Second, apocalypses contain bizarre, symbolic visions. The future is described, not in straightforward and prosaic terms, but in mystical and often metaphorical terms. Often though the symbols are transparent when read in light of the book's owned historical context. Let me give you a couple of examples from the Book of Revelation, a couple of the more famous of the bizarre images that one finds here and show how they can be interpreted in light of Revelation's own context. Often the author of an apocalypse will give you hints about how to interpret his vision. You have to read very carefully though to pick up on the hints.

In chapter 17 of the Book of Revelation, the author sees a bizarre vision. He sees the great whore of Babylon—chapter 17. The prophet says he carried me away in the spirit into a wilderness and I saw a woman sitting on a scarlet beast that was full of blasphemous names and it had seven heads and 10 horns. A woman in the wilderness sitting on a beast with seven heads and 10 horns. The woman was clothed in purple and scarlet and adorned with gold and jewels and pearls. Holding in her hand a golden cup full of abominations and the impurities of her fornication. And on her forehead was written a mystery, a name, Babylon the great, mother of whores and of earth's abominations. And I saw that the woman was drunk with the blood of the saints and the blood of the witnesses to Jesus.

A very peculiar vision. In the King James Bible, by the way, in the next verse the author is expressing his reaction to this vision. In the King James version the next verse says, "When I looked upon her, I admired her greatly," which is an Elizabethan way of saying I was greatly astonished; back in Elizabethan times when you say I admired something, it means you were astonished by it. The new Revised Standard Version says I looked upon her and I was greatly amazed.

What is this vision, this great whore of Babylon—this one who is bedecked in fine clothes and jewelry, who is drunk with the blood of martyrs, who is the mother of whores? In fact, the vision is not all that hard to interpret given the hints within the text itself. We are told that this beast has seven heads. The angel who shows the prophet this beast explains in verse 8 that these seven heads, I'm sorry verse 9, these seven heads represent the seven mountains on which the woman is seated. The woman is seated on seven mountains. Moreover, at the end of the chapter, in verse 18, we are told that the woman is the great city that rules over the kings of the earth. Who then is this great whore who has committed fornication with all the kings of the earth, which is bedecked with all these fine clothes and jewelry, who is drunk with the blood of the martyrs? Which city ruled the world at the end of the 1st century, when this book was written, a city that had persecuted the Christians, leading to the flow of their blood, a city in fact that was known throughout antiquity to have been built on the seven hills? The city of Rome. Any ancient reader would have recognized this imagery. And so what he is seeing is he's seeing the judgment of the great city that is the enemy of God and his people. Eventually in this account, of course, Babylon, the city of Rome, is going to be destroyed. It's called Babylon, by the way, because in the Hebrew Bible, the enemy of the people of God was the city of Babylon, which destroyed Jerusalem in the 6th century B.C. and destroyed the first temple. So Babylon became a code name for the enemy of God and so now it's applied here to the city of Rome, which is a modern Babylon. And so you see, the bizarre symbolic vision can be explained in light of what the text itself says within its own historical context. It's not talking about something future for us, it is talking about something in the author's own day.

Or consider what is probably the most famous puzzle of the Book of Revelation. The great enemy of God, the anti-Christ, who's described in chapter 13 of this book. In chapter 13, the author talks about having another vision, in which he sees a beast arising out of the sea having 10 horns and seven heads. Seven heads. Well, we've seen this already, we saw it in chapter 17. And then he describes what this beast is like. The beast was given a mouth that utters haughty and blasphemous words. It makes war on the saints to conquer them. It's given authority over every tribe and people and language and nation. And it urges all the inhabitants of the earth, in fact requires all the inhabitants of the earth to worship it. We are also told that this beast has experienced a mortal wound from which it will be healed. At the end of the chapter then comes probably the best known image from the Book of Revelation, where the author tries to identify the beast by saying this calls for wisdom, let anyone with understanding calculate the number of the beast. For it's the number of a person, its number is 666, or 6-6-6. As I indicated in an earlier lecture, we don't have the original copy of any of the manuscripts of the New Testament. We have Greek manuscripts that were produced centuries after the originals themselves. In some of the Greek manuscripts, including one that has just been discovered, at least published, this year, the number of the beast is not given as 666, it's given as 616.

What does it mean that the number of the beast is 666 or 616? Any reader in antiquity would probably understand full well what the author is talking about. There was an ancient practice in Judaism called Gamatria, which calculated the number of a word based on the numerical equivalencies of the letters found in the word. In ancient languages, most ancient languages, they did not use a separate number system from the alphabet. The alphabet serves as the numbers. In English, for example, A would be 1, B would be 2, C would be 3, D would be 4, etc. This worked in Greek—alpha - 1, beta - 2, gamma - 3. If you wanted to write a number then, you would write the letters that would correspond to the numbers, and you'd put a little tick above it to show that this is a number. You could take any word then and add up the number of the letters and you would come up with the calculation for the numerical equivalency of the word.

This author is telling us that the number of the name of the anti-Christ—it's a human name he says—if you add up the numerical equivalencies of the letters, you will total 666. Now this is probably a significant number in itself. In the Bible, and especially in the Book of Revelation, the number seven is particularly significant as the number of perfection. The number of God. Six is one less than seven, it's the number of imperfection. It's the number of humans. This person is 666—the totality of imperfection. In fact, he is the anti-Christ, the one who is opposed to God. But how do you get 666?

Well, as scholars have long recognized, there is probably a way to figure out this name in the author's own historical context. Who was the beast? Well, it has seven heads, seven hills—the city of Rome. Who was the first emperor of Rome to persecute the Christians? It was Emperor Nero who persecuted the Christians, as we have seen already, in the 60s A.D. When you spell the name Caesar Nero in Hebrew letters and add up the letters, it adds up to 666. Moreover, there are two ways to spell Kaiser Nero. One with a final "n" at the end of the word, final "Nun," and one without. If you take the "Nun" off, the numbers add up to 616. What's the number of the beast? It appears to be the number of Kaiser Nero, who persecuted the Christians and who was believed in some Jewish circles, according to texts we have from the 1st and 2nd century, to be about to come back from the dead to again rule Rome and to persecute the people of God. Remember this anti-Christ is going to recover from a mortal wound. This appears to be referring to Kaiser Nero.

This may not be as exciting as thinking that the anti-Christ is someone living in our own day or someone who is soon to come. Over the past 50 years we've had devoted Christian authors arguing that 666 must refer to Hitler or Mussolini or the Pope or Henry Kissinger or Saddam Hussein, or back in the 80s there were some liberal Christians who pointed out that Ronald Wilson Reagan's name each had six letters in them: 6-6-6. But if we are interested in knowing what the author himself meant, it makes sense to think that he is talking about something going on in his own world. Apocalypses, then, used bizarre symbolic visions, which can be interpreted in light of their own historical context.

So far I have given two characteristics of apocalypses—they're pseudonymous, they include bizarre symbolic visions. Third, apocalypses are characterized by violent repetitions, by which I mean, not just that violence goes on in the text, although that's true as well, but I mean that the repetitions themselves violate any literal chronological sequencing of the events. There are repetitions that just don't make sense if you try and lay things out chronologically. For example, at one point in the Book of Revelations, when God's wrath strikes the earth, we're told that there are cosmic disasters—the sun turns dark, the moon turns to blood, the stars fall from the sky, the sky itself is rolled back. You'd think we are at the end of all things; but, in fact, we are only in chapter 6. There are 12 more chapters of disaster to occur, with the sun, moon, and stars still shining in full force. Repetitions, then, of these disasters are for effect, they can't be taken as a literal sequence.

Fourth, apocalypses are characterized by triumphalistic movement from cataclysm to utopia, from horrendous suffering on earth to the restoration of peace and harmony. Suffering in these books can reach unimaginable heights, but the entire course of events is in fact being directed by God himself, who is going to bring triumph out of suffering. That makes sense if we realize that these books are written particularly for those who are already suffering in unimaginable ways. The point of these books is that the suffering is overseen by God himself, who will soon bring it to an end.

And so the fifth characteristic: These books stress that the end of all things is imminent, suffering is not going to last long because God is going to bring all history to a resounding climax. In the Book of Revelation the emphasis is on just this point as the text says itself, Lord Jesus come quickly.

Sixth and finally, characteristic of apocalypses, the overarching themes of the books are encouragement and admonition. The author of Revelation, as the author of most apocalypses, was writing to encourage his readers in the midst of their own suffering. God is sovereign and in control. It may not look like it, but he is, don't give up hope. In many respects, then, the ultimate point is not to give a precise blueprint of future events or an itemized timetable of when they will occur, it's to give hope for those for whom life in the present was virtually unbearable. God can be trusted to bring an end to all things, a happy ending to present suffering.

And so by way of a quick conclusion, let me reaffirm that the Book of Revelation was not written to describe our own future, it wasn't written in the context of 21st century America, but in the context of 1st century Rome. In that context, the enemy of God was Rome, its emperor was the anti-Christ. He was responsible for intense suffering the Christians were experiencing. In that context, an author named John wrote an apocalypse like other apocalypses before him and others since. It was filled with bizarre dreams and strange symbolism. It was written to assure his readers that at the end of the day, God himself was sovereign and he was soon going to bring the suffering of the Christians to an end. Christians living in a context of intense suffering need to realize that God is ultimately in control and that he, rather than the forces of evil aligned against him, will have the last word.

Do We Have the Original New Testament?
Lecture 24

> We can say with some confidence that we don't have the original text of any of the books of the New Testament. ... There is no alternative to this situation and there never will be unless by some unbelievable stroke of luck we discover the original text themselves.

We do not have the originals of any of the books that were later canonized into the New Testament. What we have are copies of the originals, or better yet, copies of the copies of the copies of the originals—copies made for the most part hundreds of years after the originals themselves. These copies are all written by hand, the literal meaning of the term *manuscript*. Unfortunately, all of these surviving copies contain mistakes. For that reason, it is often difficult to know what words were in the original texts. And that's an important matter, because it's impossible to interpret what an author meant if you don't know what he said. Let me illustrate the problem by giving a solitary example of how things worked.

When Paul wrote his first letter to the Corinthians, someone in the community must have copied it by hand, one word at a time. That copy was then copied, possibly in Corinth, possibly in some other community that found out about the letter and wanted a copy. That copy was then copied, as were later copies. Before long, there were a large number of copies in circulation in different communities throughout the Mediterranean. In this long process of copying and recopying, the original was eventually lost, worn out, burned, or otherwise destroyed. No one saw the need to keep the original when copies were readily available. Had they been more aware of what happens to a manuscript that gets copied by hand, they may have been more diligent in preserving the original. What happens is that copyists, especially untrained specialists (like most of the early Christians who served as copyists), make mistakes. A subsequent copyist will reproduce the mistakes and introduce new mistakes—or else he will try to correct mistakes, sometimes doing so in a way that creates even further mistakes. We don't have the original of 1 Corinthians, or its first copy, or the copy made of the copy… The first copy of 1 Corinthians we have is a fragment of a manuscript that dates to around

A.D. 200—nearly 150 years after Paul had written it. We don't have complete manuscripts of the books of the New Testament until about 150 years after that (mid-4th century A.D.) and, in all the intervening years, the text was copied slowly by hand, one copy from another, with mistakes creeping in all along the way. The question, then, is how can we take the copies that we do have and establish the text as Paul originally wrote it? (The same applies, of course, for all the books of the New Testament.)

To address this, we must have some basic background information. We have some 5,400 Greek manuscripts of the New Testament, not to mention the thousands of copies of the New Testament as translated into Latin—which was the language of the Middle Ages when most manuscripts were produced—and in other ancient languages, such as Syriac, Coptic, and Armenian. The earliest of these manuscripts are tiny fragments of papyrus, many of which were discovered by archaeologists in the trash heaps of Egypt. Papyrus was the ancient writing material used before the invention of paper, manufactured out of reeds that grew in Egypt. Sometimes the papyrus was scrolled or put into a book form called a *codex*; most Christian writers used this latter form.

The earliest manuscript is a tiny scrap the size of a credit card, written on front and back, that originally came from a full codex manuscript of the Gospel of John.

The earliest manuscript is a tiny scrap the size of a credit card, written on front and back, that originally came from a full codex manuscript of the Gospel of John. It is called P52, because it was the 50-second papyrus manuscript to be discovered and catalogued in modern times. P52 contains a few lines from John 18, Jesus' trial before Pilate. It was probably produced in the early part of the 2nd century, possibly within 30 to 40 years of the publication of John's Gospel. Complete manuscripts were eventually written on vellum—a material made out of animal skins—starting in the 4th century A.D. The majority of our manuscripts derive from the Middle Ages, from the 7th century onwards. It appears that all these manuscripts, large and small, early and late, contain mistakes. The evidence is virtually unassailable: Among all these thousands of Greek manuscripts, with the exception of the smallest fragments, there are no two that are exactly alike. That is to say, they all differ in their wording in places. It is difficult to know how many differences there are among the surviving manuscripts. Some scholars think there are 200,000; others believe the number could be 300,000 or more. It's easiest to put the matter in comparative terms: There are more differences among our manuscripts than there are words in the New Testament.

There is a subdiscipline of New Testament scholarship called *textual criticism*. This discipline seeks to determine which of the different readings found among our manuscripts are mistakes and which represent the original words as penned by the authors. It helps to know just what kinds of mistakes were typically made by New Testament scribes. Many mistakes were pure accidents. The most common mistake is immaterial to the meaning: Scribes misspelled words even more than most people do today. Sometimes scribes inadvertently left out words, lines, or sometimes entire pages. This was especially common when two lines ended with the same words. The scribe would copy the first, but when his eye returned to the page, it sometimes would fall inadvertently on the second, causing him to leave out all the words between the two.

This kind of problem was exacerbated by the fact that, in ancient texts, scribes did not use paragraph divisions, small case letters, punctuation, or even spaces to separate the words. Everything was run together in a jumble that could create havoc both for copyists and for those who simply wanted to read the text (e.g., try to read: lasnighatdinnerisawabundanceonthetable). Occasionally, scribes would insert a marginal note they found in their copies, thinking that the previous scribe had inadvertently left out a line of text and added it in the margin, when in fact the scribe had simply been making a note to himself (e.g., Corinthians 14 and the *Codex Vaticanus* version of Hebrews 1:3).

Scribes also introduced mistakes intentionally. This happened when scribes thought the text they were copying made some kind of factual mistake. For example, in Mark 1:2, the reference to Isaiah is really comprised of a quote from Malachi, Exodus, and Isaiah. Some modern versions merely say "the prophets." In Mark 2:25, Jesus says that David entered into the temple when Abiathar was the high priest. It is clear from the passage in the Hebrew Bible to which he was referring (1 Sam 21:1–7), however, that it was not Abiathar, but his father, Ahimelech, who was high priest at the time. Some scribes changed the text to eliminate the discrepancy. Sometimes scribes would try to "harmonize" two accounts in the Gospels so that they read in the same way. For example, both Matthew and Luke have the Lord's Prayer, but only Matthew gives it in the full form that people are accustomed to today; Luke is lacking several of the petitions. A number of scribes resolved the difference by adding Matthew's petitions to Luke as well. Even more interesting are items that scribes took to be theological errors that they then corrected. For example, Luke's Gospel has the story of Jesus visiting Jerusalem as a 12-year old, along with Joseph and Mary. They begin the long trek home, only to discover three days later that Jesus is not with them. After tracking him down in the temple, Mary says to him "Why have you treated us like this? Your *father* and I have been looking all over for you." Your *father* and I? Scribes who believed in the virgin birth and thought that Joseph was not Jesus' father, changed the text to "*we* have been looking all over for you." Or consider the passage in which Jesus gives his apocalyptic teachings in Matthew's Gospel and indicates that no one knows exactly when the end will come "not the angels in heaven, nor even the Son, but only the Father" (Matt. 24:36). Scribes who thought that Jesus is divine and knows all things changed the text by dropping out the words "nor even the Son."

From some of these examples, it should be clear that some textual changes are of no real importance for interpretation (for example, the misspelled words), but others are highly significant. The oldest and best manuscripts of the Gospel of John do not contain the famous story of the woman taken in adultery (where Jesus utters his famous line: "let the one without sin among you be the first to cast a stone at her"). This was not added until the 12th century. The best witnesses of the Gospel of Mark do not include the final 12 verses, in which Jesus appears to his disciples (in these manuscripts, the text ends with the women fleeing the empty tomb in fear, telling no one what they have seen) (see Lecture Five). The only verses in the entire New Testament that provide an explicit affirmation of the traditional doctrine of the Trinity— that the three divine beings are one (1 John 5:7–8)—is not found in the text of any Greek manuscript until around the time of the invention of printing in the 15th century.

Textual critics apply a number of criteria to determine the original reading of the text in any given instance. The number of manuscripts supporting a reading is usually not of much use. We might have two manuscripts, but one may have been copied 100 times and the other not at all—and even that may have nothing to do with which of the two is the more accurate copy. The age of a manuscript is of some importance, though, because older manuscripts are obviously closer to the originals. The geographical spread of the manuscripts is important, because if one form of a text is found in only one location and another form is found throughout Christendom, the localized form may simply represent a local variant. The quality of the manuscripts is important, because like human beings, some are more likely to be reliable and faithful than others. When a manuscript is reliable in places where you are certain of the original reading, it is also more likely to be reliable in places where you are not certain. It is important to consider which readings are harmonious, less grammatically problematic, and less theologically offensive—not because those readings are more likely to be the original ones, but because precisely they are the ones that scribes would have been likely to change! That is, the more difficult reading is more likely to be original. It is also important to consider which readings coincide more closely with the New Testament author's own writing style and theology, because words that are more like those he usually wrote are more likely the words that he probably did write.

In conclusion, we can say with some confidence that we do not have the original texts of any of the books of the New Testament. Scholars trained in textual criticism devote themselves to examining the surviving manuscripts of the New Testament to see where scribes have made mistakes, in an effort to reconstruct what the authors originally wrote. In many instances, there is little dispute about what the original text was, but in other instances, there remains considerable doubt—and sometimes these are passages of real significance for the interpretation of the text. There is no alternative to this situation and never will be, unless by some unbelievable stroke of luck, we discover the original texts themselves. ■

Essential Reading

Brown, *Introduction to the New Testament*, chap. 3.

Ehrman, *The New Testament: A Historical Introduction*, chap. 28.

Parker, *The Living Text of the Gospels*.

Supplemental Reading

Ehrman, *The Orthodox Corruption of Scripture*.

Greenlee, *An Introduction to New Testament Textual Criticism*.

Metzger, *The Text of the New Testament*.

Questions to Consider

1. Suppose a rather long story (for example, the last 12 verses of Mark or the woman taken in adultery) were known not to have been part of the original text of the New Testament. Should the story still be considered part of the New Testament canon?

2. Many Christians today believe that God inspired the very words of the New Testament. How would that belief be affected by the fact that in some cases we don't know what the words were?

Do We Have the Original New Testament?
Lecture 24—Transcript

We have now nearly concluded our survey of the writings of the New Testament. I would like to devote this final lecture to a rather broad topic that can be expressed in terms of a question. Do we have the original New Testament? The answer may come as a surprise to many people. In one very real sense we do not. As we have already seen in this course, we do not have the originals of any of the books that were later canonized into the New Testament. What we have are copies of the originals or better yet, copies of the copies of the copies of the originals—copies made for the most part hundreds of years after the originals themselves. These copies were all written by hand, which is the literal meaning of the term manuscript—written by hand.

Unfortunately, all of our surviving manuscripts contain mistakes. For that reason in many cases it's difficult to know what words were in the original texts of the New Testament, and that's an important matter because it's impossible to interpret what an author meant if you don't know what he said. Let me illustrate the problem by giving a solitary example of how things work. When Paul wrote his first letter to the Corinthians, someone in the community must have copied it by hand, one word at a time. The copy itself was then copied, possibly in Corinth, possibly in some other community that found out about the letter and wanted a copy for itself. That copy was then copied as were later copies. Before long there were a large number of different copies in circulation in different communities through Mediterranean. In this long process of copying and recopying, the original text of the book was eventually lost, worn out, burned, or otherwise destroyed.

No one evidently saw the need to keep the original when copies were readily available. Had they been more fully cognizant of what happens to a manuscript that gets copied by hand though, they may have been more diligent to preserve the original. What happens is that copyists—especially untrained copyist as were most of the early Christians who served as copyists—copyists make mistakes. And a subsequent copyist will not only reintroduce new mistakes, but will reproduce the mistakes of the copy that he copies, or else he will recognize that there has been a mistake that's been made and he'll try to correct the mistake. Sometimes in doing so, he creates even further mistakes.

We don't have the original copy of 1 Corinthians. We don't have the first copy of the copy, or the copy made of the first copy of the copy. We don't have the copy of the copy of the copy of the copy. The first copy of 1 Corinthians that we have is a fragment of a manuscript that dates to around A.D. 200; that is, nearly 150 years after Paul originally wrote the letter. We don't have complete manuscripts of all of the books of the New Testament until about 150 years after that—the middle of the 4th century. In the intervening years, the text of the New Testament was copied slowly by hand, one copy from another, with mistakes creeping in all along the way. The question then is how can we take the copies that we do have and establish the text as Paul originally wrote it for 1 Corinthians or as the other authors wrote their own books?

In order to explore this question further, it might help to give some background information on our surviving copies of the New Testament. We have at present some 5,400 Greek manuscripts of the New Testament—5,400 copies in Greek—not to mention the thousands of copies of the New Testament as translated into Latin, which was the language of the Middle Ages, when most manuscripts were produced and copies found in other ancient languages like Syriac, Coptic, and Armenian. The earliest of our manuscripts are tiny fragments, many of which were discovered by archaeologists in the trash heaps of Egypt.

The earliest manuscripts are made out of papyrus. Papyrus was a writing material that was used in antiquity. It was made out of reeds that grew around the Nile and was, in fact, a very good writing substance. Some people today think of papyrus as being not very useful for writing on because it is so brittle. The reason they think this is because they see papyrus manuscripts that are 2,000 years old and they are naturally brittle. In fact, papyrus is a very good writing material, not that much worse actually than paper. The way they would manufacture papyrus sheets for writing was by taking this papyrus plant—it grew about 12 or 15 feet high and was about as wide as a person's wrist. They would peel off the outer parts in strips, which they would cut uniformly and lay down, and then they would lay across, perpendicular to this layer of strips, another layer of strips. They would press them together, and there's a substance that functions kind of as a glue that would bring them together and keep them together. They would cut out large sheets of these and roll them up and dry them out, and then they would sell them as sheets of writing material. As I said, it's a pretty good writing substance because for one thing, if you write on one side of this, you already have lines provided for you, you didn't have to line the paper, because the strips themselves provided the lines. Most books in antiquity were written in the form of scrolls. They would roll up papyrus and then unroll it to write on, and so it would only be written on one side and so it would be just written on the side where you would have the lines.

As we'll see the early Christians wrote their books apparently not in scroll form, but in codex form. Codexes [codices] were produced by taking sheets of papyrus or other writing substances and folding them together and writing on both sides so that if you have one sheet you could actually have four pages by folding the sheet together and writing on both sides—four pages. And then if you had several of these, you could sew them together and create a book, called a codex. Most Christian documents were written in codex form.

Back to our early manuscripts. Our earliest ones were written on papyrus. The earliest manuscript of any kind from the New Testament that we have is a tiny scrap that's about the size of a credit card. It's written on the front and back. It originally came from a full manuscript of the Gospel of John. In other words, somebody produced the Gospel of John and had a full manuscript of this, all that survives of this is this little credit-card-sized scrap that was apparently discovered in a trash heap in Egypt. The fact that it's written on front and back is significant because this shows that this particular manuscript was a codex rather than a scroll. This little fragment is called P-52. It's P-52 because it is written on papyrus—that's the "P"—and it was the 52nd papyrus manuscript to be discovered and catalogued in modern times. This little fragment, P-52, contains a few lines from John, chapter 18, Jesus' trial before Pilate. This little fragment was probably produced in the early part of the 2nd century. Most scholars date this papyrus to around the year 125 give or take 40 or 50 years, so that—well actually give or take 25 years—so it could have been written as early as 100 or possibly as late as the year 150. In any event, it looks like this particular manuscript of John was written within 30 or 40 years of John's Gospel. Unfortunately, we don't have the whole manuscript, just this one little scrap.

Complete manuscripts eventually were written on velum, which is writing material created not out papyrus, but out of animal skins. These complete manuscript start appearing in the 4th century A.D. The vast majority of our manuscripts derive from the Middle Ages, starting with the 7th century onwards when the manuscripts of the New Testament were being copied in monasteries.

It appears that all of our surviving manuscripts, both great and small, early and late, contained mistakes. The evidence is virtually unassailable. Among all of these thousands of Greek manuscripts that we have, with the exception of the smallest fragments, there are no two that are exactly alike in all of their particulars. That is to say, they all differ in their wording in places. It's difficult to know how many differences there are among our surviving manuscripts of the New Testament. It's difficult to know because nobody has been able to count all of the differences. Some scholars think that there might be 200,000 differences, other say 300,000 or more. It's probably easiest though to put the matter in comparative terms. There are more differences among our manuscripts than there are words in the New Testament.

There is a subdiscipline of New Testament scholarship called textual criticism. It's the task of textual criticism to determine which of the different readings found among our manuscripts are mistakes and which represent the original words penned by the authors. It helps to know first of all what kind of mistakes were made typically by New Testament scribes. Many mistakes were pure accidents. The single most common mistake that is found in our manuscripts, the single most common mistake is completely immaterial for the meaning of these texts. Scribes misspelled words even more than most people do today. Scribes, of course, will be excused for this, they are living in an age before spell check, in fact they are living in an age before there were dictionaries. Most scribes didn't have any access to anything like a dictionary, and they often would spell the same word in different ways. Well most of the differences in our manuscripts, the majority of them, are actually just misspelled words.

Sometimes scribes would inadvertently leave out words. Sometimes they would leave out entire lines. On occasion they would leave out entire pages. Scribes would be tired or they would be incompetent, or their attention would be distracted and so they would leave some things out. This was especially common when a scribe would be copying a text and there would be two lines that ended with the same words. Sometimes what would happen is the scribe would copy the first set of words on the upper line, but then when his eye returned to the page, it would come to the words that were written on the second line, and he would think those were the words he had just copied and so he would proceed on below, leaving out the lines in between. And so this was common kind of mistake, one that is relatively easy to detect. This kind of problem was exacerbated by the circumstance that in ancient texts, scribes did not use paragraph divisions, small case letters, punctuation, or even spaces to separate the words from one another. This would make everything run together into a jumble that would create havoc, both for copyists and for those who simply wanted to read the text. It is very hard to read a text when there aren't any spaces between the words and so this occasionally led to problems when the scribes were copying the text.

Sometimes, speaking more about accidental mistakes the scribes would make, sometimes scribes would inadvertently insert a note that they found in the margin of the copy that they were copying, thinking that the scribe who made the note, had inadvertently left out a line of the text and had simply put it in the margin, when in fact the scribe may have been making a note to himself. This is probably what happened, as I argued in an earlier lecture, with the passage in 1 Corinthians, chapter 14 that says women ought to be silent in the churches. It makes sense if this was a marginal note that some scribes inserted into the text, some of them in one place, others in another place.

Other marginal notes did not get inserted into manuscripts, luckily enough for us. One of my favorite marginal notes occurs in a 4th century manuscript of the New Testament. This is a very famous manuscript called Codex Vaticanus. This particular page is one of the more amusing pages we have among our manuscripts, in fact I have it framed and hanging in my living room. The text is of the Book of Hebrews, chapter 1. The manuscript gives three columns of writing. Between the first and the second columns there is a marginal note that explains something going on in the next. In Hebrews, chapter 1, verse 3, the original author of Codex Vaticanus wrote out the line which says: Christ manifests all things by the word of his power. That is what the 4th century scribe wrote. A few centuries later, another scribe came along, looked at this manuscript, and erased the word manifests and put in the word that is found in all the other Greek manuscripts, which is that Christ bears all things by the word of his power. It's a similar looking Greek word. Some centuries later, a third scribe came along, saw what had happen, erased the second scribe's correction and put back in the text that the original scribe had written—Christ manifests all things by the word of his power. And in the margin he inserted a note saying to his scribal predecessor: Fool and knave, leave the old reading, don't change it. Well fortunately that didn't make its way into any text.

Scribes made a number of mistakes by accident. Somewhat more interesting though are mistakes that scribes appear to have made intentionally. I don't mean that the scribes meant to make a mistake, I mean that they changed the text on purpose even though they changed it away from the original text. This would happen, for example, whenever a scribe thought that the text they were copying itself had made some kind of factual error and the scribe then was trying to correct it. Several examples come readily to mind. Mark, chapter 1, verse 2, the author of Mark says, "as is written in Isaiah the prophet," and then he quotes a passage. Unfortunately, the passage that he quotes isn't found in Isaiah. Part of the passage comes from Exodus, part of the passage comes from Malachi, and then a third part of the passage comes from Isaiah. Some scribes later appear to have thought that there was a mistake here and so they changed the text of Mark 1:2 from saying "as is written in Isaiah the prophet," to say, "as is written in the prophets," correcting a possible mistake. And even clearer mistake occurs in Mark, chapter 22, verse 25. Jesus has been accused of breaking the Torah. He wants to point out that in fact there is biblical precedent for breaking the Law in some respect at some time. He points out that David entered into the temple when Abiathar was the high priest in order to eat the shew bread. The problem textually is that when you read the passage in the Hebrew Bible, 1 Samuel, chapter 21, it turns out that David did this, not when Abiathar was the high priest, but when his father, Ahimelech, was. Some scribes who knew their Hebrew Bibles quite well changed the text in order to make Jesus not make a factual error.

Sometimes scribes would make intentional changes in the text in order to harmonize two or more accounts of the Gospels. As we've seen, the Gospels sometimes would tell the same story in two different ways. Scribes sometimes solve the problem of having discrepancies simply by harmonizing accounts. As a famous example, Matthew and Luke both have the Lord's Prayer. But only Matthew gives the Lord's Prayer in the full form that people are accustomed to today. Luke lacks several of the petitions found in Matthew, including such things as "thy will be done" and "deliver us from evil." Scribes copying Luke were familiar with the Lord's Prayer, they themselves said it in church and as they knew it from Matthew's Gospel, and added these petitions to Luke's Gospel to make it harmonize with Matthew.

There were other problems that scribes tried to take care of by changing their texts. Some of the most interesting are places where scribes thought the text had made some kind of theological error that they then tried to correct. As one interesting example, Luke's Gospel gives us the only story in the New Testament of Jesus as a boy. It's the account of Jesus as a 12-year-old, who with his family has visited Jerusalem during a festival. The family goes home thinking that Jesus is with them in the caravan, only to discover three days later that he is not with them, that he has been left behind. They search for him back in Jerusalem and finally track him down in the temple. Mary then says to Jesus, why have you treated us this way, your father and I have been looking all over for you. Your father and I? Jesus, of course, in the Christian doctrine was born of a virgin. Joseph wasn't his father. Scribes knowing this full well, realizing there might be a problem in the text because Mary calls Joseph Jesus' father, changed the text, and so in some manuscripts instead of your father and I have been looking all over for you, the text reads: We have been looking all over for you.

Or as another example of a passage that has been changed because of its theological implications: In Matthew's Gospel we have an account of Jesus' delivering his apocalyptic teachings in which he indicates that the end of the age is imminent, that the end of the age is going to involve all sorts of cosmic disasters, but the end of the age is going to come even though it's eminent at a time that nobody really knows. As Jesus says in Matthew 24, no one knows the day or the hour, when the end will come—not the angels in heaven, nor even the Son, but only the father—Matthew 24:36. Some scribes thought that this was a peculiar thing to say. How could it be that if Jesus himself were really divine, he didn't know when the end was going to come. Scribes who thought that Jesus was divine solved the problem by changing the text—dropping out the words "nor even the Son."

From some of these examples it should be clear that whereas there are some textual changes that are of no real importance for interpretation, for example, the misspelled words, others are highly significant. [I'll] give you a couple of examples of ones that are extremely significant. The oldest and best manuscripts of the Gospel of John do not contain the famous story of the woman taken in adultery, which of course has been one of the most popular stories about Jesus in modern times. It occurs in every Hollywood film about Jesus. There's a woman who has been caught in the act of adultery. They bring her to Jesus and they say the Law commands that we stone one such as this, what do you say that we should do. And Jesus stoops down and begins writing on the ground, and he looks up and he says let the one without sin among you be the first to cast a stone at her. And he begins writing on the ground again. They each become embarrassed, realizing that they too have sinned, one by one they leave, Jesus looks up and sees that nobody is there except for the woman, and he says is there no one left to condemn you. The woman replies, no Lord, no one. Jesus says neither do I condemn you, go and sin no more. It's a brilliant story filled with pathos, a story that was used throughout the ages to show that one should be merciful to sinners, even the worst of sinners. Unfortunately, the story was not originally in the Gospel of John. As I've indicated, it's not found in the oldest and best manuscripts. Moreover, the writing style of this story isn't at all like found in the rest of the Gospel of John. The first church father to quote this text in Greek as appearing in the Gospel of John isn't until the 12th century. It was only in the Middle Ages that this story was added to John, and the manuscripts that did have this in John were the manuscripts that were used then by the King James translators, and so it entered into English translation.

Or a second example. As I have indicated in an earlier lecture, the best manuscripts of the Gospel of Mark do not include its final 12 verses where

Jesus actually appears to his disciples, so that in these manuscripts, the text of Mark ends with the women fleeing the tomb in fear telling no one what they have seen or heard. No one in this Gospel ends up seeing Jesus after he has been raised from the dead. That's how that Gospel ends.

Third example of a significant one. There is only one verse in the entire New Testament that contains the traditional orthodox doctrine of the Trinity—that there are three members in the Trinity and the three members are one. It's a passage found in 1 John, chapter 5, verses 7 and 8. Unfortunately, it's a passage that is not found in the text of any Greek manuscript until around the time of the invention of printing in the 15th century. The manuscripts that it is found in were the manuscripts that were used by the King James translators and so that passage came again into the English Bible. Most modern translations though won't include it, or if they include it, they will put it as a footnote saying that it is not original to the text. I am not saying that the doctrine of the Trinity is wrong, I am saying that there is no passage that explicitly teaches it, even this controversial passage in 1 John, chapter 5, which wasn't original.

Textual critics recognize that we have all of these kinds of mistakes in our manuscripts of the New Testament, and they have devised a number of criteria to try to determine where the original text is wherever there are differences. The number of manuscripts that support one reading over others is usually recognized to not be of much use to scholars trying to figure out what the original is. If you originally had say two copies of a manuscript, and one of the copies was copied 100 times and the other one only once, it would sound like you'd have 100 copies would be a better witness for what the original text was. In fact, in that case, you don't have 100 witnesses against one, you've got one against one. So that the number of manuscripts isn't nearly as important as other considerations. Scholars are interested in knowing which manuscripts are the oldest manuscripts. The age of a manuscript is of particular important since the older manuscripts are closer to the original. It's important to consider the geographical spread of the manuscripts. If you have one form of the text that is attested in manuscripts that were copied throughout the entire Mediterranean, it's more likely to be original than the form of the text found in only one place in the Mediterranean .

The quality of the manuscripts generally is an important consideration. Manuscripts, like people, are either more or less reliable so that manuscripts that can be shown to be reliable where we know what the original text is, are more likely to be original when we are uncertain. When you have different readings among the manuscripts it's important to determine which of the readings is more like what the original author would have said based on things like the grammar of the verse, the vocabulary of the verse, the theological perspective of the verse. It is also important to consider which of the different readings would have been more attractive to a scribe. If you have two readings and one of them is less harmonious or more theologically offensive, ironically that will be the reading that is more likely to be original, because that is the kind of reading a scribe would have changed, so that the more difficult reading generally is more likely to be original. These are the kinds of criteria that textual critics have devised to help them determine what the authors of the New Testament originally wrote.

In conclusion, we can say with some confidence that we don't have the original text of any of the books of the New Testament. Scholars trained in textual criticism devote themselves to examining the surviving manuscripts in order to see where scribes made mistakes in an effort to reconstruct what the authors originally wrote. In many instances there is little dispute about what the original text was. In other instances though, there remains considerable doubt. And sometimes these are passages of real significance for the interpretation of the text. There is no alternative to this situation and there never will be unless by some unbelievable stroke of luck we discover the original text themselves.

Timeline

1800 B.C.? .... Abraham.

1400 B.C.? .... Moses.

753 B.C. .... Traditional date for founding of Rome.

750 B.C.? .... Homer

750–500 B.C.? .... Prophets of Hebrew Bible.

587 B.C. .... Babylonian conquest of Jerusalem.

510 B.C. .... Expulsion of kings/beginning of
                                                    Roman Republic.

400 B.C. .... Plato.

333–323 B.C. .... Conquests of Alexander the Great.

145 B.C. .... Book of Daniel (final book of
                                                    Hebrew Bible).

140 B.C. .... Rise of Jewish Sects.

63 B.C. .... Conquest of Palestine by Romans.

44 B.C. .... Assassination of Julius Caesar.

40–4 B.C. .... Herod, King of the Jews.

27 B.C.–A.D. 14 .... Octavian Caesar Augustus as Emperor.

4 B.C.? .... Jesus' birth.

4 B.C.–A.D. 65 .... Seneca.

A.D. 14–37.................................... Emperor Tiberius.

A.D. 26–36.................................... Pilate as Governor of Judea.

A.D. 30?....................................... Jesus' death.

A.D. 33?....................................... Conversion of Paul.

A.D. 37–4..................................... Emperor Caligula.

A.D. 41–54.................................... Emperor Claudius.

A.D. 50–60?.................................. Pauline epistles.

A.D. 50–60?.................................. Q Source.

A.D. 50–70?.................................. M and L Sources.

A.D. 54–68.................................... Emperor Nero.

A.D. 56–117?................................ Tacitus.

A.D. 61/62–113............................. Pliny the Younger.

A.D. 65?....................................... Gospel of Mark.

A.D. 66–70.................................... Jewish Revolt and destruction of Temple.

A.D. 69–79.................................... Emperor Vespasian.

A.D. 79–81.................................... Emperor Titus.

A.D. 80–85?.................................. Gospels of Matthew and Luke, Book of Acts.

A.D. 80–100? .... Deutero-Pauline Epistles, 1 Peter, Hebrews, James.

A.D. 81–96 .... Emperor Domitian.

A.D. 85–105? .... Pastoral Epistles.

A.D. 90–95? .... Gospel of John.

A.D. 95? .... Book of Revelation.

A.D. 98–117 .... Emperor Trajan.

A.D. 110–130? .... Gospels of Peter and Thomas.

A.D. 120? .... 2 Peter.

A.D. 129–199 .... Galen.

A.D. 160–225 .... Tertullian.

A.D. 190 .... Melito of Sardis (death).

A.D. 249–251 .... Emperor Decius.

A.D. 285–337 .... Constantine.

A.D. 312? .... "Conversion" of Constantine.

Timeline

Glossary

antitheses: Literally, a "contrary statement." As a technical term, it designates six sayings of Jesus in the Sermon on the Mount (Matthew 5:21–48), in which he states a Jewish Law ("You have heard it said..."), then places his own interpretation on it ("But I say to you...").

apocalypse: A literary genre in which an author, usually pseudonymous, describes symbolic and often bizarre visions that reveal the heavenly mysteries that make sense of earthly realities.

apocalypticism: A world view held throughout the ancient world by many, Jews and Christians, that claimed that the present age is controlled by forces of evil, which would be destroyed at the end of time, when God would intervene in history to bring in his kingdom. This event was thought to be imminent.

apostle: From a Greek word meaning "one who is sent." In early Christianity, the term designated emissaries of the faith who were special representatives of Christ. See **disciple**.

autograph: The original manuscript of a document, from a Greek word that means "the writing itself."

Beatitudes: Literally, "blessings." The Beatitudes are the sayings of Jesus that begin the Sermon on the Mount (e.g., "Blessed are the poor in spirit...," Matthew 5:3–12).

canon: From a Greek word that means "ruler" or "straight edge." The term is used to designate a recognized collection of texts; the New Testament canon is the collection of books that Christians have accepted as authoritative.

Christ: See **Messiah**.

Christology: Any teaching about the nature of Christ.

contextual credibility, criterion of: Commonly used to establish historically reliable material from the life of Jesus. If a saying or deed of Jesus does not plausibly fit into a 1st-century Palestinian context, then it cannot be accepted as authentic.

cosmos: The Greek word for "world."

covenant: An agreement or treaty between two social or political parties. Ancient Jews used the term to refer to the pact God made with the Jewish ancestors to protect and preserve Israel as his chosen people in exchange for their devotion and adherence to his Law.

cult: Shortened form of "cultus deorum," a Latin phrase that literally means "care of the gods." The term is generally used for any set of religious or liturgical practices of worship, such as sacrifice and prayer.

Dead Sea Scrolls: A collection of ancient Jewish writings discovered in several caves near the northwest edge of the Dead Sea. The scrolls are widely thought to have belonged to a group of apocalyptically minded Essenes who lived in a monastic-like community from the mid-2nd century B.C. up through the Jewish War of 66–70 C.E. See **Essenes**, **Qumran**.

Deutero-Pauline Epistles: Ephesians, Colossians, and 2 Thessalonians, letters that have a "secondary" (= deutero) standing among the Pauline epistles because scholars debate whether they were actually written by Paul.

disciple: A follower, one who is "taught" (as opposed to an "apostle" = an emissary, one who is "sent"). In the New Testament, a common designation of one of Jesus' "12" specially chosen followers.

dissimilarity, criterion of: Used to establish historically reliable material from the life of Jesus. If a saying or deed of Jesus appears to conflict with the vested interests of Christians who preserved the traditions, it is likely to be authentic.

Essenes: An apocalyptically oriented Jewish sect, some of whom started their own monastic-like communities to preserve their purity in anticipation of the coming end of the world; e.g., the community at Qumran, whose members are widely believed to have produced the Dead Sea Scrolls.

Fourth Philosophy: A group of Jews who insisted on violent opposition to the foreign domination of the Promised Land, e.g., by the Romans.

gentile: A Jewish term for a non-Jew.

Gnosticism: A group of ancient religions, closely related to Christianity, that maintained that sparks of a divine being had become entrapped in the present, evil world and could escape only by acquiring the appropriate secret *gnosis* (Greek for "knowledge") of who they were and how they could escape. This *gnosis* was generally thought to have been brought by an emissary descended from the divine realm.

Greco-Roman world: The lands and culture of the Mediterranean from Alexander the Great through the early Roman Empire (c. 300 B.C. to A.D. 300).

Hellenization: The spread of Greek language and culture (Hellenism) across the Mediterranean, starting with the conquests of Alexander the Great.

Holy of Holies: The innermost room in the Jewish Temple in Jerusalem, separated from the rest of the Temple by a thick curtain, where God was believed to dwell. No one was allowed to enter this room, except the High Priest on the Day of Atonement to make a sacrifice for the sins of the people.

independent attestation, criterion of: Used to establish historically reliable material from the life of Jesus. If a saying or deed of Jesus is attested by more than one independent source, it is more likely to be authentic.

judicial model: One of the two models of salvation used by Paul, especially in his letter to the Romans. The model conceives of salvation as a legal process, in which God, who is both lawmaker and judge, treats humans as "not guilty" for their sins (i.e., acts of disobedience) against his Law because he has accepted Jesus' death as a substation for payment. See **participationist model**.

justification by faith: The idea that lies at the heart of Paul's "judicial model." A person is "made right" (= justified) with God by having faith in Christ's death and resurrection, rather than by doing what is required of Jews in the Law of Moses.

L source: A document (or documents), which may have been written or oral and no longer survives, that provided Luke with traditions that are not found in Matthew or Mark.

M source: A document (or documents), which may have been written or oral and no longer survives, that provided Matthew with traditions that are not found in Mark or Luke.

manuscript: Any handwritten copy of a text.

Melito: A 2nd-century Christian leader from Sardis (in Asia Minor) whose eloquent sermon on the Old Testament story of Exodus casts harsh recriminations against the Jews, accusing them of committing deicide.

Messiah: From a Hebrew word that means "anointed one," which translates into Greek as *Christos* (whence our English word, *Christ*). The 1st century A.D. saw a variety of expectations of what this future anointed one might be look like. Some Jews expected a future warrior king like David; others, a cosmic judge from heaven; others, an authoritative priestly interpreter of the Law; and others, a powerful prophet from God, like Moses.

Mishnah: A collection of oral traditions that goes back to the oral laws of the Pharisees. These traditions were passed on by generations of Jewish rabbis until they were put into writing around 200 A.D. See **Talmud**.

Nag Hammadi: Village in Upper (South) Egypt, near the place where a collection of Gnostic writings, including the Gospel of Thomas, was discovered in 1945.

paganism: Any of the polytheistic religions of the Greco-Roman world; an umbrella term for ancient Mediterranean religions other than Judaism and Christianity.

papyrus: A reed that grows around the Nile; used in antiquity to manufacture a paper-like writing surface.

participationist model: One of the two models of salvation used by Paul, especially in his letter to the Romans. This model understood sin to be a cosmic force that brought people into slavery. Salvation was seen as a liberation from the bondage to sin, which came by participating in Christ's death through baptism. See **judicial model**.

Passion: From the Greek word for "suffering." The Passion is used as a technical term for the traditions of Jesus' last days, including his crucifixion (hence, the "Passion narrative").

Passover: The most important and widely celebrated annual festival of ancient Jews, which commemorated the Exodus from Egypt under Moses.

Pastoral epistles: New Testament letters that Paul allegedly wrote to two pastors, Timothy (1 and 2 Timothy) and Titus, concerning their pastoral duties. Most critical scholars doubt whether Paul actually wrote them.

Pauline Corpus: All the letters of the New Testament that claim Paul as their author, including the Deutero-Pauline and Pastoral epistles.

Pentateuch: Literally, the "five scrolls." The term designates the first five books of the Hebrew Bible, also known as the Law (or *Torah*) of Moses.

Pentecost: A Jewish agricultural festival that was celebrated 50 days after Passover (the Greek word for 50 is *pentakosia*).

Persephone: Daughter of the Greek goddess Demeter, reported to have been abducted to the underworld by Hades but allowed to return to life every year to be reunited temporarily with her grieving mother; also known as Kore.

Pharisees: A Jewish sect during the days of Jesus that emphasized strict adherence to the laws of the Torah and developed a set of "oral" laws to help them follow this "written" law of Moses.

pseudonymity: The practice of writing under a "false name," as is evident in a number of pagan, Jewish, and Christian writings from antiquity.

Q source: Source used by Matthew and Luke for the sayings and stories they did not derive from Mark. The source is called Q from the German word *quelle*, "source." The document is hypothetical (it no longer exists) and is reconstructed by studying the traditions in Matthew and Luke that are not found in Mark.

Qumran: Place where the Dead Sea Scrolls were discovered, near the northwest shore of the Dead Sea; in antiquity, it was evidently the home of a the community of Essenes who used the scrolls as part of their library.

Roman Empire: All the lands (including Palestine) that were conquered by Rome and were ruled, ultimately, by the Roman emperor, starting with Caesar Augustus in 27 B.C. Before Augustus, Rome was a republic, ruled by the Senate.

Sadducees: A Jewish sect associated with the Temple cult and the Jewish priests who ran it. The sect appears to have been made up of the Jewish aristocracy in Judea. Their leader was the High Priest, who served as the highest-ranking official in Jerusalem and the chief liaison with the Roman governor.

scribes, Christian: Christians who copied their sacred Scriptures.

scribes, Jewish: Highly educated experts in the Jewish Law who possibly also copied it.

Sermon on the Mount: Found only in Matthew 5–7, this sermon preserves many of Jesus' best known and most memorable sayings (including Matthew's version of the Beatitudes, the antitheses, and the Lord's Prayer).

Son of God: In most Greco-Roman circles, a person who was born to a god and a mortal and who was, as a result, able to perform miracles or deliver superhuman teachings. In Jewish circles, a person who was chosen to stand in a special relationship with God, including the ancient Jewish Kings.

Son of Man: A term used by Jesus, and some other apocalypticists, to refer to a cosmic judge who would appear from heaven at the end of time.

synagogue: From a Greek word that literally means "being brought together." A synagogue was a Jewish place of prayer and worship.

Synoptic Gospels: The Gospels of Matthew, Mark, and Luke, which tell many of the same stories, sometimes in the same words, so that they can be placed side by side to "be seen together" (the literal meaning of *synoptic*).

Talmud: The great collection of ancient Jewish traditions that includes the Mishnah and the Gemarah (later commentaries written on the Mishnah). There are two different Talmuds, one produced in Palestine in the early 5th century A.D., the other, more authoritative one, produced in Babylon a century later.

textual criticism: A discipline that attempts to establish the original wording of a text on the basis of its surviving manuscripts.

Torah: A Hebrew word meaning "guidance," "direction," or more woodenly, "law." It is often used as a technical term for the Law of God given to Moses or for the first five books of the Hebrew Scriptures, which were sometimes ascribed to Moses: Genesis, Exodus, Leviticus, Numbers, and Deuteronomy.

Undisputed Pauline epistles: Romans, 1 and 2 Corinthians, Galatians, Philippians, 1 Thessalonians, and Philemon. Scholars are mostly unified in judging that these letters were actually written by Paul. See **Deutero-Pauline Epistles** and **Pastoral Epistles**.

Biographical Notes

Alexander the Great

Alexander of Macedonia, otherwise known as Alexander the Great was born in 356 B.C., son of King Philip of Macedonia, upon whose assassination he succeeded to the throne at the age of 22. He set out to conquer Greece before moving his armies eastward to overcome Asia Minor, Palestine, and Egypt. His major conquest came over Darius, ruler of the Persian Empire, which extended his territories well into what is modern-day India. Alexander's real historical significance lies in his use of military conquest to spread a previously unheard of cultural unity to the lands around the Mediterranean, the process of *Hellenization*. It played an enormous role in the history of Western civilization The New Testament, was rooted in Hellenistic culture and written in Greek.

Caesar Augustus (Octavian)

Octavian was the first of the Roman emperors, who transformed Rome from a republic (ruled by a Senate) to an empire (ruled, ultimately, by the emperor). He was born in 63 B.C. to the niece of Julius Caesar and was later adopted as the son of his great-uncle. When Caesar was assassinated in 44 B.C., Octavian left Greece (where he was being educated) to avenge his death. He was a member of the first so-call "triumvirate" of power. After defeating fellow triumvir Antony (and Cleopatra) in battle, he emerged as the sole ruler of Rome, and was given the honorific titles "Augustus" (= most revered one) and *Princeps* (= "first citizen"). Augustus used his enormous and unparalleled power and influence to bring stability throughout the empire after many years of internal, to extend the influence of Roman power, and to promote a conservative social agenda that stressed traditional virtues of marriage, family, morality, hard work, and simple living. This was the beginning of what some historians have referred to as the *Pax Romana* (the Roman Peace), an extended period of internal tranquility in the empire. Octavian's rule lasted over 40 years (27 B.C.–A.D. 14).

Constantine the Great

Constantine is not significant for the study of the New Testament except insofar as he was the first emperor, some three centuries after the birth of Jesus, to accept Christianity, to bring to an end its persecution, and to begin to bestow favors on the church that ultimately led to its triumph over the pagan religions of Rome. Born in A.D. 285, Constantine was involved in the early 4th century, as one of Rome's principal generals, in a complicated set of power struggles over the ultimate rulership of Rome. According to his own account delivered to Eusebius, the father of church history and his own biographer, when Constantine marched against his rival Maxentius in Rome in 312 he had a vision of the cross and the words "in this conquer." He took this as a divine sign and, having successfully overcome his opponent in battle, began openly to favor the Christian religion.

His real commitment to Christianity is open to question, as he continued to evidence devotion to pagan deities as well. But he certainly brought an end to persecutions, and once he had consolidated his power, bestowed numerous benefits on the church that made it clearly beneficial for others among the empire's upper classes to convert. From being a still small minority of possibly five per cent of the empire's population at the beginning of the 4th century (demographic numbers are nearly impossible to reach with any certainty), Christians by the end of the century—due in large part to Constantine's conversion—comprised nearly half the populace and became the "official" religion of the state. Constantine died in 337, after receiving baptism on his deathbed.

Jesus

We do not know when Jesus was born, but if it was during the reign of King Herod of Israel, as recorded in the Gospels of Matthew and Luke then if must have been sometime before 4 B.C., the date of Herod's death. Jesus was raised in a Jewish home in the small village of Nazareth in Galilee, the northern part of what is now Israel.

Biographical Notes

As an adult he engaged in an itinerant preaching ministry in largely rural areas of Galilee; there is no record of him visiting any large cities until his fateful journey to Jerusalem at the end of his life. His message was comparable to that found in the prophets of the Hebrew Bible: the people of Israel must repent or they will be faced with judgment. Jesus, though, gave this message an apocalyptic twist – as did many other religious Jews of his day: the coming judgment would be of cosmic proportions and brought by an emissary from heaven, the Son of Man, who would overthrow the forces of evil and establish God's kingdom on earth. When this happened, there would be a serious reversal of fortunes: those in power now would be destroyed and those who suffered and were oppressed now would be exalted. People needed to prepare for this historical cataclysm by turning back to God and keeping his Law, especially as interpreted by Jesus himself.

Despite Jesus' reputation as a healer and exorcist, he was not viewed favorably by Jewish leaders. At the end of his life he came to Jerusalem during a Passover feast, caused a disturbance in the Temple, and raised the ire and fears of the ruling party, the Sadducees, who were intent on keeping the peace and avoiding any riots during such tumultuous times. They had Jesus arrested and turned him over to the Roman governor, Pontius Pilate, who ordered him crucified as a trouble maker. Scholars dispute the precise year of his death, but it must have been some time around A.D. 30.

Josephus

Josephus was born to an aristocratic Jewish priestly family in A.D. 37 in Palestine who wrote two important works (one being *The Antiquities of the Jews*, detailing the history of the Jewish People), and the other being an account of the Roman-Jewish wars of the 1st century A.D. that occurred after the life of Jesus. His accounts are among the only non-Scriptural references we have to Jesus. He was highly educated and became an important figure in Judean politics and played a leading role in the Jewish war against Rome A.D.–A.D. 70. He was captured and told the conquering Roman general Vespasian that he would become emperor, which happened after the suicide of Nero. As a reward for his prophetic insight, Vespasian granted Josephus an annual stipend and appointed him to work as a court historian.

Paul the Apostle (Saul of Tarsus)

Paul was a Hellenistic Jew born and raised outside of Palestine. We do not know when he was born, but it was probably sometime during the first decade A.D. Through his own letters and the encomiastic account found in the book of Acts, we can learn something of his history. He was raised as a strict Pharisaic Jew and prided himself on his scrupulous religiosity. At some point in his early adulthood, he learned of the Christians and their proclamation of the crucified man Jesus as the messiah. Incensed by this claim, Paul began a rigorous campaign of persecution against the Christians—only to be converted himself to faith in Jesus through some kind of visionary experience.

Paul then became an ardent proponent of the faith and its best-known missionary. He saw his call as a missionary to the Gentiles and worked in major urban areas in the regions of Asia Minor, Macedonia, and Achaia to establish churches through the conversion of former pagans. A distinctive aspect of his message was that all people, Jew and Gentile, are made right with God through Jesus' death and resurrection and by no other means. The practical payoff was that Gentiles did not need to become Jewish to be among the people of the Jewish God—in particular, the men did not need to become circumcised.

We know about Paul principally through the letters he wrote to his churches when problems arose that he wanted to address. Seven letters in the New Testament indisputably come from his hand; six others claim him as an author, but there are reasons to doubt these claims. According to the book of Acts, Paul was eventually arrested for socially disruptive behavior and sent to Rome to face trial. An early tradition outside of the New Testament indicates that Paul was martyred there, in Rome, during the reign of the emperor Nero, in A.D. 64.

Bibliography

Beker, J. Christiaan. *The Heirs of Paul: Paul's Legacy in the New Testament and in the Church Today.* Philadelphia: Fortress, 1991. A clear assessment of the theology of the Deutero-Pauline and Pastoral epistles, which tries to understand these books in light of the undisputed Pauline epistles.

Brown, Raymond. *The Birth of the Messiah: A Commentary on the Infancy Narratives in Matthew and Luke,* 2nd ed. Garden City, NY: Doubleday, 1993. A massive and exhaustive (but highly popular) discussion of the birth narratives of Matthew and Luke. Suitable for anyone who wants to know everything about every detail of the passages.

————. *An Introduction to the New Testament.* Anchor Bible Research Library. New York: Doubleday, 1997. A full and authoritative introduction to all the major issues pertaining to the study of the New Testament, by one of the premier New Testament scholars of the second half of the 20th century. It includes extensive and up-to-date bibliographies.

Carter, Warren. *What Are They Saying About Matthew's Sermon on the Mount?* New York: Paulist, 1994. The best introductory sketch of the scholarly debates about the Sermon on the Mount, Jesus' best known set of teachings.

Cohen, Shaye. *From the Maccabees to the Mishnah.* Philadelphia: Westminster Press, 1987. Perhaps the best place for beginning students to turn for a clear overview of Jewish institutions, practices, and beliefs from roughly the mid-2nd century B.C. to A.D. 200.

Collins, Adela Yarbro. *Crisis and Catharsis: The Power of the Apocalypse.* Philadelphia: Westminster, 1984. A superb discussion of the authorship, social context, and overarching message of the Revelation of John.

Donfried, Karl P., ed. *The Romans Debate,* 2nd ed. Peabody, MA: Hendrikson, 1991. A significant collection of essays by eminent New Testament scholars, each of whom discusses the occasion and purpose of Paul's letter to the Romans, often from different perspectives.

Ehrman, Bart D. *Jesus: Apocalyptic Prophet of the New Millennium*. New York: Oxford University Press, 1999. Written by the instructor, this study considers all the evidence for the historical Jesus—including recent archaeological discoveries and noncanonical sources—and argues that he is best understood as an apocalyptic prophet who expected God soon to intervene in the course of history to overthrow the forces of evil and bring in his good kingdom.

————. *The New Testament: A Historical Introduction to the Early Christian Writings*. 2nd ed. New York: Oxford University Press, 1999. Written by the instructor, this volume provides a historically oriented introduction to all the issues dealt with in this course. It is designed both for use as a college-level textbook and as a resource for anyone interested in the New Testament.

————. *The New Testament and Other Early Christian Writings: A Reader*. New York: Oxford, 1998. A collection of all the writings by the early Christians from the 1st century after Jesus' death (i.e., written before A.D. 130), both canonical and noncanonical. It includes the noncanonical Gospels of Peter and Thomas discussed in this course.

————. *The Orthodox Corruption of Scripture: The Effect of Early Christological Controversies on the Text of the New Testament*. New York: Oxford University Press, 1993. A study of the ways scribes were influenced by doctrinal disputes in the early church and how they modified their texts of the New Testament to make them conform more closely with their own theological views. It is best suited for more advanced students.

Fitzmyer, Joseph. *Pauline Theology: A Brief Sketch*. 2nd ed. Englewood Cliffs, NJ: Prentice Hall, 1989. A brief and concise, but superb, overview of the major aspects of Paul's theological views.

Frend, W. H. C. *Martyrdom and Persecution in the Early Church*. Oxford: Blackwell, 1965. This classic is the best full-length study of Christian persecution and martyrdom during the first three centuries A.D. The book tries to understand Christian views of martyrdom in light of the martyrdoms in the Jewish tradition.

Furnish, Victor Paul. *Jesus According to Paul*. Cambridge: University Press, 1993. This slim book provides a concise and insightful discussion of Paul's understanding of Jesus, including the question of how much Paul actually knew about Jesus' life. It is an ideal book for beginning students.

————. *The Love Commandment in the New Testament*. Nashville, 1972. A standard study of the role played by the command to love among the authors of the New Testament.

Gager, John. *The Origins of Anti-Semitism*. Oxford: University Press, 1983. An important and fascinating study of the rise of anti-Semitism among Christians in the early centuries A.D.

Gamble, Harry. *The New Testament Canon: Its Making and Meaning*. Philadelphia: Fortress, 1985. A clearly written and informative overview of the formation of the canon that shows how, why, and when Christians chose the current 27 books to include in their sacred Scriptures of the New Testament.

Greenlee, J. Harold. *An Introduction to New Testament Textual Criticism*, 2nd ed. Peabody: MA: Hendrickson, 1995. This slim volume provides a fine introduction to the problems and methods involved in reconstructing the original text of the New Testament.

Hooker, Morna. *The Message of Mark*. London: Epworth, 1983. A clearly written introductory discussion of the most significant features of Mark's Gospel. It is well suited for those just beginning in the field.

Juel, Donald. *Luke–Acts: The Promise of History*. Atlanta: John Knox, 1983. A clearly written discussion of the background of Luke–Acts and the overarching themes found in the two books; ideal for beginning students.

Keck, Leander. *Paul and His Letters*. Philadelphia: Fortress, 1979. An insightful overview of Paul's theology as expressed in his letters. The book makes an excellent resource for those who are new to the field.

Kingsbury, Jack Dean. *The Christology of Mark's Gospel*. Philadelphia: Fortress, 1983. A useful discussion of Mark's view of Jesus from a literary perspective; examines the flow of the narrative to find clues to the meaning of the text.

Kysar, Robert. *John the Maverick Gospel*. Atlanta: John Knox, 1976. One of the best introductions to the distinctive features of John's Gospel, paying particular attention to how John differs from the Synoptics in many of its major perspectives on Jesus.

Lane Fox, Robin. *Pagans and Christians*. New York: Alfred A. Knopf, 1987. A long but fascinating discussion of the relationship of pagans and Christians during the first centuries of Christianity; especially valuable for its brilliant sketch of what it meant to be a "pagan" in the 2nd and 3rd centuries A.D.

Lindars, Barnabas. *The Theology of the Letter to the Hebrews*. Cambridge: University Press, 1991. A clear statement of the major theological perspectives found in the epistle to the Hebrews.

Meier, John. *A Marginal Jew: Rethinking the Historical Jesus*, vol 1. New York: Doubleday, 1991. An authoritative discussion of the historical Jesus (only the first two volumes are currently available) by a highly knowledgeable scholar. The first volume includes the clearest and most up-to-date discussion of the extra-canonical sources for Jesus' life and the methods used by scholars to determine which traditions in the New Testament are historically accurate.

Metzger, Bruce M. *The Text of the New Testament: Its Transmission, Corruption, and Restoration*, 3rd ed. New York: Oxford University Press, 1992. All in all, this is the best introduction to the history, data, and methods of New Testament textual criticism. Portions of the book require a basic knowledge of Greek, but all English readers can use the book as a tremendous resource.

Musurillo, H., ed. *The Acts of the Christian Martyrs*. Oxford: Clarendon, 1972. An intriguing collection of 28 accounts of Christian martyrdom in English translation, taken from eyewitness sources of the 2nd to 4th centuries.

Pagels, Elaine. *The Gnostic Gospels*. New York: Random, 1976. An enormously popular and provocative account of the views of some of the early Gnostics in relation to emerging Christian orthodoxy.

Parker, David. *The Living Text of the Gospels*. Cambridge: Cambridge University Press, 1998. Perhaps the best introduction to New Testament textual criticism for beginners. The author argues that the modifications made by the Christian scribes who copied the text show that they did not see it as a dead object but as a living tradition.

Pilch, J. *What Are They Saying About the Book of Revelation?* New York: Paulist Press, 1978. A clear and useful overview of the perspectives of modern scholars on the book of Revelation.

Powell, Mark A. *What Are They Saying About Acts?* New York: Paulist, 1991. An accessible overview of modern scholarship on the Book of Acts, suited especially for beginning students.

————. *What Are They Saying About Luke?* New York: Paulist, 1989. An excellent survey of modern scholarly views of Luke's Gospel, suited especially for beginning students.

Ruether, Rosemary. *Faith and Fratricide: The Theological Roots of Anti-Semitism.* New York: Seabury, 1974. This compelling and controversial study by a prominent feminist theologian argues that early Christian claims about Jesus as the messiah were, by their very nature, necessarily anti-Semitic.

Roetzel, Calvin. *The Letters of Paul: Conversations in Context*, 3rd ed. Atlanta: John Knox, 1991. Perhaps the best introductory discussion of the Pauline epistles available. The book includes an examination of the issues of authorship and date, as well as a sketch of the major themes of each letter.

Sanders, E. P. *The Historical Figure of Jesus*. London: Penguin, 1993. One of the best introductions to the life and teachings of the historical Jesus. It is well suited for beginning students.

————. *Judaism Practice and Belief, 63 B.C.E.-66 CE*. London and Philadelphia: SCM Press/Trinity Press International, 1992. This is a full, detailed, and authoritative account of what it meant to be a Jew immediately before and during the time of the New Testament, by one of the great New Testament scholars of our generation.

Sandmel, Samuel. *Anti-Semitism in the New Testament?* Philadelphia: Fortress, 1978. A clear and interesting discussion, from the perspective of a prominent Jewish scholar of the New Testament, of whether parts of the New Testament should be viewed as anti-Semitic.

————. *Judaism and Christian Beginnings*. New York: Oxford University Press, 1978. A well-written, clear, and insightful sketch of the Jewish religion from the time of Jesus; suitable for those who are relatively new to the field.

Schrage, W. *The Ethics of the New Testament*. 2nd ed. Philadelphia: Fortress, 1988. Covers the major aspects of the ethical teachings found in New Testament writings and their contemporary relevance, by a prominent German scholar.

Schweitzer, Albert. *The Quest of the Historical Jesus*. New York: Macmillan, 1968. This is the classic study of the major attempts to write a biography of Jesus up to the first part of the 20th century (the German original appeared in 1906). It is also one of the first and perhaps the most important attempt to portray Jesus as a Jewish apocalypticist.

Senior, Donald. *What Are They Saying About Matthew?* New York: Paulist Press, 1983. An overview of what scholars in recent years have concluded about Matthew's Gospel; an excellent resource for beginning students.

Shelton, Jo-Ann, ed. *As the Romans Did: A Source Book in Roman Social History*. New York/Oxford: Oxford University Press, 1988. A highly useful

Bibliography

anthology of ancient texts that deals with every major aspect of life in the Roman world, including religion.

Sloyan, Gerard S. *What Are They Saying About John?* New York: Paulist, 1991. An accessible sketch of the modern scholarly debates concerning major aspects of John's Gospel.

Smith, D. Moody. *The Theology of John.* Cambridge: University Press, 1994. A clearly written and incisive discussion of the major themes of John, by one of the premier scholars of the Fourth Gospel.

Tatum, W. Barnes. *In Quest of Jesus: A Guidebook.* Atlanta: John Knox, 1982. A superb introduction to the problems and methods involved in establishing historically reliable traditions in the Gospels.

Turcan, Robert. *The Cults of the Roman Empire.* Oxford: Blackwell, 1996. A superb introduction to some of the major religious cults in the Roman Empire from roughly the time of early Christianity (and before).

Vermes, Geza. *Jesus the Jew: A Historian's Reading of the Gospels.* New York: Macmillan, 1973. A readable but very learned study of Jesus in light of traditions of other Jewish "holy men" from his time, written by a prominent New Testament scholar at Oxford.

Wedderburn, A. J. M. *The Reasons for Romans.* Edinburgh: T & T Clark, 1988. The most complete book-length discussion of the reasons that Paul wrote his letter to the Romans: to explain his gospel of salvation apart from the Law to the predominantly Gentile Roman Christians, in light of the tensions between Jews and Gentiles there and of his own impending journey to Jerusalem.

Wenham, David. *Paul: Follower of Jesus or Founder of Christianity?* Grand Rapids: Eerdmans, 1995. This book emphasizes the close ties between Paul and Jesus and tries to counter the view that Paul radically altered the religion he had inherited through the Christian tradition.

Wilken, Robert. *The Christians as the Romans Saw Them.* New Haven: Yale University Press, 1984. A popular and clearly written account of the mainly negative views of Christians held by several Roman authors; particularly suitable for beginning students.